Values and Revaluations

The Transformation and Genesis of
'Values in Things' from Archaeological and
Anthropological Perspectives

Edited by

Hans Peter Hahn, Anja Klöckner
and Dirk Wicke

Oxford & Philadelphia

Published in the United Kingdom in 2022 by
OXBOW BOOKS
The Old Music Hall, 106–108 Cowley Road, Oxford, OX4 1JE

and in the United States by
OXBOW BOOKS
1950 Lawrence Road, Havertown, PA 19083

© Oxbow Books and the individual contributors 2022

Paperback Edition: ISBN 978-1-78925-813-4
Digital Edition: ISBN 978-1-78925-814-1

A CIP record for this book is available from the British Library

Library of Congress Control Number: 2021951814

All rights reserved. No part of this book may be reproduced or transmitted in any form or by any means, electronic or mechanical including photocopying, recording or by any information storage and retrieval system, without permission from the publisher in writing.

Printed in the United Kingdom by Short Run Press

Typeset in India by Lapiz Digital Services, Chennai.

For a complete list of Oxbow titles, please contact:

UNITED KINGDOM	UNITED STATES OF AMERICA
Oxbow Books	Oxbow Books
Telephone (01865) 241249	Telephone (610) 853-9131, Fax (610) 853-9146
Email: oxbow@oxbowbooks.com	Email: queries@casemateacademic.com
www.oxbowbooks.com	www.casemateacademic.com/oxbow

Oxbow Books is part of the Casemate Group

Front cover: (Clockwise, from top left) Copenhagen, NY Carlsberg Glyptotek, Inv. 2782; neg. nr. 436a (photo J. Selsing; Courtesy NY Carlsberg Glyptotek, Copenhagen); St Petersburg (RUS) (photo after: Zalesskaya 2010, 235 no. 275); Bad Deutsch-Altenburg, Archäologisches Museum Carnuntinum, inv. CAR-S-98 (© ÖAI-IKAnt. Photo: Gabrielle Kremer); Berlin, Antikensammlung – SMB inv. Misc. 7928 (photo: Norbert Franken, Antikensammlung – SMB); London, British Museum inv. 1889,0410.1-5 (©The Trustees of the British Museum. All rights reserved); (photo: Thomas Widlok).
Back cover: (Left to right) (photo: Thomas Widlok); (© S. Harris with kind permission); Paris, Cabinet des médailles, coll. Beistegui 233 (© Wikimedia Commons (Siren-Com)); (© Tim Mitchell and Lucy Norris).

This book is an outcome of the academic work of the Research Training Group 'Value and Equivalence' (http://www.value-and-equivalence.de/) (GRK 1576). The printing of the book has been sponsored by the German Research Foundation (DFG)

Contents

List of contributors..v
Preface..vi

Part I: Values and value

1. Introduction to Part I: Values and value: some approaches
   to the concept of 'values in things'...3
   Hans Peter Hahn

2. Learning new styles, quickly: an examination of the Mittani–middle
   Assyrian transition in material culture..29
   Federico Buccellati

3. Changing exchange values in Solomon Islands..47
   Ben Burt

4. Objects with (a) history: observations on reworking and
   re-using ancient bronzes...59
   Norbert Franken

5. The value of things: textiles in the Iron Age...87
   Susanna Harris

6. Negotiating the value of ethnographic cultural heritage: between
   scholarship, entertainment, sentimentality and nationalism...................107
   Ivan Maksimovic

7. The gift as an open question..123
   Guido Sprenger

Part II: Re-evaluations

8. Introduction to Part II: Re-evaluations..143
   Anja Klöckner and Dirk Wicke

9. Recycling Egypt? The phenomenon of secondary re-use of Egyptian imports in the Northern Levant during the 2nd millennium BCE 151
   Alexander Ahrens

10. Beyond the bones: relics in Greek temples 175
    Andreas Hartmann

11. The 'Altar of the Emperors' from Carnuntum 193
    Gabrielle Kremer

12. How do materials matter? 209
    Lucy Norris

13. From antiquities to art: why has classical archaeology ignored Marcel Duchamp? 227
    James Whitley

14. When secondary is primary: on *Halbzeug* and other objects of continual re-evaluation 251
    Thomas Widlok

List of contributors

ALEXANDER AHRENS
German Archaeological Institute, Berlin
Alexander.ahrens@dainst.de

FEDERICO BUCCELLATI
Free University, Berlin
Fab.urkesh@gmail.com

BEN BURT
British Museum, London
benburt@live.co.uk

NORBERT FRANKEN
Johannes Gutenberg University, Mainz
franken@uni-mainz.de

HANS PETER HAHN
Johann Wolfgang Goethe University,
Frankfurt am Main
hans.hahn@em.uni-frankfurt.de

SUSANNA HARRIS
University of Glasgow
Susanna.Harris@glasgow.ac.uk

ANDREAS HARTMANN
University of Augsburg
Andreas.hartmann@philhist.uni-augsburg.de

ANJA KLÖCKNER
Johann Wolfgang Goethe University,
Frankfurt am Main
kloeckner@em.uni-frankfurt.de

GABRIELLE KREMER
Austrian Academy of Sciences, Vienna
Gabrielle.kremer@oeaw.ac.at

IVAN MAKSIMOVIC
Ethnographic Museum, Belgrade
imaksimovic89@gmail.com

LUCY NORRIS
University College, London
Lucy.norris@ucl.ac.uk

GUIDO SPRENGER
Ruprecht Karls University, Heidelberg
sprenger@eth.uni-heidelberg.de

JAMES WHITLEY
Cardiff University
whitleya@cardiff.ac.uk

DIRK WICKE
Johann Wolfgang Goethe University,
Frankfurt am Main
wicke@em.uni-frankfurt.de

THOMAS WIDLOK
University of Cologne
Thomas.widlok@uni-koeln.de

Preface

In times when the material becomes the ephemeral and the virtual seems to be the real bearer of value and meaning, this volume gains an unexpected topicality. While the uncertainty about the value of material things in the present and the past is becoming more and more evident, it is an everyday reality that virtual links, access rights and the possibilities of the internet are held in the highest esteem.

This book confronts this trend and uses numerous examples to show the values and revaluations of material things. The common starting point of all contributions in this volume is the assumption that there are things of value in every society. Value-in-things is a universal observation, which, however, is always concretised quite differently in different cultures. Of equal importance is the fundamental observation that there are such values, as well as the observation that appreciation and depreciation occur again and again. It is, of course, not possible in this book to deal with this topic in any kind of exhaustive way, however, the carefully researched case studies stand for the extraordinary range of different processes of valuation, revaluation or recognition of value-in-things.

The editors would first like to thank all contributors for their texts and for their willingness to engage with such an extraordinarily complex topic. The editing of the present volume has taken considerably more time than expected, partly due to Corona. In its present form, the volume combines contributions from two international conferences organised by the Research Training Group (RTG) 'Value & Equivalence' at Goethe University in Frankfurt am Main, Germany.

Furthermore, we would like to thank the German Research Foundation (DFG) for making these conferences possible and for financially supporting the work on this publication. The funding of the RTG was the basis for an extensive, always creative and sometimes also critical dialogue between the disciplines involved, i.e. the archaeologies and social anthropology, which is also reflected in the present volume.

Last but not least, the editors would like to thank the editorial team, without whose careful editing of all the contributions the present book could not have been published. Mareike Chudaska, Cornelia Voelsch and Hans Voges took great care to give the contributions their final form.

The editors wish this volume an interested readership who will be inspired by the sometimes surprising ways in which things are valued.

Hans Peter Hahn
Anja Klöckner
Dirk Wicke
Frankfurt am Main, October 2021

Part I

Values and value

Chapter 1

Introduction to Part I: Values and value: some approaches to the concept of 'values in things'

Hans Peter Hahn[1]

> *Value is a conception, explicit or implicit, distinctive of an individual or characteristic of a group, of the desirable which influences the selection from available modes, means and ends of action.*[2]

Introduction

The task of understanding the value of material objects and to describe it in an objectifying way is a problematic and at times contradictory one. This statement is true despite everyone's everyday experience that many things of our personal property receive appreciation and valuation to different degrees. One factor for this might be the financial expenditure of its acquisition, i.e., its price. Despite the obviousness of such everyday value assignments to material things, a cultural science analysis should go further and deal with the question of which forms of generating value-in-things are effective.

From an analytical point of view, it is difficult to separate in a categorial manner value-in-things and values of a society in general. As will be shown more thoroughly throughout this introduction, socially and culturally defined values are often inextricably linked to material objects. Furthermore, every statement about the value of an item is a relational statement. It is equally a matter of the characteristics of an item and of the person who makes such a statement.[3] The value sort of floats between

---

[1] This contribution is based on the work of the Research Training Group 'Value and Equivalence' (DFG-GRK 1576) from 2010–2019. Many thanks go to the German Research Foundation (DFG) as sponsoring institution. The final version has been established in the context of a CAS-fellowship of Munich University in September 2021. Special thanks to the hosts, Ruth Bielfeld and Philipp Stockhammer for providing an excellent environment for the final steps of writing.
[2] Kluckhohn 1952, 395.
[3] Rezsohazy 2001.

the person and the object, i.e. the mind and the material, the abstract and the concrete. Thus it is impossible to define exclusive realms of values like the 'immaterial values' or the 'material values'.

Various models are used to illustrate the connection between value and material thing. A much-quoted metaphor is the one of the 'Semiophore'.[4] It suggests that meaning could be filled into things and kept in it like in a vessel. Thereby, objects would first be sign vehicles (semaphores), whereby these 'signs' are an indicator for the value. Another model refers back to the onion model and describes different 'layers' of meanings for which – depending on the relative position – different contexts are relevant, respectively. Societal meaning, discussed in the public sphere, would, according to this, be the 'outer layer'. In contrast, subjective and mostly rather personal meanings are situated closer to the imagined 'core'. Even if it is not always clear if such 'layers' can be clearly differentiated, the input of such an image no doubt helps in raising awareness for the complexity of value assignments. Many things are considered to be valuable for more than one reason!

A third group of metaphors foregrounds the emblematic function: things 'crystallise' meanings, they function – similar to national flags – as recognisable emblems which mirror complex and often even highly emotional meanings in a condensed form. The talk of 'crystallising'[5] implies such a form of condensation of meaning in an object. Different connotations are closely related to each other and are no longer discerned in everyday life. Meaning and appreciation are felt but cannot be explained in detail.

It is not the aim of this introduction to discuss the advantages and disadvantages of these and similar metaphors, although several contributions in this volume draw on such images and thereby offer graphic examples of the connection of value, meaning and object. The centre of the following considerations shall, rather, be examinations of the processes of value assignment and at the same time moments of culturally conceivable 'evaluation' of things. In a first approach, we can establish with David Graeber: values are discernible and describable only insofar as they are connected with certain actions or certain practices in the pertaining society.[6] The pivotal question of this volume is therefore: how is it possible to recognise the value-in-things connected with material objects within a society? And, subsequently, which actions or contexts allow to draw conclusions about the fact that things are seen as being connected with value?

At the same time, the reversed question is also of importance: what do values do to people? Basically, it should be considered that values can be seen as powerful agents

---

[4] Pomian 1978.
[5] Miklautz 1996.
[6] Graeber 2001; in accordance with Fred Myers (2001, 8), this text is not about introducing 'classifications' of valuable objects but about emphasising the processes which are assumed to be the origin of value assignment. According to Myers (2001, 10–11), culturally productive and highly dynamic processes are e.g., the conversion of coins to jewellery or the conversion of objects of everyday life to 'art' or the transgressive mobilisation of objects (cf. Chapter 8).

which massively influence opportunities for action of individuals or groups.[7] The tension between the opportunities for action of individuals or groups with reference to the formation of values on the one hand and value as a pre-defined, seemingly objective, norm on the other hand describes the essential dualism in the definition of the term 'value'. It will be the focus of the present introduction.

This text cannot deal with testing the credibility of the correlation of values and things nor with presenting the plausibility of certain connections in contrast to others. According to Nathalie Heinich,[8] it should, rather, be emphasised that objectivity in the description of value-in-things is only achievable by refraining from a further evaluation of the assignment in a first step of approximation.[9] All chapters in this book deal with empiric evidence for such generally acknowledged and accepted links between things and different forms of value. The contributions gathered here examine how such links between value and material thing are generated and turned into an accepted fact by agents of a society. However, it is not about the question whether the values which are described are plausible, legitimate or in any other manner objectifiable.

Against the background of the general indivisibility of material versus immaterial value, it seems sensible to first go into some selected approaches in the development of value theories.

Theoretical approaches to 'value'

Without exaggeration, it is possible to state that humanities today are unthinkable without taking a position concerning the question of what counts as 'value' or 'system of values' within a society and what does not.[10] At the same time, however, it can be determined that the concept of value in a broader sense is far more recent than the thinking about the appropriate price of an item. Whereas Aristotle already wrote on price and value of artisanal products,[11] the notion of an abstract social and cultural value only emerged in the late 18th century, according to Jürgen Gebhardt.[12] At the

---

[7] Rezsohazy 2001.
[8] Heinich 2017, 21.
[9] The assumption of a cross-cultural objectivity of value is often connected with a perception of immanence of value in material things. Examples of it are things of gold or other rare and expensive materials. However, even gold has a history (Grewe 2009; Hahn 2014b) and, therefore, culture-specific and differing contexts.
[10] According to Joas (2000), contemplation on the concepts of 'value' is the foundation of cultural sciences in general.
[11] Bertram Schefold (1992) examined more closely the theory of economy and assessment of value of goods in Aristotle. As he shows, Aristotle already distinguished between use value and market value. The artisanal produced shoe can thereby count as a *leitmotif* in the philosophical debate on a fair price. Whereas Aristotle gives priority to the value of working hours (Franz 2006), Marx stresses the special character of the value of commodities (Marx 1867, 84). Heidegger finally abstracts from the value of commodities and points out how much the appreciation of a shoe depends on its usability (Porath 2002).
[12] Gebhardt 1989, 36.

same time, Gebhardt warns about the tendency inherent to the concept of value to absolutise the values of a particular culture or society. Therefore, talk about a 'system of values' often implies a historical amnesia and a problematic equation of intentions and normative demands.[13] As Gebhardt explains – with reference to Herman Lotze – the term 'value' in humanities has developed in consequence of Immanuel Kant's distinction between *a priori* and *a posteriori*.[14] 'Values' are at the same time a justification of the subjective 'I' and absolute, unquestionable issues of a society. Thus, the distinction essential for this introduction between subjective, actor-centred conceptions of value in contrast to objectifiable concepts has become a key argument once more. As shall be shown, this basic dualism influences the discussion on the concept of value to the present day.

Studies of culture and society are based on the perception that certain aspects have a higher cultural or social value, whereas others have a rather low one. Already in the 19th century, during the phase of the formation of many relevant disciplines, the thinking about the basis of a society was deeply influenced by the insight that certain valuable perceptions, ideologies and also objects should be defended and their value emphasised.[15] The discussion on 'values' concerns the core of humanities.

Starting with Aristotle and via Karl Marx and Max Weber, it would be possible to quote a long list of thinkers whose position can be understood as a justification or, also, a rejection of certain values. Alongside Marx' distinction between use value and commodity value, many other, often derivated or secondary values emerged within the decades after the publication of his works. Each was respectively useful or necessary for the explanation of certain cultural criteria. The so-called 'marginalists' underlined the relevance of subjective elements into economic thinking and lead, in the long run, to the belief in mathematical models, so much cherished by many economists. Only if a certain good has become scarce, its value rises, which can be deduced by the price it is able to achieve.[16] However, within studies of society, the abstract description of such a relation was soon found insufficient.

Whereas, in economy, the concept of value is usually substantiated in price, scholars of humanities insist on a concept of values that is different and clearly distinguishable

---

[13] Gebhardt 1989, 38.
[14] Hermann Lotze (1864, 473) insists on the capacity of every human individual to distinguish between the more or less valuable, according to his subjective preferences. He develops this deeply idealistic worldview in contradiction to the category of Kant's *a priori*.
[15] Thus, e.g., the approach of Emile Durkheim can be understood. His original desire was to describe the social solidarity as a phenomenon of special value (Hahn 2012).
[16] According to the 'theory of marginal utility', developed in the 19th century, the success of economic actions depends on keeping supply and demand in perfect ratio. Chris Gregory (2000) describes cultural anthropology's way away from such universal economic theories towards own approaches. Anthropological approaches in the early 20th century, advocated by Raymond Firth, Bronislaw Malinowski and Marcel Mauss, among others, emphasise the meaning of social obligations and thereby formulate a criticism of the orientation at price (Hahn 2021).

from 'economic value'.[17] In so doing, their hypotheses about the value of things usually refer to social conventions and norms, as e.g., the value of tradition, of authenticity, of locality and many more. Therefore, economic value and cultural values emphasised by humanities become more and more separated.[18]

The problematic process of the multiplication of values implies that, from the point of view of humanities, there is usually no effort to try to interrelate with economic processes, market models or value concepts.[19] 'Values in society' thereby becomes a separated area whose claim to describe a shared perception is not always accepted by supporters of different positions. A cultural value is often also to be understood as a political value.

Thus, whereas cultural values are not consistently drawing back on an economically defined concept of value anymore, it is also evident on the part of the economists that the values discussed in humanities are observed as being rather marginal.[20] From the economists' point of view, the culturally defined value is missing important characteristics like objectivity and predictability.[21] Social negotiations about the economic value of an appreciated material object or a desirable trait or institution are at best categorised as 'institutional economics'.[22] This approach investigates the effects of dominant taste or appreciation, and the social pressure within a society to fulfil the expectations of class and milieu. Quite early, Thorstein Veblen critically reported the distortions of overvaluing particular things as means of distinction.[23]

Although the assumption that any evaluation of a culture (as compared to another) is impossible can be deduced from the concept of cultural relativism,[24] anthropologists have intensively contributed to the discussion on the concept of value, especially by examining the practices of value assignment or the defence

---

[17] Knight 1963.
[18] Hahn 2014a.
[19] Cf., however, the special issue by Ehmer and Reith (2004).
[20] According to Joas (2000, 13–19), the dominating paradigm in economy was mostly 'utilitarianism', which does not include a concept of generating value. Economists, respectively 'utilitarians', therefore delegated the question of value to the so-called 'normativists', subsuming historians, sociologists, philosophers and cultural anthropologists.
[21] However, it is worth here to mention the mathematician Daniel Bernoulli. Already in the 18th century, he pointed to the impossibility of an objective, purely economic determination of value. As Bernoulli explains, the value of every single object in possession is dependent on the composition of said possession. Without context, a determination of value is impossible (Bernoulli 1738).
[22] García del Hoyo and Jiménez de Madariaga (2016) argue in this sense. The authors are economists and predict a reconciliation of economy and anthropology. They substantiate their prognosis with a rising acceptance of a broadened spectrum of 'needs'.
[23] Veblen 1899.
[24] The ambivalences of cultural relativism are also applicable to the question about the values in a society. According to Brown (2008), we need to ask critically: up to which degree is it possible to abstain from the own values in looking at another culture? Despite these problems, anthropology should not renounce relativism, since it sharpens the attention to the fact that there are different living environments. Relativism also has a humanistic potential: it enables the analysis of foreign cultures without assimilating them to one's own culture.

of value within individual societies. According to Graeber, the question of values in a society has always been important in the history of cultural anthropology. However, Graeber also states that the theories have failed without exception, since they ended in a circular argument:[25] a principle or object which is meaningful and important is also valuable. These theories were specific to explaining values by the fact that something is assigned to it which is deemed important. Despite this rather frustrating disciplinary history, more recently several studies and special issues have been published pointing to the eminent historical meaning of value theories for the history of cultural anthropology.[26]

The present volume, in assuming the theoretic position that 'value' is to be understood not as an abstract principle but as a catalyst of actions, follows some basic considerations of Daniel Miller's much-quoted paper on 'The Uses of Value'.[27] Miller views the assignment of values through specific actions or through a special dealing with certain things as something universal. All societies do have practices of value assignment or value articulation, even if their content and meanings differ. Therefore, the specific task of humanities is not merely to list values but rather to investigate which practices and strategies of legitimisation are used and prove to be effective.

According to Miller, whoever wants to know what particular object has 'value' needs, in the first place, to observe what people do. Thereby, 'money' can serve as a measure of value but does not need to.[28] As Miller explains, value assignments that deny any equivalence to price can be observed in everyday life in every family and in every household. In addition, he states that there is a basic willingness in all societies to widen the areas of the validity of equivalence relations. For instance, what can be commodified, i.e., offered as commodity, will eventually, one day in the future, also appear in such a context.[29]

There is an important addendum to this last point: people can neither assign values as they please nor is it socially acceptable to extend the equivalence relations indefinitely. On the contrary, controversies about the question which material objects are legitimately valuable and which other items are not to be priced, belong

---

[25] Graeber 2001, 20.
[26] Eiss and Pedersen 2002; Hénaff 2002; Pels *et al.* 2002; Werner and Bell 2004; Foster 2008; Pedersen 2008; Graeber 2013; Palomera 2014; Derix *et al.* 2016.
[27] Miller 2008.
[28] Already in Marx, 'work' was the primary means of measuring value. Neo-Marxian approaches in anthropology point to the fact that Marx saw money as a means of communication. The exchange value, i.e., the money, thereby mainly produces relations of value. Money as semaphore thus stabilises relations of value (Turner 2008).
[29] With this, Miller's argument takes up the old debate on spheres of trade. As already Paul Bohannan (1955; 1959) established, there are valuable things in every society which can be grouped and assigned to different spheres. Values systems structured into such spheres are striking because there are hardly ever relations of equivalence between such spheres. Already Bohannan described this phenomenon while at the same time emphasising how much money destroys such distinctions. As Paul Sillitoe (2006), among others, has shown, such spheres are very common. Thereby, societies with inequality manifest social differences with such limits of equivalence relations.

to the fundamental political conflicts in all societies worldwide. On the basis of the question if certain items are allowed to take the character of commodities and what a reasonable price would be for them, the relationship of economy and politics is negotiated time and time again. Controversies about the 'appreciation' and also the rejection of evaluations belong to the pivotal social dynamics by means of which social and cultural change can often be recognised quite well.[30]

Against the background of such extensive and ubiquitous debates, it is impossible to give an even approximately complete overview of the topics relevant to it. However, it seems to be sensible to point to a work which discusses the term value in a very basic way and also stands for the wide acceptance of economic anthropology within the US-American cultural anthropology. It is the essay by Clyde Kluckhohn about 'value-orientation' already quoted in the epigraph.

Value-Orientation Theory (VOT)

Is there even a possibility of a purely subjective attribution of value – beyond the aforementioned political negotiations? Tilman Habermas's work *Geliebte Objekte*[31] constitutes a widely accepted and differentiated study which shows how certain material objects can have a high subjective value through embeddedness in a personal biography or also through a specific standing within the ensemble of the individual possession of things. A broader concept, described by the term 'cultural psychology of things', includes ideas like 'transitory object'[32] or 'biographic object'[33] and, not least, the 'flow-experience'.[34]

However, such approaches to the appreciation of material things neglect the aspect of necessary negotiations. Even evaluations which are felt to be more-or-less subjective, are, at least to a certain extent, dependent on the acceptation within society. In other words: the fact that a stuffed animal can have a high value for an individuum is definitely accepted in a broader social framework.[35] Possibly, the highly important paradigm of 'favourite objects' or of 'personal valuables' is linked to social norms far more than is perceptible from subjective statements.[36]

---

[30] Hahn 2019.
[31] Habermas 1992.
[32] Winnicott 1953.
[33] Hoskins 1998.
[34] Rochberg-Halton 1984.
[35] Cf. Hahn 2016. It is one of the recurring topics in the works of Daniel Miller to point to the necessity of outer acceptance of subjectively valuable items. Miller thus refers to the term 'objectification' (1987, 19–33; 1992; 2001b). Only in succeeding to get the social environment to accept the appreciation, does a certain object really contribute to the status of the person concerned. However, Miller's derivation of 'objectification' from Hegel and his concept of *Entäußerung* constitutes a problematic semantic shift (Hahn 2005, 65; Tilley 2006). A necessary condition (Hegel) turns into an act of will (Miller).
[36] According to Watson *et al.* (2002), Americans have lower values in affective autonomy and harmony than, for instance, New Zealanders. As their empiric study shows, there are differences in value which, however, do not express themselves directly in the valued things. Americans rather appreciate useful

An early text by Kluckhohn has special merit for having elaborated the already mentioned tension between subjective and objective assignment of value.[37] More explicitly than anyone else, he pointed out that 'value' is a basis of culture in general. The 'Value Orientation Theory' (VOT) named by him, is, in its essence, an attempt to go beyond older, purely descriptive accesses to culture and at the same time preserve the idea of cultural relativism. People in a society learn what is valuable, and value is the – often only indirectly identifiable – inciting factor for actions.

According to Kluckhohn's model, there is a 'value orientation' (or system of values) in every society; to identify it is the most important task of a sociological, anthropological or archaeological analysis. By highlighting this task, Kluckhohn has formulated in a generic way what is basically already found in the classic monography of Bronislaw Malinowski, namely the question for the triggering actions for the socially accepted attribution of value to certain objects.

Obviously, Malinowski's book, entitled *The Argonauts of the Western Pacific*[38] deals with objects of value whose special character is immediately evident for the outsider. However, the character as something of the kind of value-in-things is also obvious to the members of the societies in which these objects are passed on and traded. We are talking about necklaces (*Mwali*) and bracelets (*Soulava*) which are involved in an exchange of rings which is called 'Kula' and which reaches from island to island over several hundred kilometres. Whereas the necklaces (*Mwali*) are traded in a clockwise direction, the direction of trade of the bracelets (*Souvala*) is the other way around (Fig. 1.1). The meetings between the inhabitants of different islands, which are necessary for such a trade, are planned meticulously. They sometimes involve several-day-long expeditions in canoes with outriggers through the open seas. In the light of the already-mentioned remarks on the generation of value, one could say that the complete book by Malinowski is a description of the actions which contribute to the public acceptance of value-in-things.[39]

Although Malinowski's approach basically sticks to culture relativism, in his monograph, he compares necklaces and bracelets from the Southern Pacific to the crown jewels of the Queen of England.[40] However, he immediately limits this comparison: whereas the crown jewels gain their special value through the fact that they have been kept safe for a long time and are not passed on (except for within the succession), the objects in the Southern Pacific are valued due to their continuous

---

things, whereas New Zealanders rather appreciate sentimental family objects which stand for a personal relationship. Nevertheless, they may be the same things (e.g., a house) whose appreciation is justified differently according to culture.

[37] Kluckhohn 1952.
[38] Malinowski 1922.
[39] Contrary to Malinowski's expectation, the Kula ring exchange did not come to an end with the spread of money. This form of circular exchange is still in existence today (Kuehling 2017).
[40] Malinowski 1922, 90.

1. Introduction to Part I: Values and value

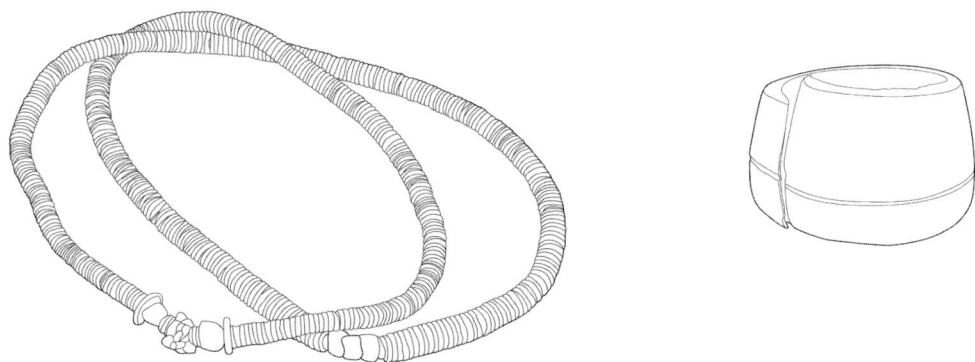

Figure 1.1. Soulvala *(left) and* mwali *(right) can be considered as the archetypical 'value objects' in ethnography and anthropological theories. First described by Bronislaw Malinowski (1922), they are used as gifts in a circular exchange system in the south-eastern Pacific (line drawings: Saira Tumpa © 2021).*

change of owners and their mobility.[41] Every bracelet, every necklace, is a unique copy because of factors like size, accuracy in workmanship, etc. Often-times, such objects have their own names. In order to increase the owner's prestige, he needs to pass on these objects after an appropriate amount of time – usually not longer than a few months. He can expect to gain in exchange another unique piece of the other category. Tales about the acts of exchange and about previous owners increase the value of a bracelet or a necklace.

On the Trobriand Islands, the personal experience of gaining reputation by personal possessions is complementary to the social appreciation which is gained by the passing on of valuable material objects. Whoever subjectively overestimates his property and therefore acts hesitantly in trade, will lose prestige as trade partner. Thereby, social obligations and personal appreciation are connected in a unique way. Malinowski not only recognised the particularity in this ring exchange, he also suggested a functional explanation for it: the specific practice of meticulously prepared meetings contributed to the stabilisation of a precarious neighbourly relationship between the groups of the islands. While trading or exchanging gifts, no one conducts war. As if to confirm his thesis, Malinowski reports on warlike conflicts among the southern neighbours of

---

[41] The paradoxon of 'passing on' and at the same time appreciating has lately resulted in an extensive debate in cultural anthropology. While some authors, like Annette B. Weiner (1992) view the theories of 'giving and receiving' as an original western thought which is problematic to apply to the Southern Pacific, others, like Mark S. Mosko (2000), for instance, argue for a specific embeddedness of such practices in the cultures of the region.

the Trobriands on Dobu, one of the Amphlett Islands.[42] Whenever a Kula expedition was coming up, a peace agreement was settled, at least temporarily.

It is of minor significance whether Kula is seen as a religious, political or economic institution. It is of secondary importance whether necklaces and bracelets are viewed as valuable objects because of this reason or that one. In the context of a concept about value-in-things it is much more important to acknowledge the complementary nature of rather subjective evaluation and merely culturally objectifiable actions.

The objects of value in Kula do not have a 'price'. Nevertheless, there are, according to Malinowski, practices of bargaining and evaluation; however, in contrast to a market trade, which, is to be expected according to European economy, there is no free negotiation about prices.[43] The aspect of relinquishing an exact price formation was further elaborated by Marcel Mauss in his essay on gifts, which was published a few years after the work of Malinowski.[44] Mauss's main thesis concerns a double reason for appreciation: to receive a gift is, on the one hand, a factor of personal acknowledgement; the resulting obligation for reciprocal response, on the other hand, is a cultural norm. Mauss further explains this argument by assuming that a society as a whole is kept together through gifts and their response. This is why Mauss views the observance of the rules for gifting, which is always based on the acceptance of value-in-things, as a basis for a society as a whole.

The complementary character of value as 'self'-accomplishment and at the same time the transgression of the self is emphasised by Hans Joas,[45] although without taking into consideration the anthropological discussion on this topic. Joas deplores the inability of current sociology to provide an explanation for the emergence of such values which do not centre on the subject or the individual. In a globalised world coined by cultural diversity, means of self-fulfilment come forth as the most important factor in generating values. What is appreciated is what serves the evolvement of the individual.[46] At the same time, it is beyond all question that such values which lie beyond the interests of the individual are of major importance for the continued existence of society.

---

[42] 'The function of the Kula in Trobriand society and politics is fully understood only when it is grasped that this institution fulfils a dual role: it provides socially sanctioned occasions for the assertion of individual self-interest; and it provides the idiom in terms of which the corporate units of Trobriand society can work out their political relations' (Uberoi 1962, 97).
[43] Strathern and Stewart 2005.
[44] Mauss 1954.
[45] Joas 2000.
[46] For his diagnosis, Joas refers to central works of the sociology of globalisation, among others by Zygmunt Bauman. In the context of this chapter, it is not possibe to explain more in detail Joas's thesis about a currently ongoing change in value orders. Nevertheless, the question about the role of shared social values is more important than ever.

Values and value. Subjectivity and objectivity in object evaluation

In his reflection on the history of value theories, Joas[47] refers to the important contribution of Talcott Parsons,[48] who in turn adopts the 15-year-older definition by Kluckhohn already mentioned in the previous section. However, Parsons speaks for a broadening of the definition by assuming that every society has a specific grid of different value-commitments.[49] So, while Kluckhohn still assumed that there is one 'system of values' for the whole society, Parsons adds another level of differentiation. With that, he can explain how different groups in a society are each ready to take on a different commitment of certain values for themselves.[50] For example, consumers perceive other commitments as politicians, wealthy members of society have other values than the impoverished part of the population.

According to a provisional historic classification of value theories, Parsons' text refers to a different perspective on values, which has also been of extraordinary importance in the history of these theories. In contrast to Kluckhohn, it does not deal with the values of a society as a whole but with the specific actions and values of social groups within a society.

From this point of view, an attribution of value is always the outcome of a social negotiation, whereby only a basic pattern of values is mandatory for all.[51] Integrity, money and power are parts of such a pattern. These aspects of value can be activated if needed; who follows them receives a positive sanctioning. By focusing on the possibility of different individual strategies and the freedom of the individual to decide for one or another value-commitment, Parsons opens up the space for a diversity of value orientations which is somehow similar to the theory of social milieus and the habitus of Pierre Bourdieu (see below). Subjective freedom of choice for one value or another and collective value patterns can thus be connected to each other.

Here we can see again how much the history of theories of value-in-things as a whole is characterised by the dualism of the opposition of 'value as subjective determination' versus 'value as objective fact'. From this perspective two lines of theories evolve in the succession of Kluckhohn's already-mentioned seminal article; up to today, both are defended by experts in the field of value theories and are developed further without there being an agreement on their validity. In the following, some anthropological authors shall be mentioned (Fig. 1.2).

---

[47] Joas 2000, 17–18.
[48] Parsons 1968.
[49] Parsons 1968, 136.
[50] The concept of values as an expression of commitment enables Parsons' original definition of money: it is no more than a 'generalized symbolic medium' for the expression of value – but not a value in itself (Parsons 1968, 141). Money is therefore a kind of symbol. Financial transactions are comparable to a language (Dodd 2014, 34).
[51] Parsons 1968, 140.

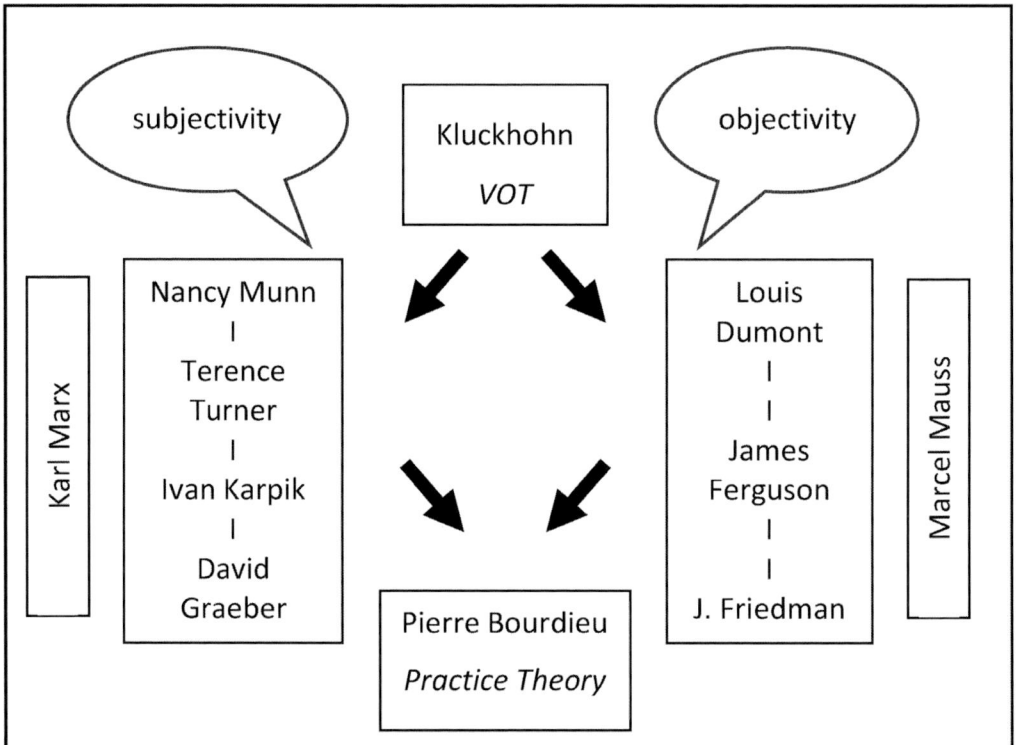

Figure 1.2. Diagram with the principal positions in anthropological value theories: underlining the subjectivity of values goes along with a focus on negotiations, whereas the objectivity approach considers the individual as being exposed to pre-existing orders of value (drawing: Hans Peter Hahn © 2021).

The subjective identification with valuable objects and the stressing of individual achievements is clearly perceptible, for instance, in the work of Nancy Munn.[52] She focuses on insignia of power and objects connected to prestige in the societies of the Gawa island, part of the Massim Archipelago in the Pacific, north of Papua New Guinea, already mentioned by Malinowski. Her thesis, first presented in the context of the Henry-Louis-Morgan-Lecture in 1976, follows exactly Parsons, since she also understands the commitment to a valuable object as a strategic action: valuables are a means of communication about the foundations of society.[53] According to Munn, it is the chiefs who refer to hereditary jewellery and thereby, at the same time, point to the value of these objects and also emphasise their specific position of power.

---

[52] Munn 1986.
[53] The thesis that valuable and elaborated objects are at the same time signs of the status of the owner is also advocated in archaeology (Bailey and Mills 1998).

Therefore, certain objects are a means to achieve prestige beyond the boundaries of the island. At the same time, we are dealing with transformations of value: from the value connected to a thing arises a value of prestige of a person. Value is a sign. Semiotically speaking, it is a 'qualisign', sometimes attached to things, sometimes to people. Graeber[54] points to the obvious parallels between this argument and the studies of Terence Turner about the Kayapo in the rainforest of Brazil.[55] The form of the houses, their spatial arrangement, the alignment of the village square – all form a cosmogony which is understood as being the aesthetic realisation of social order.[56] The value of these things lies in their analogy to social hierarchy.[57] In both studies, the one from Munn and that from Turner, Graeber distinguishes parallels with the concept of the formation of value in Marx. The substantiation of value, the prestige objects of the chiefs from Gawa or the arrangement of houses of the Kayapo is always also a symbolic order, the same as Marx saw 'value' not only in the work needed for the production of an object but also in the symbolic order underlying this work, which forces the labourers to sell their work.[58] Obviously value-in-things, considered as valuable material symbol is an outcome of communication. A pre-condition of such a valuation is the acknowledgement of the meaningful character of the object for as many members of the society as possible.[59]

The perception of the subjective and active production of value was up to now demonstrated by reference to the ethnographies of Munn and Turner but also with reference to Marx' statements on value.[60] This concept, put forward by Graeber in this context, could be further evidenced in the theory of the unique by Lucien Karpik.[61] In Karpik's concept, it is also actions of certain individuals or groups, i.e., subjective initiatives, which help a valuable object gain acceptance. In view of the art market, where the 'unique' is often specifically emphasised, Karpik is interested in the concept of 'connoisseurship'.[62] However, how is it that this 'connoisseurship' applies in some

---

[54] Graeber 2013, 221.
[55] Turner 1995; 2003.
[56] Turner 2003, 20.
[57] 'These moieties are crucial in the realization of value, since the consummate value—what Kayapo call "beauty"—is embodied most of all in great communal rituals in which sponsors from one moiety give names and present heirloom jewellery to initiates from the other side, and the community expresses its ultimate solidarity and unity' (Graeber 2013, 226–227).
[58] Graeber 2013, 225.
[59] 'An important aspect of what makes something valuable is its capacity to preserve, increase, or transform its worth as it moves in time and space …, which often has the effect of altering scales of value or constructing them in complex ways' (Narotzky and Besnier 2014, 5).
[60] Without referring to Graeber, Michael Heinrich (2020) has examined the connection of material objects and the rhetoric on 'value' in Marx. He stresses that Marx always emphasises the social character of the determination of value. The table which is raised to an expensive commodity fetish only receives this trait in the eyes of wealthy consumers who are willing to pay for it. The seemingly intrinsic value of a commodity fetish is basically a social value (Dant 1999, 41, 46).
[61] Karpik 2010.
[62] Kraemer 2016; paradoxically, it is frequently especially old things which have a special value. Lowenthal (1990) developed for this the concept of 'value of age'.

contexts, in others, by contrast, not? Here, Bourdieu and his concept of habitus is relevant again: 'connoisseurship' as part of habitus contributes to accumulating a cultural capital. This shall be explained further in the next section.

However, it is essential for the context that in all authors named in the last paragraphs, 'values' are understood as communication about social status and prestige. This is a political argument and emphasises the fields of action of those who are interested in generating, accepting and visualising value-in-things. It also plays a role in the definition of markets. In this context, 'market' is less a place of objective determination of value but rather a place of communication about value.[63] Thus, stories become a core feature in the process of valuation of things.[64] Ultimately, all literature on marketing can be assigned to the area of 'subjective' values-in-things, influenceable by communication about such material objects and especially commodities.

In contrast to this stands another line of theory which can also be connected to Kluckhohn's value orientation theory (VOT) but targets the cultural commitment of values. In that regard Louis Dumont, an eminent French anthropologist, is the classic reference., who has investigated the Indian caste system. In his important study, published first in 1966, he states that the caste system is based on an ideology thousands of years old and is only to be understood as a whole.[65] For him, the holistic approach has priority over the perspective of certain agents or social groups, precisely because the caste system has been in existence for so long.

Based on this, Dumont insinuated a radical separation of the perception of value between pre-modern and modern societies.[66] In an essay with the simple title 'On Value', he emphasises the hierarchic character of values which elude any comparison from the point of view of the persons affected. Whereas the modern world distinguishes between reality and ideals ever since Kant, the 'good' is a part of the life of every individual in pre-modern times. According to Dumont, Weber's concept of a value-free science is a radical contradiction to the embodiment of values by the people in pre-modern societies. The hierarchic structure implies that there is always a highest value to which all other values are subordinate. Dumont adduces as an example the Indian society, in which 'purity' is always more important than 'power'. It is not the decision of the individual to define such a value hierarchy but the system of the culture. An example: although today, it is generally known that left and right form a symmetrical pair, most people worldwide accept an imbalance and perceive the right side as superior.

Obviously, actions, intentions and strategies of individuals or groups have little room in such a structure. Human beings are born into a system of values and have

---

[63] Hahn 2018.
[64] This is shown impressively by Glenn and Walker (2012). Their book describes how things of very low value experience a substantial gain in value by adding stories to them. See also Miller (2000) on the issue of 'appropriateness' of contexts for particular things.
[65] Dumont 1970, 39.
[66] Dumont 1980.

to accept it. In a certain way, Mauss's theory of the gift[67] can be connected to this concept, since it claims differentiations between relationship, religion and politics to be less important than obligations resulting from gifts: all other rules are subordinate to this very norm. Gift receiving and gift giving in return is superior to any other value within this value hierarchy.

The concept of the hierarchic system of values with a top value mandatory for all members of a society can also be found in more recent case studies. For example, James Ferguson,[68] in the context of a rural society in Lesotho, describes that farmers are forced to enlarge their herds of cattle. They need to act this way and therefore refrain from using their money from labour migration in other (more profitable) ways, since only cattle are perceived as an appropriate sign of wealth. The farmers are captured within a value system which does not open up economically sensible options for them. With the help of an impressive diagram, Ferguson shows that, due to the local value system, different indicators of wealth (consumer goods, house building, field cultivation, cattle farming) are by no means equivalent.[69]

In a sense, the studies of Jonathan Friedman on 'La Sape'[70] can also be viewed as the description of a hierarchic and unquestioned value system. The desire to make huge efforts to acquire European luxury clothes and thereby defer other investments, perhaps more sensible in an economic way, could be understood as an expression of accepting a very specific highest and most important value. For Friedman, the members of the urban working class in the Republic of Congo are subjected to a global world order without being aware of it.[71] According to him, globalisation is not so much the freedom of new possibilities of mobility and communication but rather the enforcement of a neo-liberal world order. In this case, value-in-things is identical with globally distributed commodities.

With these two important case studies and the related interpretations, the over 50-year-old VOT by Kluckhohn proves to be relevant to this day and inspiring for the understanding what value-in-things means. Turner, Munn, Karpik and, in a broader sense, Graeber have here been used as examples for authors who pay attention to the subjectivity of individuals or groups and investigate their actions, intentions and strategies. Contrary to them, there is a series of authors, including Dumont, Ferguson and Friedman who, rather, emphasise the relevance of culture as a whole for a value order and see little room for individuals or groups to change this order.[72]

---

[67] Mauss 1954.
[68] Ferguson 1992.
[69] Ferguson 1992, 70.
[70] Friedman 1994; 2004.
[71] Friedman 1995; 1998.
[72] The compilation of 'objective' or holistic value concepts partly follows an explanation of Joel Robbins (2013) who in turn, refers to a classic essay by Durkheim. According to Durkheim, values (in a society) have the same degree of reality as things. At the same time, Durkheim acknowledges the tension between individual experiences and objective assertiveness: 'On the one hand, all value presupposes appreciation by an individual in relation with a particular sensibility. What has value, is in some way good; what is

Both perspectives are no doubt eligible. Within the specific context of the analysis of a single case study, it is the responsibility of each expert to make a choice for one or the other interpretation.

Mobility and value dynamics

However, there are more factors influencing value-in-things. One of the most important dynamics by which the value of material things is changed is the mobility of goods and commodities.[73] Thereby, we are dealing with mobility in a spatial sense and with the embeddedness in various contexts. First, we shall go into the shift from one context to another a little more thoroughly.

Worldwide, things experience new attributions of value as soon as they change from one cultural sphere into another. Whereas Paul Bohannan, in his classic study already mentioned, holds the opinion that the introduction of money leads to the destruction of other spheres of value attribution, other authors presented extensive ethnographic evidence for the fact that spheres of exchange persist even if money as a means of payment has long been established.[74]

In the light of a broadened theoretic framework, we can state that the perception of money as universal tool for the measurement of value forms an ideology of its own.[75] Money is by no means a 'measure of value' and neither does it work as an instrument for levelling. Although money is available worldwide, there are restrictions as to its applicability in societies. Not everything which is purchasable using money or what has been purchased using money is seen as the value equivalent of a price. Miller[76] gives a series of descriptive examples: personal gifts – e.g., for a birthday – are usually more valuable than their merchandise value suggests. The art market can also serve as an example: no matter which price may be called up, a piece of art is often more valuable to a specialised collector than the amount appointed for it.[77] The transition from the sphere of commodities to the sphere of personal gifts or art expertise are only examples; there are many more to accompany them: e.g., it is not acceptable to

---

good is desired, and all desire is a psychological state. Nevertheless, the values under discussion have the objectivity of things.' (Durkheim 2010, 43).

[73] Hahn and Weiss 2013.
[74] Shipton 1989; Werthmann 2001; Walsh 2003.
[75] Hart and Ortiz 2014; already Mary Douglas has shown this using the example of raffia fabrics in the Congo: although people are very willing to trade livestock or valuable objects for the acquisition of such a fabric, it is hardly possible to find a piece of raffia for sale. Only in emergency situations, are these objects of prestige sold.
[76] Miller 2001a.
[77] Michael Hutter and David Throsby deal extensively with ways of assigning value to art objects. Their list includes the following: (1) value through meaning; (2) value via innovation or uniqueness; (3) valuating temporal continuity; (4) value by ranking (in a broader category of established works or art); (5) valuation through politics, especially politics of art (Hutter and Throsby 2008, 9–15).

buy medication or drugs with money. Objects classified as pieces of art of national relevance may not be sold outside of the country, no matter the price.[78]

As Miller emphasises, it is not about subjective evaluations but about normative processes which restrict the commodity character of certain goods. Thus, there is the generally accepted rule that a birthday gift cannot be sold (even if it is possible and sometimes does occur). It is generally known that the purchase of drugs is illegal. Naturally, it does happen anyway; however, if you get caught doing it, you should not try to withstand a confiscation by the police.[79]

In all cases mentioned up to now, mobility and the restriction of mobility concern the transfer from one sphere into another: commodities become gifts, art objects become commodities. Other examples (classified pieces of art, drugs) show the interest of the legislator to disallow such forms of mobility between spheres.

Concepts which describe a strategic transformation of goods and values from one sphere to another belong to the standards of humanities. Basically, such concepts are also the core of the theory of 'habitus' by Bourdieu. In this framework, individuals have cultural and social capital, that is, the competence for dealing with valuable or at least highly appreciated goods.[80] Due to this ability, named 'habitus', they are able to convert the possession of such goods and its appropriate usage into economic capital. Bourdieu calls this 'conversion'.[81] It can also be labelled as transformation of one kind of capital in another. The ability to proceed to such transformation can be considered as 'doing value', i.e., generation value via socially acknowledged activities.[82] An art dealer who is well versed in good wine can use this ability to persuade an art buyer, who is also into good wines, to a beneficial purchase. A tasteful furnishing of an apartment presented during an informal meeting will convince business partners of the reliability of the other and will therefore be beneficial to a business transaction. Taste in wine or nice furnishing are goods whose value is higher than the price of this specific bottle of wine or that specific piece of furniture.

---

[78] Restrictions of value transformations are sensitive political decisions (Klamer 2004). A good example for such a revaluation is collecting. Collecting is often a strategy of revaluation, since as soon as a collection gains public appreciation it gains a special value of uniqueness. Susan Pearce (1995) therefore classifies collecting as a policy of value generation.

[79] Here, it is important to point to this from the already-mentioned psychological study by Tilmann Habermas (1992). While Habermas focuses on the subjectivity, Miller is oriented towards normative expectations of appreciation: a birthday present shall be praised, the relinquishment of selling national cultural goods should be accepted as patriotic norm. In a cross-cultural comparison, Wallendorf and Arnould (1988) asked about the most valuable goods in the Republic of Niger and in the USA. In the first case, it was jewellery which was most valuable, in the USA, by contrast, it was family photos. Obviously, there are culture specific rules which can simultaneously be perceived as subjective priorities.

[80] Bourdieu 1979.

[81] Bourdieu 1986, 252.

[82] Kornberger et al. (2015) provide an exhaustive list of such activities. These authors are critical against mathematical models of measuring value. They insist on the fact that every criterium for 'value' is the product of a social negotiation. Value is a fictitious category insofar as it is constructed.

Such conversions are relevant examples for the mobility of things between spheres (here: cultural, social and economic sphere). Strikingly, Bourdieu takes an intermediate position between subjective and objectifying conceptions of value against this background. As Paul Costey describes,[83] Bourdieu insinuates that actors in a society adapt themselves; they internalise the exterior and thereby correspond to whatever is respected as a rule in a certain milieu. At the same time, however, they have strategies available which stay rather implicit.

With regard to spatial mobility, we have already pointed to Malinowski's classic study on the Kula ring exchange in the south-eastern Pacific. Indeed, the central phenomenon here is mobility, namely especially over long distances, even if such an exchange of the already-mentioned Kula objects of value may also happen between different villages on one island. Trade between different ethnic groups within a region or across the boundaries of regions can without a doubt be counted as one of the most important and universal aspects of generating value. A special, even unusual, aspect is the high degree of consensus in the evaluation of the specific Kula objects. Even if the trading partners live at a distance of several hundred kilometres from each other, the connotations of gender and prestige are very similar in all participants.[84]

For the title of his study, Malinowski uses a reference to Greek mythology by calling the seafarers in the Pacific 'Argonauts'. It is certainly not too far-fetched to assume a particular hypothesis here. Is the *Odyssey* not a basic metaphor for enrichment on goods which come along with a voyage? This is at least how Mary Helms[85] interprets the myth, and she applies this to relationships of long-distance trading in antiquity in general. According to Helms, it is the search for foreign knowledge, for honour and prestige and the liberation from local social obligations which causes the special appeal of exotic goods and therefore long-distance trading. In search of explanations on why people in ancient Greece made sea voyages of over 100 km as early as in the 3rd millennium BCE, Cyprian Broodbank also refers to the Kula exchange and supposes that there had to be a special adventurous spirit.[86] He insinuates that a specific cultural group of long-distance traders had a higher willingness to take risks and undertook these dangerous several-day-long voyages in order to transport hewn marble and other trading goods to their destination.[87] The particular role of long-distance traders as a specialised group has also been noted in Central and Western Africa.[88]

---

[83] Costey 2004.
[84] While Kula objects are always embedded in rituals of time-delayed gift exchange (return gifts occur only months later), participants at the same time know trade, e.g., with crops, dried fish or artisan products. Thereby, immediate counter-performances are demanded about which there is also bargaining (Geffray 2001).
[85] Helms 1988.
[86] Broodbank 1993.
[87] At this point it can, by all means, remain open if we are dealing with commodities or gifts to the host in the context of the *Odyssey*. Political gifts can be economically sensible or simply grant the secure passage from one island to the next (Wagner-Hasel 2000).
[88] Saul 2018.

The appreciation of goods from afar or the preference for exotic goods can frequently be observed in the past and the present.[89] It is, at the same time, an important topic of European cultural history where imports from Japan or China as a means of distinction have played a major role since the early modern age.[90] It is significant that European goods were already viewed as valuable objects in China in the 19th century.[91] Nevertheless, Marshall Sahlins[92] warns about viewing the appreciation of well-travelled goods as universal. Behind such a worldview of global commodity circulation might be capitalism projected on all societies worldwide.

From a historic point of view, it is surely right to assume a continuity in the appreciation of mobile things and especially in the material goods implied in far-distance trading between pre-modernity, early modern times and the current globalisation.[93] Such an epoch-spanning view includes western and non-western societies and impressively proves the high continuity in the appreciation of mobile goods.[94]

In present times, the global circulation of commodities has taken on such a ubiquitous dimension that consumers are often not aware of the ways a good has travelled before it is provided as commodity. To the consumer, it is mostly unknown on which continent different parts of a car have been produced and hardly anyone knows where the blue jeans they are wearing are coming from.[95] So, whereas the characteristic of origin is currently losing importance in many areas, subjective characteristics gain importance: the actual origin of a commodity does no longer count, but rather the supposed properties whose value ensues from the identity of the consumers.[96]

Thus, it becomes apparent that the relationship of subjective values versus an objective 'system of value' explained in the last section does also play a role here: whoever mainly looks at the value of identification acts as individual agent or group. In contrast, who looks at the objective characteristic of 'origin' as value indicator thereby prioritises an objective property, namely the way the object has travelled.

---

[89] Arnould and Wilk 1984; Orlove 1997; Wilk 1999.
[90] Suberbère et al. 2016; Siebenhüner 2017.
[91] Dikötter 2006.
[92] Sahlins 1988.
[93] Ertl 2008; Gerritsen and Riello 2016.
[94] To these observations belongs a reference to the continually growing volumes of transport. As Jürgen Osterhammel (2021) has shown in a historic comparison, technical accomplishment of transport tasks promoted the long-distance trade and therefore the development of new lifestyles again and again during the last 500 years.
[95] Miller and Woodward 2012; Rieger 2013; numerous examples for travelling objects might be added here. This includes jewels and gold and also medications and globally distributed drinks like *Coca Cola* and coffee. Quite often, such cultural histories of mobile goods reveal inequalities due to the conditions of global trading.
[96] Thompson 2013.

Conclusion

There is an established field of study in the history of philosophy named 'axiology'.[97] It deals with the justifiably good things in the world. For good reasons, the present introduction did not take up this term and instead focused on the question about the actions, processes and dynamics connected to the generation or confirmation of value. In order to distinguish oneself from Max Scheler and other philosophers, it should be noted that the search for the 'invariable good' is an empirically rather unproductive endeavour. In contrast, the explanations in this introduction, concurrent with Edmund Husserl and other phenomenologists, assume that 'value' only emerges or gets perceivable through action. However, there are also different positions within phenomenology:[98] does value-in-things originate in structures? Or can the actions of individuals or groups produce value?

In this introduction, both positions have been introduced and illustrated by some ethnographic and archaeological case studies. They are, on the one hand, connected with the notion of subjective valuation and the centring on actors, on the other hand with the concept of cultural (value) orders. Whereas the subjective position very frequently examines the question of the bargaining and strategies of individuals or groups, the concept of the culturally given value order looks at the consequences of certain acceptances of value for the individual. The latter concept, assuming the culturally inflicted objectivity of values, often insinuates that the persons affected do not know in what way their actions are connected to a value order. Values in this objective sense are structures which every individual is subjected to and to which they need to adjust. Concepts which conflate both approaches to values are important: according to Bourdieu, the outer, seemingly objective, demand to take on a certain habitus can be connected with subjective strategies of acquisition of cultural or social capital.

Of similar importance are the historic genesis or respectively the processes of acceptance and enforcement of values. Like any historic consideration on this term inevitably shows, values are bound to certain developments which are dependent on availability and technical abilities. Thereby, value-in-things is usually only indirectly related to the question of desires or luxury goods.[99]

In the centre of any reflection on values should stand the question about the relations between humans and things which are generated by them: to gain or to keep valued things might be an important motive for action. However, it is also possible that the confrontation with a valuable good or its inaccessibility can pose a problem for humans. Thus, value-in-things can be a motive for actions; however,

---

[97] Heinich 2019.
[98] Zhang 2010.
[99] The extensive literature on 'luxury' cannot be integrated here. It might suffice the indication that numerous investigations show how luxury objects become goods of everyday life and as a consequence thereof the standards of necessity or desire are constantly changing (Hugh-Jones 1992; Hofmeester and Grewe 2016).

value-in-things can also pose a challenge and complicate the actions of the individual, or even render them impossible.

References

Arnould, E. J. and Wilk, R. 1984. Why do the natives wear Adidas? *Advances in Consumer Research* 11, 748–753

Bailey, D. W. and Mills, S. (eds) 1998. *The Archaeology of Value. Essays on Prestige and the Processes of Valuation* (Oxford)

Bernoulli, D. 1738 *Specimen Theoriae novae de Mensura Sortis* (Petersburg)

Bohannan, P. 1955, Some principles of exchange and investment among the Tiv. *American Anthropologist* 57(1), 60–70

Bohannan, P. 1959. The impact of money on an African subsistence economy. *Journal of Economic History* 19(4), 491–503

Bourdieu, P. 1979. *Distinction. A Social Critique of the Judgement of Taste* (London)

Bourdieu, P. 1986. The forms of capital. In: J. G. Richardson (ed.), *Handbook of Theory and Research for the Sociology of Education* (New York), 241–258

Broodbank, C. 1993. Ulysses without sails. trade, distance, knowledge and power in the Early Cyclades. *World Archaeology* 24(2), 315–331

Brown, M. F. 2008. Cultural relativism 2.0. *Current Anthropology* 49(1), 363–383

Costey, P. 2004. Pierre Bourdieu, penseur de la pratique, Tracés. *Revue de Sciences humaines* 7, 11–25

Dant, T. 1999. *Material Culture in the Social World. Values, Activities, Lifestyles* (Buckingham)

Derix, S., Gammerl, B., Reinecke, C. and Verheyen, N. 2016, Der Wert der Dinge. Zur Wirtschafts- und Sozialgeschichte der Materialitäten, *Zeithistorische Forschungen/Studies in Contemporary History* 13(3), 387–403

Dikötter, F. 2006. *Exotic Commodities. Modern Objects and Everyday Life in China* (New York)

Dodd, N. 2014. *Social Life of Money* (Princeton NJ)

Dumont, L. 1970. *Homo Hierarchicus. The Caste System and Its Implications* (Chicago IL)

Dumont, L. 1980. On value. *Proceedings of the British Academy* 66, 207–240

Durkheim, E. 2010 Value judgments and judgments of reality. In: E. Durkheim (ed.), *Sociology and Philosophy* (1st edition 1911) (London), 42–51

Ehmer, J. and Reith, R. 2004. Märkte im vorindustriellen Europa. *Jahrbuch für Wirtschaftsgeschichte* 45(2), 9–24

Eiss, P. K. and Pedersen, D. 2002. Introduction. Values of value. *Cultural Anthropology* 17(3), 283–290

Ertl, T. 2008. *Seide, Pfeffer und Kanonen. Globalisierung im Mittelalter* (Darmstadt)

Ferguson, J. 1992. The cultural topography of wealth. commodity paths and the structure of property in rural Lesotho. *American Anthropologist* 94, 55–73

Foster, R. 2008. Commodities, brands, love and Kula. Comparative notes on value creation. In honor of Nancy Munn, *Anthropological Theory* 8(1), 9–25

Franz, M. 2006. Aneignungslogik und imaginäre Bedeutung. Alfred Sohn-Rethel und Cornelius Castoriadis. In: R. Heinz and J. Hörisch (eds), *Geld und Geltung. Zu Alfred Sohn-Rethels soziologischer Erkenntnistheorie* (Würzburg), 112–121

Friedman, J. 1994. The Political economy of elegance. An African cult of beauty. In: J. Friedman (ed.), *Consumption and Identity, Studies in Anthropology and History* 15 (Chur), 167–189

Friedman, J. 1995. Global system, globalization and the parameters of modernity. In: M. Featherstone (ed.), *Global Modernities* (London), 69–90

Friedman, J. 1998. Transnationalization, socio-political disorder and ethnification as expressions of declining global hegemony. *International Political Science Review* 19, 233–250

Friedman, J. 2004. Anthropology of the global, globalizing anthropology. A commentary. *Anthropologica* 46, 231–240

García del Hoyo, J. J. and Jiménez de Madariaga, C. 2016. The debate on the concept of value. interpretations from the perspective of economics and social anthropology, *Mediterranean Journal of Social Sciences* 7(2), 11–20

Gebhardt, J. 1989. Die Werte. Zum Ursprung eines Schlüsselbegriffs der politisch-sozialen Sprache der Gegenwart in der deutschen Philosophie des späten 19. Jahrhunderts. In: R. Hofmann, J. Jantzen and H. Kuhn (eds), *Anodos. Festschrift für Helmut Kuhn* (Weinheim), 35–54

Geffray, C. 2001. *Trésors. Anthropologie Analytique de la Valeur* (Strasbourg)

Gerritsen, A. and Riello, G. 2016. The global lives of things. Material culture in the first global age. In: A. Gerritsen and G. Riello (eds), *The Global Lives of Things. The Material Culture of Connections in the First Global Age* (London), 1–28

Glenn, J, and Walker, R. 2012. *Significant Objects. 100 Extraordinary Stories about Ordinary Objects* (Seattle WA)

Graeber, D. 2001. *Toward an Anthropological Theory of Value. The False Coin of our Own Dreams* (New York)

Graeber, D. 2013. It is value that brings universes into being. *HAU, Journal of Ethnographic Theory* 3(2), 219–243

Gregory, C. A. 2000 Anthropology, economics, and political economy. A critique of Pearson. *History of Political Economy* 32(4), 999–1009

Grewe, B.-S. 2009 Gold. In: A. Iriye and J.-Y. Saunier (eds), *The Palgrave Dictionary of Transnational History* (Basingstoke)

Habermas, T. 1992 *Geliebte Objekte. Symbole und Instrumente der Identitätsbildung* (Munich)

Hahn, H. P. 2005 Dinge des Alltags – Umgang und Bedeutungen. Eine ethnologische Perspektive. In: G. M. König (ed.), *Alltagsdinge. Erkundungen der materiellen Kultur* (Tübingen), 63–79

Hahn, H. P. 2012 Durkheim und die Ethnologie. *Paideuma* 58, 261–282

Hahn, H. P. 2014a Notizen zur Umwertung der Werte. Perspektiven auf ökonomische Konzepte im interdisziplinären Diskurs. In: I. Klein and S. Windmüller (eds), *Kultur der Ökonomie. Materialität und Performanz des Wirtschaftlichen* (Bielefeld) 17–36

Hahn, H. P. 2014b Die Sprache des Glanzes. Wert und Werte als Kontext von Gold. In: H. Meller, R. Risch and E. Pernicka (eds), *Metalle der Macht. Frühes Gold und Silber* (Halle [Saale]), 21–31

Hahn, H. P. 2016 Geliebt, geschätzt, verachtet. Zur Dynamik der Be- und Umwertung materieller Dinge. *Beiträge zur Mittelalterarchäologie in Österreich* 31, 9–16

Hahn, H. P. 2018. Markets as places. Actors, structures and ideologies. In: H. P. Hahn and G. Schmitz (eds), *Market as Place and Space of Economic Exchange. Perspectives from Archaeology and Anthropology* (Oxford), 1–18

Hahn, H. P. 2019 The values of things, pragmatically, symbolically and emotionally. Some remarks on object appreciation. In: G. Jaritz and I. Matschinegg (eds), *My Favourite Things. Object Preferences in Medieval and Early Modern Material Culture* (Berlin), 21–35

Hahn, H. P. 2021 Die versteckte Gabe. Über einige Irrtümer zum Konzept der 'Gabenökonomie'. *Zeitschrift für Wirtschafts- und Unternehmensethik* 22(1), 28–45

Hahn, H. P. and Weiss, H. (eds) 2013 *Mobility, Meaning and Transformations of Things. Shifting Contexts of Material Culture through Time and Space* (Oxford)

Hart, K. and Ortiz, H. 2014 The anthropology of money and finance: between ethnography and world history. *Annual Review of Anthropology* 43, 465–482

Heinich, N. 2017 *Des valeurs. Une approche sociologique* (Paris)

Heinich, N. 2019 Axiologie du Precieux, Gradhiva. *Revue d'anthropologie et d'historie des arts* 30, 92–107

Heinrich, M. 2020 'Gespenstige Gegenständlichkeit'. Wie Marx im Kapital das phantastisch-reale Dasein des Werts analysiert. In: M. Bies and E. Mengaldo (eds), *Marx konkret. Poetik und Ästhetik des 'Kapitals'* (Göttingen), 111–121

Helms, M. W. 1988 *Ulysses' Sail. An Ethnographic Odyssey of Power, Knowledge, and Geographical Distance* (Princeton NJ)

Hénaff, M. 2002 *Le prix de la vérité. Le don, l'argent, la philosophie* (Paris)

Hofmeester, K. and Grewe, B.-S. 2016 *Luxury in Global Perspective. Objects and Practices (1600-2000)* (New York)

Hoskins, J. 1998 *Biographical Objects. How Things Tell the Stories of People's Lives* (London)

Hugh-Jones, S. 1992 Yesterday's luxuries, tomorrow's necessities. Business and barter in northwest Amazonia. In: S. Hugh-Jones and C. Humphrey (eds), *Barter, Exchange and Value. An Anthropological Approach* (Cambridge), 42–74

Hutter, M. and Throsby, D. (eds) 2008 *Beyond Price. Value in Culture, Economics and the Arts* (New York)

Joas, H. 2000 *The Genesis of Values* (Cambridge)

Karpik, L. 2010 *Valuing the Unique. The Economics of Singularities* (Princeton NJ)

Klamer, A. 2004 Cultural goods are good for more than their economic value. In: V. Rao and M. Walton (eds), *Culture and Public Action* (Stanford CA), 138–162

Kluckhohn, C. 1952 Values and value-orientations in the theory of action. In: T. Parsons and E. A. Shils (eds), *Toward a General Theory of Action* (Cambridge), 388–433

Knight, F. H. 1963 Value and Price. In: D. L. Sills (ed.), *International Encyclopedia of the Social Sciences* (New York), 218–225

Kornberger, M., Justesen, L., Madsen, A. K. and Mouritsen, J. 2015 Introduction. In: M. Kornberger, L. Justesen, A. K. Madsen and J. Mouritsen (eds), *Making Things Valuable* (Oxford), 1–17

Kraemer, K. 2016 Lucien Karpik. Mehr Wert. Die Ökonomie des Einzigartigen. In: K. Kraemer and F. Brugger (eds), *Schlüsselwerke der Wirtschaftssoziologie* (Wiesbaden), 507–513

Kuehling, S. 2017 'We Die for Kula'. An object-centred view of motivations and strategies in gift exchange. *Journal of the Polynesian Society* 126(2), 181–207

Lotze, H. 1864 *Microcosmos* (Leipzig)

Lowenthal, D. 1990 Forging the past and authenticity. *APOLLO. The International Magazine of the Arts* 131(337), 152–157

Malinowski, B. 1922 *Argonauts of the Western Pacific. An Account of Native Enterprise and Adventure in the Archipelagoes of Melanesian New Guinea* (London)

Marx, F. 1867 *Das Kapital. Kritik der politischen Ökonomie* (Hamburg)

Mauss, M. 1954 *Gift. Forms and Functions of Exchange in Archaic Societies* (1st edition 1925) (Glencoe IL)

Miklautz, E. 1996 *Kristallisierter Sinn* (Munich)

Miller, D. 1987 *Material Culture and Mass Consumption* (Oxford)

Miller, D. 1992 Imported goods as authentic culture. In: R. Eisendle (ed.), *Produktkulturen. Dynamik und Bedeutungswandel des Konsums* (Frankfurt am Main), 271–288

Miller, D. 2000 Introduction. The Birth of Value. In: P. Jackson, M. Lowe and D. Miller (eds), *Commercial Cultures. Economies, Practices, Spaces* (Oxford), 77–83

Miller, D. 2001a Alienable gifts and inalienable commodities. In: F. R. Myers (ed.), *The Empire of Things. Regimes of Value and Material Culture* (Santa Fe NM), 91–115

Miller, D. 2001b Possessions. In: D. Miller (ed.), *Home Possessions. Material Culture Behind Closed Doors* (Oxford), 107–121

Miller, D. 2008 The uses of value. *Geoforum* 39, 122–132

Miller, D. and Woodward, S. 2012 *Blue Jeans. The Art of the Ordinary* (Los Angeles CA)

Mosko, M. S. 2000 Inalienable ethnography. keeping-while-giving and the Trobriand case. *Journal of the Royal Anthropological Institute* NS 6, 377–397

Munn, N. 1986 *The Fame of Gawa. A Symbolic Study of Value Transformation in a Massim (Papua New Guinea) Society* (Cambridge)

Myers, F. R. 2001 Introduction. In: F. R. Myers (ed.), *The Empire of Things. Regimes of Value and Material Culture* (Santa Fe NM), 1–61

Narotzky, S. and Besnier, N. 2014 Crisis, value, and hope. Rethinking the economy. *Current Anthropology* 55, suppl. 9, S4–S16

Orlove, B. S. 1997 *The Allure of the Foreign. Imported Goods in Postcolonial Latin America* (Ann Arbor MI)

Osterhammel, J. 2021 Warenökonomie und Mobilitätsfolklore. *Zeitschrift für Ideengeschichte* 15(1), 5–13

Palomera, J. 2014 Reciprocity, commodification, and poverty in the era of financialization. *Current Anthropology* 55, suppl. 9, S105–S115

Parsons, T. 1968 On the concept of value-commitments. *Sociological Inquiry* 38, 135–160

Pearce, S. M. 1995 *On Collecting. An Investigation into Collecting in the European Tradition* (London)

Pedersen, D. 2008 Introduction. Toward a value theory of anthropology. *Anthropological Theory* 8(1), 5–8

Pels, D., Hetherington, K. and Vandenberghe, F. 2002 The status of the object. Performances, mediations, and techniques. *Theory, Culture and Society* 19(5/6), 1–21

Pomian, K. 1978 Zwischen Sichtbarem und Unsichtbarem. Die Sammlung. In: K. Pomian, *Entre l'invisible et le visible. la collection. Enciclopedia Einaudi III* (Turin), 15–59

Porath, E. 2002 Die Frage nach der Dinglichkeit. Heidegger und das Geschlecht der Dinge zwischen Entzug und Ereignis. In: G. Ecker, C. Breger and S. Scholz (eds), *Dinge. Medien der Aneignung, Grenzen der Verfügung* (Königstein), 256–272

Rezsohazy, R. 2001 Values, sociology of. In: N. J. Smelser and P. B. Baltes (eds), *International Encyclopedia of the Social & Behavioral Sciences* 23 (Amsterdam), 16153–16158

Rieger, B. 2013 *The People's Car. A Global History of the Volkswagen Beetle* (Cambridge)

Robbins, J. 2013 Monism, pluralism and the structure of value relations. A Dumontian contribution to the contemporary study of value. *HAU. Journal of Ethnographic Theory* 3(1), 9–115

Rochberg-Halton, E. 1984 *Object Relations, Role Models, and Cultivation of the Self. Environment and Behavior* 16(3), 335–368

Sahlins, M. D. 1988 Cosmologies of capitalism. The Trans-Pacific sector of 'The World System'. *Proceedings of the British Academy* 74, 1–51

Saul, M. 2018 Markets in West Africa. Karl Polanyi, or what sort of social formation. In: H. P. Hahn and G. Schmitz (eds), *Market as Place and Space of Economic Exchange. Perspectives from Archaeology and Anthropology* (Oxford), 127–151

Schefold, B. 1992 *Studien zur Entwicklung der ökonomischen Theorie XI* (Berlin)

Shipton, P. 1989 *Bitter Money. Cultural Economy and Some African Meanings of Forbidden Commodities* (Washington DC)

Siebenhüner, K. 2017 Die Mobilität der Dinge. Ansätze zur Konzeptualisierung für die Frühneuzeitforschung. In: A. C. Cremer and M. Mulsow (eds), *Objekte als Quellen der historischen Kulturwissenschaften* (Cologne), 35–46

Sillitoe, P. 2006 Why spheres of exchange? *Ethnology* 45(1), 1–23

Strathern, A. and Stewart, P. J. 2005 Ceremonial exchange. In: J. G. Carrier (ed.), *Handbook of Economic Anthropology* (Cheltenham), 230–245

Suberbère, S., Audinet, G. and Derlon, B. 2016 *Si loin si proche. Objets d'ailleurs dans les intérieurs européens* (Rome)

Thompson, C. J. 2013 The politics of consumer identity work. *Journal of Consumer Research* 40(5), iii–vii

Tilley, C. 2006 Objectification. In: C. W. Tilley, W. Keane and S. Kuechler (eds), *Handbook of Material Culture* (London), 60–73

Turner, T. 1995 Social body, embodied subject. Bodiliness, subjectivity, and sociality among the Kayapo. *Cultural Anthropology* 10(2), 143–170

Turner, T. 2003 The beautiful and the common. Inequalities of value and revolving hierarchy among the Kayapó, Tipití. *Journal of the Society for the Anthropology of Lowland South America* 1(1), 11–26

Turner, T. 2008 Marxian Value Theory. An anthropological perspective. *Anthropological Theory* 8(1), 43–56

Uberoi, J. P. S. 1962 *Politics of the Kula ing. An Analysis of the Findings of Bronislaw Malinowski* (Manchester)
Veblen, T. 1899 *The Theory of the Leisure Class. An Economic Study of Institutions* (New York)
Wagner-Hasel, B. 2000 *Der Stoff der Gaben. Kultur und Politik des Schenkens und Tauschens im archaischen Griechenland* (Frankfurt am Main)
Wallendorf, M. and Arnould, E. J. 1988 'My favorite things'. A cross cultural inquiry into object attachment, possessiveness, and social linkage. *Journal of Consumer Research* 14, 531–547
Walsh, A. 2003 'Hot money' and daring consumption in a northern Malagasy sapphire-mining town. *American Ethnologist* 30, 290–305
Watson, J. J., Lysonski, S., Gillan, T. and Raymore, L. 2002 Cultural values and important possessions. A cross-cultural analysis. *Journal of Business Research* 55, 923–931
Weiner, A. B. 1992 *Inalienable Possessions. The Paradox of Keeping-While-Giving* (Berkeley CA)
Werner, C. and Bell, D. (eds) 2004 *Values and Valuables. From the Sacred to the Symbolic* (Walnut Creek CA)
Werthmann, K. 2001 Gefährliches Gold und bitteres Geld. Zum Umgang mit einer außergewöhnlichen Ressource in Burkina Faso. *Africa Spectrum* 36(3), 363–381
Wilk, R. R. 1999 'Real Belizean food'. Building local identity in the transnational Caribbean. *American Anthropologist* 101(2), 244–255
Winnicott, D. W. 1953 Transitional objects and transitional phenomena. A study of the first not-me possession. *International Journal of Psycho-Analysis* 34, 89–97
Zhang, W. 2010 Wertapriori und Wertsein in der materialen Wertethik Max Schelers. *META. Research in Hermeneutics, Phenonemology, and Practical Philosophy* 2(2), 178–194

Chapter 2

Learning new styles, quickly: an examination of the Mittani–middle Assyrian transition in material culture

Federico Buccellati

During the 2nd millennium BCE, the area known today as Mesopotamia was controlled by two political entities – first the Mittanian and then the middle Assyrian. The period of transition between the two was brief, since Mittani ended abruptly with a major military loss to a Hittite army which came from Anatolia. After their victory, the Hittites did not stay and attempt to control the region but, instead, withdrew once the Mittani military might had been crushed. This defeat and subsequent withdrawal left a power vacuum which the Assyrians quickly filled. These two periods are particularly interesting from the historical and archaeological perspectives because of the markedly different forms of political control and cultural dissemination espoused by the two regional powers.

The vicinity, in terms of space and time, between these two states is surprising: within a few decades at most, the political power controlling the Jezireh changed dramatically – the Assyrian king Eriba-Adad I is a Mittani vassal and sees his liege-lord fight and lose to the Hittites. His successor, Ashur-uballit, is an independent ruler, seizes large portions of what was Mittani territory and has the military might to conquer Babylon.

The distance, in terms of material culture and mechanisms of territorial control, between these two states is equally surprising. The Mittani presence is, on the whole, marked by a few monumental structures and a few unique aspects of material culture in areas which otherwise demonstrate a continuity of local traditions. The middle Assyrian presence, in contrast, is much more widespread, building on the Mittani administrative districts and to a much more complex administrative system under Shalmanasser I.

In what follows, the Mittani and middle Assyrian evidence will be discussed, followed by the aims of the Mittani–Middle Assyrian Transition Project, an ongoing research project being carried out at the Freie Universität Berlin by the author.

Mittani presence in the Jezireh

The Jezireh area has long been identified with the Mittani heartland due to the presence of the two capital cities, Taidu and Washukanni. Washukanni has been potentially identified as the modern Tell Fekheriye (also spelled Tell Fakhariyah and Fakhariya)[1] and Tell Hamidiye as Taidu,[2] although Tell Farfara and Üçtepe are other proposed locations.[3]

Many important sites with levels dating to the Mittani period have been discovered, both in the Jezireh and in Syro-Mesopotamia as a whole.[4] The list of sites is longer than one might think – about 34 have been identified while doing preliminary research, including: Arbid, Ashara, Bazi, Bi'a, Chuera, Fakhar, Fekheriye, Giricano, Hamidiya, Kurd Qaburstan, Mozan, Rimah, Sabi Abyad, Üçtepe, Um el Marra and Ziyaret Tepe.

The material culture of the Mittani period is distinguished by several aspects,[5] particularly glyptics, architecture and ceramics. A definition of Mittani material culture can be, at times, difficult to identify vis-à-vis local traditions, as the distribution of Mittani material culture over the area of control is limited; as Peter Akkermans and Glenn Schwartz put it, 'excavations at major tells with Mitannian [sic] period occupation exhibit a pattern of large-scale elite buildings on mound summits with little evidence of occupation elsewhere on the site.'[6] Thus it is in glyptics, architecture and ceramics that Mittani traditions can best be discovered.

The glyptic evidence from the Mittani period includes studies focused on material from specific sites,[7] collections[8] and studies of specific iconographic elements,[9] as well as being part of the general volumes on glyptic, such as that by Anton Moortgat.[10] Edith Porada's study compares elements of Mittani and middle Assyrian glyptic as well.[11]

Architectural studies in Mittani periods have focused in particular, due to discoveries in the archaeological record, on residential houses, e.g. in Nuzi[12] and Bazi[13] and on monumental architecture, e.g. at Brak[14] and again at Nuzi.[15] The architecture from Tell Chuera is of particular relevance, as Chuera has elements from both periods, e.g. the Mittani-Bau excavated in 1974[16] (Fig. 2.1).

---

[1] Opitz 1927.
[2] Haas and Wäfler 1985.
[3] Köroğlu 1998; Ristvet and Weiss 2005.
[4] Cancik-Kirschbaum *et al.* 2014.
[5] Evans 2008; Schwartz 2014.
[6] Akkermans and Schwartz 2003, 346.
[7] Porada 1947; Stein 1993–1997; 2001; 2010.
[8] Teissier 1984.
[9] Kantor 1945.
[10] Moortgat 1966.
[11] Porada 1979.
[12] Novák 1994.
[13] Otto 2014.
[14] Oates 1990.
[15] Starr 1939; Heinrich 1984.
[16] Moortgat and Moortgat-Correns 1976.

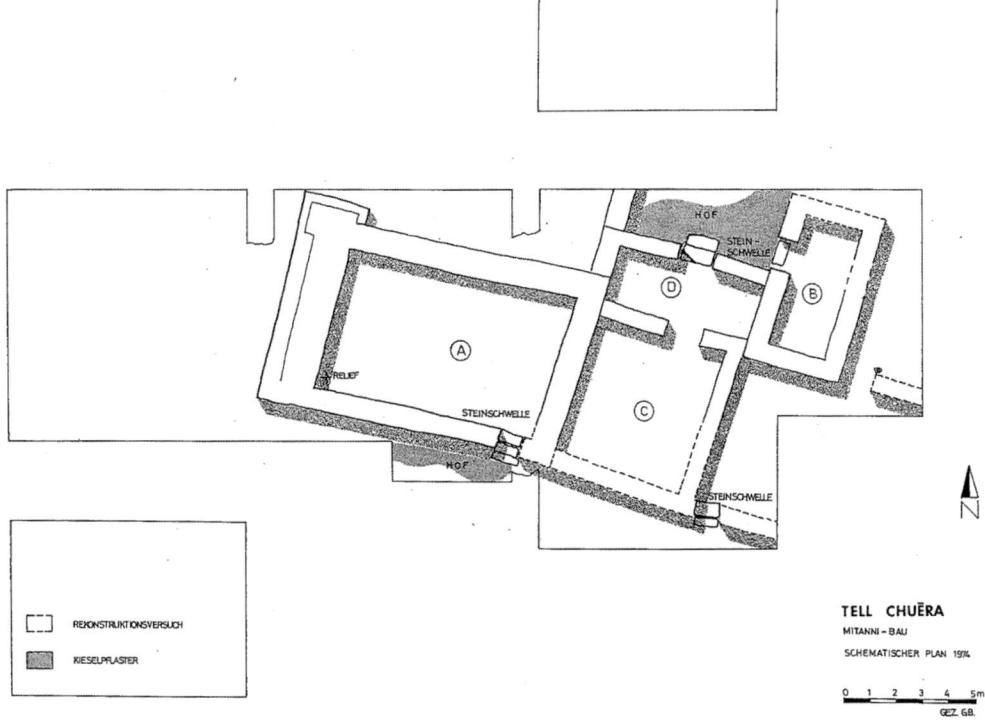

Figure 2.1. Plan of the 'Mittani-Bau' from Tell Chuera (Moortgat and Moortgat-Correns 1976, map V).

The ceramic assemblage associated with the Mittani period has elements of continuity from the preceding Khabur assemblage,[17] and yet the demographics of the region between Khabur and Mittani change (based on survey data).[18] Also, the wide distribution of 'Nuzi Ware' (arriving all the way to Alalakh) is, in part, linked to the Mittani political expansion;[19] this distribution is not, however, a litmus test for Mittani presence,[20] and other, more common, ceramic types are not necessarily indicative of Mittani (or middle Assyrian) presence either.[21] For an example of Mittani ceramics from Tell Mozan, see Figure 2.2. Despite these difficulties, by putting ceramics together with glyptic evidence and architecture, one can identify commonalities of presence/absence which are not apparent when considering ceramics alone. The problem of the identification of Mittani material culture is in part mitigated by the

---

[17] Stein 1984.
[18] Akkermans and Schwartz 2003, 331; Lyonnet and Faivre 2014.
[19] Akkermans and Schwartz 2003, 329.
[20] Schwartz 2014.
[21] Pfälzner 1995.

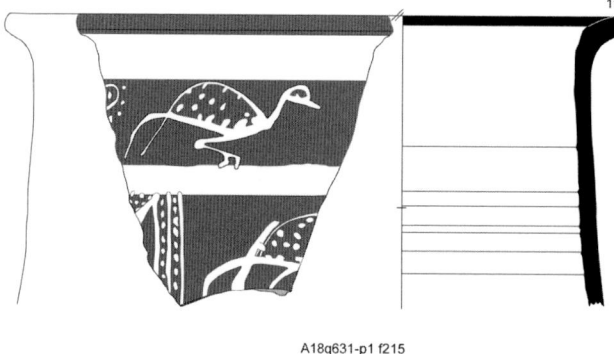

Figure 2.2. Drawing of potsherd A18q0631-p1 from Tell Mozan, depicting peacocks (© Tell Mozan/Urkesh Archaeological Project).

inclusion of material from the Tell Fekheriye project, material from the Mittani heartland and thus a definitive meter by which to measure material from other areas.

Our understanding of the area under Mittani control is shaped by discoveries in the archaeological record, including a large number of tablets coming from this period, of either Mittani origin or from other political players from the same time period.[22] These give a broader understanding of the mechanisms of control within the area dominated by Mittani. The picture which emerges is one of indirect control, where a local king is set up as a vassal of the Mittani state; cases where a polity is reduced to direct control from Mittani are few, notably the city of Halab where a real danger of rebellion existed, which direct control would have hindered.[23]

Several monographs exist exploring the history and material culture of the Mittani period, most notably Gernot Wilhelm's *The Hurrians*[24] (with Diana Stein's chapter on Art and architecture) and Jacques Freu's *Histoire du Mitanni*,[25] while questions of chronology related to Nuzi are raised by Michael Klein.[26] However, in these volumes the aspects of material culture tend to be overshadowed by the political and historical framework.

One of the primary and immediate causes of the downfall of Mittani is the continuing conflict with the Hittite state; a series of military defeats at the hand of the Hittite king Suppiluliuma I lead to the eventual subjugation of Mittani.[27] This is an interesting echo of the rise of the Mittani state, which filled a power vacuum after the Old Hittite kings defeated Yamhad.[28] As the Hittites were primarily interested in the region to the west of the Euphrates, these defeats created a power vacuum which was quickly filled by the Assyrians, who, up to that point, had been subjects (albeit

---

[22] Richter 2003.
[23] von Dassow 2014.
[24] Wilhelm 1989.
[25] Freu 2003.
[26] Klein 2013.
[27] Bryce 2011, 478.
[28] Liverani 2014, 291.

rebellious subjects, particularly at the end under the Assyrian king and Mittani vassal Eriba-Adad I) of the Mittani state.[29]

The middle Assyrian conquest

The middle Assyrian state seized large portions of territory formerly under Mittani control and went so far as to attack and defeat the Babylonian power to the south, even taking the city of Babylon – all of this under the first independent king, LUGAL (šarru), of the newly independent Assyrian state, Ashur-uballit.[30] Subsequent kings conquered most of the territory once held by Mittani (Adad-nirari I), defeated the Hittites at the Euphrates river (Tukulti-Ninurta I) and boasted that they received tribute from lands as far as Arwad and Byblos (Tiglath-pileser I).[31]

The archaeological record relating to the middle Assyrian period in the Jezireh and the wider Syro-Mesopotamian area is at least as rich as the Mittani one, including another 40 sites (several overlapping with Mittani sites) such as: Ali, Assur, Barri, Bderi, Billa, Chuera, Fekheriye, Halaf, Hammam et-Turkman, Mozan, Hariri (Mari), Satu Qala, Sheik Hamad, Shemamok.

The material culture of the middle Assyrian period[32] can also be particularly defined in terms of glyptics, architecture and ceramics. Glyptic evidence from the middle Assyrian period is present in tombs and in other areas of Assur, but several other sites have yielded further evidence, particularly ar-Rimah,[33] Fekheriye[34] and Tell Billa[35] (see Fig. 2.3 from Tell Fekheriye, for instance). Other studies consider middle Assyrian glyptic by chronological period or as a whole.[36] The glyptic evidence from these sites is of particular interest as they are from stratigraphic contexts and can also be tied to texts that aid in defining the chronological framework. Texts from this period also often contain seal impressions, e.g. the middle Assyrian texts published by Helmut Freydank.[37] Further glyptic evidence comes from collections such as the Marcopoli Collection;[38] Beatrice Teissier notes that 'Mitannian [sic] influence is discernible in much of the iconography of early Middle Assyrian glyptic art, which is otherwise characterized by symmetrical and formal compositions.'[39]

---

[29] Herles 2007.
[30] Bryce 2003, 14; 2011.
[31] Singer 1985; Grayson 1991, 2:2:37, 53; Bryce 2011, 85–86; Fales 2011.
[32] Pedersén 1986.
[33] Parker 1977.
[34] Kantor 1958; Bonatz 2021.
[35] Matthews 1991.
[36] Moortgat 1941; 1944; 1966; Beran 1957; Matthews 1990; 1992.
[37] Freydank 2001; Freydank and Feller 2010.
[38] Teissier 1984.
[39] Teissier 1984, 30.

Figure 2.3. Drawing of composite seal impression M.As 1 from Tell Fekheriye (Bonatz 2021, 14).

Architectural evidence for the middle Assyrian period is in abundance, with major excavations at several sites such as Sheik Hamad, Rimah and Sabi Abyad,[40] where large numbers of texts give an unparalleled look into the administrative structure of the state from the Grand Vizier to a fortified farmhouse. The archaeological evidence has been presented in several publications relating to the individual sites, as well as an overview of the archaeological evidence published by Aline Tenu[41] and a review of palatial architecture by Mario Liverani.[42]

The ceramics of the middle Assyrian period present a clearer picture than the Mittani one. Anacleto D'Agostino writes:

> Whenever we talk about Mitannian [sic] pottery we mean the pottery used at Tell Barri during the period of the Mitannian [sic] hegemony in the Khabur area, while the Assyrian pottery discovered at Tell Barri is a locally produced pottery belonging to a chronological phase happened [sic] after the conquest of the city by the Assyrian kings and tightly bound to a new political dimension of the settlement.[43]

Peter Pfälzner's work on the Mittani and middle Assyrian pottery integrates not only the typological aspects, but also provides an index to changes within the middle

---

[40] Akkermans *et al.* 1993; Postgate *et al.* 1997; Akkermans 2006; Kühne 2010.
[41] Tenu 2009; 2013.
[42] Liverani 2012.
[43] D'Agostino 2008a, 525 n. 1.

Assyrian state as reflected in its material culture.[44] Other studies include material from Sabi Abyad[45] and the ceramic evidence from sites with continuous occupation levels like Barri.[46] Kim Duistermaat's 2015 article on middle Assyrian pottery is of particular use in understanding the complexity of the ceramic evidence.[47] The middle Assyrian tombs from Assur are especially helpful in understanding the material culture of this period; the tombs were published originally by Arndt Haller,[48] but the material has been reworked and augmented by Friedhelm Pedde.[49]

The Assyrian administrative system of dividing territory into districts has its origins in the Mittani districts.[50] This system becomes more complex and divides the territory in a three-tiered system: *ālu* – city, *birtu* – fort, *dunnu* – (fortified) farmstead.[51] A further tier was added during the reign of Shalmanasser I, who places the entire area of Hanigalbat (representing most of the territory once held by the Mittani state) under a Grand Vizier; the reasons for such a change are unclear, as is the effect on the political relationship between Hanigalbat and Assur.[52] A number of studies aim to present comprehensive analyses relating to the administrative aspects and geographic extension of the middle Assyrian state, either in specific areas or for the entire political structure;[53] the evidence from Tell Fekheriye is of particular importance in considering the impact of middle Assyrian material culture at a site combining texts with architectural, glyptic and ceramic evidence.[54] Clearly there are marked differences between the administrative structure under the various middle Assyrian kings (during the reign of Shalmanasser I in particular, a number of changes can be discerned) but the basic structure of a distributed administrative system is present from the beginning.

The end of the middle Assyrian state has been discussed by several scholars, who cite internal pressures as well as the Aramean threat as causes for its dissolution.[55] This dissolution cannot be pinned to a specific point, and scholars disagree on the moment at which the middle Assyrian state ends.[56]

---

[44] Pfälzner 1995; 1997; 2007.
[45] Akkermans and Duistermaat 2001; Duistermaat 2008.
[46] D'Agostino 2008b.
[47] Duistermaat 2015.
[48] Haller 1954.
[49] Pedde 2011/2012; 2012; 2015; see also Lundström 2008.
[50] Radner 2004, 113; Fales 2011, 19.
[51] Al-Khalesi 1977; Herles 2007; Shibata 2007; Postgate 2010; Fales 2011; Llop 2012; Brown 2014; Cancik-Kirschbaum 2014.
[52] Cancik-Kirschbaum 1996, 29; Wiggermann 2000, 171.
[53] Machinist 1982; Harrak 1987; Liverani 1988; Kühne 1995; Cancik-Kirschbaum 2000; Lyon 2000; Jakob 2003; 2009; Novák 2007; 2013; Kertai 2008/2009; Llop-Raduà 2009; Llop 2011; Pongratz-Leisten 2011; 2015; Politopoulos 2012; Shibata 2012; Postgate 2013; Düring 2015; Mühl 2015.
[54] Bartl and Bonatz 2013.
[55] Postgate 1992; Szuchman 2007; Fales 2011; Brown 2013.
[56] Pfälzner 1995.

The Mittani–Middle Assyrian Transition Project

The questions that arise when looking at this evidence include: to what extent is the cultural impact of these two states different in polities under their control? Are local traditions in material culture present alongside those of the regional power? Is the diversity in representation of material culture related, directly or indirectly, to the mechanisms of political control? Does the quantity and quality of the dissemination of material culture play a role in the way scholars apply the modern terms of Empire, Kingdom or State to such societies?

Political control does not necessarily mean the physical presence of administrators, a garrison or foreign merchants – the kind of people who facilitate the transmission of material culture. The Mittani form of political control seems to involve few individuals, limiting the cultural 'footprint' to one or few large-scale buildings and controlling territory through vassal kings. The middle Assyrian cultural 'footprint' seems to be much larger, perhaps related to the larger administrative apparatus which marks the Assyrian presence. What then do these two states tell us about the relationship between the distribution of material culture and the mechanisms of political control?

The stylistic characteristics inherent in elements of material culture are not inseparable from the objects or their makers, nor are they immutable. The polities which fall under Mittani and/or Assyrian control have their own traditions and style; how are these affected by the arrival of new stylistic impulses? Are those elements which are Mittani or Assyrian affected at all, on a local level, by local traditions or availability of material?

Where local material culture is present or even predominant, is there a direct correlation with the absence of a strong cultural pressure from outside? Inversely, is the ubiquity of one society's material culture related to the mechanisms of control? If these tendencies can be seen in one element of material culture (e.g. glyptics or ceramics), is it automatically present in the others? How do these pressures affect smaller communities, such as towns or villages? Another factor is represented by the active/passive role of these pressures – are local populations adapting on their own to styles and objects newly arrived in their region (but not directly at their site) in a piecemeal fashion, or are representatives of these political powers actively imposing changes in material culture in sites where they are in direct control as a mechanism of integration?

Clearly, these questions apply only to those sites which are subsequently taken over by an external power – the material culture from sites such as Fekheriye, which lie in the Mittani heartland, have inherently Mittani traits. As the Mittani elements of material culture are less clearly defined in the literature to date, the inclusion of sites from the Mittani heartland provide an important 'Mittani control group' for the identification of local traditions. To this aim the inclusion of unpublished material from Fehkeriye linked to an uninterrupted stratified sequence is fundamental – and this is the focus of my current research.

The terms Empire and Kingdom are modern definitions which attempt to describe political relationships in territorial states. Can a parallel study of the Mittani and middle Assyrian periods validate or undermine our use of these terms in these contexts? There are studies on empire in general and on specific political entities in the ancient Near East[57] or other regions,[58] but none considers Mittani and middle Assyrian polities in comparison as proposed here; for a particularly interesting consideration of the sequence of these two polities at the same site see Dominik Bonatz's article on Fekheriye.[59] Another study intertwining archaeological, historical and anthropological facets in a way similar to the research I have undertaken, albeit for a different region and period, is Lisa Cooper's volume on the polities of the Euphrates.[60]

It is because of the unique situation in the Jezireh, where these two diverse states follow so closely on one another, and perhaps even overlap when considering elements of material culture, that these broader questions can be meaningfully approached. Two sets of sites can be discussed: one for Mittani and one for middle Assyrian. In unifying them into a single list, the number of sites with settlement periods during the period of control of either Mittani or middle Assyrian is clear.

Data. Breadth and depth

To return to the basic research question: to what extent is the cultural impact of the Mittani and middle Assyrian states different in polities under their control? It is to answer such a question that I have undertaken a long-term research project that aims at bringing together the large body of data available, on which then to build a comprehensive study of the underlying political and cultural implications. As is apparent from the brief overview I have given here, the body of data that is available has a very considerable breadth and depth. The breadth is represented by the large number of published sites with material from the Mittani and/or middle Assyrian periods. These sites will lead to a definition of what is Mittani and middle Assyrian, as different from elements of the local material culture. On the basis of these definitions, the presence or absence of material culture can be determined for polities under direct or indirect political control and the link evaluated. Parallel to the breadth of sites under study, the depth of material is represented by the wealth of unpublished material from Tell Chuera which spans both periods. This portion of my research will provide data for an analysis which looks at the change over time from Mittani to middle Assyrian in the same polity. It is in this combination of a broad perspective and a detailed analysis that a new approach to this important research question can be found.

---

[57] Gorny 1995; Parker 2001; 2009; Glatz 2009.
[58] Sinopoli 1994; 2001.
[59] Bonatz 2014.
[60] Cooper 2006.

Here, one sees that a total of 64 sites have settlement levels from the Mittani and/or middle Assyrian periods; 18 sites have settlement levels from both. There are several questionmarks and some of these sites may have textual evidence but not archaeological levels – I am currently carrying out an in-depth study of these publications to determine each one's relevance to the project's research question. Furthermore, just because a site has a settlement dating to the Mittani or middle Assyrian period does not mean that there are elements of material culture which may be attributed to either state – it is possible that some of the sites have exclusively local traditions. The first question, then, is how to identify what material should be used to define Mittani and middle Assyrian in the context of this project. The answer lies in the use of textual evidence, which allows one to determine which sites had members from these political entities present; the commonality in material culture between these sites would be the point of departure for defining what is Mittani and/or middle Assyrian. From that basis, then, the other sites would be queried in order to discern what is local and what is indicative of the presence (in material culture) of these political entities. While it is true that some of the sites have very limited material, and some publications may lack some of the material needed for such a study, I submit that one of the strengths of my research lies in the breadth of sites, an analysis of which enables new results. Certainly, these published materials have been available to scholars for years if not decades – what is innovative and productive is the understanding which only a broad macro-regional study can provide, hand-in-hand with a deeper study of the unpublished material from select sites, as described below.

In fact, in order to best isolate which elements of material culture are representative of the larger society and which are local or micro-regional, a macro-regional approach is needed for this portion of the project. It is for this reason that some of the sites on the list are quite far from the Jezireh, including sites like Alalakh or Nuzi; these sites give a macro-regional view to the distribution of material culture, so as to aid in the identification of those elements of material culture tied to the territorial control of a regional power. Thus the danger of a circular argument is avoided – sites which are Mittani (or middle Assyrian) in date do not define the Mittani material culture which might (wrongly) then be used to define other Mittani sites. Instead, the broad distribution across the macro-region is what is used to define elements as belonging to Mittani, leaving other elements as local or micro-regional. Additionally, the inclusion of material from Fekheriye (as discussed also above) gives my research a firm foundation of Mittani material from the centre, where the local culture is Mittani, against which other Mittani settlements can be compared.

While a macro-regional view gives an understanding of the distribution of material across the territory under control, an in-depth look at one site is also needed in order to explore the network of objects over time within a single community. To this aim, the (mostly) unpublished material from Tell Chuera excavation areas M and V forms a crucial part of my research.

Area M was excavated by Moortgat during the 1974 and 1975 seasons; a brief report was published in the 1976 volume,[61] but a large amount of unpublished material is present in the Moortgat archive. The major architectural find within this excavation area was a large building dated to the Mittani period. The Oppenheim Stiftung was recently bequeathed a large body of notes, excavation diaries, photographs and drawings tied to Moortgat's excavations at Tell Chuera; this material is currently housed at the Institute of Archaeology at the Goethe University, Frankfurt am Main and is under the care of the Director of the Tell Chuera Archaeological Project, Jan-Waalke Meyer. These excavations cover many years of fieldwork in areas dating to the early historical era, including several areas with finds from the Mittani and middle Assyrian periods, including area M. The Moortgat archive contains over 120 elements of documentation, including excavation diaries, reports, photos, drawings and plans. The material from area M is, understandably, spread out throughout the archive, as excavations and object analysis were carried out in different points during the field seasons. The primary excavation notes come from three main excavation diaries but part of the proposed project involves a detailed culling of the material from area M held within the archive.

While preliminary excavation reports relating to these discoveries were published, these covered only the main finds of those excavations and did not include the documentary evidence which has become the standard in modern archaeological publication. The archive was not catalogued by Moortgat, having grown organically year by year as the excavations at Tell Chuera progressed. Thanks to the bequest of the Moortgat archive, this information is not lost but can still be gleaned from those records. For a recent consideration of Moortgat's impact on the field, see the edited volume by Rita Dolce.[62]

Area V was excavated during the 2001 season under the direction of Meyer and has, in a single excavation area, levels dating to both the Mittani and middle Assyrian periods.[63] The architecture of this area is residential in nature, so that it is an ideal area in which to explore elements of continuity and change between the two periods.

Area G is a further excavation area of Tell Chuera which is relevant to this study, as it contains the middle Assyrian palace. The data from this excavation area is currently being prepared for publication by the excavators and will be included when available.

Learning new styles, quickly

The challenge here is to be able to identify change within the archaeological record across multiple sites. The strength of the project is also a potential limitation: the brief period of time between the end of Mittani and the beginning of the middle Assyrian periods means that identifying the transition in the archaeological record can be

---

[61] Moortgat and Moortgat-Correns 1976, 35–51.
[62] Dolce 2010.
[63] Stoyke and Heinzle 2001.

difficult. Further, changes in material culture will have occurred in diverse moments at the sites under analysis, depending on several factors, including importance of the site and the presence of Mittani or middle Assyrian actors.

As the research progresses, I am testing my guiding hypothesis that there are varying degrees of rapidity in change in the three categories of material culture which I am examining as benchmarks for the change. Ceramics changes rapidly because the vessels in use break easily and must be replaced frequently. Seals, on the other hand, are durable and become a symbol of identity for the seal owner; at the same time, an influx of foreign seal owners with their own style would create a desire to imitate the new fashion and to adapt to it on the part of the local population. Architecture is the slowest because buildings last longer and are more expensive to replace.

By examining the overlap of change in these three aspects, I am gaining a relative measure of the time frame within which change occurred. By examining this time frame against the backdrop of the historical data available from several sites, a scenario is emerging that serves to test, in depth and with a rich amount of data, the basic hypothesis regarding their distribution.

Outlook

The analysis of the transition between the Mittani and middle Assyrian periods outlined here will show not only how changes in material culture can be found to parallel changes in political control, but also how the distribution and dissemination of that material culture is related to the presence or absence of representatives of the governing polity. The full results will be published as a monograph within the *Berliner Beiträge zum Vorderen Orient* series, and the datasets will be made available online at www.mit-ma.net (hosted on GitHub and mirrored at Zenodo for data longevity). The project is associated with the 'Researching Oriental Despotism' Research Center at the Freie Universität Berlin (Deutsche Forschungsgemeinschaft – Center for Advanced Studies in the Humanities and Social Sciences #2615); thanks to this collaboration, the results will resonate within a wider research framework dedicated to understanding forms of governance within the ancient Near East.

Acknowledgements

It is with great pleasure that I contribute to this volume, a publication of a final workshop of the Research Training Group 'Value and Equivalence'. The time I spent in the Research Training Group was fundamental for my scholarly development; first and foremost, I would like to thank Jan-Waalke Meyer – I cannot imagine a more supportive, thoughtful, generous and insightful mentor. Thomas Richter's comments always started a deeper discussion which inevitably enriched my work. Franziska Lang was my mentor for the Post-Doctoral period during which this project was born, and

I am very grateful for her help in formulating the research path. Peter Breunig, Hans Peter Hahn and Hans-Markus von Kaenel were all supportive in different moments of my work, and to them as well as the other professors go my heartfelt thanks. The other members of the first 'cohort' helped create an environment where we could all work well and learn from each other as well. Last but by no means least, Annabel Bokern was fundamental in creating this environment and supporting my and the other candidates' growth over the time spent together. Thanks as well to the Institute of Near Eastern Archaeology at the Freie Universität Berlin for hosting my current project, and to Dominik Bonatz for his support.

References

Akkermans, P. M. M. G. 2006 The fortress of Ili-pada. Middle Assyrian architecture at Tell Sabi Abyad, Syria. In: P. Butterlin, M. Lebeau, J.-Y. Monchambert, J. L. Montero Fenollós and B. Muller (eds), *Les Espaces Syro-Mésopotamiens. Dimensions de l'expérience Humaine Au Proche-Orient Ancien. Volume d'hommage Offert à Jean-Claude Margueron*, Subartu 17 (Turnhout), 201–211

Akkermans, P. M. M. G. and Duistermaat, K. 2001 A middle Assyrian pottery kiln at Tell Sabi Abyad, Syria. In: J.-W. Meyer, M. Novák and A. Pruß (eds), *Beiträge zur Vorderasiatischen Archäologie. Winfried Orthmann gewidmet* (Frankfurt am Main) 12–19

Akkermans, P. M. M. G. and Schwartz, G. M. 2003 *The Archaeology of Syria. From complex hunter-gatherers to early urban societies (c. 16,000–300 BC)*, Cambridge World Archaeology (Cambridge)

Akkermans, P. M. M. G., Limpens, J. and Spoor, R. H. 1993 On the frontier of Assyria. Excavations at Tell Sabi Abyad, 1991 *Akkadica* 84/85, 1–52

Al-Khalesi, Y. M. 1977 Tell al-Fakhar (Kurruḫanni). A dimtu-Settlement. *Assur* 1(6), 1–42

Bartl, P. V. and Bonatz, D. 2013 Across Assyria's northern frontier. Tell Fekheriye at the end of the Late Bronze Age. In: K. A. Yener (ed.), *Across the Border. Late Bronze-Iron Age Relations between Syria and Anatolia. Proceedings of a Symposium Held at the Research Center of Anatolian Studies, Koç University, Istanbul. May 31-June 1, 2010*, Ancient Near Eastern Studies Suppl. 42 (Leuven), 263–292

Beran, T. 1957 Assyrische Glyptik des 14. Jahrhunderts. *Zeitschrift für Assyriologie und Vorderasiatische Archäologie* 52, 141–215

Bonatz, D. 2014 Tell Fekheriye in the Late Bronze Age. Archaeological investigations into the structures of political governance in the Upper Mesopotamian Piedmont. In: D. Bonatz (ed.), *The Archaeology of Political Spaces. The Upper Mesopotamian Piedmont in the Second Millennium BCE*, Topoi. Berlin Studies of the Ancient World 12 (Berlin), 61–84

Bonatz, D. 2021 *Middle Assyrian Seal Motifs from Tell Fekheriye (Syria)*. Tell Fekheriye Excavation Reports 1 (Berlin)

Brown, B. 2013 The structure and decline of the middle Assyrian State. The role of autonomous and nonstate actors. *Journal of Cuneiform Studies* 65, 97–126

Brown, B. 2014 Settlement patterns of the middle Assyrian State. Notes toward an investigation of state apparatuses. In: D. Bonatz (ed.), *The Archaeology of Political Spaces. The Upper Mesopotamian Piedmont in the Second Millennium BCE*. Topoi. Berlin Studies of the Ancient World 12 (Berlin), 85–105

Bryce, T. 2003 *Letters of the Great Kings of the Ancient Near East*. The Royal Correspondence of the Late Bronze Age (London)

Bryce, T. 2011 *The Routledge Handbook of the Peoples and Places of Ancient Western Asia. The Near East from the Early Bronze Age to the Fall of the Persian Empire* (London)

Cancik-Kirschbaum, E. C. 1996 Die mittelassyrischen Briefe aus Tall Šēḫ Ḥamad. *Berichte der Ausgrabung Tall Šēḫ Ḥamad/Dūr-Katlimmu* 4 (Berlin)

Cancik-Kirschbaum, E. 2000 Organisation und Verwaltung von Grenzgebieten in mittelassyrischer Zeit. Die Westgrenze. In: L. Milano, S. de Martino, F. M. Fales and G. B. Lanfranchi (eds), *Landscapes. Territories, frontiers and horizons in the ancient Near East. Papers Presented to the XLIV Rencontre Assyriologique Internationale, Venezia, 7-11 July 1997 2. Geography and Cultural Landscapes.* History of the Ancient Near East. Monograph 3(2) (Padua), 5–8

Cancik-Kirschbaum, E. 2014 From text to tell. Governance and the geography of political space according to middle Assyrian administrative documents. In: D. Bonatz (ed.), *The Archaeology of Political Spaces. The Upper Mesopotamian Piedmont in the Second Millennium BCE.* Topoi. Berlin Studies of the Ancient World 12 (Berlin), 107–116

Cancik-Kirschbaum, E., Brisch, N. and Eidem, J. (eds) 2014 *Constituent, Confederate, and Conquered Space. The Emergence of the Mittani State.* Topoi. Berlin Studies of the Ancient World 17 (Berlin)

Cooper, L. 2006 *Early Urbanism on the Syrian Euphrates* (New York)

D'Agostino, A. 2008a Between Mitannians and middle-Assyrians. Changes and links in ceramic culture at Tell Barri and in Syrian Jazirah during the end of the 2nd millennium BC. In: J. Córdoba, M. Molist, C. Pérez, I. Rubio and S. Martínez (eds), *Proceedings of the 5th International Congress on the Archaeology of the Ancient Near East. Madrid, April 3-8 2006.* (Madrid), 525–547

D'Agostino, A. 2008b Pottery production and transformation of the social structure in an 'Assyrian' settlement from the Late Bronze Age to the Iron Age. The Tell Barri case. In: H. Kühne, R. M. Czichon and F. J. Kreppner (eds), *Proceedings of the 4th International Congress of the Archaeology of the Ancient Near East. 29 March-3 April 2004, Freie Universität Berlin II. Social and Cultural Transformation. The Archaeology of Transitional Periods and Dark Ages. Excavation Reports* (Wiesbaden) 47–63

Dassow, E. von 2014 Levantine polities under Mittanian hegemony. In: Cancik-Kirschbaum *et al.* (eds) 2014, 11–32

Dolce, R. (ed.) 2010 *Quale Oriente? Omaggio a un maestro. Studi di arte e archeologia del vicino Oriente in memoria di Anton Moortgat a trenta anni dalla sua scomparsa* (Palermo)

Duistermaat, K. 2008 *The Pots and Potters of Assyria. Technology and Organisation of Production, Ceramic Sequence and Vessel Function at Late Bronze Age Tell Sabi Abyad, Syria.* Papers on Archaeology of the Leiden Museum of Antiquities 4 (Turnhout)

Duistermaat, K. 2015 The pots of Assur in the land of Hanigalbat. The organization of pottery production in the far west of the middle Assyrian Empire. In: B. S. Düring (ed.), *Understanding Hegemonic Practices of the Early Assyrian Empire. Essays Dedicated to Frans Wiggermann.* Uitgaven van het Nederlands Instituut voor het Nabije Oosten 2015 (Leiden), 125–152

Düring, B. S. 2015 The hegemonic practices of the middle Assyrian Empire in context. In: B. S. Düring (ed.), *Understanding Hegemonic Practices of the Early Assyrian Empire. Essays Dedicated to Frans Wiggermann.* Uitgaven van het Nederlands Instituut voor het Nabije Oosten 2015 (Leiden), 299–315

Evans, J. M. 2008 The Mitanni State. In: J. Aruz, K. Benzel and J. M. Evans (eds), *Beyond Babylon. Art, Trade, and Diplomacy in the Second Millennium B.C.* Exhibition catalogue, New York (New York), 194–199

Fales, F. M. 2011 Transition. The Assyrians at the Euphrates between the 13th and the 12th century BC. In: K. Strobel (ed.), *Empires after the Empire. Anatolia, Syria and Assyria after Suppiluliuma II (ca. 1200-800/700 B.C.),* Eothen 17 (Florence), 9–59

Freu, J. 2003 *Histoire du Mitanni, Collection KUBABA.* Série Antiquité 3 (Paris)

Freydank, H. 2001 *Mittelassyrische Rechtsurkunden und Verwaltungstexte IV.* Tafeln aus Kār-Tukultī-Ninurta, Wissenschaftliche Veröffentlichungen der Deutschen Orient-Gesellschaft 99 (Saarbrücken)

Freydank, H. And Feller, B. 2010 *Mittelassyrische Rechtsurkunden und Verwaltungstexte IV.* Wissenschaftliche Veröffentlichungen der Deutschen Orient-Gesellschaft 125 (Wiesbaden)

Glatz, C. 2009 Empire as network. Spheres of material interaction in Late Bronze Age Anatolia. *Journal of Anthropological Archaeology* 28, 127–141

Gorny, R. L. 1995 Hittite imperialism and anti-imperial resistance as viewed from Alişar Höyük. *Bulletin of the American Schools of Oriental Research* 299/300, 65–89

Grayson, A. K. 1991 *Assyrian Rulers of the Early First Millennium BC. I (1114-859 BC). The Royal inscriptions of Mesopotamia. Assyrian Periods 2* (Toronto)

Haas, V. and Wäfler, M. 1985 Möglichkeiten der Identifizierung des Tall Al-Ḥamīdīya. In: S. Eichler, V. Haas, D. Steudler, M. Wäfler and D. Warburton, Tall *Al-Ḥamīdīya I. Vorbericht 1984, Orbis Biblicus et Orientalis.* Series Archaeologica 4 (Fribourg), 53–76

Haller, A. 1954 *Die Gräber und Grüfte von Assur.* Wissenschaftliche Veröffentlichungen der Deutschen Orient-Gesellschaft 65 (Berlin)

Harrak, A. 1987 *Assyria and Hanigalbat. A Historical Reconstruction of Bilateral Relations from the Middle of the Fourteenth to the End of the Twelfth Centuries B. C.* Texte und Studien zur Orientalistik 4 (Hildesheim)

Heinrich, E. 1984 *Die Paläste im alten Mesopotamien.* Denkmäler antiker Architektur 15 (Berlin)

Herles, M. 2007 Assyrische Präsenz an Euphrat und Balīḫ. Grenzkontrolle gegen Feinde des Reiches und nomadische Gruppierungen, Ugarit Forschungen. *Internationales Jahrbuch für die Altertumskunde Syrien-Palästinas* 39, 413–449

Jakob, S. 2003 *Mittelassyrische Verwaltung und Sozialstruktur. Untersuchungen.* Cuneiform Monographs 29 (Leiden)

Jakob, S. 2009 *Die mittelassyrischen Texte aus Tell Chuēra in Nordost-Syrien, Vorderasiatische Forschungen der Max Freiherr von Oppenheim-Stiftung.* Ausgrabungen in Tell Chuēra in Nordost-Syrien 2(3) (Wiesbaden)

Kantor, H. J. 1945 Plant Ornament. Its origin and development in the Ancient Near East. Unpublished Ph.D. dissertation, University of Chicago

Kantor, H. J. 1958 The glyptic. In: C. W. McEwan, L. S. Braidwood, H. Frankfort, H. G. Güterbock, R. C. Haines, H. J. Kantor and C. H. Kraeling, *Soundings at Tell Fakhariyah.* Oriental Institute Publications 79 (Chicago IL), 69–85

Kertai, D. 2008/2009 The history of the Middle-Assyrian Empire, Talanta. *Proceedings of the Dutch Archaeological and Historical Society* 40/41, 25–51

Klein, M. 2013 *Hurri-Mittani-Hanigalbat. Untersuchungen zu Geschichte, Sprache und Kultur der Hurriter. Heft 4. Die Palastarchive von Nuzi. Die peripheren Archive II. Texte und Kommentar* (Munich)

Köroğlu, K. 1998 *Yeni kazı ve yüzey bulguları ışığında Diyarbakır. Üçtepe ve çevresinin yeni Assur dönemi tarihi coğrafyası.* Türk tarih kurumu yayınları 5, 45 (Ankara)

Kühne, C. 1995 Ein mittelassyrisches Verwaltungsarchiv und andere Keilschrifttexte. In: W. Orthmann (ed.), *Ausgrabungen in Tell Chuēra in Nordost-Syrien I. Vorbericht über die Grabungskampagnen 1986–1992.* Vorderasiatische Forschungen der Max Freiherr von Oppenheim-Stiftung 2 (Saarbrücken), 203–225

Kühne, H. (ed.) 2010 *Dūr-Katlimmu 2008 and Beyond.* Studia Chaburensia 1 (Wiesbaden)

Liverani, M. 1988 The growth of the Assyrian Empire in the Habur/Middle Euphrates area. A new paradigm. *State Archives of Assyria Bulletin* 2, 81–98

Liverani, M. 2012 'I Constructed palaces throughout my country'. Establishing the Assyrian provincial order. The motif and its variants. *Revue d'Assyriologie et d'archéologie Orientale* 106, 181–191

Liverani, M. 2014 *The Ancient Near East. History, Society and Economy* (trans. S. Tabatabai) (Abingdon 2014)

Llop, J. 2011 The creation of the Middle Assyrian provinces. *Journal of the American Oriental Society* 131, 591–603

Llop, J. 2012 The development of the Middle Assyrian provinces. *Altorientalische Forschungen* 39(1), 87–111

Llop-Raduà, J. 2009 *Mittelassyrische Verwaltungsurkunden aus Assur. Texte aus den 'großen Speichern' und dem Ubru-Archiv.* Wissenschaftliche Veröffentlichungen der Deutschen Orient-Gesellschaft 124 (Wiesbaden)

Lundström, S. 2008 From six to seven royal tombs. The documentation of the Deutsche Orient-Gesellschaft Excavation at Assur (1903–1914). Possibilities and limits of its reexamination. in: J. Córdoba, M. Molist, C. Pérez, I. Rubio and S. Martínez (eds), *Proceedings of the 5th International Congress on the Archaeology of the Ancient Near East. Madrid, April 3–8 2006* II (Madrid), 445–463

Lyon, J. D. 2000 Middle Assyrian expansion and settlement development in the Syrian Jazira. The view from the Balikh Valley. In: R. M. Jas (ed.), *Rainfall and Agriculture in Northern Mesopotamia. Proceedings of the Third MOS Symposium. Leiden 1999.* Publications de l'Institut historique-archéologique néerlandais de Stamboul 88 (Leiden), 89–126

Lyonnet, B. and Faivre, X. 2014 The settlement pattern of the western Upper Khabur from the Old Babylonian period to the end of the Mittani era. In: Cancik-Kirschbaum *et al.* (eds) 2014, 213–245

Machinist, P. 1982 Provincial governance in middle Assyria and some new texts from Yale. *Assur* 3(2), 1–36

Matthews, D. M. 1990 *Principles of Composition in Near Eastern Glyptic of the Later Second Millennium B.C. Orbis Biblicus et Orientalis. Series Archaeologica* 8 (Fribourg)

Matthews, D. 1991 Middle Assyrian Glyptic from Tell Billa. *Iraq* 53, 17–42

Matthews, D. 1992 The random Pegasus. Loss of meaning in middle Assyrian seals. *Cambridge Archaeological Journal* 2(2), 191–210

Moortgat, A. 1941 Assyrische Glyptik des 13. Jahrhunderts. *Zeitschrift für Assyriologie und Vorderasiatische Archäologie* 47, 50–88

Moortgat, A. 1944 Assyrische Glyptik des 12. Jahrhunderts. *Zeitschrift für Assyriologie und Vorderasiatische Archäologie* 48, 23–44

Moortgat, A. 1966 *Vorderasiatische Rollsiegel. Ein Beitrag zur Geschichte der Steinschneidekunst* (Berlin)

Moortgat, A. and Moortgat-Correns, U. 1976 *Tell Chuēra in Nordost-Syrien. Vorläufiger Bericht über die siebente Grabungskampagne 1974.* Schriften der Max Freiherr von Oppenheim-Stiftung 9 (Berlin)

Mühl, S. 2015 Middle Assyrian territorial practices in the region of Ashur. In: B. S. Düring (ed.), *Understanding Hegemonic Practices of the Early Assyrian Empire. Essays Dedicated to Frans Wiggermann.* Uitgaven van het Nederlands Instituut voor het Nabije Oosten 2015 (Leiden), 45–58

Novák, M. 1994 Eine Typologie der Wohnhäuser von Nuzi. *Baghdader Mitteilungen* 25, 341–446

Novák, M. 2007 Mittani Empire and the question of absolute chronology. Some archaeological considerations. In: M. Bietak and E. Czerny (eds), *The Synchronisation of Civilisations in the Eastern Mediterranean in the Second Millennium B.C. III. Proceedings of the SCIEM 2000 – 2nd EuroConference. Vienna, 28th May–1st June 2003*/ Österreichische Akademie der Wissenschaften. Denkschriften der Gesamtakademie 37/Contributions to the Chronology of the Eastern Mediterranean 9 (Vienna), 389–401

Novák, M. 2013 Upper Mesopotamia in the Mittani Period. In: W. Orthmann, P. Matthiae and M. al-Maqdissi (eds), *Archéologie et Histoire de la Syrie I. La Syrie de l'époque néolithique à l'âge du fer, Schriften zur Vorderasiatischen Archäologie* 1(1) (Wiesbaden), 345–356

Oates, D. 1990 Tell Brak. The Mitanni Palace and Temple. In: S. Eichler, M. Wäfler and D. Warburton (eds), *Tall Al-Ḥamīdīya II. Symposion. Recent Excavations in the Upper Khabur Region. Berne, December 9–11, 1986.* Orbis Biblicus et Orientalis. Series Archaeologica 6 (Fribourg), 149–157

Opitz, D. 1927 Die Lage von Waššugganni *Zeitschrift für Assyriologie und verwandte Gebiete* 37, 299–301

Otto, A. 2014 The organisation of residential space in the Mittani Kingdom as a mirror of different models of governance. In: Cancik-Kirschbaum *et al.* (eds) 2014, 33–60

Parker, B. 1977 Middle Assyrian seal impressions from Tell al Rimah. *Iraq* 39, 257–268

Parker, B. J. 2001 *The Mechanics of Empire. The Northern Frontier of Assyria as a Case Study in Imperial Dynamics* (Helsinki)

Parker, B. J. 2009 Ašipâ Again. A Microhistory of an Assyrian Provincial Administrator. In: M. Luukko, S. Svärd and R. Mattila (eds), *Of God(s), Trees, Kings, and Scholars. Neo-Assyrian and Related Studies in Honour of Simo Parpola.* Studia Orientalia 106 (Helsinki), 179–192

Pedde, F. 2011/2012 Die mittel- und neuassyrischen Gräber und Grüfte. *Alter Orient Aktuell* 12, 44–45

Pedde, F. 2012 The Assur Project. The Middle and Neo-Assyrian graves and tombs. In: R. Matthews and J. Curtis (ed.), *Proceedings of the 7th International Congress on the Archaeology of the Ancient Near East. 12 April-16 April 2010 The British Museum and UCL London I. Mega-Cities & Mega-Sites. The Archaeology of Consumption & Disposal. Landscapes, Transport & Communication* (Wiesbaden), 93–108

Pedde, F. 2015 Gräber und Grüfte in Assur II. Die mittelassyrische Zeit. *Wissenschaftliche Veröffentlichungen der Deutschen Orient-Gesellschaft* 144 (Wiesbaden)

Pedersén, O. 1986 *Archives and Libraries in the City of Assur. A Survey of the Material from the German Excavations.* Acta Universitatis Upsaliensis. Studia Semitica Upsaliensia 8 (Uppsala)

Pfälzner, P. 1995 *Mittanische und mittelassyrische Keramik. Eine chronologische, funktionale und produktionsökonomische Analyse.* Berichte der Ausgrabung Tell Šēḫ Ḥamad/Dūr-Katlimmu 3 (Berlin)

Pfälzner, P 1997 Keramikproduktion und Provinzverwaltung im mittelassyrischen Reich. In: H. Waetzoldt and H. Hauptmann (eds), *Assyrien im Wandel der Zeiten. XXXIXe Rencontre Assyriologique Internationale Heidelberg 6.-10. Juli 1992.* Heidelberger Studien zum Alten Orient 6 (Heidelberg), 337–345

Pfälzner, P. 2007 The Late Bronze Age ceramic traditions of the Syrian Jazirah. In: M. Al-Maqdissi, V. Matoïan and C. Nicolle (eds), *Céramique de l'âge du bronze en Syrie II. L'Euphrate et la région de Jézireh.* Bibliothèque archéologique et historique 180 (Beirut), 231–291

Politopoulos, A. 2012 From Mitanni to Middle Assyrians. Changes in Settlement Patterns and Agriculture in the Land of Hanigalbat. Unpublished MA Thesis, University of Leiden

Pongratz-Leisten, B. 2011 Assyrian royal discourse between local and imperial traditions at the Hābūr. *Revue d'Assyriologie et d'archéologie Orientale* 105, 109–128

Pongratz-Leisten, B. 2015 *Religion and Ideology in Assyria.* Studies in Ancient Near Eastern Records 6 (Boston MA)

Porada, E. 1947 Seal impressions of Nuzi. *The Annual of the American Schools of Oriental Research* 24, 1–138

Porada, E. 1979 Remarks on Mitannian (Hurrian) and Middle Assyrian glyptic art. *Akkadica* 13, 2–15

Postgate, C., Oates, D. and Oates, J. 1997 *The Excavations at Tell Al Rimah. The pottery.* Iraq Archaeological Reports 4 (Warminster)

Postgate, J. N. 1992 The Land of Assur and the Yoke of Assur. *World Archaeology* 23, 247–263

Postgate, J. N. 2010 The debris of government. Reconstructing the middle Assyrian state apparatus from tablets and potsherds. *Iraq* 72, 19–37

Postgate, N. 2013 *Bronze Age Bureaucracy. Writing and the Practice of Government in Assyria* (New York)

Radner, K. 2004 *Das mittelassyrische Tontafelarchiv von Giricano/Dunnu-ša-Uzibi.* Ausgrabungen in Giricano 1, Subartu 14 (Turnhout)

Richter, T. 2003 Das 'Archiv des Idanda'. Bericht über Inschriftenfunde der Grabungskampagne 2002 in Mišrife/Qaṭna. *Mitteilungen der Deutschen Orient-Gesellschaft zu Berlin* 135, 167–188

Ristvet, L. and Weiss, H. 2005 The Hābūr region in the late third and early second millennium BC. In: W. Orthmann (ed.), *The History and Archaeology of Syria* I (Saarbrücken), 1–26

Schwartz, G. M. 2014 Reflections on the Mittani emergence. In: Cancik-Kirschbaum *et al.* (eds) 2014, 265–277

Shibata, D. 2007 Middle Assyrian administrative and legal texts from the 2005 excavation at Tell Taban. A preliminary report. *Al-Rāfidān* 28, 63–74

Shibata, D. 2012 Local power in the Middle Assyrian period. The 'Kings of the Land of Māri' in the Middle Habur region. In: G. Wilhelm (ed.), *Organization, Representation, and Symbols of Power in the Ancient Near East. Proceedings of the 54th Rencontre Assyriologique Internationale at Würzburg 20-25 July 2008* (Winona Lake IN), 489–505

Singer, I. 1985 The Battle of Niḫriya and the end of the Hittite Empire. *Zeitschrift für Assyriologie und Vorderasiatische Archäologie* 75, 100–123

Sinopoli, C. M. 1994 The archaeology of Empires. *Annual Review of Anthropology* 23, 159–180

Sinopoli, C. M. 2001 Empires. In: G. M. Feinman and T. D. Price (eds), *Archaeology at the Millennium. A Sourcebook* (New York), 439–471

Starr, R. F. S. 1939 *Nuzi. Report on the Excavations at Yorgan Tepa near Kirkuk, Iraq* (Cambridge)

Stein, D. L. 1984 Khabur Ware and Nuzi Ware. Their origin, relationship, and significance. *Assur* 4(1), 1–64

Stein, D. L. 1993-1997 s.v. Mittan(n)ni B. Bildkunst und Architektur. In: *Reallexikon der Assyriologie und Vorderasiatischen Archäologie* 8 (Berlin, Boston), 296–299

Stein, D. L. 2001 Nuzi Glyptic. The eastern connection. In: W. W. Hallo and I. J. Winter (eds), *Seals and Seal Impressions. Proceedings of the XLVe Rencontre Assyriologique Internationale II* (Bethesda ML), 149–183

Stein, D. 2010 The Nuzi elite. Iconography of power and prestige. In: J. C. Fincke (ed.), *Festschrift für Gernot Wilhelm anläßlich seines 65. Geburtstages am 28. Januar 2010* (Dresden), 355–367

Stoyke, S. and Heinzle, G. 2001 Grabungen im Bereich V (unpublished report, Frankfurt)

Szuchman, J. J. 2007 Prelude to Empire. Middle Assyrian Hanigalbat and the Rise of the Aramaeans. Unpublished Ph.D. dissertation, University of California, Los Angeles

Teissier, B. 1984 *Ancient Near Eastern Cylinder Seals from the Marcopoli Collection* (Berkeley CA)

Tenu, A. 2009 L'expansion médio-assyrienne. Approche archéologique. *British Archaeological Report* S1906 (Oxford)

Tenu, A. 2013 Imperial Culture. Some reflections on middle Assyrian settlements. In: L. Feliu, J. Llop, A. Millet Albà and J. Sanmartín (eds), *Time and History in the Ancient Near East. Proceedings of the 56th Rencontre Assyriologique Internationale at Barcelona. 26-30 July 2010* (Winona Lake IN), 575–584

Wiggermann, F. A. M. 2000 Agriculture in the Northern Balikh Valley. The case of middle Assyrian Tell Sabi Abyad. In: R. M. Jas (ed.), *Rainfall and Agriculture in Northern Mesopotamia. Proceedings of the Third MOS Symposium. Leiden 1999*, Publications de l'Institut historique-archéologique néerlandais de Stamboul 88 (Leiden), 171–231

Wilhelm, G. 1989 *The Hurrians* (Warminster)

Chapter 3

Changing exchange values in Solomon Islands

Ben Burt

Solomon Islands is a group of six large and many small islands in Melanesia, home to 600,000 people of about 80 local languages and cultures (Fig. 3.1). The islands were introduced to the global economy through trade and labour migration in the latter 19th century, colonised by the British in the 1890s, large areas planted with coconuts in the early 20th century, fought over by the Japanese and Americans in the Second World War, and made an independent state in 1978. Since then the country has continued to develop economically through the export of natural resources, with benefits and problems familiar in so many former colonies.

Over this century and a half, Solomon Islands society has been transformed from networks of independent local communities, empowered by the spirits of their ancestors and constantly feuding, to a nation of Christians under the rule of government law. But the process has been gradual and uneven, fraught with contradictions between the local values of inherited *kastom* (custom or tradition) and the values of commerce and capitalism. This includes changes in how people have valued their local artefacts.

When Solomon Islanders continue to use the things they make for themselves it is often because they cannot afford to substitute convenient and prestigious imported goods for ordinary everyday necessities. Baskets and mats of plaited leaf, bowls and canoes carved of wood, cordage and cloth made from bark, flasks of bamboo, roofs and walls of palm-leaf, knives and spoons of shell, can all be replaced with manufactured goods by those who 'live by money', meaning cash (*selene* or shillings), as Solomon Islanders say of Europeans. But there are also local artefacts that are made and used, or just kept safe, because they are still needed for the things that, as Europeans say, 'money can't buy'. Research in 2014 into the Solomon Islands' collections of the British Museum resulted in *The Things We Value*, a book by local experts and foreign academics demonstrating how such objects were valued for mediating relationships and identities.[1] That book is the basis for this chapter.

---
[1] Burt and Bolton 2014a.

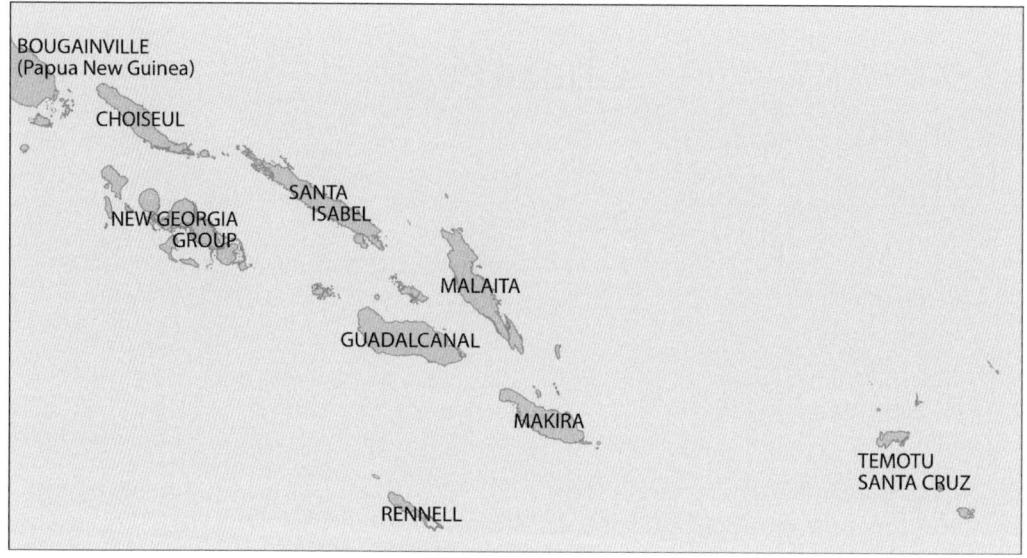

Figure 3.1. Solomon Islands (map: Ben Burt).

In former times, much Solomon Islands material culture was ephemeral, as testified by the scant remains of stone and shell fragments in archaeological sites. The land- and sea-scape of forests and reefs endured to be divided and claimed by successive generations of families and clans and was marked by durable signs, both natural features and simple stone-works, but it also absorbed most everyday artefacts. Food gardens were mostly temporary clearings in the forest, settlements were moved as buildings decayed and artefacts of wood, fibre and leaf decayed and were discarded. If objects endured over lifetimes, it was because they were deliberately made and preserved for their social value. Relationships between persons, living and dead, were vested in these valuable things, some of which played a crucial role in the reproduction of society. The objects people preserved included relics ranging from the skulls and bones of ancestors and unusually shaped spirit-stones to personal possessions such as weapons, utensils, ceremonial objects and old carvings. Such things were kept in houses and shrines as memorials of ancestors and their works, mediating continuing relationships that provided spiritual support and discipline to the living and maybe channeled spiritual power.

Local moneys

While relics were precious symbols of relationships inherited through dead ancestors, conferring rights and identities within families and clans, the on-going maintenance and development of relationships depended more on objects moving through exchanges among the living. Such movements have been analysed as operating in different spheres and modes (in theories synthesised by Akin and Robbins)[2] but for simplicity we can distinguish between exchanges as purchases and as presentations. Both were facilitated by standardising certain artefacts, mostly derived from certain kinds of body ornaments worked from shell and teeth, as currency with recognised values. These were distinguished as different denominations and could be exchanged for goods and services such as foodstuffs, pigs and artefacts, labour and ritual procedures. Hence Islanders and colonials agreed in calling them 'local money' or 'home money', as distinct from state money or cash. Although many of them could be exchanged at standard rates for colonial cash, in higher denominations they were also used to transact major relationships through presentations for marriages and funerals, restitution and compensation, alliances and warfare, in ways that cash was inadequate to accomplish.

Throughout Solomon Islands and beyond into Bougainville and the islands of Papua New Guinea, similar kinds of artefacts of shell and teeth were valuable possessions, but in different islands and localities some of these gained more standard values in exchange for other things and were preferred as local moneys. Certain communities specialised in producing them, diverting considerable labour from subsistence production to sawing and grinding large shells for rings, chipping, drilling and grinding smaller shells for beads and drilling teeth for stringing.

In the western Solomons, the preferred local moneys were rings of clamshell of a size to wear on the arms (Fig. 3.2), with the more valuable kinds worn as pendants. One centre of production was Roviana in the New Georgia group, where raiding in large, fast canoes around the western Solomons killed many people for trophy heads and captured others to increase the workforce making rings. Other valuables given in presentations included more elaborate carvings of clamshell, mostly based on, derived from, or including such money rings, and also whale teeth strung as pendants. Smaller rings of coneshell could be used for minor exchanges, including symbolic gifts to spirits.[3] These were also used on charms and body ornaments, sewn in rows on collars of red braid and, the smallest, strung as beads on ornaments including larger rings and teeth, which could be exchanged for or instead of standard money-rings. Choiseul island participated in the shell-ring exchange network dominated by the New Georgia group but also had its own distinctive local money of clamshell cylinders, which were exchanged for important transactions within the island but not worn or displayed.[4] The military and political dominance of the New Georgia group in the late 19th century led to its shell rings being exchanged and worn in similar ways in Isabel island, but here teeth from dolphins, cuscus and bats were also important local moneys. These were drilled, strung and woven into straps to wear around the head, neck or waist, their value measured in numbers of teeth. Certain communities specialised in hunting dolphins and trading the drilled teeth to other areas, including

---
[2] Akin and Robbins 1999.
[3] Sheppard and Walter 2014.
[4] Richards 2014.

Figure 3.2. Western Solomons money rings worn as arm rings and a pendant by Ingova, warrior chief of Roviana in the New Georgia group, and his wife in 1902 (photo: George Brown).

neighbouring Malaita island, where they were obtained and used in the same way.

While the western islands preferred shell rings, in the south-east Solomons shell beads were more important, strung in denominations valued by the length and number of strings and the proportion of more valuable red beads. A major centre of production for this 'shell money' was Langalanga in Malaita, where people living on offshore islands with little access to garden land were economically dependent on making it for sale according to the specifications of various districts around Malaita and neighbouring islands.[5] A less widespread kind of money bead was made by inland people of the southern half of the island from small coneshells. Makira and Guadalcanal islands had their own production centres for shell bead money, but also imported the Langalanga money and made similar use of dolphin teeth and also dog teeth, worn as ornaments in similar local styles.

Denominations of most kinds of shell money could be worn as prestigious ornaments on important occasions, but the beads were also made up into bandoliers and woven straps for head, arms, waist and legs. Like shell rings and a variety of other body ornaments, these could be valued in terms of shell money denominations and teeth.[6] Throughout the Solomons, such ornaments contributed the glamour of wealth to public display, but they were less acceptable for exchange than recognised denominations of local money. However, the distinction was not always clear and in the first published study on the subject by a Solomon Islander, George Bogesi listed the ornaments of his home area in Isabel as well as shell rings and teeth, as 'currency'.[7]

---

[5] Guo 2014.
[6] see Burt 2009.
[7] Bogesi 1948, 228.

Further east in the Santa Cruz and Reef islands, a distinctive money of red feathers, bound on coils of fibre as large denominations, was used for purchases and presentations including brideprice and restitution for disputes and offences.[8] This 'feather money' circulated around the island group, carried on trading voyages to purchase local products from canoes to courtesans, but exchange with other parts of the Solomons was precluded by distance, Santa Cruz being closer to the neighbouring country of Vanuatu.

Purchase and presentation

There has been much academic discussion about distinctions between currencies and moneys and how far Solomon Islands valuables were either, but the significant consideration is the system of economic relationships in which they were used.[9] Formerly Solomon Islanders lived in what Graeber calls 'human economies' which are '… primarily concerned not with the accumulation of wealth, but with the creation, destruction and rearranging of human beings'.[10] In Solomon Islands, communities based on inter-related families and local clans, goods and services such as food, hospitality and casual labour would be exchanged as sharing and assistance, to be returned informally through enduring relationships in a spirit of goodwill. The failure of so many village retail businesses due to customers' reluctance to pay for goods testifies to the scope and strength of such relationships even within the encroaching commercial economy. Beyond this sphere of mutual obligations, local money could mediate single exchanges of equivalent value by purchase from acquaintances and strangers. The teeth of Isabel and the southeast Solomons, counted in tens and hundreds, and the shell beads of the south-east, measured by length against the arm, could purchase small portions of food, minor artefacts and services. Larger denominations could be used to commission or purchase gardens of food, pigs or catches of fish, as were the shell rings of the western Solomons. In this respect local moneys functioned like cash in being portable, durable, storable, dividable and liquid, and valued as a general purpose medium of exchange.[11]

But in the often fractious dealings among autonomous local communities, far reaching and long lasting relationships depended less on short term transactions of purchase than on presentations to be returned under long term agreements in which local moneys acted as what Graeber calls 'social currencies'.[12] The organisers of major public events, such as festivals celebrating clan ancestors and the inauguration of ceremonial buildings and canoes invited contributions from other communities near and far, to be returned on similar occasions in the future, building networks of

---

[8] Samou 2014.
[9] Akin and Robbins 1999.
[10] Graeber 2011, 130.
[11] Akin 1999, 109.
[12] Graeber 2011, 130.

enduring mutual obligations. Marriages drew in contributions from a man's relatives to the bride-price presented in exchange for his wife and then distributed among her relatives, creating obligations to be recalled in bride-price for later marriages and maintained between families over generations. Restitution for offences, from swearing and theft to adultery and bloodshed, created or called in obligations from relatives as contributions to presentations reconciling the parties and preventing further conflict. Clan land was shared with outsiders, children were adopted and enemies killed, in exchange for presentations that created long term alliances. Trading between distant communities around and between the islands also depended on establishing and maintaining amicable relations through presentations to create partnerships with potential enemies who had goods and services to exchange. All such transactions required appropriate kinds and quantities of local moneys as well as other goods, mainly food and pigs to be shared in feasts confirming mutual goodwill in the mediation of important relationships between communities.

The differences between modes of exchange as purchase or presentation became more obvious as local economies were disrupted by colonial imports of desirable new goods. From the latter 19th century, steel tools, tobacco, cloth and novel luxuries became available by purchase from Europeans, for local goods at home and for labour on distant plantations overseas, in exchanges increasingly mediated by colonial money. Providing small goods and services in return for local money or credit had enabled people to save up for the larger denominations required for presentations within and between local communities. Participation in such exchanges created and discharged the obligations which underlay the authority of community leaders and the reputations of everyone else, as local money circulated among them. The commercial economy enabled young men in particular to shortcut this system by obtaining imported goods and cash from labouring abroad without incurring such obligations and using this wealth to purchase or substitute for local money. As the sector expanded with a shift to coconut plantations in the Solomons from the early 20th century, these new forms of wealth increasingly challenged local money systems and the vested interests they supported. Although Europeans would deal in local money when convenient, they undermined its value by using cash to purchase labour, sell imported goods and extract government taxes. The imposition of government authority, suppressing feuding and violent sanctions for offences, reduced the need for local money presentations as restitution or compensation, which was also often discouraged on theological grounds as people converted to Christianity. The process was gradual and uneven and during the 20th century, as some local moneys became redundant in some districts and islands, others continued to be made and used for major presentations, or even for minor purchases.

Insofar as some Solomon Islands local moneys have remained social currencies, this is mainly because people have managed to separate more socially significant presentations from simple purchases. In Malaita, local moneys are still required for bride-price and restitution presentations, in recognition of the need to involve networks of families and clans as contributors and recipients in major transactions that bring them together over generations of reciprocal obligations. Cash is increasingly included but, although shell money can be purchased for cash in markets and stores, cash itself is still regarded as less appropriate as it can be diverted to impersonal purchases rather than circulating to maintain social obligations. For this reason, in the conservative Malaitan enclave of Kwaio, until the early 21st century only local money was allowed for purchases as well as presentations and cash earnings had to be converted by purchasing imported goods abroad and selling them for shell money at home.[13] At the same time, in the suburbs of the Solomon Islands capital Honiara in Guadalcanal, where everyone is heavily dependent on the cash economy, brideprice in shell money is contributed and distributed to build relationships in the new communities created by immigration from Malaita.[14] Despite a century of church attempts to abolish or severely limit the size of brideprice presentations, the quantity has been increasing among families enriched by the cash economy (Fig. 3.3).

Figure 3.3. A large Malaita brideprice presentation of shell moneys and banknotes in Honiara in 2011 (photo: Clive Moore).

Other local moneys have fared less well. In the western Solomons and Isabel, shell rings and straps of teeth are no longer made but enough are still kept to serve in important presentations such as bride-price and land transfers, if only as symbolic additions to cash and other goods. Higher value moneys are kept as mementos of former exchanges for persons or land in otherwise abandoned ancestral shrines or domestic houses as evidence of continuing relationships. As ancestral relics, maybe imbued with spiritual power, their former exchange value is less relevant than the family and clan histories they evoke and testify to in issues such as inheritance and land tenure. The shell cylinders of Choiseul are now seldom exchanged at all and have also become more like ancestral relics than local moneys. In Santa Cruz, concern for the use of cash for bride-price has led to community efforts to make and promote feather money, but with limited success.[15] In Isabel, in the 2010s, a research

---

[13] Akin 1999.
[14] Kwa'ioloa and Burt 2012, 85–115.
[15] Samou 2014.

Figure 3.4. Local moneys kept as family treasures in Maringe, Isabel, in 2010 (photo: Christian Kokomana).

programme for local people to rediscover their ancestral culture demonstrated the change of values. Objects kept as mementos of past times included local money valuables but also more mundane artefacts, some still in use, such as food bowls, bark cloth beaters and walking sticks, all treated as 'family treasures'. The local moneys might be brought out when needed as evidence of ancestral history and land claims, but they were valued as heirlooms rather than as a medium of exchange (Fig. 3.4).[16]

Commodification

As cash took over purchases and intruded into presentations, local moneys also became commodities for purchase, revalued in terms of the Western art and antiquities market. This market dates back to the late 19th century, when artefacts were used to purchase desirable manufactured goods from visiting ships, colonial traders and residents, ultimately supplying overseas collectors and museums such as the British

---

[16] Tetehu 2014.

Figure 3.5. The Solomon Islands High Commissioner to the United Kingdom, H. E. Eliam Tangirongo of Guadalcanal, and his wife Anna of Malaita in 2019, wearing regalia of shell money beads made in Langalanga (photo: Ben Burt).

Museum. People began to make the most popular artefacts for export, later encouraged by the demand for souvenirs by American troops during the Second World War. Since then, new styles of artefacts have been developed to meet the preferences of colonial residents and visitors for portable carvings and Solomon Islands versions of 'primitive art'. From the 1970s, new styles of export artefacts were influenced by European art teachers in the national secondary schools, who encouraged painters and carvers to use Solomon Islands motifs regardless of their own local traditions. With influences from popular exports from other parts of the world such as New Guinea and Africa, this led to the development of a generic Solomon Islands art style in the latter 20th century, featuring in public works and art displays in Honiara as well as sales to foreigners.[17] This new tradition is still negotiating its position among the Western art-world categories of 'folk', 'tourist' and gallery 'fine' art that affect its value in commercial terms. At the same time a few communities have revived and

---

[17] Kupiainen 2014.

Figure 3.6. In 2021, a Malaitan accused of killing a Guadalcanal man in the civil conflict of 1998–2003 and still serving a prison sentence, presented a large shell money with garden food and a pig to the family of the dead man in a formal reconciliation ceremony. Official recognition of the ceremony was expected to facilitate his long overdue parole. The accused, with the white scarf and dark glasses, was supported by his brothers, with the bereaved at the other end of the money.

adapted their own local artefacts for the export market, such as body ornaments from Malaita and woodcarvings from Makira.[18] Malaita shell workers in Langalanga, still producing shell money (Fig. 3.5), have branched out into new styles of shell-bead body ornaments which have become popular with foreign visitors as well as Islanders in Malaita and beyond.[19] There are also deliberate fakes presented as antiques, such as money-ring carvings from the western Solomons and body ornaments from Malaita.

Although Solomon Islanders often express regret at the demise of local artefact traditions, most are too committed to the commercial economy and its products to do much about it. From selling their artefacts, including local moneys and heirlooms, to obtain manufactured imports, they gradually ceased to replace them for their own use or for sale, in a loss of ancestral heritage that has also been a devaluation of local material culture. There are still things in Solomon Islands 'that money can't buy', but as people increasingly 'live by money' they find cash buying more of the things that they should not sell.[20] The material benefits of the European lifestyle,

---

[18] Akin 2014; Revolon 2014.
[19] Guo 2014.
[20] Kwa'ioloa 2014

first observed during labour migration in the 19th century, have become increasingly available to their own indigenous elite and emerging middle class from the latter 20th century. Unfortunately, the price paid in things of local value is high. Not only ancestral relics but even the land inherited from their ancestors, the foundation of Solomon Islanders' livelihood and identity, is being sacrificed for the cash available from destructive logging and mining. As people say cynically, 'cash is all that talks' (*selene nomoa toktok*).

New values for old artefacts

It is a sad irony that so many artefacts, once but no longer valued for their role in the constitution of Solomon Islands societies, are now treasured by the museums of the former colonisers who did so much to diminish their local value. There they are valued instead for their exotic, artistic or academic interest, which is also measured in their purchase price in cash as determined by the collectors' market. But as museums revalue their collections in attempts to 'decolonise' themselves in response to claims from source communities, they are increasingly recognising the responsibilities and rewards of repatriating the cultural knowledge vested in their collections, if not the collections themselves. The question remains what the value of the artefacts now is for these communities. If artefacts are no longer used as they were, will they be valued merely as museum pieces, in the Solomons as they are abroad? Will they be used to restore local artefact production, help inspire the new styles of painting and carving, enrich local and national culture, or merely become subjects of historical academic interest?

Whatever the case, it seems unlikely that the repatriation of cultural knowledge or even artefacts will do much to restore the value of things like local moneys. Solomon Islanders concerned by this might look instead to Malaita, where shell moneys are still valued as social currencies. Furthermore, Langalanga shell money has gained new value as a symbol of Solomon Islands national identity, as large denominations are presented to foreign dignitaries and the beads are made into ornaments for dancers, national sports teams, beauty queens and political leaders, as well as souvenirs for tourists. More significantly, during the civil conflict at the turn of this century between Guadalcanal islanders and immigrants drawn from Malaita by the economic development focused on Honiara, Malaita shell money became a powerful symbol of reconciliation between the two sides (Fig. 3.6). While militia groups extorted huge payments in cash from government and businesses in the name of restitution and compensation, it was shell money that was presented in ceremonies of reconciliation between their politicians and community leaders. When British residents from various parts of the Solomons were consulted recently on how their country should be represented in an exhibition in the British Museum, they all agreed that it should feature Malaita shell money. We displayed a ten-string denomination that had been presented to the Queen's representative in 1978 at the celebration of Solomon Islands independence from British colonialism.

Acknowledgements
Thanks to Lissant Bolton, David Akin and Hans Peter Hahn for constructive comments on earlier drafts of this paper.

References
Akin, D. 1999 Cash and shell money in Kwaio, Solomon Islands. In: D. Akin and J. Robbins (eds), *Money and Modernity: state and local currencies in Melanesia,* 103–130 (Pittsburgh PA)
Akin, D. 2014 Regenerating local arts at the Kwaio Cultural Centre. In: Burt and Bolton (eds) 2014, 93–101
Akin, D. and Robbins 1999 An introduction to Melanesian currencies. In: D. Akin and J. Robbins (eds), *Money and Modernity: state and local currencies in Melanesia.* (Pittsburgh PA, 1–40)
Bogesi, G. 1948 Santa Isabel, Solomon Islands. *Oceania* 18, 208–232, 327–357
Burt, B. 2009 *Body Ornaments of Malaita, Solomon Islands.* (London)
Burt, B. and Bolton, L. 2014a Solomon Islands Artefact Traditions and their Contemporary Transformations. Introduction. In: Burt and Bolton (eds) 2014, 1–13
Burt, B. and Bolton, L. (eds) 2014b *The Things We Value: culture and history in Solomon Islands.* (Canon Pyon)
Graeber, D. 2011 *Debt: the first 5,000 years.* (London & New York)
Guo, P. 2014 Bata: the adaptable shell-money of Langalanga, Malaita. In: Burt and Bolton (eds) 2014, 56–61
Kupiainen, J. 2014 Artistic Bellona in the contemporary art of Solomon Islands. In: Burt and Bolton (eds) 2014, 130–139
Kwa'ioloa, M. 2014 Traditional money and Artefacts in Malaita. In: Burt and Bolton (eds) 2014, 48–53
Kwa'ioloa, M. and Burt, B. 2012 *The Chiefs' Country: leadership and politics in Honiara, Solomon Islands* (St Lucia, Queensland)
Richards, R. 2014 *Kesa and other shell valuables from Choiseul* (St Lucia, Queensland)
Revolon, S. 2014 The trade in wood carvings from Aorigi. In: Burt and Bolton (eds) 2014, 117–127
Samou, S. 2014 Santa Cruz feather-money. In: Burt and Bolton (eds) 2014, 15–23
Sheppard, P. and Walter, R. 2014 Shell valuables and history in the western Solomon Islands. In: Burt and Bolton (eds) 2014, 33–45
Tetehu, E. 2014 Some family treasures of Santa Isabel. In: Burt and Bolton (eds) 2014, 81–91

Chapter 4

Objects with (a) history: observations on reworking and re-using ancient bronzes

Norbert Franken[1]

Compared with artworks and utensils made of other durable materials, ancient statues, vessels and utensils made of bronze or brass are, as is well known, preserved only in smaller numbers.[2] Not without reason, this is usually explained by the common 'recycling' practice in Late Antiquity and the Middle Ages: bronzes which were no longer useful but still had monetary value due to their material were collected, chopped up and melted down as systematically as possible in order to – depending on necessity – either mint small change or cast new useful items like cannons or church bells from them.

Whereas numerous observations on the melting down have already been published, either within the analyses of depots of statue fragments or by indirectly proving the re-use with the help of metal analysis,[3] 'upcycling' (i.e. the intentional reworking and re-using of ancient bronzes, much rarer to observe) has to my knowledge never been analysed on a broad material basis from a classical archaeological point of view. This is astonishing, particularly as the principle of practical re-use seems to be not just a

---

[1] Many thanks to Hans Voges for his help in translating my text.
[2] This study is part of an ongoing project of the German Research Foundation (DFG) on ancient figurative bronzes in the Near East and the Arabian Peninsula conducted by Detlev Kreikenbom at the Johannes-Gutenberg-Universität Mainz since July 2017. I thank the organisers for the invitation to the concluding conference of the Research Training Group 'Value and Equivalence' at the Goethe-Universität Frankfurt/Main. For references and discussion I am grateful to Marianne Bergmann, Gunnar Brands, Boris Burandt, Jutta Dresken-Weiland, Anja Klöckner, Árpád M. Nagy, Barbara Niemeyer, Stephanie Pearson, Gertrud Platz-Horster (†), Agnes Schwarzmaier, Rüdiger Splitter, Thomas M. Weber-Karyotakis and Erika Zwierlein-Diehl. New insights on the candelabra I owe to a project conducted by Ruth Bielfeldt and carried out by her jointly with Nele Schröder-Griebel and Johannes Eber and, not to forget, work campaigns approved by Valeria Sampaolo and Paolo Giulierini at the National Archaeological Museum Naples.
[3] A high proportion of gold contained in the alloy indicates the recycling of gold-plated bronzes: Willer et al. 2016, 83–86.

typical phenomenon in times of crisis, even if some of us may remember, either by own experience or on the basis of stories told to us, the hardship and deprivation of the post-war period, when cooking pots were made out of steel helmets and wedding dresses out of parachute silk. However, against the background of a conscious critique of the prevailing consumer and throw-away society, a noticeable counter-movement towards a sustainable interaction with the limited resources is presently taking place. Moreover, in scientific discourse, the use of spolia and the continued use and re-use of Greek and Roman architecture and art during the Middle Ages has been increasingly researched during the last years.[4] In addition, Martin Baumeister with his study on metal recycling in early history has already presented an instructive investigation within the frame of pre- and early history which also treats cases of the reworking of prehistoric metal finds.[5]

Prompted by the friendly invitation to participate in the final conference of the Research Training Group 'Value and Equivalence' at the Goethe-University Frankfurt in May 2019, I would like to approach, for the first time, the subject of 'reworking and re-use' with special attention to Roman bronzes (statues, devices, vessels, inscriptions). After three rather cursory introductory sections I will content myself to present a few, in my opinion particularly typical, groups of materials and instructive individual examples whereby, especially in sections 5 and 6, the methodological problem of a reliable delimitation from modern *pasticci* should not go unmentioned.

My contribution is divided into the following ten sections:

1. 'Upcycling' Greek bronzes
2. On the re-use of bronze portrait statues
3. How statues change into lamp holders
4. On the re-use of cut-up inscription plates as military diploma
5. Reworked in antiquity or modern times?
6. From candelabra to cult equipment?
7. Secondary weights of Roman steelyards
8. The charms of the antique. Re-use after more than 1,500 years
9. A reworked relief container from Amorgos
10. Summary

1. 'Upcycling' of Greek bronzes

A secondary use of older, specifically Orientalising bronzes is already established for early Greek art. An impressive example is provided by three *sphyrelata* from

---

[4] On this, cf. e.g. Boschung and Wittekind 2008. In February 2018, an international colloquium was held in Berlin on the subject *UMGEBAUT. Umbau-, Umnutzungs- und Umbauprozesse in der antiken Architektur* (*REBUILT. Rebuilding, reusing and rebuilding processes in antique architecture*).

[5] Cf. e.g. the socketed spearheads of the Early Bronze Age reworked into mullers and fishing spears: Baumeister 2004, 76, 247 fig. 30. Clearly tied to a particular time and ideologically overloaded seems to be the new study by Stefan Schreiber (Schreiber 2018). On 're-uses' see Schreiber 2018, 164–169.

Olympia, found in many fragments, elaborately restored and published in detail by Brigitte Borell (for the Greek metal sheets) and Dessa Rittig (for the oriental metal sheets).[6] As a result, a group of three images of deities, composed of an approximately life-sized statue of unknown gender and two female statues with a height of about 1.20 m could be restored. In the second quarter of the 7th century BC artists,[7] probably originating from the island of Crete, produced the figures by combining newly made Greek sheets with engraved figurative representations for the fronts and with re-used embossed oriental sheets for the backs. According to the excavation finds, the statues must have stood at an unknown location in the sanctuary of Olympia until at least the first quarter of the 5th century BC before they were cleared out and their remains buried.

Already in the 6th century BC, the hammered legs of geometrical tripods had been occasionally cut up within the Zeus sanctuary of Olympia in order to re-use the undecorated reverse of these parts as an ideal basis for epigraphy.[8] An example for such use is different kinds of bronze lot tokens (*pinakia*). They were used to determine Athenian judges. Often traces of earlier inscriptions naming the proper names and the demos of the candidate have been found on them.[9]

The re-use of embossed reliefs on folding mirrors of Late Classical and Hellenistic times, researched by Agnes Schwarzmaier, which were formerly parts of weapons and other equipment, attained nearly industrial production levels.[10] Take as an arbitrary example a mirror of the Berlin Antiquities Collection which shows a relief of the abduction of the boy Ganymede by Zeus in the guise of an eagle (Fig. 4.1).[11] As a recent investigation on Greek decorated cuirasses by Raimon Graells i Fabregat has confirmed,[12] the reliefs, which were cut into shape to be used on folding mirrors probably originally served as cheek flaps or forehead appliqués of helmets, epaulettes (*epomides*) of armour, horse bridles forehead plates (*prometopidia*) and similar defensive arms and as appliqués of vessels and other devices as well. Since the manufacture of folding mirrors was a demanding and highly specialised craft, one may expect a relatively limited number of workshops. In fact, Schwarzmaier postulated only four large centres for the manufacture of folding mirrors, namely Euboea, Corinth, southern Italy (Taranto) and Athens.[13] Therefore, it is conceivable that large numbers of defensive arms which had been rejected as damaged or taken from the enemy after a victorious battle were repeatedly delivered or sold to a mirror workshop.

---

[6] Borell and Rittig 1998.
[7] Borell and Rittig 1998, 154–161.
[8] Maass 1978, 2 n. 12.
[9] Kroll 1972, 69–90.
[10] Schwarzmaier 1997, 18–24.
[11] Berlin, Antikensammlung – SMB inv. Misc. 7928: Franken 2011 (with extensive literature).
[12] Graells i Fabregat 2018.
[13] Schwarzmaier 1997, 232–233.

Figure 4.1. Greek folding mirror. Berlin, Antikensammlung – SMB inv. Misc. 7928 (photo: Norbert Franken, Antikensammlung – SMB).

Yet perhaps there is a much simpler explanation for the frequent use of older reliefs, if we take into consideration that it was the same artists who produced reliefs of such high quality for the arms industry and for the mirror workshops and other toreutic businesses. Even if nothing more detailed is known about the organisation of the workshops, it seems most probable that already the coexistence of the involved artisans could have facilitated the later exchange of artistically successful antique specimens. But also, beyond the well-known art centres, the replacement of damaged or lost reliefs would not have caused trouble to an artisan who was less specialised but experienced in everyday dealings with metal.

However, we have to imagine this scenario and whichever reasons might have been decisive, in the end the re-use was for sure carried out with the intention to grant the elaborately worked and therefore precious bronze reliefs a second and, this time, far more 'peaceful', life.

2. On the re-use of bronze portrait statues

I will also only briefly touch on a subject of whose fundamental importance everyone is aware, particularly as it is already mentioned in ancient sources.[14] We are talking about bronze portrait statues whose heads had been replaced once or even several times. For Pliny the Elder (c. AD 23/24–79), who, in his *Natural History*, talks of '*statuarum capita permutantur*',[15] the replacement of heads of statues must also have been common practice. Perhaps even the conspicuously frequent preservation of individual portrait heads is owed to this habit.[16] In order to keep open the option of a later exchange, the heads taken off were possibly not immediately destroyed but, for the moment, hidden in a safe place and eventually forgotten.

The subject of the re-use of Greek and Roman portrait statues has been dealt with by Horst Blanck on a broad material basis, discussing, as his sole bronze example, the togate statue of 'Caius Julius Pacatianus' found in Vienne (France) in 1874.[17] The stylistic discrepancy between the body dated by him to Claudian times and the Severan portrait head is obviously indicative of a secondary use of the statue about 150 years after the first installation.

A very impressive example is offered by the armoured statue found in Amelia (Umbria) in the 1960s, which, in the last period it was in use, carried the head of Germanicus (15 BC–AD 19). However, according to researcher Giulia Rocco, it had been previously used for the representation of other historical figures, namely Mithridates VI of Pontus (135–63 BC) and Sulla (138–78 BC) (Fig. 4.2).[18] In his recently published study, John Pollini did not have any doubts about an exchange of the head but he believes that the statue once carried a portrait of Caligula (AD 12–41).[19]

Without being able to take a glimpse at the interior of a statue, one can rarely prove the replacement of a portrait head. Even in cases in which several overlapping phases of surface leading are discernible it is hard to decide with certainty if one is dealing, in fact, with traces of two portrait heads mounted in succession or if it is probably only a renewal of the attachment of the first portrait. Also problematic are proofs of stylistic discrepancies between head and body in the individual case, especially as the rarity of bronze armoured statues not only complicates a firm dating but also the formation of stylistic series.[20]

The fact that the replacement of portrait heads on bronze statues had probably not been rarer than on marble statues – on which the experienced eye may discern

---

[14] Blanck 1969, 21 on the bronze equestrian statue of Arcadius reworked into a portrait of Iustinian.
[15] Plin. *Nat. Hist.* 35, 2.
[16] Among the heads assembled by Lahusen and Formigli (2001), many certainly also belonged to portrait busts freely erected on plinths or herms.
[17] Blanck 1969, 29–32 cat. A 5 pls 4b–5; Lahusen and Formigli 2001, 263–265 no. 163 figs 1–4.
[18] Cf. Lahusen and Formigli 2001, 90–92 no. 41 figs 1–4; Rocco 2008.
[19] Pollini 2017.
[20] A re-use of the torso of Hadrian from Tel Shalem at Beth Shean in Jerusalem, Israel Museum, seems convincing: Gergel 1991; Lahusen and Formigli 2001, 194–197 no. 116 figs 1–8.

Figure 4.2. Armoured statue with portrait head of Germanicus. Amelia, Museo Archeologico (Franken 2000, 219 fig. 4).

reworkings much more easily – is shown by a well-known example in the form of the bronze equestrian statue of Domitian (reign AD 81–96) changed into Nerva (reign AD 96–98) from Misenum in the Gulf of Naples.[21] Interestingly, it was not the entire head that was exchanged but only the face with the ears of Domitian cut off and subsequently replaced by the face of his successor. Naturally, one could not have used a randomly chosen portrait of Nerva. Rather, the face of the new emperor had to be adapted exactly to avoid unsightly discrepancies in height and width at the transitions. The latter should be the explanation for the fact that this process of an ancient portrait transformation cannot be observed more frequently.

Regardless of whether one replaced only the face or the entire head of a portrait statue, two advantages at least are obvious. Thus, one spared not only the repetition of costs, efforts and risks which were usually associated with the cast and installation of a complete statue. Moreover, the sole replacement of head or face was much quicker to contrive so that the patron of the statue could present the effigy of the new ruler just a few days or weeks after the inauguration and thus, at the same time, demonstrate his loyalty.

3. How statues change into lamp holders

A sophisticated living comfort in Late Hellenistic and early Imperial times included so-called silent servants, sometimes life-sized bronze statues, often in the form of naked boys or youths, which either served as tray supports or as lamp holders. The latter especially have recently been the subject of archaeological investigations.[22]

---

[21] Pozzi 1987; Lahusen and Formigli 2001, 175–176, 178 no. 105 figs 1–4.
[22] Mattusch 2017, fig. 8, 1–8.

Therefore, the question of whether the function of lamp holder is a primary or secondary one arises on a case-by-case basis.

While there is no doubt about life-sized bronze statues of naked or dressed 'negro' boys having the primary function of 'silent servant', and this being highly probable for most of the youths in classicistic style as well, there are statues which were obviously transformed into such functional figures only secondarily. Especially disconcerting is the use as a lamp support (*lychnophoros*) in the statue found in rescue excavations in Zeugma on the Euphrates (eastern Turkey) in 1999/2000 and exhibited today in the Archaeological Museum of Gaziantep (TR): it shows a helmeted naked youth with curly hair in divine pose with the right hand holding an erect lance; we might take him for a youthful Mars (Fig. 4.3).[23] As neither the demanding posture nor the weapon have found a parallel among all 'silent servants' known until now, it can well be presumed that the statue, slightly under life-sized with its height of *c.* 1.50 m, served as a lamp support only in a secondary use.

4. On the re-use of cut-up inscription plates as military diplomas

According to modern knowledge, not very numerous but all the more interesting seem to be tablets of military diplomas made from cut-up bronze plates with fragments of letters

Figure 4.3. Bronze statue of Mars as lychnophoros. *Gaziantep, Arkeoloji Müzesi (photo: Michel Feugère).*

---

[23] Başgelen and Ergeç 2000, 45; Nardi and Önal 2003; Parlasca 2005, 237 figs 3 and 4; Dieudonné-Glad *et al.* 2013, 158–159 no. 915 fig. 74.

of older inscriptions, with which the ancient historian and epigraphist Werner Eck has most recently dealt with in detail.[24] Starting from a diploma[25] found in Serbia, he reviews the examples known up to now and finds that most of the older inscriptions probably belonged to bases of portrait statues installed in private houses: these were sold not only in Late Antiquity but already in Middle Imperial times by later owners of the houses and then brought to their secondary context. The scribes of the diplomas always paid careful attention that the letters of the older inscription were only on the inside of the unopened document given to the honourably discharged soldiers, with the result that the use of a cheap 'recycling plate' could remain hidden for a long time.

The secondary use also remained hidden in a *tabula ansata* from Rome which the Berlin Antiquities Collection acquired together with the collection of the epigraphist and numismatist Heinrich Dressel (1845–1920). The bronze plate carries on one side an older, now erased, inscription and on the other an, up to now, unedited dedication to Bona Dea[26] (Fig. 4.4). Remains of mortar stuck to it favour the assumption that the tablet in its secondary use was implemented in such a way that the scraped-out older inscription was no longer visible. However, to what extent the intended concealment of the older inscription can be regarded as a generally valid feature of re-used Roman bronze inscriptions has to be decided on a broader material basis.[27]

The use of scrap pieces on externally invisible spots could be recently proven on a fragment of a gilded Roman statue from Groß-Gerau (Hesse) by the restorer Frank Willer: for stabilisation, the shattered fragments of an older statue had been riveted to the inside of a new one.[28] As the alloy of the statue and of the repair pieces match, and thus both probably come from the same workshop, the pieces of repairing were most probably not part of an older shattered statue but of a previous faulty casting of a statue part.

5. Reworked in antiquity or in modern times?

Interesting mainly for the history of culture and collections, modern *pasticci* seem at first glance less productive for ancient monuments themselves and thus for our research question. Concerning this question, some archaeologists and restorers have recently gained great merit with the detailed presentations of materials by drawing attention to montages, etc., which cannot possibly fit together for chronological

---

[24] Eck 2000, pl. 9; cf. also Weiß 2000, pl. 9 – to be added is a military diploma in Munich: Kruse 2003, 111–113 no. 90 with fig. p. 110.
[25] Mirković 2000, pls 7 and 8.
[26] Berlin, Antikensammlung – SMB inv. 30894, 59. From Rome. 22.7 × 9.4 cm: Galerie Helbing 1910, 55 no. 716 fig. (drawing); Franken 2011 sub 30894, 59 (with fig. of front and reverse side).
[27] Cf. also a small plate, twice inscribed, in Leiden, Rijksmuseum van Oudheden inv. 1 1932/12.1a: Bechert 2007, 38 fig. 23.
[28] Willer 2014, fig. 1.

Figure 4.4. Bronze tabula ansata from Rome. Berlin, Antikensammlung – SMB inv. 30894, 59 (photo: Norbert Franken, Antikensammlung – SMB).

reasons alone.[29] Yet the fashion of de-restoring,[30] beginning in the late 19th century and still going on, poses a great danger. This is especially true if ancient and post-antique manipulations of objects cannot be reliably told apart or the persons involved start from false premises and so, in the end, only unappealing rubble is left from previously highly esteemed pieces.

---

[29] Cf. Briguet 1977; Descamps-Lequime 2012.
[30] On an early case of de-restoring see Dostert et al. 2008.

Figure 4.5. Roman bronze vessel (state before 'de-restoration'). Kassel, Antikensammlung (Bieber 1915, 87 no. 374, pl. 51).

An example in this sense is the case of a bronze lidded vessel at Kassel (Fig. 4.5) which, according to the evidence of a Piranesi engraving and historical photos, was once decorated with relief attachments.[31] After restoration conducted at the Helms-Museum in Hamburg-Harburg in the 1960s had shown that the attachments were soldered on in modern times and the vessel had served originally as an *autepsa*, i.e., as a Roman samovar, the attachments were completely removed.[32] The removed parts have long been considered lost, but as Rüdiger Splitter, the director of the Kassel antiquities collection kindly informed me, they happened to reappear when the store rooms moved in August 2021.

Apart from the fact that modern traces of soldering alone do not principally exclude an essentially ancient reworking, as perhaps only temporarily detached attachments could have been refastened with the help of modern soldering,[33] I would go so far as to declare the ancient manufacturing of the supposed *pasticcio* not only possible but thoroughly probable. Thus, on the basis of otherwise inexplicable mounting holes on the medallions of Roman silver vessels, it had already been proposed in the past that some middle emblems had originally served as *phalerae* (first on the bridle of mounts, later as military medals) before they were incorporated into the vessels.[34] From a contemporary point of view, it seems well conceivable that the *autepsa* from Kassel was a historically and culturally comparable case: in antiquity, a set of *phalerae* – as a means of permanent remembrance – had been fastened on an already discarded bronze vessel of no use as an *autepsa* so as to presumably give it to the one honoured by the *phalerae* as an urn to put into his grave. Actually, in the historical photos of the Kassel *autepsa*, one can see small holes

---

[31] Kassel, Antikensammlung. Acquired in Rome in 1777. H: (total, previous) 68 cm. Bieber 1915, 87 no. 374 pl. 51.
[32] Gercke *et al.* 1967, pl. 48.
[33] The fact that individual attachments had indeed temporarily come off a container is proven by an engraving of Piranesi. Piranesi 1778, fig. 12.
[34] Gregarek 1997, 92–93; Niemeyer 2007, 46–47.

or nail heads on the margin of the supposedly soldered discs, which might come from an earlier phase of use and would thus necessarily refute the assumed modern manufacture. Moreover, there are comparable bronze *phalerae* with a similar low relief decoration, on which obviously nothing at all indicates a modern manufacture.[35]

A similar principle of decoration may be observed in a large casserole in the Boston Museum of Fine Arts, presumably from Western Asia Minor, on the walls of which up to eight different Roman coins might have been once applied.[36] Even if, without the possibility of a personal inspection and because of a missing find report, nothing reliable can be said about the moment of reworking or improvement, it must be emphasised that in this case, a modern manipulation of the finding has up to now never been taken into account.

Apart from the awful, although currently unprovable, suspicion that in the case of the Kassel *autepsa* a unique document of Roman memory culture was destroyed due to over-eagerness or to sheer ignorance, one can fundamentally ask how much more aesthetic and attractive a highly imaginative and wrongly compounded but historically interesting *pasticcio* might be for the educated museum visitor, if as an alternative he is confronted with an old pot completely stripped of its decoration and, in the end, no longer worthy of an exhibition.

In any event, it will have to become a requirement that supposedly modern parts which were removed from an object by the restorer should also be permanently kept for reasons of verifiability. Furthermore, concerning bronzes from historical collections and art trade whose original find context is unknown but who feature chronologically non-related parts, the author likes to plead insistently for not immediately considering a modern *pasticcio* as the only contemplable explanation but always also considering the possibility of an ancient reworking. In general, the archaeologist should learn to appreciate and to respect the modern phases of an ancient object more, provided that this is not already 'common sense' with the responsible persons at most museums and collections.

In the case of a construct assembled from a Mercury bust–*tintinnabulum* of the 1st or 2nd century AD and a lamp of the 3rd or 4th century AD, which is in the former Pierpont Morgan Collection at the Wadsworth Atheneum in Hartford (CO, USA)[37] (Fig. 4.6), we can only hope that it is kept as an exhibit of highest appeal: especially as seen from afar, the chains matching the dating of the lamp do not seem to completely exclude a reworking in Late Antiquity.[38]

---

[35] Cf. a Roman bronze *phalera* with imperial portrait (Nero?) in profile facing to the left: Sotheby's 1990, without pagination, no. 63 with illustration.
[36] Comstock and Vermeule 1971, 340–342 no. 479 with illustration.
[37] Hartford (CT), Wadsworth Atheneum acc. no 1917.890. Smith 1913, no. 84 pl. 54; Franken 2007, 10 n. 5. Cordial thanks to Edd Russo (Hartford, CT) for kind information.
[38] An autopsy, which has not been possible for the author until now, should pay attention above all to the existence or non-existence of modern chain links and to inconsistencies in the patina of individual elements of the construct.

6. From candelabra to cult equipment?

On first sight alone, a clear decision between an ancient and a modern reworking can hardly be reliably made. How little in the end remains of a highly promising idea shows the example of a new acquisition of the Israel Museum in Jerusalem (Fig. 4.7) which the author saw for the first time on a beautiful colour plate in the catalogue 'Chronicles of the Land' published in 2010.

Figure 4.6. Pasticcio (?) *from tintinnabulum and lamp. Hartford (CO), Wadsworth Atheneum (Smith 1913, no. 84, pl. 54).*

Cat. 1: *Thymiaterium*: Jerusalem, Israel Museum inv. 2006.28.112. Gift of Eleanore and Charles Stendig, New York, in memory of their fathers, Meyer Brustein and Irving Stendig. Find site unknown. H: 30.5 cm (?) or 30.9 cm (with cup-shaped attachment). W: 25 cm. (Christie's East 1999, 137 f. no. 736 with illustration. ['A Roman Bronze Tripod Stand. Circa 2nd century A.D. Composed from various elements, including a tripod base with lion-paw feet, the rectangular shaft in the form of a janiform herm of a satyr and a Pan, surmounted by an inverted bell-shaped socket. ... 30.9 cm high. Provenance: Royal Athena Galleries, New York']; Dayagi-Mendels and Rozenberg 2010, 349 (left) no 14; 278 f. fig. 14 ['candelabrum decorated with a two-faced Janus head and lion paws. 2nd–3rd century CE ...']).

It seemed immediately clear that, already in antiquity, some changes must have been made on this exciting object. The first idea was that a kind of *thymiaterium* had been created from parts of a Roman candelabrum by attaching small bowls. In fact, similar small bowls were not uncommon in the East, such as the incense shovels which were used, among other things, in Jewish worship. Yet the expectation of a secured archaeological find from the Holy Land and of an accompanying detailed find and restoration report was soon belied, as it became clear that the curious device had been acquired in the US art trade, where it was described already in a 1999 catalogue in an accurate but unprecise way as 'composed from various elements'. Examined in the cold light of day, it seemed, therefore, far more plausible that it cannot be an object already reworked in antiquity. Instead, we are probably dealing with one of those modern *pasticci* which are in many archaeological museums and collections and which we owe above all to highly imaginative 'restorers', unscrupulous art dealers or museum men of the late 18th and early 19th centuries, who were focused on pieces as well-preserved and as spectacular as possible.[39]

Figure 4.7. Thymiaterium *made of parts of several candelabra. Jerusalem, Israel Museum (Cat. 1) (Dayagi-Mendels and Rozenberg 2010, 349 (left) no. 14).*

In its present condition, the 'tripod stand' lacks a cup-shaped crowning which is reproduced in an older auction catalogue. Other than supposed in the catalogue mentioned above, the cup does not seem to have really been reworked from a statuette's plinth. It might rather have been used earlier as the crowning of a Roman candelabrum. Whether the cup-shaped top got lost or someone failed to put it on for the photo is irrelevant, in the end. A closer inspection will rapidly clarify that, in fact, a series of originally unconnected parts had been used here. The double herm in the middle was once part of a height-adjustable candelabrum, a well-documented type of lampstand which is above all known through some complete specimen in the Naples Museum and through excavations in the Balkans. The significant indication is a small eyelet under one of the residual limbs through which there ran a short chain with a hanging pin to fix the candelabrum at different heights.[40] To such a candelabrum, adjustable in height, always belonged a removable base, which gives us the certainty

---

[39] As every great museum with a collection of ancient bronzes developing over several centuries, the Berlin Antiquities collection – SMB also owns a series of remarkable bronze *pasticci* which have, up to now, been very seldomly the object of an investigation carried out or supervised by experienced restorers. Cf. e.g. three candelabra or stands of devices and a volute *krater*: Franken 2011, sub inv. Fr. 707, Fr. 710, Misc. 8574, Fr. 1654.

[40] On this cf. Franken 1996, 97–99 no. 104 figs 176–179.

that the probably also Roman base of the candelabrum presently fastened on it is not the original one because it belongs to another type. The enigmatic small bowls – when turned by 180° – are also nothing else than profiled bases as they are usually mounted under the three legs of the candelabrum base in many Roman lampstands.

This object, on first sight so apparently interesting but in reality tinkered with in recent times, can no longer be regarded as an archaeological object of scientific value.

7. Secondary weights of Roman steelyards

It is now 30 years since I first came into contact with the problem of the re-use of ancient bronzes. The reason for this was the subject of my dissertation supervised from 1987 by Nikolaus Himmelmann (1929–2013) at the University of Bonn, concluded in 1991 and published in 1994 under the title *Aequipondia. Figurative weights of Roman and Early Byzantine steelyards.*[41]

Among figurative steelyard weights there is, next to head-, bust- and figure-shaped weights that had been produced solely for this purpose, also a larger number of pieces which were only reworked into steelyard weights by the subsequent mounting of an eyelet on the upper head and the introduction of a lead filling. These had originally served other purposes. Although, in my dissertation, I dealt mainly with the so-called 'primary' steelyard weights, I did not ignore the 'secondary' examples completely, but listed a representative selection of the appropriate items in the appendices of my study.[42]

I distinguished 'secondary' steelyard weights that were made from bust-shaped medallions and the crownings (muleheads) of the *fulcra* of *klinai* of Hellenistic and Imperial times, from other bust appliqués of unknown function, from bust and figure vessels, heads of statuettes, small-format portrait busts, tripod top busts and similar parts of devices. As it was not always possible to study the original objects and, in most cases, no profile and rear views had been published, in the end there remained a certain number of 'secondary' steelyard weights of which the original function and use could not be determined or at least not with the necessary certainty.

So as not to bore the reader with an all too subtle specialist knowledge and not too interesting technical details, here are just a few significant cases instead. Weights reworked from small-format portrait busts that, in the ideal case, can be dated according to the living data of the represented person or in correspondence to the general development of the Roman portrait sculpture, deserve the greatest interest.[43] In the rare cases in which the accompanying steelyards have been preserved, the date of the reworking can be further delimited.

---

[41] Franken 1994.
[42] Franken 1994, 204–207.
[43] Cf. lately Dahmen 2001, 172 f. 198 cat. 100–103, 203, 205, pls 100–103, 203, 205.

To the exceptions last mentioned belongs a steelyard found in Pompeii in 1843, now in the Hermitage of St Petersburg, with an armoured bust of a Julio-Claudian boy, 16 cm high, as a steelyard weight (Fig. 4.8). It is possible to identify it on the basis of the individual shaping of the forelocks as Lucius Caesar (17 BC–AD 2), one of Augustus's two grandsons who died young. This differentiates it from the frequently occurring primary steelyard weights which occur in the form of armoured busts of boys and youths with hairstyle motifs following the High Classical works of the Greek sculptor Polykleitos (5th century BC), which obviously represent the Roman emperor without special features. The portrait bust in St Petersburg was reworked only secondarily as a steelyard weight. As the evidently accompanying steelyard belongs to a Roman type most common in the Vesuvian towns (the 'Pompeii type'), there can be no doubt that the small portrait bust no longer used after AD 2 was probably very soon reworked into a weight (AD 79 at the latest). Severe traces of use, as they may be observed on other steelyard weights often used for decades, are not detected on the bust in St Petersburg, which speaks more likely for a late reworking within the sketched time frame.

Figure 4.8. Portrait bust of L. Caesar with chest armour. St. Petersburg, State Eremitage (Cat. 2) (Curtius 1948, 92–93 no. A pl. 38, 1).

> Cat. 2: Armoured bust of L. Caesar: St Petersburg, State Museum Hermitage inv. B 61. Found in Pompeii in 1843. H 16 cm (Curtius 1948, 92–93 no. A pl. 38, 1; O. Neverow in: Antičnaja chudožestvennaja bronza 1973, 108 no. 288 with pl.; Boschung 1989, 121 no. 59; Franken 1994, 206 sub 7.2.7.; Dahmen 2001, 172 no. 100 pl. 100 with further literature).

A recently published new find (Fig. 4.9) from excavations in Lycian Patara (TR) deserves further attention.

> Cat. 3: Armoured bust of Vespasian: Antalya, Arkeoloji Müsezi inv. 2004.229. From Patara (Tepecik). H: 5.05 cm. (Işik 2011, fig. p. 21 (coloured reproduction of the bust from the right); Işkan et al. 2016, 119–120 fig. 99 (head from the right; *ein als Gewicht wiederverwendeter Kopf des Vespasian ... vom Tepecik*/head of Vespasian reworked as a weight ... from Tepecik); Şahin 2018, 153 no. E2 fig. and pl. 14).

Figure 4.9. Portrait bust of Vespasian with chest armour. Antalya, Arkeoloji Müzesi (Cat. 3) (Şahin 2018, 153 no. E2 pl. 14).

The armoured bust, only about 5 cm high, with the portrait features of the Roman emperor Vespasian, had been reworked into a weight as described above and connected to a steelyard of the early group of the Osterburken type.[44] We are in a convenient position which allows us to date the origin of the portrait within the reign of the emperor (AD 69–79). The type of steelyard, however, dates to within the second half of the 2nd or the first half of the 3rd century. In view of the long time span of about 70–170 years between the death of Vespasian and the re-use of his portrait, we can be sure that a special personal devotion for the dead emperor could have hardly been a cause for re-use. It must rather be supposed that the manufacture of figurative weights during the lifetime of the Osterburken type of steelyards had already clearly decreased.[45] However, it cannot be completely excluded yet that the original weight had been lost to the owner of the steelyard and he therefore had to have a new weight adjusted. The latter, however, is less probable, since the weights were calibrated at the beginning together with the steelyard, and after that the corresponding scales were registered so that the weight could not easily be exchanged. Either the steelyard weight serving as a substitute had to be exactly equivalent in weight to the lost one, or it was necessary to renew the scales in correspondence with the secondary weight – but this was technically difficult, if not even impossible.

There are indications that also bust appliqués belonging originally to the pictorial decoration of Roman equestrian statues were from time to time reworked into steelyard weights. But unfortunately, until now, not a single one of these busts has been preserved together with the accompanying steelyard. Otherwise, we might possibly gain important chronological evidence as to when the systematic destruction

---

[44] Franken 1993, 85–89 fig. 8.
[45] The existence of primary bust weights on steelyards of the type Osterburken (early group) is proven by the historical drawing only recently known to me (https://memoirevive.besançon.fr/ark:/48565/xqv4zbw105fn, accessed 13 October 2021) of a steelyard with charioteer bust found in Besançon (F) in 1734: Franken 1994, 150 no. A 174 pl. 51 d, with literature).

of statues from the imperial time or respectively their pagan pictorial decoration started.[46]

8. Charms of the antique. Re-use after about 1500 years

Between 2004 and 2012, the author conducted a re-analysis of the inventory and losses of the more than 8000 bronze, lead and iron objects in the Antiquities Collection of the Staatliche Museen in Berlin, which had got into disarray during the chaos of the Second World War. In the course of this analysis one of the most sensational results was the rediscovery of a seemingly Mycenaean, i.e., Late Bronze Age, axe of the 14th or 13th century BC which had been furnished on both sides with mysterious magic signs and inscriptions in Roman times.[47] The axe was acquired by the German archaeologist Albert Ippel (1885–1962) in Smyrna at an unknown date and entered the Berlin Antiquities Collection under the inventory number '30900' (Fig. 4.10). Apart from being briefly mentioned in the acquisition report, it was never published and had been lost since the end of the Second World War. Yet, in the end, the author could relocate the piece so long believed lost solely by means of a sketch in the inventory book and a collection document established before the evacuation (1939) and the 'war-related transfer' to the Soviet Union (since 1945) in the Museum of Fine Arts A.S. Pushkin (Pushkin-Museum) in Moscow, and could photograph it extensively.[48]

> Cat. 4: Bronze-period axe with magic inscriptions and signs: previously Berlin, Antikensammlung – Staatliche Museen zu Berlin inv. 30900 (at present Moscow, State Museum of Fine Arts A.S. Pushkin). Acquired by the archaeologist Albert Ippel (1885–1962) in Smyrna (today Izmir, TR) before 1923. L: 16.5 cm; W: 4.5 cm; D: 1.0 cm (Berliner Museen 1923, 51; Franken 2011 sub inv. 30900).

In order to be able to understand Roman magic inscriptions, a special expertise is necessary, which the author does not have. Also, a publication which has already been announced shall not be anticipated here.[49] Yet it is a bronze axe certainly originating from the 2nd millennium BC and thus of the Bronze Age that was furnished with mysterious magic signs and inscriptions in Roman imperial times and therefore at least about 1500 years later; at any rate, it is an object which wins an additional aspect beyond the subject frame of this conference. As is well known, it was not only in Roman times that supernatural power was attributed to palaeontological and archaeological chance discoveries. Already among the small

---

[46] Franken 2000; 2017.
[47] Formally very similar is an axe of only 15.4 cm length from Ledrai/Lidir – Ayia Paraskevi (Cyprus) in Berlin, ANT – SMB inv. Misc. 8103, 66; Merrillees 2012, 38–39.
[48] I like to thank the former museum director Irina Antonova (1922–2020) and staff members Ludmilla Akimova and Vladimir Tolstikov for their kind support.
[49] The magic signs of the axe are being studied at present by Kirsten Dzwiza among others within the project 'Characteres' with support of the German Research Foundation since 2017.

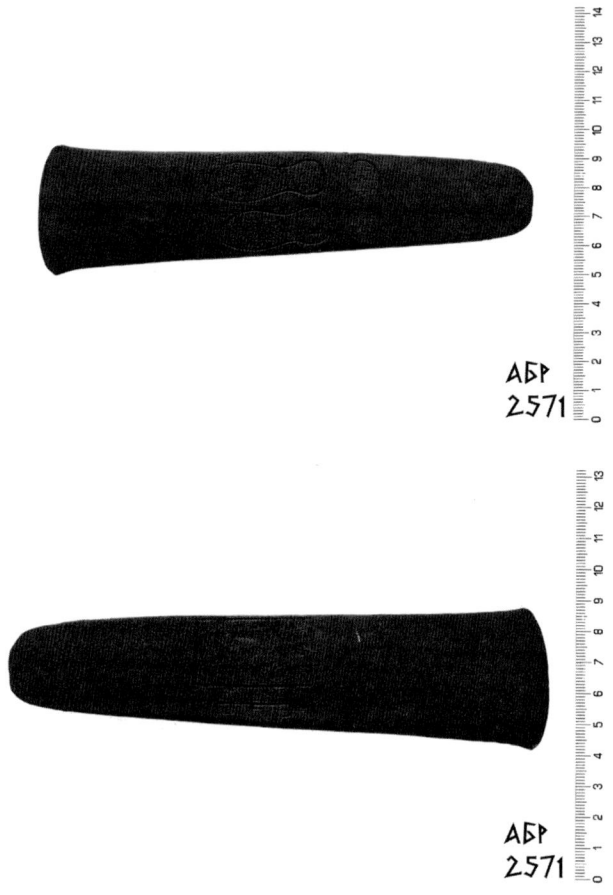

finds from the old excavations in the Apollon sanctuary of Didyma lost since the First World War there were, according to the inventory lists kept in the archive of the Berlin Antiquities Collection, several axes of polished black stone. Also well known are unusually assorted find complexes of Bronze Age weaponry from the area of Roman sanctuaries in Britain, as is demonstrated in an exemplary way by the Temple Treasury of Ashwell (Hertfordshire) in the British Museum, published in 2018.[50]

In fact – as a recent investigation of Dieter Quast has shown – examples of stone axes with magical inscriptions had become increasingly frequent since Roman times, with the inscribed axes from the so-called oracle apparatus of Pergamon being probably the most widely known.[51] Other than the bronze axe, only 1 cm thick, the Pergamon axes were cut into thin slices before they were furnished with magic inscriptions in Roman times.

Figure 4.10. Bronze axe with magic inscriptions. Berlin, Antikensammlung – SMB (Cat. 4) (photo: Norbert Franken)

9. A reworked relief vessel from Amorgos

Presumably in the 1980s, an unusual find (Fig. 4.11), which directly concerns the essentials of our topic, surfaced near Aigiale in the north-east of the Greek Cycladic island of Amorgos.

> Cat. 5: Thurible: Amorgos, Chora Museum inv. 282 (Marangou 1994) or inv. 276 (Marangou 2002). From the Bay of Aigiale. Measurements unknown (Marangou 1994, 375. 380 fig. 3 a. b; 2002, 39 f. fig. 49. 50 a–c).

---

[50] Wilkin 2018.
[51] Quast 2011; Faraone 2014.

The object was published twice by Lila Marangou without measurements and under different inventory numbers as 'an Alexandrian bronze vessel decorated with dionysiac subjects'. In its last utilisation phase, the vessel apparently served as a Late Roman or Byzantine thurible. Different devices with appropriate chain suspension, to which, apart from incense and hanging lamps,[52] also the so-called *polycandela*[53] belong, are known in large numbers, although the dating propositions often vary. It is not clear whether the author did not recognise the secondary use as thurible or whether she intentionally ignored it. However, her firm intention to prove far-reaching relations of the island in Hellenistic times with the help of the object is already indicated in the title of her investigation and the line of argument therein. A neutral observer must consider this to be naive or at least negligent, for it is neither proven nor provable at all that the container has been reworked in Amorgos. Just as easily, it could have found its way to the island much later, especially as long-distance transport over the sea is evidenced by completely pre-cast marble church fittings in shipwrecks of the Byzantine era.[54]

The thurible from Amorgos might also have belonged to the fittings of a church. Yet it differs, as can be seen, from all other specimens of this kind of equipment in that parts of an ancient item, by then already 500 years old, were used for the container. This was accomplished by taking off the mouth, the neck and the shoulder from a Late Hellenistic relief container and cutting out a wide bowl with three projecting suspension eyelets from the previously closed container.

As a result of the cutting out, the original form of the relief container can no longer be completely reconstructed. At first it calls to mind the jug (preserved without handle) from Aventicum (Avenches),[55] the ancient central place of the Helvetians in the Swiss Mittelland; however, the contour line in the lower part seems too steep for this, which is why one must rather think of a bulbous vessel like the *balsamaria* investigated by Claudia Braun.[56]

In fact, the topic of the relief decoration does not contradict this either. Under an ivy tendril, partly cut off in the upper parts, which almost surrounded the container horizontally somewhat below the expected shoulder, one recognises various Dionysian masks, *thyrsoi*, musical instruments and cult vessels arranged like a still life. Related arrangements are mainly known from Hellenistic or Roman silver and gemstone

---

[52] Cf. V. H. Elbern in: Wamser and Zahlhaas 1998, 46–49 cat. 33–38 with figs.; Wamser and Zahlhaas 1998, 49 cat. 39 with illustration.
[53] Cf. C. Schmidt in: Wamser 2004, 100 cat. 132–134 with illustrations.
[54] Cf. Ancona 2014, 127 with illustration.
[55] Bérard 1967; Leibundgut 1976, 101–102 no. 121 fig. 1 pl. 63; Kapeller 2003, 91 fig. 5; 137 no. 102 pl. 17; Franken 2018, 541–543 fig. 1 b.
[56] Braun 2001.

Figure 4.11. Late Roman–Early Byzantine thurible. Amorgos, Chora Museum (Cat. 5) (Marangou 2002, 39–40, figs 49, 50 a–c).

vessels.⁵⁷ Yet similar still lives with masks⁵⁸ also occur with bronze *balsamaria* – just as the set pieces⁵⁹ borrowed from the world of the *palaestra*.

It seems an interesting idea that the relief vessel might not have served as an 'authentic' vessel, i.e., one ready for use, but as an attribute of a statue.⁶⁰ Indeed, without autopsy, it is difficult to distinguish real vessels from merely vessel-shaped attributes of statues, for real vessels could not only be embossed but also cast.⁶¹ Unfortunately, many archaeologists today seem not to be aware of the basic difference between these object categories. But it may also be that they do not ask themselves such a question at all because then they need not answer it. However, the need for a binding definition remains, especially since, in view of the presumably very different weights, it should actually be easy to define.⁶²

In the case of a new arrangement or a re-use of a divine attribute, one could see a deliberate appropriation in the service of the new faith, just as one often intentionally occupied ancient temples and cult places when building early churches to prevent the continuation of pagan cults. Similar reasons might have played a role with a Roman bronze statuette of the childlike Bacchus, approximately 35 cm high (Fig. 4.12). The figure was found in 1864 on the banks of the Don (RUS) and today features mutilated feet and arms, a toothless mouth and empty eye sockets. According to Russian archaeologists, it was furnished with cruciform monograms at the chest and the hips and a 'belt' from a psalm verse referring to the Christian liturgy in the 8th and 9th century and was used for the storage of holy water.⁶³

Even though the object from Amorgos (Fig. 4.11), which was reworked from a Late Hellenistic relief container into a late Roman – early Byzantine thurible, lacks an expressive find context, it is at least provided with an established provenance; it is thus incomparably more valuable to us than are some bronzes coming from an old collection or the art market because with them, other than in our case, we always have to take into account the possibility of modern manipulations.

In cultural history, the later re-use of an ancient vessel is not a solitary occurrence. Moreover, it is possibly part of a phenomenon typical of its time, even if we must look beyond the narrow confines of the class of materials. Thus,

---

⁵⁷ Cf. a bronze jug with a shoulder frieze with similar motifs in Paris, Petit Palais: Oliver 2019, figs. 1, 3, 4, 6, 7.
⁵⁸ Cf e.g. a vessel in the art trade with busts and theatre masks: Braun 2001, 122 cat. 28 pl. 34.
⁵⁹ A vessel from the surroundings of Trento/I (Braun 2001, 130 cat. 43 fig. 90 pl. 47) has now a parallel of high quality in New York: Sotheby's 2004, 46 f. no. 49 with illustration.
⁶⁰ Cf. on this in general Franken 2000, 225–229.
⁶¹ A jug from Hungary, dated to the late 5th/6th century stands technically and iconographically within the antique tradition: Vida 2017; cf. also Vida 2016.
⁶² The 'Cup from Erp' in Bonn, controversial for a long time, could once also have been part of a statue's attribute. On that see Stupperich (2000, pl. 66, 2), which takes up an orally announced idea of the author and interprets the 'cup' as a possible crowning of a candelabrum.
⁶³ Zalesskaya 2010, 235 no. 275 with fig. Three obviously intentional bore-holes in the upper body of the figure remain unexplained.

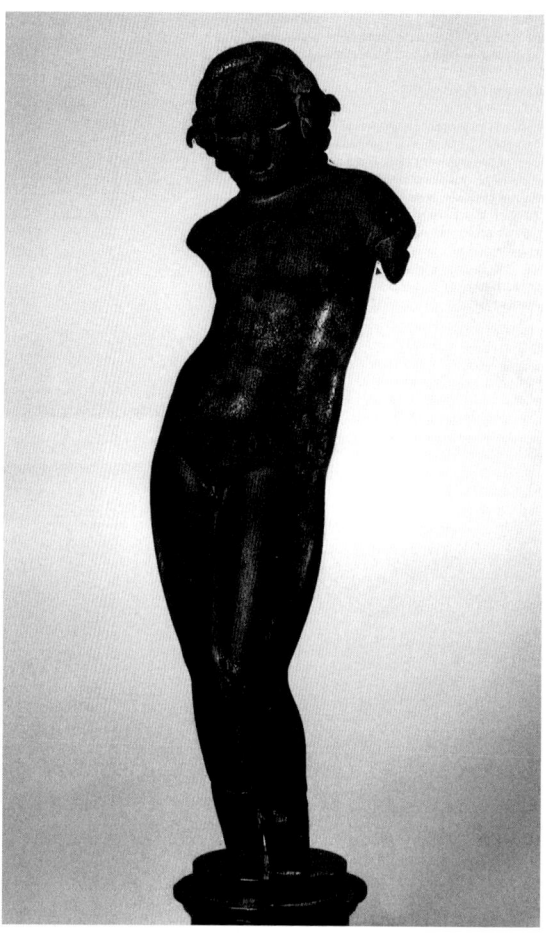

Figure 4.12. Early medieval re-used Roman Bacchus statuette. St Petersburg (RUS) (Zaleesskaya 2010, 235 no. 275).

as is well known, we encounter for instance ancient gems of secondary use on medieval gold work such as reliquaries, crosses, *fibulae* and rings.[64] Moreover, in Merovingian graves there are – apart from ancient coins, *fibulae* and pearls – also Roman glass vessels which, because of their good preservation, were believed to come from the looting of older graves.[65] The fact that precisely the re-use of ancient vessels was in accordance with a widespread practice in early Christian times is indicated in written sources mentioning the benedictions of vessels found at classical sites.[66]

But what could have been the concrete reason for the reworking of a Roman *balsamarium* and its re-use as an early Christian thurible? Was it only the material need of a remote island in the Cyclades? As thuribles with Christian relief representations are mainly known from the Syro-Palestinian area[67] one has to ask further whether in Amorgos they were content with the certainty that superficially inappropriate images for church equipment were as such unrecognisable for a distant observer or church visitor. Yet, in my view, a re-interpretation in accordance with an *interpretatio christiana* would be possible, if one interprets the masks as the heads of beheaded Christian witnesses of faith, just as one could see a Christian ordeal in the representation of the dragging of Hector on an Attic Achilles sarcophagus from about AD 240/250 (since 1828 at Woburn Abbey,

---

[64] Zwierlein-Diehl 2008.
[65] Cf. Krämer 1965, 327.
[66] Krämer 1965, 328.
[67] Cf. J. G. Deckers and J. Witt in: Stiegemann 2001, 187–189 cat. I.70 with fig. I did not have access to the unpublished study of I. Richter-Siebels (1989).

Bedfordshire),⁶⁸ placed at the 'gate of persecution' in Ephesus and probably erected in the 6th century.⁶⁹

If this idea sounds daring at first, it nevertheless bears a certain probability. As Erika Zwierlein-Diehl could show, on the basis of numerous examples, in the Middle Ages ancient intaglios and cameos were not rarely attributed a Christian re-interpretation,⁷⁰ a fact which is conclusively proven thanks to individual inscriptions on the bezels. In another context, that author mentions the monolith sardonyx-*kantharos*, known as *coupe de Ptolémée* (more rarely *coupe des Ptolémées*) in the Cabinet des Médailles of the Bibliothèque Nationale de France which was in the treasure of the abbey church in Saint-Denis near Paris until 1791⁷¹ and, for a long time, played an important role as a liturgical instrument at the coronation of the French kings. Artistically more demanding than the vessel of Amorgos but, with regard to the iconography fundamentally closely related to it, the vessel made of semi-precious stone is also adorned with the representation of a sacral idyll dominated by masks, containers and other devices. Besides an allusion to the theophoric name of Dionysius of Paris (about AD 250), one could also see this as a specific reference to his martyr's death by decapitation. Within the Catholic and Anglican churches, Dionysius is in fact worshipped as one of the '14 helpers in need' even today, and he belongs to the so-called *cephalophoroi* who, in the pictorial tradition, hold their own head in their hands. Concerning Amorgos, however, only the adoration of St Paul is testified in Agios Pavlos situated only a few kilometres south-west of Aigiale. He died the martyr's death by sword apparently in Rome under emperor Nero in AD 64.

An incomplete attempt of reworking into a thurible is documented in a bronze vessel from Emona in Ljubljana, Slovenia, decorated with relief scenes of fighting animals.⁷² In this case, one might see a '*damnatio ad bestias*' in the represented *venationes*, which was not uncommon in the period of the persecution of Christians.

10. Summary

The mending of casting defects on bronze statues, inscription tablets and utensils and all kinds of smaller repairs on *fibulae*, belt loops and similar items of everyday use were, as is known, an everyday occurrence in Roman and late antique times. The systematic destruction, collecting, smashing and renewed melting down of bronzes also prevailed from the end of antiquity. There has been much research on all these phenomena. It is different with the more rarely provable reworking and subsequent further use or re-use of bronze statues, vessels and devices. This author deals with all this while trying to trace the different motivations that might have led

---

⁶⁸ Kintrup 2017, 49–60 cat. 3 pls 34–38.
⁶⁹ Karwiese 1995, 144.
⁷⁰ Zwierlein-Diehl 2008, 241–266.
⁷¹ On that recently Del Bufalo 2016, 65 fig. 84, with literature.
⁷² Braun 2001, 119 cat. 22 pls 23–32; Plesničar Gec 2002, figs 1–6.

to the fact that an ancient or prehistoric bronze was picked up again, methodically reworked and in this way led to a new use either already after a few years or only after many centuries. It becomes evident that in Greek folding mirrors adorned with reliefs (Fig. 4.1) on which bronze sheets in repoussé technique, in many cases originating from older defensive arms, vessels or other devices are re-used, and in Roman steelyards on which not only 'primary' (that is, steelyard weights made for this purpose) but also 'secondary' (that is, bust and head weights subsequently reworked for this purpose; Figs 4.8 and 4.9) occur, we can observe an outright mass phenomenon; what mattered most for the ancient craftsmen was probably the preservation of beautiful things through re-use. Primarily political but also economic reasons must be assumed for the exchange of portrait heads on re-used statues (Fig. 4.2) widespread in Roman times yet today often hardly verifiable. Just as widespread was the renewed use of older inscription tablets by turning them around and simply using the reverse side for a new inscription (Fig. 4.4). In other cases, as for instance the thurible of the early Byzantine period from Amorgos (Fig. 4.11) or the Bronze Age axe from Asia Minor (Fig. 4.10) furnished with Roman magic inscriptions, it is rather a matter of exceptional cases which only selectively highlight diverse yet still very interesting aspects of the ancient and post-antique history of mentalities.

References

Antičnaja chudožestvennaja bronza 1973 *Katalog vystavki*. Exhibition catalogue Leningrad (Leningrad)
Başgelen, N. and Ergeç, R. 2000 *Belkis/Zeugma, Halfeti, Rumkale. A Last Look at History* (Istanbul)
Baumeister, M. 2004 *Metallrecycling in der Frühgeschichte. Untersuchungen zur technischen, wirtschaftlichen und gesellschaftlichen Rolle sekundärer Metallverwertung im 1. Jahrtausend n. Chr.* Würzburger Arbeiten zur Prähistorischen Archäologie 3 (Rahden/Westfalen)
Bechert, T. 2007 *Germania Inferior. Eine Provinz an der Nordgrenze des Römischen Reiches*, Zaberns Bildbände zur Archäologie. Sonderbände der Antiken Welt (Mainz)
Bérard, C. 1967 Art alexandrin et mystères dionysiaques. Le 'vase bachique' d'Avenches. *Bulletin de l'Association Pro Aventico* 19, 57–90
Berliner Museen 1923 *Verzeichnis der Erwerbungen im Januar und Februar* (Berlin)
Bieber, M. 1915 *Die antiken Skulpturen und Bronzen des Königl. Museum Fridericianum in Cassel* (Marburg)
Blanck, H. 1969 *Wiederverwendung alter Statuen als Ehrendenkmäler bei Griechen und Römern*. Studia Archaeologica 11 (Rome)
Borell, B. and Rittig, D. 1998 *Orientalische und griechische Bronzereliefs aus Olympia. Der Fundkomplex aus Brunnen 17*. Olympische Forschungen 26 (Berlin)
Boschung, D. 1989 *Die Bildnisse des Caligula*. Das römische Herrscherbild 4 (Berlin)
Boschung, D. and Wittekind, S. (eds) 2008 *Persistenz und Rezeption. Weiterverwendung, Wiederverwendung und Neuinterpretation antiker Werke im Mittelalter*. ZAKMIRA 6 (Wiesbaden)
Braun, C. 2001 *Römische Bronzebalsamarien mit Reliefdekor*. British Archaeological Report S917 (Oxford)
Briguet, M. F. 1977 Un lampadaire devient trépied! Réexamen de la 'suspension' étrusque Br 3142 du musée du Louvre. In: A. Neppi Modona (ed.), *La civiltà arcaïca di Vulci e la sua espansione. Atti del X convegno di studi etruschi e italici. Grosseto-Roselle-Vulci. 29 maggio-2 giugno 1975* (Florence), 65–69

Burgersdijk, D., Calis, R., Kelder, J., Sofroniew, A., Tusa, S. and van Beek R. (eds) 2014 *Sicily and the Sea* (Amsterdam), 127

Christie's East 1999 *Nineteenth Century Decorative Arts. Antiquities and Souvenirs of the Grand Tour.* Auction catalogue New York 28-29 April 1999 (New York)

Comstock, M. and Vermeule, C. 1971 *Greek, Etruscan and Roman Bronzes in the Museum of Fine Arts, Boston* (Boston)

Curtius, L. 1948 Ikonographische Beiträge zum Porträt der römischen Republik und der julisch-claudischen Familie XIV. Germanicus, *Mitteilungen des Deutschen Archäologischen Instituts* 1, 69–94

Dahmen, K. 2001 *Untersuchungen zu Form und Funktion kleinformatiger Porträts der römischen Kaiserzeit* (Münster)

Dayagi-Mendels, M. and Rozenberg, S. (eds) 2010 *Chronicles of the Land. Archaeology in The Israel Museum Jerusalem* (Jerusalem)

Del Bufalo, D. 2016 *Murrina Vasa. A Luxury of Imperial Rome* (Rome)

Descamps-Lequime, S. 2012 Un thymiatérion archaique en bronze dans les collections du Louvre. In: M. Denoyelle, S. Descamps-Lequime, B. Mille and S. Verger (eds), *Bronzes Grecs et Romains, Recherches récentes. Hommages à Claude Rolley* (Paris), 310–334, <https://journals.openedition.org/inha/4400> (accessed 28 September 2021)

Dieudonné-Glad, N., Feugère, M. and Önal, M. 2013 *Zeugma V. Les objets*. Travaux de la Maison de l'Orient et de la Méditerranée 64 (Lyon)

Dostert, A., Franken, N. and Peltz, U. 2008 'Ein seltenes und interessantes Stück'. Die erste antike Großbronze der königlichen Kunstsammlungen in Berlin und Potsdam. *Jahrbuch der Berliner Museen* N.F. 50, 9–24

Eck, W. 2000 Bronzeinschriften von Ehrendenkmälern aus Rom. Zu dem neuen Militärdiplom von der unteren Sava. *Zeitschrift für Papyrologie und Epigraphik* 133, 275–282

Faraone, C. A. 2014 Inscribed Greek thunderstones as house- and body-amulets in Roman Imperial times. *Kernos* 27, 251–278

Franken, N. 1993 Zur Typologie antiker Schnellwaagen. *Bonner Jahrbücher* 193, 69–120

Franken, N. 1994 *Aequipondia. Figürliche Laufgewichte römischer und frühbyzantinischer Schnellwaagen* (Bonn)

Franken, N. 1996 Die antiken Bronzen im Römisch-Germanischen Museum Köln. Fragmente von Statuen. Figürlicher Schmuck von architektonischen Monumenten und Inschriften. Hausausstattung, Möbel, Kultgeräte, Votive und verschiedene Geräte. *Kölner Jahrbuch* 29, 7–203

Franken, N. 2000 Zu Bildschmuck und Attributen antiker Bronzestatuen. *Kölner Jahrbuch* 33, 215–229

Franken, N. 2007 Leda und der Schwan. Beobachtungen zu Bildtradierung und Werkstattorganisation an spätantiken Bronzelampen mit figürlichem Schmuck. *Mitteilungen zur spätantiken Archäologie und byzantinischen Kunstgeschichte* 5, 9–19

Franken, N. 2011 Bilddatenbank 'Antike Bronzen in Berlin'. http://antike-bronzen.smb.museum (accessed 29 September 2021)

Franken, N. 2017 Eine Bronzebüste der Dea Roma im Museum der Bildenden Künste. Neue Beobachtungen zum Bildschmuck römischer Pferdestatuen. *Bulletin du Musée hongrois des beaux-arts* 122, 73–89

Franken, N. 2018 Nochmals zu antiken Bronzen auf frühen Fotografien. In: B. Schiller and K. Müller (eds), *Von Kreta nach Kuba. Gedenkschrift zu Ehren des Berliner Archäologen Veit Stürmer* (Berlin), 539–548

Galerie Helbing 1910 *Kunstbesitz eines bekannten norddeutschen Sammlers. Abteilung IV. Antike Bronzen und Keramik.* Auction catalogue Munich 22 February 1910 (Munich)

Gercke, P., Krug, A. and Lullies, R. 1967 Zu einer römischen Authepsa in Kassel. *Jahrbuch des Römisch-Germanischen Zentralmuseums Mainz* 14, 175–178

Gergel, R. A. 1991 The Tel Shalem Hadrian reconsidered. *American Journal of Archaeology* 95, 231–251

Graells i Fabregat, R. 2018 *Corazas helenísticas decoradas. Ὅπλα καλά, los 'Siris bronzes' y su contexto.* Studia Archaeologica 223 (Rome)

Gregarek, H. 1997 Der Hildesheimer Silberfund. In: H. Hoyer von Prittwitz und Gaffron and H. Mielsch (eds), *Das Haus lacht vor Silber. Die Prunkplatte von Bizerta und das römische Tafelgeschirr.* Exhibition catalogue Bonn (Cologne), 91–98

Işik, F. 2011 *'Caput Gentis Lyciae'. Patara. Capital of the Lycian League* (Istanbul)

Işkan, H., Schuler, C., Aktaş, Ş., Reitzenstein, D., Schmölder-Veit, A. and Koçak, M. 2016 *Patara. Lykiens Tor zur römischen Welt,* Zaberns Bildbände zur Archäologie. Sonderbände der Antiken Welt (Darmstadt)

Kapeller, A. 2003 La vaisselle en bronze d'Avenches/Aventicum, *Bulletin de l'Association Pro Aventico* 45, 83–146. https://www.e-periodica.ch/digbib/view?pid=bpa-001:2003:45::239#86 (accessed 29 September 2021)

Karwiese, S. 1995 *Gross ist die Artemis von Ephesos. Die Geschichte einer der grossen Städte der Antike* (Vienna)

Kintrup, C. 2017 Attische Sarkophage aus Ephesos. Jahreshefte des Österreichischen Archäologischen Instituts in Wien, Ergänzungsheft 16 (Vienna 2017), 49–60

Krämer, W. 1965 Zur Wiederverwendung antiker Gefäße im frühen Mittelalter. *Germania* 43, 327–329.

Kroll, J. H. 1972 *Athenian Bronze Allotment Plates.* Loeb Classical Monographs (Cambridge MA)

Kruse, T. 2003 Inschriften. In: R. Wünsche (ed.), *Die Sammlung Thun.* Exhibition catalogue Passau (Munich), 106–116

Lahusen, G. and Formigli, E. 2001 *Römische Bildnisse aus Bronze.* Kunst und Technik (Munich)

Leibundgut, A. 1976 *Die römischen Bronzen der Schweiz. II. Avenches* (Mainz)

Maass, M. 1978 *Die geometrischen Dreifüsse von Olympia.* Olympische Forschungen 10 (Berlin)

Marangou, L. I. 1994 Amorgos and Egypt in Hellenistic and Roman periods. Old and new evidence. In: M.-O. Jentel and G. Deschênes-Wagner (eds), *Tranquillitas. Mélanges en l'honneur de Tran tam Tinh* (Québec)

Marangou, L. I. 2002 *ΑΜΟΡΓΟΣ Ι. Η Μινώα. Η πόλις, ο λιμήν και η μείζων περιφέρεια* (Athens)

Mattusch, C. C. 2017 When a statue is not a statue. In: J. M. Daehner, K. Lapatin, and A. Spinelli (eds), *Artistry in Bronze. The Greeks and Their Legacy. XIXth International Congress on Ancient Bronzes. Los Angeles 2015* (Los Angeles), 69–76

Merrillees, R. S. 2012 *The 'Ochsenkrater-Grab' from Nicosia Ayia Paraskevi. Studies in Mediterranean Archaeology and Literature.* Pocket-Book 177 (Uppsala)

Mirković, M. 2000 Euphrata et Romano consulibus auf einem neuen Militärdiplom von der unteren Sava. *Zeitschrift für Papyrologie und Epigraphik* 133, 286–290

Nardi, R. and Önal, M. 2003 The Bronze Mars of Zeugma. Marginal notes on its discovery and conservation treatment. In: R. Early (ed.), *Zeugma. Interim Reports. Rescue Excavations (Packard Humanities Institute), Inscription of Antiochus I, Bronze Statue of Mars, House and Mosaic of the Synaristôsai, and Recent Work on the Roman Army at Zeugma. Journal of Roman Archaeology* Supplement 51 (Portsmouth RI), 69–78

Niemeyer, B. 2007 *Trassologie an römischem Silber. Herstellungstechnische Untersuchungen am Hildesheimer Silberfund.* British Archaeological Report S1621 (Oxford)

Oliver, A. 2019 Two Bronze Vases in the Musée du Petit Palais. *Revue Archéologique* 67, 119–135

Parlasca, K. 2005 Skulpturen aus Zeugma-Seleukeia am Euphrat. Idealplastik und sepulkrale Bildwerke. In: D. Kreikenbom – K.-U. Mahler – T. Weber (eds), *Urbanistik und städtische Kultur in Westasien und Nordafrika unter den Severern* (Mainz 2005), 231–240

Piranesi, G. B. 1778 *Vasi candelabri cippi sarcofagi tripodi lucerne ed ornamenti antichi* (Rome)

Plesničar Gec, L. 2002 The figural vessel from Emona. In: C. Mattusch, A. Brauer and S. E. Knudsen (eds), *From the Parts to the Whole II. Acta of the 13th International Bronze Congress, held at Cambridge, Massachusetts, May 28–June 1, 1996. Journal of Roman Archaeology* Supplement 39 (Portsmouth RI), 248–255

Pollini, J. 2017 The Bronze statue of Germanicus from Ameria (Amelia). *American Journal of Archaeology* 121, 425–437

Pozzi, E. (ed.) 1987 *Domiziano/Nerva. La statua equestre da Miseno. Una proposta di ricomposizione* (Naples)

Quast, D. 2011 Ein Steinbeil mit magischer Inschrift aus der Sammlung des Prinzen Christian August von Waldeck. *Archäologisches Korrespondenzblatt* 41, 249–261

Richter-Siebels, I. 1989 Die palästinensischen Weihrauchgefäße mit Reliefszenen aus dem Leben Christi. Unpublished PhD Dissertation Freie Universität Berlin.

Rocco, G. 2008 *La statua bronzea con ritratto di Germanico ad Ameria (Umbria), Atti della accademia nazionale dei lincei. Classe di scienze morali. Storiche e filologiche.* Memorie (Serie 9) 23(2) (Rome)

Şahin, F. 2018 *Patara Metal Buluntulari. Patara V(2)* (Istanbul)

Schreiber, S. 2018 *Wandernde Dinge als Assemblagen. Neo-materialistische Perspektiven zum 'römischen Import' im 'mitteldeutschen Barbaricum'.* Berlin Studies of the Ancient World 52 (Berlin)

Schwarzmaier, A. 1997 *Griechische Klappspiegel. Untersuchungen zu Typologie und Stil, Mitteilungen des Deutschen Archäologischen Instituts.* Athenische Abteilung Beiheft 18 (Berlin)

Smith, C. H. 1913 *Collection of J. Pierpont Morgan. Bronzes Antique Greek, Roman etc. Including Some Antique Objects in Gold and Silver* (Paris)

Sotheby's 1990 *Antiquities and Islamic Art.* Auction catalogue New York 20 June 1990 (New York)

Sotheby's 2004 *Antiquities.* Auction catalogue New York 9 June 2004 (New York)

Stiegemann, C. 2001 *Byzanz. Das Licht aus dem Osten. Kult und Alltag im Byzantinischen Reich vom 4. bis 15. Jahrhundert.* Exhibition catalogue Paderborn (Mainz)

Stupperich, R. 2000 Der römische 'Bronzebecher' von Erp. In: T. Mattern and D. Korol (eds), *Munus. Festschrift für Hans Wiegartz* (Münster), 297–303

Vida, T. 2016 *Late Antique Metal Vessels in the Carpathian Basin. Luxury and Power in the Early Middle Ages.* Hereditas Archaeologica Hungariae 1 (Budapest)

Vida, T. 2017 *Die frühbyzantinische Messingkanne mit Jagdszenen von Budakalász (Ungarn)* (Budapest)

Wamser, L. (ed.) 2004 *Die Welt von Byzanz. Europas östliches Erbe. Glanz, Krisen und Fortleben einer tausendjährigen Kultur.* Exhibition catalogue Munich (Munich)

Wamser, L. and Zahlhaas, G. 1998 *Rom und Byzanz. Archäologische Kostbarkeiten aus Bayern.* Exhibition catalogue Munich (Munich)

Weiß, P. 2000 Ein Prätorianerdiplom Severus Alexanders auf einer wiederverwendeten Bronzetafel. *Zeitschrift für Papyrologie und Epigraphik* 133, 283–285

Wilkin, N. 2018 Bronze Age Metalwork. In: R. Jackson and G. Burleigh (eds), *Dea Senuna. Treasure, Cult and Ritual at Ashwell, Hertfordshire.* The British Museum Research Publication 194 (London), 300–313

Willer, F. 2014 Recycling. Ein alter Hut. In: LVR-LandesMuseum Bonn, Archäologisches Landesmuseum Baden-Württemberg and Museum Het Valkhof Nijmegen (eds), *Gebrochener Glanz. Römische Großbronzen am UNESCO-Welterbe Limes.* Exhibition catalogue Bonn (2014), 210–211

Willer, F., Schwab, R. and Mirschenz, M. 2016 Römische Bronzestatuen am Limes. Archäometrische Untersuchungen zur Herstellungstechnik. *Bonner Jahrbücher* 2016, 57–207

Zalesskaya, V. 2010 Byzantium. The third ancient world. In: *Immortal Alexander the Great. The Myth. The Reality. His Journey. The Legacy.* Exhibition catalogue Amsterdam (Amsterdam), 235–239

Zwierlein-Diehl, E. 2008 Antike Gemmen im Mittelalter. Wiederverwendung, Umdeutung, Nachahmung. In: Boschung and Wittekind (eds), 237–284

Chapter 5

The value of things: textiles in the Iron Age

Susanna Harris

The value of things

The meaning and origin of the value of things have been studied intensely across the humanities and social science. In *The philosophy of money*,[1] Georg Simmel argues that value is found in what people hold as desirable and for which they are willing to sacrifice other things, their time and to take risks to have and accumulate. In studies of living societies it is broadly recognised that value is not only found in materials but is alive through the desires and actions connected to those things.[2] People judge things as desirable within holistic systems of thought, action, belief and materials; and values may be perceived differently across society. As well, value is mainly relational, one thing may be more or less desirable than something else; this is referred to as ordinal ranking. These observations have proved enduring because the value of things is not fixed but is constantly evolving according to fashion and circumstance.

Archaeologists, working without the testimony of participants, identify why and how past people desired things through the material manifestations of thoughts and actions. Value is attributed to objects that are rare, have exotic origins or were made with high levels of crafting. Wealth, as an accumulation of valuable things, is recognised in the selection of goods placed in a well-furnished burial or those things transported in a ship's cargo.[3] From an economic perspective, value is seen in the balance of supply and demand.[4] Archaeologists usually encounter value in those objects and materials that are well preserved in the archaeological record: coins, precious metals or stone axes. These have proved effective ways of recognising valuable things. However, the weakness of these approaches is that value is presented as fixed and immutable and certain categories of material and object are treated as valuable while others are not.

---

[1] Simmel 1978.
[2] e.g. Graeber 2001; Douglas and Isherwood 1979.
[3] e.g. Bartoloni 2000; Monroe 2010.
[4] van Wijngaarden 1999.

Table 5.1. Desirability and effects; the five principles by which objects are valued (from Harris 2017, 683)

Principle	Desirability	Effect
1. Material properties	Objects are desirable for their material properties. Properties are relational; it may be that a property is more effective and desirable in one context, less so in another	The value of material properties is that it enhances a person's capacity to be or act in a given situation
2. Expense and exclusivity	Objects can be expensive due to their rarity, relative quality or quantity, whether in materials, skills of the creator, or other factors. Expense makes objects exclusive, and exclusive objects are desirable due to limited accessibility	The value of exclusive objects is that they enhance and justify the dynamics of power, legitimacy and order as they demonstrate connections, networks and acquisition ability
3. Conspicuous, sensory appeal	Objects are desirable when they appeal to the senses in an agreeable way	The value of objects with conspicuous, sensory appeal is in their ability to bring pleasure and to influence the perception and behaviour of others
4. Life history or biography	History or biography enhances object desirability when it creates connections between people, places or ideas that are themselves desirable	The value of object biography is that it attaches other people to the object, a factor which extends networks and relationships
5. Fungibility	Objects are desirable when they are part of an established, standardised system of exchange	The value of fungible objects is that they can be readily exchanged for goods and services, because they systemised the transfer of payment, debts and obligations

In the last decade approaches to the materiality of value have turned to the relationship between people and things. This has brought archaeologists' attention to the significance of judgement, knowledge, material agency and the situational value of things.[5] In turn, archaeologists' evaluation of value has diversified and is recognised in a wider range of objects, people and places.[6] With growing interest in material agency, the concept of value is understood in the effects of things and the way objects enable action, as much as in their intrinsic value based on material, form and function.[7] Approaches such as James Gibson's theory of affordances have been influential in drawing attention to the way an environment affords certain opportunities for people, surfaces and substances.[8] Archaeologists working with

---

[5] Bokern and Rowan 2014.
[6] Bevan and Wengrow 2010; Papadopoulos and Urton 2012.
[7] Bokern and Rowan 2014, 4.
[8] Gibson 1977, 67–68.

Actor-Network theory have applied the concept of affordances and object agency to how objects enable people to act.[9] Such approaches connect the physical world with people, and the relationship between people's intentions enacted through objects. If this is taken back to concepts of value, where value is a judgement based on desire, then value is also in the effect of things.

Approached this way, value is found in the things people want, and people want things because of what they enable them to do, be and become. This can be seen in the emotional and physical fulfilment in life, as culturally defined. On this basis, it is argued here that value is a judgement people make about things based in desire and desire is grounded in the effects things have on and for people throughout societies. It is proposed there are five principle ways that people desire objects.[10] These are 1) material properties; 2) expense and exclusivity; 3) items with conspicuous, sensory appeal; 4) the biography or life histories of objects; and 5) as fungible products that are in some way standardised (summary in Table 5.1). The purpose of these principles is to provide a methodological framework to explore the value of things within a contextual analysis of the time and place to which they belong. These principles will be applied to appraise the value of textiles in the Iron Age societies of Etruscan and Venetic Italy in the Orientalising period, 730–580 BCE.

Etruscan and Venetic Italy, 730–580 BCE

The late 8th–early 6th century BCE (730–580 BCE, *Seconda età del Ferro*) in central and northern Italy is referred to as the Second Iron Age or Orientalising period: a Mediterranean-wide cultural phenomenon that involved the intense transportation of goods and people and that heralded major technological and social developments.[11] An emerging aristocracy was engaged in long distance trade, people started to live in early urban centres and the wealthiest buried their dead in monumental tombs with lavish grave goods.[12] If we consider the tempo of human life, the change in relationships in cities and the growth in wealth, these decades were a time of considerable attainment, much of which came through the production, possession and circulation of material goods.[13] With hierarchy comes servitude. The archaeological record is dominated by the material culture of the elite through their elaborate burials and self-representation; however, there are hints at the less wealthy, the servant class and possibly slavery, which is attested from at least the 6th century BCE in central Italy, although it may have started earlier.[14] In this complex mix of changing circumstances, and with much centred on the production, circulation and

---

[9] Van Oyen 2015, 66.
[10] Harris 2017.
[11] Sannibale 2013, 99.
[12] Riva 2010; Bietti Sestieri and De Min 2013, 48; Leighton 2013; Perkins 2014, 63–66.
[13] Gras 2000, 14.
[14] Benelli 2013, 450.

consumption of desirable goods, how was value attached to things? And importantly, how can value be recognised in archaeological remains and what was the significance of value across the social matrices? In the following sections, the five principles of value outlined above (Table 5.1) are applied to consider the desirability of one area of material culture, textiles, in Central and Northeast Italy during the late 8th–early 6th centuries BCE.

Textiles as effective materials

As a first principle of value, things are desirable for their material properties. Material properties have effects. In addition, properties are not fixed but relational, they depend on the environment and individual, a concept known as affordances.[15] The effect of materials, and for that reason their desirability, is situational and according to the individual.

What properties made textiles desirable materials? Textiles are defined as 'large, thin sheets of material made from fibre, which are soft and floppy enough to be used as coverings for people and things'.[16] Fibres are the primary materials of textiles and have a significant effect on the properties of the finished textiles. Analysis of preserved textiles from Central and north-east Italy in the Pre-Roman Iron Age demonstrate that most were made from sheep's wool (*Ovis* sp.) and fibres from the flax plant (*Linum usitatissimum*).[17]

Here we consider two sets of remarkably preserved wool garments. At the Villanovan necropolis at Lippi, Verucchio, Emilia Romagna, alongside other textiles, two semicircular shaped wool mantles were placed in Tomb 89, a well-furnished man's burial dated *c.* 700 BCE.[18] Both mantles are made from single, large, dyed textiles and of sufficient size to wrap around the upper body of an adult man.[19] Woven in one piece using fine wool threads in a weave structure called 2/2 twill, they are shaped like a segment of a circle; both are little over 250 cm in length and *c.* 80 cm wide.[20] There are small holes where fibulae were attached, showing they were worn in life and not made exclusively for the burial.[21] Their size, shape and drape suggest they were worn as lightweight, open upper body garments. This type of mantle is worn by two men in a scene painted on clay panels from the Boccanera Tomb, La Banditaccia, Cerveteri, dated 560–550 BCE, in a scene thought to represent deities (Fig. 5.1). Here wool textiles were desirable for their ability to be woven into large, fine, smooth

---

[15] Gibson 1977, 67.
[16] Barber 1991, 5.
[17] e.g. Stauffer *et al.* 2002; Gleba 2017;.
[18] von Eles 2002b, 273–275; Stauffer *et al.* 2002; Stauffer 2012.
[19] Stauffer 2012, 244–248.
[20] Stauffer *et al.* 2002, 216.
[21] Stauffer 2012, 249.

Figure 5.1. Two men, far left, wear lightweight, decorated mantles and tunics. Women wear tunics and cloaks or veils of varied length, texture and colour. Scene interpreted as the judgement of Paris. Painted clay tablets, Boccanera Tomb, La Banditaccia, Cerveteri, Height: 98–102 cm. London, British Museum inv. 1889,0410.1-5 (©The Trustees of the British Museum. All rights reserved).

fabrics and worn as lightweight garment with elegant drape and texture, as found in the tombs of the wealthy and later represented on deities.

Another remarkable find of wool clothing are two pairs of wool leggings (inner and outer leggings) and socks (inner shoes) found on the Riesenferner/Vedretta di Ries mountain pass, Bolzano/Bozen, radiocarbon dated to 794–499 BCE.[22] The two pairs of leggings are approximately 60 cm long, circumference 34 cm of tubular shape with a flap at one end to tuck into footwear. They are patched and darned and the only dyed yarn is the stitching on the knee patch.[23] The outer leggings are woven with a twill weave, like the Verucchio mantles; however, they are thicker textiles; the inner leggings are woven in plain weave (also called tabby). Wearing layered, wool-twill, patched and darned legwear at high altitude suggests these textiles were desirable for their insulative, mildly elastic properties.[24] The wool leggings were effective materials to keep the feet and legs warm in the cold mountain passes. The Riesenferner/Vedretta di Ries legwear is indicative of the type of textile clothing that was probably very common and highly desirable across society, a staple of rich and poor, in contrast

[22] Bazzanella *et al.* 2005, 152.
[23] Bazzanella *et al.* 2005, 154.
[24] Harris 2010, 107 table 18.3.

to the luxurious materials of the Verucchio mantles. The contrast of these garments suggests how value was attached to wool textiles in the Iron Age through its many material properties. For textile clothing that wraps and encloses the body both in relation to the physical and social environment is a fundamental source of value and was widely appreciated across Iron Age society.

Expense and exclusive textiles

In the second principle of value, it is proposed that things are desirable due to their expensiveness and exclusivity. Things may be expensive due to their rarity, quality or quantity, which consume resources of materials, skill and labour. Expense is relative, it depends on the resources people have available; what is expensive to a servant may be of no consequence to an aristocrat. Expense makes objects exclusive, and exclusive objects are desirable due to limited accessibility. Exclusive items are accessible only to the most wealthy, for this reason they may become signs of authority and legitimacy with the effect of creating and legitimising power.[25]

What makes textiles expensive? Analysis and experiments of spinning and weaving times demonstrate the significance labour required to produce textiles.[26] An onerous aspect of textile labour is the production of yarn (thread). In experiments with a drop spindle, two spinners who participated in experiments for the Centre for Textile Research in Copenhagen (CTR) spun 50 m of wool yarn in 1 hour using an 8 g spindlewhorl.[27] While all textiles require yarn, some textiles are denser and require more than others. The Verucchio mantles are woven using an average of 14 threads per cm in the warp and 24/cm packed into the weft.[28] The outer leggings from Vedretta di Ries are woven in herringbone twill with fewer yarns per centimetre of weaving.[29] The inner leggings are woven in plain weave using 18 threads/cm in the warp and 7 threads/cm in the weft.[30] This means the Verucchio mantles, using finer yarns, required 2–3 times more yarn to weave than the Vedretta di Ries legwear. Not only did this require more time to spin but also more time to weave, as the shuttle passes through the warp 2–3 times more often to produce the same length of textile. The progressive expense from coarse to fine textiles, simple to elaborate, can be ordered in a sequential scale, low to high; a feature known as ordinal ranking (see above). The desirability of the mantles with their fine textiles and minimal wear is that they mark the wearer out as someone with the means to have new, high quality textiles that required more labour to produce than coarse or re-used textiles.

---

[25] Joyce 2000, 70 f.
[26] Costin 2013; Jarva and Lipkin 2014; Olofsson et al. 2015.
[27] Olofsson et al. 2015, 85.
[28] Stauffer et al. 2002, 216; Stauffer 2012, 244–249.
[29] Bazzanella et al. 2005, 154.
[30] Bazzanella et al. 2005, 154.

5. The value of things: textiles in the Iron Age

Figure 5.2. Ship with sail represented in dark brown on a white ground on a jug (oinochoe). Attributed to the Pittore delle palme, active in Tarquinia 700–675 BCE. University of Missouri-Columbia, Museum of Art and Archaeology inv. 71.114 (© Museum of Art and Archaeology University of Missouri-Columbia).

As well as in quality, value is also found in quantity. The Etruscans owed their international power to control of the sea; the wealth of the aristocracy of the Veneto depended on trade along the Adriatic. Based on the representation of sails on Etruscan ceramics, from the early 7th century BCE, a variety of galleys (oared ships with square sails), from swift war ships to ample-hulled cargo ships, circulated in the Mediterranean[31] (Fig. 5.2). As in Classical times, sails were likely made of cellulosic fibres such as flax and woven from strong textiles.[32] The expense and exclusivity of sails was in their size and hence the natural and human resources and organisation of labour required to make them. Estimates of resources show the huge amount of work required to produce sails.[33]

The reconstruction of a sewn fishing boat following the mid-6th century BCE wreck Jules-Verne 9 found in Marseille, required around 5 km of thread for the sails, which in addition took 3000 hours of sewing, plus further textiles as wadding to protect the wooden joints and seams.[34] The 5th century BCE Greek *trireme*, with hull sizes of 36–41 m,[35] is estimated to require 119 m^2 of cloth for the main and foresail.[36] The Etruscan cargo ships of the Orientalising period were smaller than a *trireme*. Estimations of the amount of labour required to weave *trireme* sails suggest that it took around 18 months to produce the yarn and 1 year to weave[37] (The Grand Ribaud F, a cargo ship wrecked off the coast of Provence in the early 5th century BCE, was carrying 700–800 amphorae of Etruscan origin and had an estimated hull size of 22–30 m).[38] As the hull of the Grande Ribaud F is estimated as a third smaller than a *trireme*, it may be anticipated that the sails took around two-thirds of the time to produce. Galleys of the Orientalising period, such as the Grande Ribaud F, were exclusive items due to the extensive labour and material resources required to make and manoeuvre. Ships, with their significance for trade, as well as for defence and attack at sea, were one of the key means to control resources and power, hence highly desirable.

Conspicuous, sensory textiles

Things are desirable when they appeal to the senses in an agreeable way. This aligns to concepts such as beauty, art and aesthetic.[39] Alfred Gell's *Technology of Enchantment* emphasised the effect of dazzling technological achievements as a way to induce

---

[31] Casson 1994, 36–41; Bruni 2013, 770–771, figs 40.5; 40.7.
[32] Whitewright 2007, 289.
[33] see Bender Jørgensen 2012.
[34] Pomey and Poveda 2018, 50.
[35] Rankov 2013, 90–91.
[36] Dimova *et al.* forthcoming.
[37] Dimova *et al.* forthcoming.
[38] Long *et al.* 2006; Petrarulo 2012, 120 f.
[39] Porter 2012, 4–6.

Figure 5.3. Reconstruction of the textile of Mantle 2 from Tomb 89, Lippi Necropolis, Verucchio. The original mantle was embellished with amber and fastened with decorative metal fibulae (reconstruction of the Verucchio Mantle woven by weaver Anna Nørgaard, technical analysis and weaving description by conservator Lise Ræder Knudsen. Image © S. Harris with kind permission).

emotional responses in other people and, as a result, influence social interactions.[40] When considering textiles of 7th century BCE Italy, indicated by those deposited in burials or depicted in representation, they were often splendid, brightly coloured, lustrous and embellished with decorative tablet woven boarders, sparkling beads and fastenings.

At Poggioverde, a settlement of the minor aristocracy outside Veii, as elsewhere in Etruria and Latium, traces of textiles in women's graves show that the clothing included a long linen tunic, applied glass and amber beads and wool twill cloak with decorative tablet woven borders fastened with fibulae. Around the head of one woman, miniature fibulae were used to fasten a thin veil of fine quality wool fabric.[41] The lustre and colour of the fabrics combined with the shine of metal, amber and glass suggest a sparkling and splendid costume, which has been compared to the goddesses' costumes in Homer.[42]

---

[40] Gell 1992.
[41] De Cristofaro – Piergrossi 2017, 68–70.
[42] De Cristofaro – Piergrossi 2017, 76.

Figure 5.4. Textured, coloured tunic and mantle represented on the ceramic statues of the Tomb of the Five Chairs, Cerveteri, c. 625–600 BCE. Height: 54.61 cm. London, British Museum inv. 1873,0820.637 (© The Trustees of the British Museum. All rights reserved).

The Verucchio mantles were similarly splendid, the colours, textures and embellishments on these mantles were bright and eye-catching. The 2/2 twill weave structure creates a faint diagonal texture, enhanced by alternating thread sets in warp and weft to create a checked sheen called a spin or shadow pattern.[43] Mantle 1 contains traces of purpurin, a plant dye with a vibrant red colour.[44] Mantle 2 has traces of red and yellow dye compounds that create a red-orange colour (Fig. 5.3).[45] Both have colourful and decorative tablet woven borders. They were embellished with

---

[43] Stauffer *et al.* 2002, 216.
[44] Stauffer 2012, 247.
[45] Stauffer 2012, 248 f.; Stauffer *et al.* 2002.

amber along the curved edge. On the first, there are remnants of stitching which once attached hundreds of small amber cone-shaped beads, on the second, paired stitch holes attached a row of large amble knobs.[46] As if this were not splendid enough, Mantle 1 was covered with multiple, decorative metal fibulae.[47]

The bright colours and textures of clothing were transferred in imagery. The terracotta seated statues from the Tomb of the Five Chairs, Chiusi, Cerveteri, c. 640 BCE, are depicted wearing diagonally checked tunics and mantles that fasten on the right shoulder.[48] The tunic is painted white with red borders and the semicircular or triangular mantles are painted red with orange borders (Fig. 5.4). The conspicuous sensory appeal of textiles was used to enhance their value, not only due to the skill and resources required to achieve these effects but also in the ability of these bright, splendid textiles to enchant and create a dazzling spectacle both as worn in life and as part of magnificent burials. Where textiles are used as clothing, they became a strong personal statement that was integral to social interactions. These textiles are not only desirable for clothing, they are desirable because of their sensory appeal.

Figure 5.5. Bronze rattle (tintinnabulum) *from the Tomb of the Gold, Arsenale Militare, Bologna, dated c. 630-600 BCE. Height: 11.5 cm. Bologna, Museo Civico Archeologico (© Archivio Fotografico del Museo Civico Archeologico di Bologna).*

Textiles biographies

Things are desirable because of the people, places and ideas connected to them; and the effect of these networks in creating and demonstrating social networks. Object biography was developed in social anthropology to investigate economic exchange, originating from the concept of personal biographies to describe the birth, life and

---

[46] Stauffer 2012, 247.
[47] Stauffer 2012, 244.
[48] Bartoloni 2000, 172 f. cat. 124. 125.

death of an artefact.[49] In archaeology this broadly translates as the production, use and deposition or discard of an object. Archaeologists have developed several iterations of this approach including life histories and, recently, itineraries or trajectories of things.[50] A significant point to take from these approaches is the potential to investigate the web of social relationships surrounding objects.[51] A similar concept recognises how the trajectory (or potential) of an object shapes its future possibilities; this network of actors maintains a product's stability.[52]

In central and north-east Italy during the Orientalising period, textile production is predominantly associated with women. On a richly carved throne placed in Verucchio Tomb 89, there are scenes interpreted as men and women wool working, women weaving at an upright loom and women carrying out obscure tasks protected by guards.[53] In four scenes of textile production on a bronze rattle (*tintinnabulum*) from the Tomb of the Gold, Arsenale Militare, Bologna, 8th century BCE (Fig. 5.5),[54] women prepare the warp, distaff, spin and weave. They are seated on thrones, indicating special status. In a scene on a bronze bucket (*situla*) from tomb 244, Montebelluna-Posmon necropolis, Treviso, 6th century BCE, two women spin with drop spindles; the pictorial story is interpreted as centring on the husband and wife of high ranking families.[55] It was not only women of status who worked textiles. Spindle whorls, spools and distaffs were placed in Early Iron Age graves across central and north-east Italy (Fig. 5.6). In Osteria dell'Ossa necropolis, Latium Vetus (IIA1–IVB, *c*. 950–580 BCE), textile tools were found in 212 of 595 (36%) of tombs; while at Veii, Quattro Fontanili (IB–IIC, *c*. 900–725 BCE) in Etruria, textile tools occur in 132 (21%) of the burials.[56] Taken broadly, tools in graves appear to two patterns. Single spindlewhorls occur in burials with female attributes (understood both through osteological and grave good evidence) of all ranks and diverse ages, albeit with cemetery-specific and regional variations.[57] While most women's burials contain spinning and weaving tools and include women of varied status, the presence of multiple tools suggests the elevated status of some women, regardless of age.[58] Spinning tools in burials may signify ideological concepts of womanhood.[59] The gender and status of textile producers highlights the different ways people were connected to textiles.

Through investigating object biographies there are hints at how the value of textiles varied across society, with glimpses of how textiles may be valued by those

---

[49] Appadurai 1986; Kopytoff 1986.
[50] Hahn and Weiss 2013; Van Oyen 2015, 66.
[51] Joy 2009, 540–541.
[52] Van Oyen 2015, 66–70.
[53] von Eles 2002a; Bonfante 2013, 430.
[54] Morigi Govi 1971; Ræder Knudsen 2002, 226.
[55] Ruta Serafini and Zaghetto 2019, 56–57, 71 fig. 5.
[56] Lipkin 2013, 19.
[57] Lipkin 2013, 20.
[58] Lipkin 2013, 22.
[59] Gleba 2008, 174; Lipkin 2013, 20.

5. The value of things: textiles in the Iron Age

Figure 5.6. Grave goods including amber distaff and spindle, bone weaving tools, ceramic spools, spindlewhorls, bone, amber and blue glass beads. Tomb 3, Le Pegge Necropolis, Verucchio, 7th century BCE (image © S. Harris by courtesy of the Ministero della Cultura, Soprintendenza Archeologia, Belle Arti e Paesaggio per le province di Ravenna, Forlì-Cesena, Rimini).

of different gender, status and situation. What value were textiles for women? Where written texts exist in the Eastern Mediterranean, noblewomen such as Penelope and Helen gained fame and renown (*kleos*) through their weaving.[60] Their textile gifts had a heightened value because they wove them. In 8th and 7th century BCE Etruria and Latium it is suggested that in dress women represented the status of their families and were themselves a valuable resource.[61] What value were textiles for men? For men, textiles were a resource that came mostly through women, servants and slaves of their household, or via trade. The Verucchio mantles, most likely conceived and made by women, would have passed from women's hands, to be worn by a man. After being worn in life, the two mantles were folded and placed in the tomb along with the other desirable grave goods.[62] What value were textiles for a town? If the immense effort to produce a ship's sails relied on women's, servant's and slave's labour, then they are part of the network of people and resources creating the strategic connections

---

[60] Mueller 2010.
[61] De Cristofaro and Piergrossi 2017, 76.
[62] Stauffer 2012, 254 figs 10–17; Stauffer *et al.* 2002, 216. 220.

and trade networks for the town's inhabitants. What this seems to indicate is that textile products, and the skills and resources to produce them, may have had value to aristocratic women's networks, but they may also have been part of systems of exploitation where skills of servants or slaves were valued differently from those of aristocrats.

Standardised, fungible textiles

Those goods that are standardised, which can be readily substituted one for another, are described as fungible. Fungible goods operate in systems of exchange because there is a means of quantifying equivalence based in measurement.[63] Trade, gift exchange and barter all incorporate standardised products of negotiable value and equivalence. The desirability, and hence value, of standardised products is that they are effective in facilitating transactions which are fundamental in bargaining for goods and trading one for another.

Across the Mediterranean and Near East from at least the 2nd millennium BCE, literary evidence and inventories testify that palaces and temples had textiles assets that were traded, given as gifts, accumulated into dowries and even offered as ransoms.[64] In the absence of substantive written sources in Etruria and the Veneto during the Orientalising period, the role of textiles as standardised products and items of equivalence must be evaluated from material culture evidence. In representation, the repetition of certain dress combinations; three-quarter to ankle length tunic and shaped mantle for men, long tunic and headscarf for women[65] is evidence not only of identity, but also that textiles required in dress were consistent, if varied, products. For example, the Verucchio mantles are a similar size. Mantle 1 is 257 cm long and 82 cm wide and was originally a few centimetres larger. Mantle 2 is 259 cm long and 79 cm wide.[66] In consumption, the similar size of the two mantles may be in part because they were woven to fit the same man. The similar shape and colour of the Verucchio mantles to those in representation, as those worn by the men in the plaque from Boccanera Tomb, La Banditaccia, Cerveteri, 560–550 BCE (Fig. 5.1) raises the possibility that to weave and dye a mantle of a certain quality was a known quantity of work. Was a mantle a type of standardised product?

The quantity of textile required to clothe a household or equip a ship means these were collaborative efforts, involving more than one weaver, possibly multiple household units and their dependents. The classical sources refer to sail makers as sail-stitchers, because sails were stitched together from multiple textiles.[67] Evidence of rare fragments of Roman sailcloth provide an idea of the technical specification of

---

[63] Papadopoulos and Urton 2012, 3–5; Renfrew 2012, 253.
[64] see for summary Gleba 2014.
[65] Bonfante 2003. 32–33 figs 4–6, 11, 14–16.
[66] Stauffer *et al.* 2002, 216.
[67] Spantidaki 2019.

sails, as relatively coarse textiles woven from plant fibre yarns.[68] Textiles woven to the same specifications then stitched into sails may be another example of standardised textiles. The evidence for standardised textiles in central and north-east Italy in the Orientalising period is inconclusive, yet it is important to investigate these possibilities. Standardised or fungible products of the 7th and 6th centuries BCE in central Italy, such as the amphorae in the Grand Ribaud F shipwreck or *aes rude* uncoined metal,[69] were part of systems of trade, exchange and cult offering; roles also associated with textiles.

Conclusion

The Iron Age textiles of central and north-east Italy, 730–580 BCE, offer a rich opportunity for archaeologists to examine the value of things in past societies. Textiles are an example of value found in materials that perish, that can be produced in many places, in small quantities of goods and that circulate widely. Through applying five principles of object value, the evidence is examined from multiple perspectives. This methodological device draws out a comprehensive range of possibilities, covering economic, aesthetic, societal and material goals.

Taking a definition of value where value is a judgment based in the desirability of things based in their effects, the archaeologist is tasked with examining how, why and by whom certain textiles were desirable in these aristocratic and early urban societies. By emphasising the relationship between people and things, it is easier to see how value exists in many forms and why it fluctuates. As materials, textiles were ubiquitous in clothing. This is recognised in the widespread tools of production and the representation of textile clothing in paintings and statues. As clothing, textiles were valued for their material properties, whether as working clothes to protect the body from the hostility of a cold, mountain environment or as appropriate dress for the body in the competitive circles of social elites. This demonstrates how textiles were valuable across the social matrices, not only in stores of the wealthy. Through tracing object biographies, value is found in the way textiles create and stabilise social relationships. In central and north-east Italy in 730–580 BCE these networks are recognisable in the ideological and practical position of textile production as women's work. Through this dynamic it is possible to question the desirability of textiles in creating and stabilising marriage partnerships, households and even the power and influence of towns in the interconnected Mediterranean cultures (*koine*). Here textiles are desirable not only for what they are, but in how they connect people and create dependencies. In production, it is possible to recognise relational value and how textiles were more expensive and exclusive than others. The exclusivity of a ship's sails is a prime example of how time and resource consuming textile products

---

[68] Dimova *et al*. forthcoming.
[69] Murgan 2014, 66–67.

provide an exclusive access to power, to transport goods and to defend and attack at sea. For those textiles that were traded, whether locally or long distance, their fungibility provided a resource through which to obtain other items and turn one resource into another.

Value judgements depend on the overarching values of the societies to which people contribute and belong. For central and north-east Italy in the Orientalising period, such value would have depended on the situation and ambitions of the individual or unit, whether aspiring aristocrat, servant or slave, according to gender, age and the ambitions, household or town. The ubiquity of textiles in Iron Age Europe suggests all people had an interest in textiles, all people valued textiles in one way or another. The role of the archaeologist is to be able to recognise these varied perspectives and through this understand how value changes because the effects, roles and purposes of objects change according to time, place and person.

Acknowledgements

The research for this paper received funding from the European Research Council under the European Union's Seventh Framework Programme (FP/2007-2013-312603) within the scope of the project *Production and Consumption: Textile Economy and Urbanisation in Mediterranean Europe 1000–500 BCE (PROCON)*, PI Dr Margarita Gleba. Thanks to Prof. Dr Fleur Kemmers for the invitation to speak at the conference in Frankfurt, the audience for their insightful questions, Prof. Dr Hans Peter Hahn and Dr Sophia Adams for commenting on an earlier version of the manuscript and Pippa White for proof reading. This paper was written as Lecturer in Archaeology at University of Glasgow during the global pandemic with the support of the Glasgow Archaeology writing group.

References

Appadurai, A. 1986 Introduction. Commodities and the politics of value. In: A. Appadurai (ed.), *The Social Life of Things. Commodities and the Politics of Value* (Cambridge), 3–63

Barber, E. 1991 *Prehistoric Textiles. The Development of Cloth in the Neolithic and Bronze Age with Special Reference to the Aegean* (Princeton NH)

Bartoloni, G. 2000 *Principi etruschi. Tra Mediterraneo ed Europa* (Bologna)

Bazzanella, M., Dal Ri, L., Maspero, A. and Tomedi, I. 2005 Iron Age textile artefacts from Riesenferner/Vedretta di Ries (Bolzano/Bozen – Italy). In: P. Bichler, K. Grömer, R. Hofmann-de Keijzer, A. Kern and H. Reschreiter (eds), *Hallstatt Textiles. Technical Analysis, Scientific Investigation and Experiments on Iron Age Textiles* (Oxford), 151–160

Bender Jørgensen, L. 2012 The introduction of sails to Scandinavia. Raw materials, labour and land. In: R. Berge, M. E. Jasinski and K. Sognnes (eds), *N-TAG TEN. Proceedings of the 10th Nordic TAG conference at Stiklestad, Norway 2009* (Oxford), 173–181

Bevan, A. and Wengrow, D. 2010 *Cultures of Commodity Branding* (Walnut Creek CA)

Benelli, E. 2013 Slavery and Manumission. In: J. MacIntosh Turfa (ed.), *The Etruscan World* (London), 447–456

Bietti Sestieri, A. M. and De Min, M. 2013 Il Veneto fra l'Età del Bronzo Finale e il VII secolo A.C. In: M. Gamba, G. Gambacurta, A. Ruta Serafini, V. Tiné and F. Veronese (eds), *Venetkens. Viaggio nella terra dei Veneti antichi* (Padua), 44–50

Bokern, A. and Rowan, C. 2014 *Embodying Value? The Transformation of Objects in and from the Ancient World*. British Archaeological Report S2592 (Oxford)

Bonfante, L. 2003 *Etruscan Dress* (updated edition) (Baltimore MD)

Bonfante, L. 2013 Mothers and Children. In: J. MacIntosh Turfa (ed.), *The Etruscan World* (London), 426–446

Bruni, S. 2013 Seafaring. Ship building, harbours, the issue of piracy. In: J. MacIntosh Turfa (ed.), *The Etruscan World* (London), 759–777

Casson, L. 1994 *Ships and Seafaring in Ancient Times* (London)

Costin, C. L. 2013 Gender and textiles production in prehistory. In: D. Bolger (ed.), *A Companion to Gender Prehistory* (Hoboken NJ)

De Cristofaro, A. and Piergrossi, A. 2017 The clothes make the (wo)man. Historical and anthropological considerations of Etruscan female costumes between 8th and 7th century BC. In: M. Gleba and R. Laurito (eds), *Contextualising Textile Production in Italy in the 1st Millennium BC*. Origini. Preistoria e protostoria delle civiltà antiche 40 (Rome), 65–82

Dimova, B., Gleba, M. and Harris, S. forthcoming Naval power and textile technology. Sail production in Ancient Greece. *World Archaeology* 53 DOI 10.1080/00438243.2021.2015428

Douglas, M. and Isherwood, B. 1979 *The World of Goods. Towards an Anthropology of Consumption* (New York)

Eles, P. von 2002a Il trono della tomba 89 come strumento di comunicazione. Proposta per una analisi ed una interpretazione. In: P. von Eles (ed.), *Guerriero e sacerdote. Autorità e comunità nell'età del ferro a Verucchio. La Tomba del Trono* (Florence), 235–272

Eles, P. von 2002b La cronologia della t. 89/1972 Lippi. In: P. von Eles (ed.), *Guerriero e sacerdote. Autorità e comunità nell'età del ferro a Verucchio. La Tomba del Trono* (Florence), 273–276

Gell, A. 1992 The technology of enchantment and the enchantment of technology. In: J. Coote and A. Shelten (eds), *Anthropology, Art and Aesthetics* (Oxford), 40–63

Gibson, J. J. 1977 The theory of affordances. In: R. E. Shaw and J. Bransford (eds), *Perceiving, Acting, and Knowing* (Hillsdale MI), 67–82

Gleba, M. 2008 *Textile Production in Pre-Roman Italy*. Ancient Textiles Series 4 (Oxford)

Gleba, M. 2014 cloth worth a king's ransom. Textile circulation and transmission of textile craft in the ancient Mediterranean. In: K. Rebay-Salisbury, A. Brysbaert and L. Foxhall (eds), *Knowledge Networks and Craft Traditions in the Ancient World. Material Crossovers* (London), 83–103

Gleba, M. 2017 Tracing textile cultures of Italy and Greece in the early first millennium BC. *Antiquity* 91, 1205–1222

Graeber, D. 2001 *Toward an Anthropological Theory of Value. The False Coin of Our Own Dreams* (New York)

Gras, M. 2000 Il Mediterraneo in Etè Orientalizzante. Merci, Approdi, Circolazione. In: G. Bartoloni (ed.), *Principi etruschi. Tra Mediterraneo ed Europa* (Venice), 14–26

Hahn, H. P. and Weiss, H. 2013 Introduction. Biographies, travels and the itineraries of things. In: H. P. Hahn and H. Weiss (eds), *Mobility, Meaning and the Transformations of Things. Shifting Contexts of Material Culture Through Time and Space* (Oxford), 1–14

Harris, S. 2010 Smooth and cool, or warm and soft. Investigating the properties of cloth in prehistory. In: E. Andersson Strand, M. Gleba, U. Mannering, C. Munkholt and M. Ringgaard (eds), *North European Symposium for Archaeological Textiles* 10 (Oxford), 104–112

Harris, S. 2017 From value to desirability. The allure of worldly things. *World Archaeology* 49(5), 681–699. https://doi.org/10.1080/00438243.2017.1413416 (accessed 8 October 2021)

Jarva, E. and Lipkin, S. 2014 Ancient textiles were expensive. How do you know that? *Faravid* 38, 23–38

Joy, J. 2009 Reinvigorating object biography. Reproducing the drama of object lives. *World Archaeology* 41(4), 540–556

Joyce, R. A. 2000 High culture, Mesoamerican civilization, and the Classic Maya tradition. In: J. E. Richards and M. Van Buren (eds), *Order, Legitimacy, and Wealth in Ancient States* (Cambridge), 64–87

Kopytoff, I. 1986 The cultural biography of things. Commoditization as process. In: A. Appadurai (ed.), *The Social Life of Things. Commodities in Cultural Perspective* (Cambridge), 64–91

Leighton, R. 2013 Urbanization in southern Etruria from the tenth to the sixth century BC. The origins and growth of major cities. In: J. MacIntosh Turfa (ed.), *The Etruscan World* (London), 134–150

Lipkin, S. 2013 Textile making in central Tyrrhenian Italy. Questions related to age, rank and status. In: M. Gleba and J. Pásztókai-Szeoke (eds), *Making Textiles in Pre-Roman and Roman Times. People, Places, Identities*. Ancient Textiles Series 13 (Oxford), 19–29

Long, L., Gantès, L.-F. and Rival, M. 2006 L'épave Grand Ribaud F. Un chargement de produits étrusques du début du Ve siècle avant J.-C. In: *Gli etruschi da Genova ad Ampurias atti del XXIV convegno di studi etruschi ed italici Marseille Lattes 26 septembre–1 octobre 2002* (Pisa), 456–495

Monroe, C. M. 2010 Sunk costs at Late Bronze Age Uluburun. *Bulletin of the American Schools of Oriental Research* 365, 19–33

Morigi Govi, C. 1971 Il tintinnabulo della 'Tomba degli ori' dell'Arsenale militare di Bologna. *Archeologia Classica* 23, 212–235

Mueller, M. 2010 Helen's Hands. Weaving for Kleos in the Odyssey. *Helios* 37(1), 1–21

Murgan, A. M. 2014 Heavy metal in hallowed contexts. Continuity and change in aes deposits in central Italy and Sicily. In: A. Bokern and C. Rowan (eds), *Embodying Value? The Transformation of Objects in and from the Ancient World* (Oxford), 65–75

Olofsson, L., Andersson Strand, E. and Nosch, M.-L. 2015 Experimental testing of Bronze Age textile tools. In: E. Andersson Strand snd M.-L. Nosch (eds), *Tools, Textiles and Contexts. Investigating Textile Production in the Aegean and Eastern Mediterranean Bronze Age*. Ancient Textiles Series 21 (Oxford), 75–100

Papadopoulos, J. K. and Urton, G. (eds) 2012 *The Construction of Value in the Ancient World* (Los Angeles CA)

Perkins, P. 2014 Processes of urban development in northern and central Etruria in the Orientalizing and Archaic periods. In: E. C. Robinson (ed.), *Papers on Italian Urbanism in the First Millennium B.C. Journal of Roman Archaeology* Supplementary Series 97 (Portsmouth RI), 62–80

Petrarulo, G. 2012 New considerations regarding the seascape fresco in the Tomb of the Ship (Tomba della Nave) at Tarquinia. *Etruscan Studies* 15(2), 115–145

Pomey, P. and Poveda, P. 2018 Gyptis. Sailing replica of a 6th-century-BC archaic Greek sewn boat. *International Journal of Nautical Archaeology* 47(1), 45–56

Porter, J. I. 2012 The value of aesthetic values. In: Papadopoulos and Urton (eds) 2012, 336–353

Rankov, B. 2013 Ships and shipsheds. In: D. Blackman and B. Rankov (eds), *Shipsheds of the Ancient Mediterranean* (Cambridge), 76–101

Ræder Knudsen, L. 2002 La tessitura a tavolette nella tomba 89. In: P. von Eles (ed.), *Guerriero e sacerdote. Autorità e comunità nell'età del ferro a Verucchio. La Tomba del Trono* (Florence), 220–234

Renfrew, C. 2012 Systems of value among material things. The nexus of fungibility and measure. In: Papadopoulos and Urton (eds) 2012, 249–260

Riva, C. 2010 *The Urbanisation of Etruria. Funerary Practices and Social Change, 700–600 BC* (New York)

Ruta Serafini, A. and Zaghetto, L. 2019 L'attesa della signora Le filatrici sulla situla della tomba 244 di Montebelluna. In: G. Cresci Marron, G. Gambacurta and A. Marinetti (eds), *Il dono di Altino Scritti di archeologia in onore di Margherita Tirelli* (Venice), 57–71

Sannibale, M. 2013 Orientalizing Etruria. In: J. MacIntosh Turfa (ed.), *The Etruscan World* (London), 99–133

Simmel, G. 1978 *The Philosophy of Money* (trans. T. B. Bottomore and David Frisby) (London)
Spantidaki, S. 2019 Investigating maritime textiles in Classical Greece. Sails and rigging of the Athenian fleet. In: M. S. Busana, M. Gleba, F. Meo and A. R. Tricomi (eds), *Textiles and Dyes in the Mediterranean Economy and Society, Purpureae Vestes 6, Proceedings of the VIth International Symposium on Textiles and Dyes in the Ancient Mediterranean World Padova - Este - Altino 17-20 October 2016* (Zaragoza), 75–86
Stauffer, A. 2012 Case study. The textiles from Verucchio, Italy. In: M. Gleba and U. Mannering (eds), *Textiles and Textile Production in Europe. From Prehistory to AD 400*. Ancient textiles Series 11 (Oxford), 242–253
Stauffer, A. Wouters, J., Vanden Berghe, I. and Maquoi, M. C. 2002 Tessuti. In: P. von Eles (ed.), *Guerriero e sacerdote. Autorità e comunità nell'età del ferro a Verucchio. La Tomba del Trono* (Florence), 192–220
Van Oyen, A. 2015 Actor-Network Theory's take on archaeological types. Becoming, material agency and historical explanation. *Cambridge Archaeological Journal* 25(1), 63–78
Whitewright, J. 2007 Roman rigging material from the Red Sea port of Myos Hormos. *The International Journal of Nautical Archaeology* 36(2), 282–292
Wijngaarden, G.-J. van 1999 An archaeological approach to the concept of value. Mycenaean pottery at Ugarit (Syria). *Archaeological Dialogues* 6(1), 2–23

Chapter 6

Negotiating the value of ethnographic cultural heritage: between scholarship, entertainment, sentimentality and nationalism

Ivan Maksimović

Introduction

A museum is, by definition, home to things of value. Regardless of whether it is funded by public or private money, a substantial budget is required to invest in maintaining, researching and presenting the things that are kept there. Moreover, a museum is a nexus of interactions involving people and things, much like a marketplace. However, there are significant differences as to what form these interactions take. In the case of marketplaces they usually boil down to exchange of one type or other, which is time-restricted and mediated by money. Most importantly, the value of things takes the form of either use value or exchange value (as expressed through price).[1] At the same time, the context of a museum seems to reveal more complexity both in terms of interactions involved and the understanding of value itself. A museum setting enables, and even demands, from us that we approach the concept of value of things in a more holistic fashion, going beyond the economic sphere of use value and exchange value. It is precisely for this reason that the question of how we perceive value of things deserves to be addressed from a museum perspective. Still, to my knowledge, there has been no comprehensive theory of value to emerge that is informed by this viewpoint. I can only hope that this paper will take the first steps in that direction, much like Rosita Henry, Ton Otto and Michael Wood,[2] as formulating a comprehensive theory of value is, in general, a task so difficult that it has rarely been attempted, if at all successfully.[3]

Arguably, this may be even more the case for a museum of ethnographic provenance, where things that are housed are extremely diverse in nature, from the

---

[1] Bestor 2001, 9227.
[2] Henry *et al.* 2013.
[3] Graeber 2001.

materials used, their age, modes and technologies of production, whether they are unique or not, not to mention their biographies before becoming part of the museum's fund. Therefore, I will use my experience as curator at the Ethnographic Museum in Belgrade and especially my involvement in the preparation of an exhibition of new accessions – work that has allowed me to approach the understanding of value from multiple perspectives – to investigate the various ways in which things can be valued. More narrowly, what interests me is how value is transformed when objects change hands, or, for instance, when time passes, but also to what ends (political, economic and so on) valuing objects or entire collections can be used.

The exhibition of new accessions, set to cover the 6-year period between 2014 and 2019, was in its final stages of preparation by the time this paper was being written. For the purpose of this exhibition, a colleague and myself have taken a closer look at several thousand objects added to the collections of the Ethnographic Museum in Belgrade throughout this period and examined thoroughly some 100-odd objects that we narrowed our selection to.

This experience has allowed me not only to look at specific object histories but also to analyse current accessioning practice and directly communicate with prior owners of items for a better grasp on how value could be transformed. Aside from that, I base my findings on documents produced by museum staff, predominantly exhibition catalogues and articles published in the museum's Bulletin (*Glasnik Etnografskog Muzeja*). Many of these include presentations of specific collections, reports on the museum's activity and discussions of relevant issues. Furthermore, unpublished documents from the museum's archive also assisted in shedding a light on the core issues of this essay.

Before tackling these central questions, I will have to go through some necessary steps. First, I will indicate the previous theoretical conceptualisations of value with which I am operating. Secondly, given that a museum is a heterogeneous body influenced by countless factors both within and without, I will present the history and trajectory of the Ethnographic Museum in Belgrade as thoroughly as possible for the uninformed readers so that they may better understand the context in which it is operating and the historical transformations affecting it. Several large-scale political changes in the Serbian society throughout the 119 years of the museum's existence have thoroughly affected its collecting and exhibiting practices. It has been argued before that the Ethnographic Museum in Belgrade as an institution of culture reflects political goals on the national level,[4] and I will certainly contribute to that discussion as well. In addition to large-scale socio-political and economic factors, internal debates and differing approaches, both within the museum itself and the discipline of ethnology and anthropology on all levels, affect the day-to-day practice of museum work. These debates will also be mentioned in brief.

---

[4] e.g. Simić 2006; Gavrilović 2007a; Lukić-Krstanović 2016.

The indicated factors have all certainly contributed to the dynamism of the conceptualisations of value in regard to the museum's artefacts and collections. By taking them into consideration, I expect to prepare the field for a worthwhile approach to understanding how we value things, why we do it and in what ways do we do it. Hopefully, this chapter will contribute not only to understanding the value of things in a museum context or the value of things in general, but also to help illuminate the interplay between the value of things and collective identification.

Value as a complex phenomenon

Among the myriad of vague concepts whose many-sidedness disconcerts social scientists, value is one that is notoriously difficult to theorise. How to approach something that has many meanings and refers to diverse phenomena, from abstract ideas considered worth pursuing to concrete things considered worth having? According to David Graeber, the attempts to present a theory of value failed due to focusing only on one aspect and neglecting others.[5]

The complexity of the colloquial understanding of value has been highlighted by Daniel Miller as its very essence – since it bridges the understanding of the term in singular, i.e. an object's place in the system of exchange or consumption (price of a commodity) and its plural form which refers to concepts irreducible to monetary evaluation.[6] In other words, we should not beat our heads against the wall trying to separate the two, but rather see them as two sides of the same coin, as complementary concepts working together. The work they are doing can be interpreted as preventing a full conceptual split between the sphere of economy and the sphere of everyday life. However, the very fact that the value of things today is almost always (among other things) exchange value, this topic of study has traditionally fallen under the purview of economy. The focus on exchange forces us to think of the matter as a study of market relationships, one often posited as reflecting a quintessential human need. Anthropological research challenged this dogma somewhat, at least when it came to illustrating that not only there are other modes of circulation for material objects than purely market exchange but also that the same things circulating in the market at one point might at other times be barred from the market and vice versa.

In his seminal paper on cultural biographies of things, Igor Kopytoff defined commodity as 'a thing that has use value and that can be exchanged in a discrete transaction for a counterpart, the very fact of exchange indicating that the counterpart has, in the immediate context, an equivalent value'.[7] This equivalent value makes the thing comparable to another thing, the realisation that two things exist on common terms. In addition, money makes markedly dissimilar things comparable by providing

---

[5] Graeber 2001.
[6] Miller 2008.
[7] Kopytoff 1986, 68. Let us briefly ignore the fact that not only material goods but also entirely intangible services could be commodified.

the common terms. On the other end of the spectrum are things that are unique or so uncommon that they could not be compared. However, Kopytoff's point is that the criteria of comparison are context-relative. A specific situation can establish criteria of comparison where there were none previously. Therefore, an object has the capacity to have both use value and exchange value, only use value, or none.

At the core of this argument is an understanding that value can be transformed. Besides Kopytoff, several other authors comment on an object's transformation of value as caused by different factors.[8] Although their approaches and conclusions differ somewhat, a general consensus exists that exchange, travel and simple passage of time with or without visible material deterioration all may bring about different perceptions of value. Similarly to Kopytoff's idea of things moving between being exchangeable and unexchangeable, Michael Thompson anticipates transformations between a status of definable value to a status of rubbish – i.e. entire lack of value. Ultimately, Hans Peter Hahn and Hadas Weiss (improving on Kopytoff) observe things on the move, propelled by humans and other forces from one point in space and time to another where their value always finds new modes of expression.

Clearly, these are different modes of saying that things are valued differently in different contexts, or rather that different social actors, shaped by the social context they are part of, determine the value of things based on their needs, capabilities and understanding of the world. Hidden within these observations, again, is an understanding that value is relative.

To return to the museum perspective, I once more argue that it allows us to observe examples of all these transformations, although the examples are by no means exhaustive of all the possibilities. By investigating situations in which the objects' value status has changed, the social nature of ethnographic items in the context of this particular museum will be made clearer. It will, ultimately, lead to asking further questions in terms of what these objects mean for different people in different situations. In the majority of works dealing, whether exclusively or not, with value of museum collections, particular artefacts or museum objects in general, value itself as a concept is rarely defined, never theorised.[9] So, what kind of value can museum objects carry? Henry, Otto and Wood,[10] when writing about Aboriginal artefacts collected for several different Australian museums, show us that collected items have different facets of value for different actors: collectors, museums where the objects ended up and members of the contemporary Aboriginal population who use the objects to make political statements. Authors focused on natural history museums have, in contrast, attempted to demonstrate that biological collections in both museums and academic institutions positively contribute to research benefiting

---

[8] Just to name a few: Thompson 1979; Hahn and Weiss 2013; Henry *et al.* 2013; Hahn 2018.
[9] e.g. Penny 2002; Henry *et al.* 2013.
[10] Henry *et al.* 2013.

public health policies and thus have incalculable value in saving human and non-human lives or preventing potentially hazardous situations.[11]

In order to best determine how value is conceived in the case of artefacts and collections in the possession of the Ethnographic Museum in Belgrade, we should focus on ways in which their significance has been formulated and communicated. Barbara Kirshenblatt-Gimblett states that objects are ethnographic 'by virtue of the manner in which they have been detached, for disciplines make their objects and in the process make themselves'.[12] It sensitises us to the notion that there is nothing in objects that makes them inherently ethnographic. A similar sentiment is shared by Johannes Fabian, perhaps slightly more elucidated: 'To have been ethnographically collected, that is, removed from its context of production and consumption, is of the essence of the ethnographic item'.[13] This statement leads us more toward our current goal which is to determine the transformation of value from commodity to museum piece and the 'regimes of value'[14] that come with it.

Ethnography or heritage?

In the western world, ethnographic museums have experienced a revival due to the renewed interest in the study of material culture and, with it, new and exciting ways to approach, analyse and exhibit it.[15] One of the key dilemmas of the new era is that of representation and the issue of the extent to which the culture of the displayed 'Other' is distorted through the act of representation by carefully curated objects.[16] The debate mirrored similar debates that tackled the problem of representation in ethnography in general, as volumes such as James Clifford's and George Marcus' *Writing Culture*[17] began challenging anthropological scientific authority.

Such debates have mainly bypassed museum ethnographers in Serbia, because Serbian ethnography did not, it was widely assumed, deal with the 'Other'. Unlike western anthropology which originated in Enlightenment principles and was largely enabled by colonial infrastructure, Serbian ethnology belonged to the camp which was much more under the influence of Romantic thought. Inspired by the German scientific tradition of *Volkskunde*, and in many cases educated in this context at German Universities, early Serbian ethnologists found their object of study in the rural communities of their nation, predominantly of the same ethnic identity, although they did show some interest in minority populations such as the Roma. Although later

---

[11] Suarez and Tsutsui 2004.
[12] Kirshenblatt-Gimblett 1991, 387.
[13] Fabian 2004, 51. Fabian insists on a semantic difference between ethnographic artefact and ethnographic object, a distinction I do not find entirely necessary for this essay, but for the reader's sake I point to the explanation: Fabian 2004, 49.
[14] Cf. Appadurai 1986.
[15] Fabian 2004.
[16] Durrans 1992.
[17] Clifford and Marcus 1986.

defined by some as the 'internal other',[18] the peasant population was held to be the core element of the national being, since the young nation at the time ethnology as a discipline was established in Serbia had a relatively small urban population.

In fact, ethnology in Serbia was instituted in 1901 by the establishment of the Ethnographic Museum in Belgrade, with the department of ethnology at the University of Belgrade opening only in 1906. The first lecturers at the University were Jovan Erdeljanović, who studied in Vienna and Prague, where he was supervised by Lubor Niederle, and Tihomir Đorđević, educated in Vienna and Munich. The first director of the Ethnographic Museum in Belgrade was Sima Trojanović who studied botany and zoology in Zurich and Heidelberg.[19] The Ethnographic Museum in Belgrade was and has remained the foremost and exclusively ethnographic museum at a national level. Stojan Novaković, member of the Serbian Learned Society which later became the Academy of Arts and Sciences, originated the idea of creating a Serbian historical-ethnographic museum already in 1872, which he presented in the meeting of the Society's historical and governmental department – a museum needed 'in order to study the national life in all its aspects, both in the past as well as the present'.[20] The National Museum, established in 1844, originally collected primarily historical and archaeological artefacts but eventually began collecting ethnographic material as well, leading to the creation of a separate, ethnographic collection. The conditions to create an independent museum were met, as mentioned before, in 1901. This was the year when the museum received its first home, the house bequeathed by former Prime Minister Stevan Mihajlović. Although Mihailović died in 1888, the house was occupied by his wife until 1901.[21]

From around 1000 objects that the Museum had in its inception, its collections grew to almost 60,000 by the time this article was being written, a figure which does not include almost the same number of other museum objects not included in the main fund, such as photographs (in both positive and negative), paintings, drawings and sketches, old and rare books, archival records, ethnographic films and so forth. Most of the original objects (clothing items and textile household items, jewellery, metal vessels, etc.) came with barely any information, not even data of origin.[22]

A common expression one can find when referring to museum artefacts, an expression which denotes their priceless status without making an explicit statement on their value, is 'treasure'. It is indeed a frequent term that often finds a place in publications such as catalogues or other works that intend to present part of the museum's fund to the public. Had I been writing any other text aside from this one, I might have used the same term myself, but the topic obliges me to be more careful. This is especially obvious when one takes into consideration '[t]he very ubiquity of

[18] Stocking Jr 1982.
[19] Kovačević 2015.
[20] Drobnjaković 1926, 12.
[21] Cvetić 1926, 2.
[22] Drobnjaković 1926, 15.

the kinds of objects that interest ethnographers'[23] or, in other words, mundane things that might not be valued much in the first place. Therefore, it will now be useful to see what is it that makes them treasure.

Going back in time to the first year of the museum's activity, guidelines for collecting materials for the first international costume exhibition in Saint Petersburg provide us with an insight into the criteria of value when it comes to prioritising certain objects over others. Serbia's participation mobilised the entire state apparatus a year before the opening of the exhibition, with every branch fulfilling its role in representing the country in Russia. Although it was not the Ethnographic Museum *per se* that was the standard bearer, its director and head curator Trojanović was named one of the members of a board set up for the purpose of organising Serbia's participation, along with Nikola Zega, the second curator of the museum. In a letter to him by the minister of economy, attention was drawn to the effort that has to be made in order to represent the country with dignity, with an explicit mention to try at least to match Bulgaria's display, if not outdo it.[24] Trojanović and Zega had police constables and local clerks at their disposal when travelling the selected areas for the purposes of obtaining artefacts for the exhibition. It was up to these officials to expedite the search by actually making sure that the museum curators were met in each place by four middle-aged men, four middle-aged women, two elderly women, two younger men, two younger women and one newly married woman with different costumes each: it was required of them to arrive dressed in work clothes and carry with them their formal and winter clothes. It was also recommended to local authorities to be certain to find the most emblematic costume for a given area and, failing that, to identify two elderly women who could organise getting one made for that purpose, for which effort they would receive material compensation.

Not all costumes were made equally, however. Since the exhibition dealt with both contemporary and historical attire, the collectors should make sure to have enough of each category. When it came to contemporary clothing, all fabrics were to be represented: wool, linen, hemp, silk, mixed and waterproof ones. Animal hides, tanned and untanned, were also to be included. When it came to the list of individual garments, it would be a waste of space to name them all, as practically every type of clothing item was represented, including accessories, but also make-up and similar products. Instructions for collecting historical garments were much less comprehensive, though. Criteria were not specified, and it can be consequently concluded that the contemporary costume was considered both diverse and representative enough.

For the purposes of this essay, the list of garments is less interesting than the criteria according to which garments and items should be selected. Home-made items were preferred to those made by craftsmen. Even visibly damaged clothing had

---

[23] Kirshenblatt-Gimblett 1991, 410.
[24] Bižić-Omčikus 2002.

to be accepted, with the instruction that they were not to be cleaned or mended at any cost. The call for participation was public, but the turnout was ostensibly poor. Still, many notable figures contributed to the collection, including Queen Natalija Obrenović. Yet, the majority of the items were obtained by Trojanović and Zega. Upon returning to Serbia in 1903, all these items enriched the collections of the newly-formed museum which also included the showcases in which the objects were exhibited in Saint Petersburg.[25]

However, this is not the first international exhibition to which Serbia sent its ethnographic material. Thirty-four years before the museum was founded, the All-Russian Ethnographic Exhibition took place in the Manezh exhibition hall in Moscow. Despite its name, invitations were extended to all Slavic nations, including the Principality of Serbia, and institutions which represented Serbia in Austria-Hungary. Such a decision was apparently justified, as the reflection of a need to have a 'direct and immediate point of comparison' to the Russian people in order to study them better, along with the fact that members of these nations were also present in the Russian Empire in large numbers, a fact which demanded recognition.[26] In any case, hundreds of items, of which 160 survive to this day, were sent to Russia and are now part of the fund of the Russian Museum of Ethnography in Saint Petersburg. President of the Organisational committee Vasily Andreyevich Dashkov said of the exhibition's purpose:

> From the very inception of the idea about this exhibiting, its goal was entirely scientific: to inform the masses with data of the study of man; to familiarize it with representatives of Russia's diverse population as well as that of friendly countries; to awaken an interest for the study of their populations and ways of life, and to make it all possible and clear with the help of a museum.[27]

Since it was primarily up to individuals to send contributions for the exhibition, the Serbian government published an open call with instructions on what and how was to be exhibited. The instructions were received directly from the organisers in Moscow, with the specific request that the costumes be presented in their entirety and that they be characteristic of each 'tribe' (in this case, the Serbs). Unlike the 1902 first international costume exhibition in Saint Petersburg there was not much room for recognising regional varieties, as all the costumes were to be part of the same tableaux (the recommendation was: five or six people gathered around a blind gusle player).[28]

As the examples from the early days of the museum show, when it came to collecting costume the main criterion was its mode of production. It was expected

---

[25] Drobnjaković 1926, 15.
[26] Knight 2001, 16.
[27] Karpova 2005, 14.
[28] Inscribed in the UNESCO Representative List of the Intangible Cultural Heritage of Humanity in 2018, singing to the accompaniment of the stringed implement, the gusle, is defined as an 'ancient art of performing primarily heroic epics practised for centuries as a form of historical memory and an expression of cultural identity' (UNESCO Convention 2018); Bižić-Omčikus 2005.

that home-made items had a priority, since it reflected the ethnographers' interest in studying self-sufficient rural populations which were believed to have lived almost unchanged for centuries. These communities, organised around the system of *zadruga* (cooperative),[29] resorted to their immediate environment and their extended kin for survival. However, already in the 19th century, the market economy started to permeate and re-organise the economy of *zadruga*, a development which was not adequately recognised by most Serbian ethnographers. The study of material culture thus served a scientific purpose but also to reinforce an exhibiting practice that attempted to accomplish a political goal: helping to substantiate the young nation's claims for sovereignty over the lands where Serbs lived.

That an ethnographic museum should be first and foremost a scholarly institution, as evident from Dashkov's statement, is an idea that was embraced in the first years of the Ethnographic Museum in Belgrade as well. Arguing for stronger ties between the museum and the university in 1926, in order to improve the state of the study of Serbian culture, Erdeljanović meticulously lists reasons why, in his view, a museum is a superior institution to the academy in the sense of providing students with opportunity for practical scientific work: both in terms of studying directly from artefacts and offering opportunities to conduct fieldwork.[30] At that time, the Kingdom of Serbs, Croats and Slovenes was already established, and Serbian ethnographers joined forces with their colleagues in Bosnia, Croatia and Slovenia – whose ethnographic museums were founded in the state capitals in 1913, 1919 and 1921, respectively – so that a comprehensive study of South Slavic tribes might be conducted in an organised, structured and above all scientific fashion.

The scientific extent of ethnology in Serbia at the time, whether practised at university or museum level, was limited, according to some.[31] The entire effort failed to produce any valid theory or attempts at interpretation and was merely reduced to 'collecting' – objects and information. A transformation of the status of ethnology was brought about a few decades after the Second World War. Around that time, social anthropology as a separate discipline began developing at the university and, out of fear of being superseded, ethnology profiled itself as a historical science, interested in the study of cultural history. This was made possible by the fact that, in the new Socialist Federation of Yugoslavia, *zadruge* were rapidly becoming more and more a thing of the past. According to Ivan Kovačević, a veritable breakthrough of sorts occurred in the realm of material culture studies, where descriptive approaches to folk costume were eventually replaced by interpretive approaches to studying transformations of this phenomenon – all in all placing it in a temporal context and abandoning the more or less implied understanding of an unchanging society.[32]

---

[29] see Halpern *et al.* 1996.
[30] Erdeljanović 1926.
[31] Kovačević 2015.
[32] Kovačević 2015.

Still, such an understanding was always implicitly present in the museum's practice. Writing on the occasion of the institution's centenary, ethnologist Slobodan Zečević complimented the progress made by research teams in covering more and more parts of the country.[33] Team-based fieldwork was initiated in the 1960s, and its intent was to study holistically the populations of smaller administrative or historical-geographical units, such as townships or regions. Much effort was dedicated towards studying folklore, as was traditionally the case: costume, oral traditions, customs. Sveral decades had passed between the first team-based research and Zečević's text. Nevertheless, museum professionals were still expected to carry on their research as if Eastern Serbia of the 1960s and Western Serbia of the early-2000s were parts of the same dataset.

In the last two decades of the 20th century, anthropology as an academic discipline tried to catch up quickly with western theories from structuralism to post-structuralism, ethnology and anthropology formally merged at the university level in the purview of a single department and museum ethnologists timidly started adopting more modern approaches to their research of material culture. Research was becoming more and more open towards studying phenomena of social change, urban or at least peri-urban populations, and issues that were until then considered more of interest to sociologists or social anthropologists were now being tackled. This is also reflected in accessioning practices, with objects of industrial production becoming increasingly present in collections. However, the majority of museum artefacts were items of traditional culture, even if not entirely made using traditional methods.

When it comes to accessioning in general, there are four ways an object can become property of the Ethnographic Museum in Belgrade, depending on the place in which the transaction occurs and whether the transaction was financial in nature or not. Therefore, an object can be 1) bought by a museum curator during fieldwork, 2) received as a gift during fieldwork, 3) offered to the museum for sale by a private person or institution and, ultimately, 4) offered to the museum as a gift by a person or institution. Aside from these common ways of procurement, there is also the exchange between institutions, for instance when an institution being shut down disposes of its inventory by giving it to the relevant main institution.[34] The data on this are imprecise – for instance, during the period before the Second World War it was seemingly not a custom to specify the manner of procurement, or the documents were simply not preserved, except in cases of notable benefactors such as the royal family. Still, we can make out some regularities. Despite more recent trends, purchase of artefacts, usually in the field, was the most common way of procurement. This makes sense, as the research goal of the museum remained more or less the same in socialist times

---

[33] Dušković 2001.
[34] This was especially the case in the decade or two after the Second World War, when many endowments, foundations and institutions that were considered bourgeois, reactionary or simply irrelevant, were shut down, for instance women's societies that did not belong to the revolutionary women's associations (see Dušković 2001).

as it was in the period beforehand: a meticulous collection of artefacts belonging to the rural populations for the purpose of a comprehensive display of their way of life.

One of the rarer situations when museum objects are subjected to a form of market principles is in the case of acquisition through purchase. Usually, a committee designed to deliberate on such purchases schedules meetings several times per year, relative to the demand or offers of purchase. Notes from these committee sessions offer a view into how curators evaluate objects they are generally discouraged to evaluate on other occasions. For instance, when silverware is concerned, jewellers are consulted in order to reach a fair price. There are, however, much more complex cases than that and, as a rule, items are sold to the museum beneath market value. Now, how is market value determined is a difficult question, one that would deserve thorough investigation on its own, because ethnographic artefacts (when considered marketable) exist in a grey area between archaeology and applied art.

In any case, during purchase committee sessions, the interested curators must reach a unanimous decision whether an artefact will be purchased and thus added to the museum collection. The same committee deliberates gifts, as many are denied on various grounds. When purchases are concerned, the collective either reacts on a price offer or has to make an offer itself. In both cases, different criteria come into play. First, comparative methods are used. Curators generally try to keep discrepancies between likely items low. If a vest was purchased for, e.g., 5000 dinars, a similar vest should not exceed that price greatly. Larger sums can be offered if an item is unique in a way but is always constructed relative to prices common for other items of the same genus. All these criteria, however, fall under the umbrella of one rule: systematic enrichment of the collection.[35] Each and every potential contribution should be valued according to how it contributes to the collection and how it broadens its scope in space and time; that is to say, how they contribute to a comprehensive presentation of social life.

From this perspective, the aforementioned designation of all ethnographic artefacts as 'treasures' is more clear. Two items that could have had drastic differences in value as commodities before becoming singularised and incorporated into the museum's fund are now of equal value: they both attest to a certain way of life with equal strength. It is the data they now carry with them that brings added value. Also, it is unimportant if something is mundane and common; a simple pickaxe is important because of the stories it can tell not because of its potential market value. However, that is not to say that just because each item has the same unquantifiable amount of value that it has the same kind of use value. Highly decorated formal costumes were exhibited, especially abroad and with great pride, in order to send a message of dignity and wealth. An unobtrusive household item, however, served a different function: it spoke of modesty, frugality or asceticism of the day-to-day existence.

---

[35] Simić 2006.

Meanwhile, even though research objectives did not change significantly, exhibiting practices were shaped by the political ambitions of that time. Much as the showcases of the museum in the first decades were an advertisement of what was seen as Serbian national virtues (the dexterity and genius of embroiderers, the inventiveness and resourcefulness of the peasant etc.), the period of socialist Yugoslavia was characterised by a demonstration of different political goals. The artefacts were exhibited in such a way as to integrate Yugoslav nationalities by representing them equally. At the same time, as the museum collections started to grow it was now possible to exhibit discrete aspects of a culture: pottery, carpet-weaving and so on.

In the last days of the socialist period, an exhibition took place that caused some controversy among museum professionals; controversy that deserves to be mentioned because it illuminated implicit standards that the exhibition violated. The year was 1986 and a group of students lead by a member of the faculty was given the liberty to present the topic of their choice. Instead of peasants, they wanted to show football fans. According to the exhibition's lead author, current head of the department of ethnology and anthropology at the University of Belgrade, opposition to it was manifested, first, in the museum's decision not to print a catalogue, which was an odd choice contrary to usual procedure. Secondly, the authors were unable to arrange for a museum curator to formally open the exhibition and had to do it themselves, which was not only equally unusual but also against usual decorum of humility.[36] Fan gears had no place in the Ethnographic Museum and therefore no value in it. Adding them to the collections was never considered.

Almost two decades later, another event illustrated that the museum did not deviate from its course. On the 109th anniversary of the museum, an exhibition titled *Plastic Nineties* opened, a testament to the overall socio-economic collapse in the last decade of the 20th century, as evident from the everyday objects chosen for display. The objects, as the title suggests, were predominantly cheap industrial items made of plastic, the opposite of what the museum fostered. Although the exhibition was given sufficient media and public coverage, there were dissenting voices within the museum itself.[37]

As mentioned earlier, the notion of the ethnographic object is not a given. Ethnographic objects are contextualised as such by ethnographers (or ethnologists/anthropologists). In the Serbian context, the debate between two camps revolved around the understanding of the nature of the ethnographic item: whereas for one group it could only mean items made in the so-called traditional culture (even if this traditional mode of production was invariably changed by new forms of production and commerce, i.e. use of fabrics such as velvet, previously unavailable to historical

---

[36] Kovačević 2011.
[37] Kovačević 2011; Jakovljević-Šević 2014.

rural communities), the other considered any item of the everyday as suitable for ethnologists.[38]

Given the need to define priorities within diverse and numerous collections while, at the same time, respecting the complexity of value as a concept, many bodies try to formulate guidelines for institutions and professionals in assessing value.[39] No such guidelines exist for museum professionals in Serbia and museums generally try to reach a consensus regarding what they need to acquire. As we have seen from recent debates on the nature of ethnographic items, such a consensus has not been reached, and current accessioning practices move in both directions, with one giving attention to rural and the other to artefacts of urban culture. In 2006, during an assembly of museum ethnologists, members of the Museum Association of Serbia,[40] it was generally agreed upon that museum ethnologists should direct museum ethnographic practice towards 'acting within the frames of historical, socio-economical and cultural context of today and the near past' in order for them to 'stop being mere collectors of national treasures, and become instead interpreters of cultural symbols which, together, make up the identity of a certain culture, and by that a certain ethnos'.[41]

Similar voices were heard during the discussions on the possibility of a new permanent exhibition with the opinions published later in an edited volume.[42] Besides technical matters of making the exhibition more accessible or more effective in the communication of its message there were also strong opinions on the necessity of abandoning the antiquated notion of traditional culture and stepping back into the present from self-imposed exile into the realm of history.[43] However, other forms of criticism could be heard.[44] The current permanent exhibition is a modification of the one from 1984 which sought to represent Yugoslav nationalities in their diversity. It appears that the most radical change is a political one, since the permanent exhibition from 2001 abandoned the principle of 'brotherhood and unity', which generally died with Yugoslavia in 1991, and decided to represent only Serbs. Instead of being confined to the administrative border of the Republic of Serbia it shows Serbs from throughout the Yugoslav space, both from regions where they live in majority and those where they are a minority. This especially refers to areas where Serbs fled or were exiled from during the 1990s, enabling us to read this exhibition as a political statement that protests the outcome of the Yugoslav wars.

It is around this time, i.e. after the wars, that the accessioning practice at the museum began to skew more in favour of gifts, especially gifts brought to the

---

[38] Gavrilović 2007b.
[39] e.g. Cultural Heritage Agency 2014.
[40] The Museum Association of Serbia is a voluntary association of museum professionals, the only one existing on the national level.
[41] Romeljić 2006, 128 (my emphasis).
[42] Matić 2016.
[43] Prelić 2016.
[44] Erdei 2016; Lukić-Krstanović 2016.

museum, instead of given to the curator during fieldwork. Part of the reason for it was a reduced budget which prohibited large-scale purchases. But another significant cause was an increasing number of Serbian refugees from Bosnia and Croatia, later also Kosovo and Metohija, who recognised the museum as a beacon of national and ethnic identity and even a place of gathering. The museum became more and more a cultural centre of sorts, where performances that celebrated national heritage took place: folk dances, gusle, traditional song …

Ultimately, there is research value, both for anthropology and other disciplines. This potential is unfortunately often left unfulfilled, as is apparently not only the case here, but also in western ethnographic museums.[45] Besides colleagues from other museums, researchers that usually ask for access to museum's data are either historians or art historians, even amateurs writing chronicles of their communities. Even though curators now still conduct research in actual living communities as much as the constrained budget allows, the Ethnographic Museum in Belgrade is still seen by some as being firmly entrenched in studying the historical, the antiquated. What is becoming increasingly common, however, are visiting students of art and design who roam the exhibition space looking for inspiration for their work. This is by no means a new development: modes of similar behaviour were present in all three distinct eras of the museum. In the early days of the Kingdom of Serbs, Croats and Slovenes, artists sought a way to contribute to nation-building by looking for inspiration for their work in folk artisanship, and the socialist era was characterised by associating the museum with industrial design.

Conclusion

Because of its inward orientation, work of the Ethnographic Museum in Belgrade was open to political influences that tried to shape the way nationhood was being defined and to build an image for visitors both from the country and abroad. This led to three distinct modes of presentation that roughly correspond with three distinct political systems that shaped the social reality. The first was characterised by a capitalist mode of production and a zeal to establish the rightful place of Serbian people – primarily Serbs, even after the founding of a unified South Slav state – among other European nations. The society of the second period, after the Second World War, was driven by a centrally-planned socialist economy. It fostered the ideology of brotherhood and unity as a way to deal with the consequences of brutal inter-ethnic struggles during the Second World War in Yugoslavia and made conscious efforts not to present any ethnic group or nationality as dominant. For that reason, the material culture of other Yugoslav ethnicities was presented in various exhibitions, including permanent ones. Ultimately, after the fall of socialism and especially after the Yugoslav wars, a

---

[45] Reynolds 1983.

resurgence of ethnic politics affected the presentation, with the prominent position now given to promoting Serbian cultural heritage.

It can thus be seen that the value of objects is differently considered in the case of research and accessioning on the one hand and exhibiting on the other. In the case of the former, a scientific (no matter how outdated) principle is the guiding force, especially the idea of classification.[46] Still, the basic foundations of understanding what makes an ethnographic object have not been laid. In that sense, a decision to look only for 'traditional material culture' is a political one, just as it is to actively seek out objects of global culture, such as sweatshirts, mass-produced Disney toys or plastic chairs. However, exhibiting practices show how the same objects can be differently valued at different times. All three periods, perhaps unfairly simplified and generalised here, demonstrated different ways of approaching nation-building through cultural practice. Or rather, attempts at nation-building through national representation. On the one hand, they used objects that had value before entering the museum, especially for the habitually poor rural population, such as highly decorated costumes that turned them into a testament of national spirit. On the other hand, they worked with things that people were on the verge of discarding, took them in and turned them into things that their descendants now look at with respect. That truly was the work of magicians, or at least alchemists.

References

Appadurai. A. (ed.) 1986 *The Social Life of Things. Commodities in Cultural Perspective* (Cambridge)
Bestor, T. 2001 Markets. Anthropological aspects. In: N. Smelser (ed.), *International Encyclopedia of the Social & Behavioral Sciences* (Amsterdam), 9227–9231
Bižić-Omčikus, V. 2002 *Na početku* (Belgrade)
Bižić-Omčikus, V. 2005 *Kolekcija jesen/zima 1867. Srpska kolekcija iz Ruskog etnografskog muzeja u Sankt Peterburgu* (Belgrade)
Clifford, J. and Marcus, G. (eds) 1986 *Writing Culture. The Poetics and Politics of Ethnography* (Berkeley CA)
Cultural Heritage Agency 2014 *Assessing Museum Collections. Collection Valuation in Six Steps* (Amersfoort)
Cvetić, E. 1926 Stevan-Stevča-Mihailović. In : *Bulletin du Musée Ethnographique de Belgrade* 1 (Belgrade), 1–10
Drobnjaković, B. M. 1926 Musee Ethnographique de Belgrade. In : *Bulletin du Musée Ethnographique de Belgrade* 1 (Belgrade), 11–25
Durrans, B. 1992 Behind the Scenes. Museums and Selective Criticism. *Anthropology Today* 8(4), 11–15
Dušković, V. 2001 *Etnografski muzej u Beogradu 1901-2001* (Belgrade)
Erdei, I. 2016 Prilog diskusiji o novoj stalnoj postavci Etnografskog muzeja u Beogradu. In: M. Matić (ed.), *Ka novoj stalnoj postavci Etnografskog muzeja* (Belgrade), 211–216
Erdeljanović, J. 1926 *Stara Crna Gora; etnička prošlost i formiranje crno-gorskih plemena* (Belgrade)
Fabian, J. 2004 On recognizing things. The 'Ethnic Artefact' and the 'Ethnographic Object'. *L'Homme* 170, 47–60
Gavrilović, L. 2007a Etnografski muzeji/zbirke i konstrukcija identiteta. In: S. Nedeljković (ed.), *Antropologija savremenosti. Zbornik radova* (Belgrade), 172–189

---

[46] Simić 2006.

Gavrilović, L. 2007b *Kultura u izlogu: ka novoj muzeologiji* (Belgrade)

Graeber, D. 2001 *Toward an Anthropological Theory of Value. The False Coin of Our Own Dreams* (New York)

Hahn, H. P. 2018 Dinge als Herausforderung. Einführung In: H. P. Hahn and F. Neumann (eds), *Dinge als Herausforderung. Kontexte, Umgangsweisen und Umwertungen von Objekten* (Bielefeld), 9–32

Hahn, H. P. and Weiss, H. 2013 Introduction. Biographies, travels, and itineraries of things. In: H. P. Hahn and H. Weiss (eds), *Mobility, Meaning & Transformations of Things. Shifting Contexts of Material Culture through Time and Space* (Oxford), 1–14

Halpern, J. M., Kaser, K. and Wagner, R. E. 1996 Patriarchy in the Balkans. Temporal and cross-cultural approaches. *The History of the Family* 1(4), 425–442

Henry, R., Otto., T. and Wood, M. 2013 Ethnographic artifacts and value transformations. *HAU. Journal of Ethnographic Theory* 3(2), 33–51

Jakovljević-Šević, T. 2014 Redefining ethnographic museology. Response to the challenges of modernity. Examples from the museum practice in Serbia. *Etnoloska Istrazivanja* 18/19, 147–161

Karpova, O. 2005 Srpska kolekcija REM. In: *Kolekcija jesen/zima 1867. Srpska kolekcija iz Ruskog etnografskog muzeja u Sankt Petersburgu* (Belgrade)

Kirshenblatt-Gimblett, B. 1991 Objects of ethnography. In: I. Karp and S. D. Lavine (eds), *Exhibiting Cultures. The Poetics and Politics of Museum Display* (London), 386–443

Kopytoff, I. 1986 The cultural biography of things. Commoditization as a process. In: Appadurai (ed.)1986, 64–91

Knight, N. 2001 *The Empire on Display. Ethnographic Exhibition and the Conceptualization of Human Diversity in Post-Emancipation Russia* (Washington DC)

Kovačević, I. 2011 Muzeji i modernizacija. Dres, traktor i plastična lutka, *Issues in Ethnology and Anthropology* 6(2), 365–380

Kovačević, I. 2015 *Istorija srpske etnologije* (Belgrade)

Lukić-Krstanović, M. 2016 Aktivizam muzeja. Cirkulisanje znanje i kreativnosti. In: Matić (ed.) 2016, 231–238

Matić, M. (ed.) 2016 *Ka novoj stalnoj postavci Etnografskog muzeja* (Belgrade)

Miller, D. 2008 The uses of value. *Geoforum* 39(3), 1122–1132

Penny, H. G. 2002 *Objects of Culture. Ethnology and Ethnographic Museums in Imperial Germany* (Chapel Hill NC)

Prelić, M. 2016 Neka razmišljanja povodom buduće stalne postavke Etnografskog muzeja u Beogradu. In: Matić (ed.) 2016, 223–230

Reynolds, B. 1983 The Relevance of Material Culture to Anthropology. *Journal of the Anthropological Society of Oxford* 2, 63–75

Romeljić, Z. 2006 Ethnology in museums of Serbia at the early third millennium. *Glasnik Etnografskog muzeja u Beogradu* 70, 123–129

Simić, M. 2006 Displaying nationality as traditional culture in the Belgrade Ethnographic Museum. Exploration of a museum modernity practice. In: D. Radojičić (ed.), *Glasnik Etnografskog Instituta SANU LIV* (Belgrade), 305–318

Stocking, G. W. Jr 1982 Afterword. A view from the centre. *Ethnos* 47 (1–2), 172–186

Suarez, A. V. and Tsutsui, N. D. 2004 The value of museum collections for research and society. *BioScience* 54(1), 66–74

Thompson, M. 1979 *Rubbish Theory. The Creation and Destruction of Value* (Oxford)

UNESCO Convention 2018. *Intergovernmental Committee for the Safeguarding of the Intangible Cultural Heritage, Convention for the Safeguarding of the Intangible Cultural Heritage, December 20, 2018*. <https://ich.unesco.org/en/convention> (accessed: 17 September 2021)

Chapter 7

The gift as an open question

Guido Sprenger

Among the most striking aspects of archaeological study, from an anthropological point of view, is the geographical range of the diffusion of valuable objects. Cowrie shells, for instance, have been used as valuables in an area spreading from the Maldives across Asia, Africa and Europe for millennia.[1] In a certain way, this seems paradoxical. The value of objects – especially of items that are not for immediate consumption, like food – is a context- or culture-specific construction. It demands a degree of consensus about what is valued and why. These objects are not just objects with a value attached but represent systems of values which need some degree of coherence – value always implies a comparison of different valuables and, therefore, the value of one object is never isolated from the value of others.

However, the spread of valuables across large geographic areas indicates that they have been valued within a variety of different cultural configurations. They have transited through different regimes of value and thus were subject to different interpretations – and different usages – along the way.[2] The question, then, is how they have managed these transitions.

There are several ways of explaining this and these explanations are not mutually exclusive. For instance, one may argue for an intrinsic value of certain objects that arises from their appeal to cognitive and social universals. From this point of view, gold and gemstones are pretty to look at and, due to their durability, may work as permanent stores of value.

Another argument holds that trade is a human universal and people anywhere will figure out how to obtain things that they desire through exchange, by barter or money. This assumes that human beings act because they have needs and that social relations develop from individual desires. However, the universality of this assumption has been amply criticised. Marshall Sahlins, for instance, demonstrates how the concept of the human being as defined by needs only arose in Europe during early

---

[1] Yang 2019; see also contributions in this volume.
[2] Kopytoff 1986.

modernity.[3] This obviously does not mean that the transfer of valuables is never achieved due to individual desires but simply suggests that it is far from exhausting all possibilities. In particular, it implies that 'trade' may be a too generic term and that many transfers which look like trade or barter to the modern eye may be based on rather different principles.[4]

This chapter aims to add a further, equally non-exclusive model to the theoretical apparatus for the analysis of the spread of valuable objects. It is derived from theories of gift exchange and argues for the immanent tensions and imbalances in any value system. These tensions, which become most visible in gift exchange but are not exclusive to it, lead to an openness of value systems to innovation and external influence. Social life emerges from such irresolvable tensions between values which are specific to a cultural situation. Exchange is a crucial means for articulating and identifying these tensions. By looking at the problems and the discontents of giving and taking in different societies, we can analyse the dynamics of social life.[5]

I will argue that gift exchanges provide emic models for imagined social wholes that encompass tensions such as those between identity and alterity, or self and stranger. These models thus project moral horizons across perceived differences and therefore enable the transfer of valuables across cultural boundaries.

The instability of wholes

Gift exchange, according to classic theorist Marcel Mauss,[6] creates lasting social relationships due to three moral obligations: to give, to receive and to return a gift. It is therefore at the core of peaceful, coherent and durable social relationships. Gifts combine interest and generosity in a way that makes egoism and altruism inseparable – or rather, renders egoism and altruism inappropriate for analysing gift exchange.[7] This is because the gift represents a part of the person of the giver;[8] givers are thus not isolated as persons but distributed across their gifting relationships.[9] Gifts therefore affect and shape a substantial part of the constitutive relationships of a society and thus are '"total" social phenomena'.[10]

Systems of gift exchange therefore create society as a whole, as the three basic obligations tie people together. Yet, there is no automatism to this. More recent readings of Mauss have, more particularly, pointed out that his concept of society is dynamic and always in the making.[11]

---

[3] Sahlins 2000.
[4] Strathern 1992.
[5] see Robbins 2015.
[6] Mauss 2016.
[7] Mauss 2016, 58.
[8] Mauss 2016, 71.
[9] see also Gregory 1982; Strathern 1988.
[10] Mauss 2016, 58.
[11] Graeber 2001; Hart 2007; Därmann 2010; Hahn 2015.

This raises the question of the principles that at once create dynamics and wholeness, change and boundedness at the same time, through gift exchange. First of all, these social wholes (societies, cultures, as you may call them) are in principle virtual, restricted in their validity and changeable. By virtual I mean that such wholes become real because they are imaginations which are acted upon. The actors and parties of the exchange assume that they share a certain notion about their mutual relationship and the values that guide their actions. Then, at the moment of exchange, a whole, a community, is evoked that gives value to the exchange.[12] Each exchange which constitutes a relationship requires that the exchange partners act on the background of a – however imagined or volatile – community that recognises the exchange as valid. It is for this reason that some of the most important exchanges are highly public events.

The potentials and problematics of these social wholes will become clearer after I proceed to outline a few characteristics of the gift. Gifts constitute social wholes because relations created through gift exchange are more durable than those created by commodity exchange. There have been several attempts to explain this. Mauss stressed the delay of the return, a point I will return to below. As long as the return gift has not yet been transferred, giver and receiver remain in a relation of indebtedness.[13] However, this does not answer the question how a particular social whole is created beyond relationships between individuals.

Claude Lévi-Strauss went a step further in his concept of asymmetric marriage alliance.[14] Here, no transfer is isolated from the rest of the social whole. One group gives something to another (in Lévi-Strauss's case, the gift consists of a wife) but does not receive anything substantial in return. The cycle of transfers then provides the giver with an equivalent gift from another party: person A gives to person B, as person B gives to C, so that A knows that ultimately C will give a gift of the same kind (a wife) to him. As this kind of cycle, Lévi-Strauss argues, can contain an unlimited number of groups, it may comprise the entire society, thus creating society as a whole.

This type of totalising models has been rightfully criticised for not accounting for the complexity of any given social entity. If Lévi-Strauss's model is taken as one of social wholeness, then it assumes that affinal relations are the dominant forms of exchange and define the encompassing arena of value[15] to which everything else is subordinate. However, in any given society there are more exchanges going on than marital ones, and these other exchanges may elicit different social wholes. In particular, as Lévi-Strauss himself argues, his models demand a high degree of mutual trust in the very existence of a society-as-a-whole.[16] They will thus not be very helpful for explaining the transcultural transfer of valuables.

---

[12] see Graeber 2001, 86–88.
[13] Mauss 2016, 177.
[14] Lévi-Strauss 1993, 333–359.
[15] Graeber 2013.
[16] Lévi-Strauss 1993.

Hence, the kind of circulation analysed by Lévi-Strauss does indeed constitute a kind of whole, but it is a partial one that may not even account for all types of marriage cycles. Even this potentially totalising vision of gift exchange does not provide a model that automatically ensures that society becomes a stable whole.

Thus, more recent models have highlighted the processual and virtual character of social wholes and their inherent risks, thereby pointing at the contingency of the social.[17]

Knut Rio and Olaf Smedal, for instance, move away from the 'total social fact' as a stable given but instead emphasise the pursuit and enactment of these facts – gift exchange being just one of them – as forms of totalisation, of creating a contingent totality that could fall apart at any given moment.[18] Large public gift exchanges, Rio argues,[19] do not only make society-as-a-whole visible but at the same time stress the transience and momentary character of this whole – wholes must disappear once they have formed. For David Graeber, societies as wholes are necessary imaginations that valorise any value-oriented action.[20] The question is then what stabilises them – when delays or trust in cyclicity are not enough? This draws attention to the issue of value in exchange.

The asymmetry of values

In order to conceive gift exchange as a relationship at once stabilising and changeable, we have to look at the nature of the values which are involved. I want to argue that it is primarily the asymmetry of values that enables gift exchange relationships. Equivalence is not the same as exchangeability and is not at the core of every exchange. Rather, the two gifts represent different qualitative values which complement each other.[21]

This constitutes the dynamics of gift exchange. Three things happen at the same time: first, the two values are treated as if they form a whole made up of two heterogeneous but complementary parts. Second, this whole is at the same time incomplete, as the parts are never entirely balanced but somewhat hierarchised. Since there is no equivalence, there can be no end to the relationship. Third, the valorisation of items highlights only some of their features at the expense of others. Items, however, always contain multiple possibilities to link and compare them to others and therefore multiple potential connections.

A classic example is the symmetric marriage exchange among the Baruya of New Guinea. Ideally, Baruya men exchange sisters to give to each other as brides. Now, taken at face value, the gifts seem equivalent: a woman for a woman should balance things

---

[17] Caillé 2008.
[18] Rio and Smedal 2009.
[19] Rio 2014.
[20] Graeber 2001; 2013.
[21] Strathern 1992.

out, which would imply that there are no further obligations between the two men. However, what happens instead is that the two brothers-in-law become close allies and spend a lot of their time working together. This is because the two 'gifts' of women do not neutralise each other; each is a debt that cannot be returned but in a mutual way.[22] As a result, the two men can treat each other as equals. Thus, I suggest, what is being exchanged is not an item (two instantiations of an abstract category 'woman') but a relationship: a sister is exchanged for a wife. From a man's point of view, the relationship 'sister', with its particular values and ideas, is linked to the relationship 'wife' to form a complementary whole. This is why the relationship between the two men cannot be terminated. They are linked, as it were, by a symmetrical asymmetry. It is rather the asymmetry of the values combined in the circulation of gifts that creates permanent relationships.

This becomes even clearer when we move a step away from the exchange of persons to the transfer of valuables. This again concerns marital exchanges but this time involving bride wealth and dowry. For Lévi-Strauss, the introduction of bride wealth represents the degeneration of trust in the system of the exchange of persons. When the delay between one marriage and its return grows too long and the risk of not receiving a bride after giving away a sister increases, material valuables are introduced as a kind of replacement of persons. This immediate return only binds the intermarrying families together while removing them to a degree from the marriage cycles that unify the entirety of society.[23] Lévi-Strauss was operating from the assumption that exchange is based on equivalence, and only the assumption of equivalence may enable exchange. Giving valuables instead of women thus establishes a principle of symbolism in which the objects present stand in for something absent – they are not what really is at stake, but they enable a fiction of equivalence.[24] Lévi-Strauss implied that an asymmetry (between a symbol and what it represents) was introduced in order to retain symmetry (equivalence).

Yet, as argued above, the exchange of persons (spouses) for valuables is often based on entirely different principles, as Lévi-Strauss's early critic Jan Petrus Benjamin de Josselin de Jong has pointed out.[25] Gift exchange is asymmetric, as it is not so much equivalence but complementarity which makes the exchange of two heterogenous items possible. Spouses cannot be bought for valuables. Rather, the value of spouses needs to be complemented by the value of valuables.

A brief example from my own research among the Rmeet, an upland people in Northern Laos, may suffice. The Rmeet are segmented into patrilineal lineages formed by households that are linked in asymmetric marriage alliances. Women marry into households of lineages that have received wives from these women's houses or lineages in the past. Ideally, a woman should marry her father's sister's son, as this would

---

[22] Godelier 2011, 55–58.
[23] Lévi-Strauss 1967, 360–377.
[24] see Znoj 1995 for a model totalising the equivalence principle.
[25] de Josselin de Jong 1983.

repeat the bond created by the marriage of her father's sister. These marriages, albeit highly valued, rarely occur, but the majority of married couples claim that they have followed the basic rule in one way or another. In fact, an extensive class of cross-cousins and remote wife-giving-wife-taking relationships may be evoked to legitimise actual marriages. By tracing different genealogical connections, many relationships in the Rmeet system of kin classification can be interpreted in various ways, that is, as wife-givers, wife-takers or (unmarriageable) consanguines.

The Rmeet do not think that their marriage system forms a circle of intermarrying patrilines nor do they practice such a system. Yet, marriages are asymmetric, as the movement of women cannot be reversed. No women from a husband's house or lineage should marry into the one of a wife. Relations are also asymmetric in respect to the transfer of objects. Bride wealth given from the husband's side is obligatory and subject to extended negotiations, while dowry from the bride's side is not. Well into the 2000s, the preferred items were one buffalo and colonial silver coins in addition to bride service of the husband in his parents-in-law's household. When bride wealth is paid in modern currency, people calculate its value in terms of its equivalent in buffaloes and silver. However, this does not imply equivalence between the bride and the valuables that her husband's family provides. The most important social function of wives is the creation of new houses, that is, couples with children. Adults are called by teknonyms derived from their children's names – as the 'father of X' or the 'mother of Y' – and their houses are similarly named after their offspring. Thus, what a man acquires when he acquires a bride are relationships to future generations.

In contrast, the bride's family receives potential relationships with past generations. The most important function of buffaloes is as sacrifices to the house spirit, which is a conglomerate of the patrilineal ancestors of the current house father (the husband of the constituting couple). Silver coins are important ritual objects for various uses, including sacrificial rituals, but they have a particularly conspicuous role in mortuary rituals. At one moment, all the patrilineal male relatives of the household of a dead person place their entire stock of silver coins on the dead body. As one informant told me, the 'spirit of the money' then eats the dead person, thus making it part of itself. This suggests that the silver money which is circulating in various exchanges in Rmeet society is an anonymised representation of the dead. In any case, both silver money and buffaloes serve to cultivate relations with protective ancestor spirits which guard the houses and the health of their descendants.

It would hence be wrong to assume that bride wealth and wives are equivalent to each other. Rather, they can be exchanged because they represent mutually exclusive, yet complementary values – the value of future generations and the value of past generations. The fact that wife-givers are seen as superior to wife-takers suggests that the relationship to future generations is the higher value of the two.[26] The relationship between future and past generations defines a specific model of society as a whole

---

[26] Sprenger 2006, 144–164.

from the point of view of this exchange. Other exchanges or social processes may produce different models of the same society.[27]

This analysis, however, is just one first step. It runs the danger to create the image of a closed value system that excludes other valorisations of the relationships and items included in it. If that was the case, no marriage would be possible with people practising a different marriage system with different ideas about how to relate to the ancestors or what the value of silver coins is. For sure, the valorisations of the system I have just described circumscribe what I will call a moral horizon of exchange – a social whole that becomes imaginable due to the validity of a particular set of values, as enacted in exchange. Still, it does not amount to a clear distinction between one value system and another.

In the present case, my analysis helps explain why the Rmeet marry easily with their ethnic neighbours, the Khmu, who have a similar system of kinship and marriage,[28] but marry less with Lao or Thai, who have different systems. Still, the latter marriages do occur, and not just recently so.[29] I suggest that this is not simply due to people's readiness to sacrifice their value system when opportunities arise. If the exchange is based on a regular complementation of values, as in the Rmeet case, this is because the rules have been stabilised over many single cases. The complementation has turned from a momentary statement of exchangeability to something like an enduring 'tradition'. Still, each instantiation of marital exchange is a momentary statement. The Rmeet acknowledge the contingency of the relationship between the items of exchange by their careful and often extended bride wealth negotiations. Even when no one doubts that the marriage will occur, a semi-public discussion of its conditions marks an important part of the ritual proceedings. This signals that the value of a woman in exchange is not fixed. She is, as a person, always part of a more specific set of kin relationships that is recognised by the meticulous search for an appropriate complementation. Thus, the asymmetry of the exchange allows for, even necessitates, the openness of the value system, a lack of fixity, an insistence that items could be paired differently than done before – and thereby, I suggest, even the adoption of different value systems.

The gift as an open question

I will thus argue that gift exchange is a process that enables transcultural exchanges because of its inherent asymmetries. Generally speaking, equivalence is difficult to assert because it entails the claim that two phenomenally different entities share identity on the level of value. Asymmetries, however, are manifold. This much is implied when Lévi-Strauss, in a different field of study, demonstrates that each concrete item featuring in a myth is a bundle of traits that contains multiple

---

[27] see Barraud *et al.* 1994.
[28] Lindell *et al.* 1979.
[29] Garnier 1996, 13–14.

possibilities to be put in a structural relationship with one or another contrasting item. For example, the symbolic value of ash could be 'dead' in contrast with living plants, but it could also be 'cool' in contrast with fire. The potential combinations resulting from such multiple structural couplings are potentially endless.[30]

The same applies to the asymmetric complementation of gifts. The exchangeability made possible through the coupling of two heterogeneous items is based on their valorised difference, but this claim is contingent – each item could be coupled with a different complement. Therefore, the value of a gift, that is, its position in a specific value system, can only be determined in the moment of its – more-or-less – successful coupling with a different item. It is because gift giving is not so much based on equivalence but on asymmetry that the specific asymmetry which each gift realises will only emerge from the way it is received and returned. The gift is thus an open question, a message sent out in search of its own meaning. Its reception and the return gift may have an almost revelatory character.

What, then, does this open question pertain to? The significance of the reception and return of the gift does not just say something about its value as an isolated item but rather about the value of the relationship thus stated. The relationships of which value systems are composed represent multiple differences, and each coupling of an item with another highlights a specific one among them. Each answer to the open question of the gift thus posits it in a specific place in a given value system. Each coupling is a statement of wholeness and therefore a potential model, a metonymy for the wholeness of society. However, any specific exchange may address the value system in a new way and thereby change it.[31] This is the dynamic aspect of the virtual wholes that exchanges create.

I want to focus here on just two dimensions of the value of a relationship. The first brings back the temporal dimension of the reception, the perennial issue of delayed return. The second refers to what could be termed a spatial or synchronic dimension – the range of validity of the value system projected by the giving of a gift. Both aspects refer to the future orientation of the gift; I argue that gifts, because they are open and asymmetric, are forms of expectation.

Regarding the temporal dimension, as mentioned above, the delay in the return of the gift has raised some fundamental concerns. Mauss has already stressed the asymmetry inherent in the gift and the relationship it creates.[32] The gift puts the receiver in the role of the debtor. S/he is interested in returning the gift in order to redeem his/her debt and at the same time may be interested in retaining the relationship.

Pierre Bourdieu, in contrast, argues that the return has to be delayed in order to veil the interested character of the gift and protect the impression of generosity.

---

[30] Lévi-Strauss 1967; see also Viveiros de Castro 2016.
[31] Sahlins 1985.
[32] Mauss 2016.

The delay thus creates the fiction of a new start, making every gift an initial gift and obscuring its character as a return. At the same time, actors know that the gift really is a return and thus addresses – maintains, changes, etc. – a specific previous relationship. Importantly, Bourdieu recognises the uncertain and risky character of the gift exchange, thereby critiquing Lévi-Straussian models in which the return is fixed and unchangeable.[33] These latter models indeed make gift exchange resemble modern contracts with narrow specifications on what is given and what is returned, like those on commodity markets.[34] However, Bourdieu seeks the reason for the delay in strategic increases of capital, albeit not necessarily of the economic kind. Enduring relationships accrue as social capital, expenditure in economically meaningless ways may increase symbolic capital, etc. This again models gift exchange in terms of the maximisation strategies of modern commodity exchange and thus subordinates it to modern economic thought.

Assuming an asymmetry of exchange provides a more general approach to the delay that allows for alternatives to modern market principles. Asymmetry also accounts for the fact that delays in gift exchange occur often, but not always. Again, I refer to the marital exchanges among the Rmeet. Rmeet marriage ceremonies consist of a 'small wedding' when the husband moves into his parents-in-law's house for bride service and a 'big wedding' when the couple moves out some years later into the husband's parents' home or their own. There are immediate exchanges on both occasions but this does not end the exchange relationship. On the contrary: it is usual to delay the transfer of some items and sometimes the final transfers only occur during the mortuary rituals for either husband or wife decades later.

However, this still does not constitute a full account of the exchange. As the wife-giving side is seen as superior to their wife-takers, they have the right to ask for more bride wealth later, even beyond what has been negotiated initially. While this seems to be considered as somewhat inappropriate by some people, wife-takers are in no position to flatly turn down such demands. There is an asymmetry in their relationship that is impossible to balance out fully. Delays simply stress that the asymmetry is irresolvable.

Therefore, I argue that the delay of the return is just one possible form of many to acknowledge the interminable character of a gift exchange. In contrast to commodity exchange, in which balancing signals the potential to terminate a relationship, the asymmetry of values that constitutes gift exchanges makes ending these relationships rather difficult. In fact, while the maintenance of commodity exchange relations requires additional effort after balancing is accomplished, gift exchanges demand a reverse effort for ending them, e.g. through specific finishing exchanges.[35] In the case of the Rmeet, mortuary rituals contain an exchange between wife-givers and

---

[33] Bourdieu 1993, 180–205.
[34] Sprenger 2019, 143; see also McKinnon 2001.
[35] Sprenger *et al.* 2017.

wife-takers which publicly terminates their relationships – but even then, termination is never complete, and the relationship may be invoked again to legitimise future marriages.

The delay articulates the asymmetry of values in gift exchanges in a temporal dimension, as difficulties to end a relationship. However, asymmetry also pertains to the socio-spatial dimension of the exchange, my second point here. This directly addresses the question of transculturality.

Since gift exchanges are open and not like commercial contracts, they always run the risk of disappointment. The return gift may never materialise or come in an unexpected form. This is because different people may give different answers to the question what the appropriate complementation of a gift may be – and these perturbations may stem from mere misunderstandings to calculated attempts to manipulate or exploit the relationship. Thus, such misguided expectations may occur both among people sharing the same value system and across systems.

It is because the asymmetry of exchange implies the impossibility to ascertain its outcome that gift exchanges are not bound to singular and isolated value systems. The potential for misguided expectations often forms a continuum across the boundary of value systems. In fact, each gift is a probe into the validity of the value system, especially when people from unfamiliar (social) places are drawn into the exchange. Thus, boundaries between value systems may be impossible to determine precisely. This is particularly true if different exchanges are considered. While ideas about marriage exchange may differ fundamentally between the Rmeet and the Lao, exchanges with certain types of spirits may be quite compatible. The recognition of this state of things by the actors may facilitate experiments with the validity of exchanges. The perception that the Lao exchange differently in some but not all fields may support the acceptance of marriages with them that may or may not meet the expectations of the exchange partners.

Therefore, disappointments may occur among people who identify with the same value system but, equally, exchanges may work between people with different value systems. In the latter case, the principle of open complementation led to a benevolent but different interpretation of the exchange on each side. This constitutes an example of a structured misunderstanding, in which communication partners assume that they are talking about the same thing.[36]

The openness of the return gift thus corresponds to the openness of value systems. It is therefore too restrictive to use Mauss's term obligation for giving, receiving and returning. As I have argued elsewhere,[37] the term expectation is analytically more pertinent. Certain stabilisations of exchange relationships, like marriage among the Rmeet, make gifts expectable, and there are expectations of giving, receiving and returning. Expectations can be disappointed with less or with more disruptive effects.

---

[36] Sprenger 2016; for an example see Platenkamp 2013.
[37] Sprenger 2019.

Also, they can be more or less specific, that is, stronger or weaker. A strong expectation specifies the way a gift is received, the time and kind of return; a weak expectation allows for a variety of outcomes or specifies only some of them. Expectation thus accounts for the multiplicity of horizons that the gift opens up.

Moral horizons and the stranger

Given this analytical apparatus, gift exchanges within and across value systems – or 'cultures', if you will – are not as substantially different from each other than they may appear to be. Rather, each gift transfer, with the expectations it comes with, projects what I call a 'moral horizon'. A moral horizon outlines the possibility of congruence of shared values. A gift given opens the possibility for a response that may confirm or disappoint the expectation of a durable relationship. This potential – and not always the reality – of such durable and reliable relationships defines the horizon to which the moral commitments and values contained by the gift apply. Moral horizons may define, but also extend beyond the sphere of familiar relations and social dimensions. They may differ for each type of gift or relationship established, and, as I have argued above, they may be defined by asymmetries – asymmetries of return and asymmetries of interpretation.

The validity and the limitations of Rmeet marriage define a moral horizon which encompasses Rmeet and Khmu kinship systems but meets its limits when other systems of kinship and marriage are involved. Still, it contains a transcultural potential. First, bride wealth varies not only from marriage to marriage but the Rmeet also recognise differences between villages, for instance in the duration of standard periods of bride service. Thus, even among the Rmeet themselves, the speculative character of bride wealth is obvious. The Khmu are considered ethnically different, but the marriage systems are compatible – therefore, the transcultural potential of marriage easily expands to them as well. Marrying others is still possible but the moral horizon that the bride wealth exchanges project becomes wider and less stabilised. Ethnic Lao or Thai do have bride wealth exchanges, too, but the rituals, ensuing kin relations and the items themselves differ. However, when I explained that Germans do not pay bride wealth at all, some Rmeet suggested that Germans then are not really married, that they have 'just so' marriages.

The Kula exchange of Papua New Guinea, as described by Bronislaw Malinowski or Frederick Damon,[38] provides another example of a moral horizon which encompasses a range of cultural differences. In this exchange of 'male' for 'female' shell valuables across islands that are hundreds of kilometres apart, differences are systematically connected.[39] In some of the islands involved only nobility may join the exchange or only men; on others, commoners or women are included. Thus, the social structures

---
[38] Malinowski 1964; Damon 2000.
[39] Damon 2000, 52–53.

connected by the cycle are quite diverse but, nevertheless, the style, manners and obligations of the exchange are shared – and so are the asymmetries of exchange. The fact that remote participants may never meet each other but know their names reveals that overcoming social and spatial distance is a crucial value in this exchange.[40] The Kula is thus the model of a moral horizon that makes the social systems of various islands imaginable as a single social whole. Other types of exchange on the same islands (like those among affines), however, elicit other moral horizons that may be spatially smaller but more comprehensive:[41] while only a small number of people are involved in Kula, everyone marries.

An example that casts an even wider net are private donations from the Global North to NGOs addressing crises in the Global South, ranging from the extinction of traditions to natural disasters. The givers and the takers usually do not have an immediate relationship with each other, although advertising of such NGOs often portrays possible recipients in a way that personalises them and brings them closer to the imagination of givers.[42] These depictions invoke a sense of belonging to a global community of human beings, a moral horizon marked by shared humanity and asymmetrised by axes such as rich/poor, modern/traditional or developed/underdeveloped. Thus, several authors have understood development aid as a modern form of gift exchange which is structured by asymmetries but based on ideas of shared humanity.[43] Given that there is little discernible return in these transfers, they maintain lasting asymmetries.

Consequently, what emerges from gifts is not so much a stable and closed society but rather a virtual whole that is articulated in a particular manner but not necessarily valid for most contexts in which one usually lives. The exchange thus assumes an imagined community of shared values which is not only involved in the exchange but also witnesses, acknowledges and valorises it. Each successful exchange claims to constitute a conceptual whole, and this has the potential to serve as a model for a social whole. Society thus conceived is not simply a given which the exchange represents and continues. It is also a function of the exchange, its imagined result. This is what I mean with moral horizon: the extent of the social whole that is imaginable if the whole constituted by the exchange is considered as a model of society. Rmeet society-as-a-whole becomes conceivable as a relationship between past and future generations because marriage exchanges have worked out time and again. The moral horizon of this sociality is defined by those people and groups who practice and acknowledge this type of exchange.

Gift exchanges are thus statements of moral horizons, claims for wholeness that are realised by acting upon them. Gifts given across what actors perceive as value systems or as cultural differences have an often experimental character. They are

---

[40] Weiner 1988.
[41] Weiner 1976.
[42] Grimm 2018, 77–114.
[43] Stirrat and Henkel 1997.

forays into future possibilities with unclear outcomes, and not every member of society is willing to engage in them.

Moral horizons are therefore always moving and co-exist with each other, this is the very nature of the experiment of gift giving. The asymmetries involved in the gift can thus be matched to the difference between giver and taker. This allows connecting varying scales of difference – the giver and taker may be familiar with each other but at the same time cast in the roles of insider and outsider. Marriages in some societies in South-east Asia reveal this pattern quite clearly: brides are staged as daughters of the soil, representations of autochthony, while bridegrooms are styled as outsiders bringing gifts from afar and embodying the figure of the stranger king who makes society complete.[44] The Rmeet are once again an example: bride wealth from the husband's side represents the outside and the market – by silver coins and buffaloes that are often seen as external – while dowry from the wife's side includes local products such as rice and homemade basketry.

Therefore, it is plausible that many societies have framed exchange in terms of relations between insiders and outsiders, locals and strangers. As Graeber has observed, exchanges between different groups of Australian aborigines were accompanied by displays of aggressive behaviour or sexual license.[45] The first casts the exchanging parties in the role of enemies, but mock enemies – the two parties agree to 'play war' only. The second either stresses rules of group exogamy or signifies that the strangers are not subject to the rules of sexual conduct that apply within one's own group. All these kinds of behaviour mark the exchange partners as complementarily different – they provide a framework by which strangeness can be translated, not into plain familiarity but into an asymmetric relationship.

Various authors have thus argued that the gift is a constitutive experience of strangeness.[46] Strangeness is open and contains the potential of anomy, of namelessness. Out of the diverse set of traits of the other, exchange selects those aspects that complement the self. It turns others into strangers which stand in a definitive relationship with oneself. This is the expansive moment of moral horizons – they reach out, and by drawing strangers into them, they establish the possibility of moral relations beyond the known validity of the value system.

The wholes evoked by gifts are based on asymmetry and therefore are potential models for moral horizons that encompass strangers as their maximal difference. Each asymmetric exchange thus models exchange among strangers – but not strangers as equals but as complementation. If trade is often understood as exchange between strangers,[47] then trade may contain much more features of gift exchange than often acknowledged. Thus, the historical or archaeological record of trade may in fact document an extension of gift exchange in which strangers appear as necessary

---

[44] e.g. Sahlins 2008; Platenkamp 2016.
[45] Graeber 2012, 27–48.
[46] Moebius 2009; Därmann 2010.
[47] e.g. Sahlins 1972, 227.

complements of the self. In the moral horizons of asymmetric gifts, the identity of shared morality and the alterity of self and other coexist.

Conclusion

When the archaeological record reveals that objects travel along large distances, we, with our modern experience with trade and markets, may be inclined to interpret these processes in terms of the satisfaction of individual desires by means of an equivalent exchange among equals. This may, however, be just one possibility among many. In this text, I have laid out a few conditions and terms by which the models of gift exchange may inspire exchange across cultural and social differences. I have argued that gift exchange asymmetrically links two items just as it links two asymmetric roles, the giver and the taker, as its minimal condition. These couplings form a whole in the sense that the two items are set up as different but complementary parts constituting a social, conceptual and even cosmological microcosm.

Yet, at the same time, these wholes are essentially not closed. First, the asymmetry of the concepts and values involved may be projected unto almost any given situation. Any whole thus has an environment, any concrete exchange of gifts picks up people and things from a range of possibilities to set them in the right relationship. These may be people who are actually familiar with each other but they may just as well be strangers. In any case, exchange demands familiarity and strangeness at the same time. On the one hand, even when close relatives engage in marital exchange, they are marked as representatives of remote social domains. On the other hand, strangers are figured into moral horizons that familiarise them and subordinate their incomprehensible anomy to their function as complementation.[48]

Second, this necessitates acts of interpretation or recognition. Two items and two persons need to be understood as being in mutual complementation. Recognition here equals an act of setting into a relationship. This requires that the items and people involved are able to enter multiple relationships and be subject to different interpretations – they are bundles of aspects which are highlighted by the various relationships they are involved in. For this reason, exchange is experimental, may assume different forms and lead to different results.

Exchange is thus future-oriented. Gifts, when given, are open questions in search for a complementary response. Each gift is thrown into a moral horizon that may or may not come into being. Gifts are halves that attract other halves that may not be fully defined in advance. This is particularly the case in transcultural exchanges. The value of a gift is only revealed through its return. This experimental dimension of the gift is often obscured in models of strongly conventionalised gift giving, as they are usual in most anthropological accounts (my own ones are not necessarily an exception). However, as more recent ethnographers have noticed, gift exchanges

---

[48] e.g. Platenkamp 2013.

always run the risk of failing and remaining without return. As much as we learn about a specific cultural configuration through its conventions in exchange, there is still as much to learn about its failures and experiments.

The study of such non-sequiturs would also draw more attention to the kind of transcultural exchanges we keep observing in ethnographies and the archaeological record alike. Both those exchanges that worked and those that did not should raise our curiosity.

This also pertains to the stranger as a crucial figure in gift exchange. It is not by coincidence that so many exchanges construct strangers as kin and kin as strangers. The positions are translatable into each other – if giver and receiver constitute a momentary, virtual society-as-a-whole, the stranger will be a recurring figure of social difference, the expansion of moral horizons and the speculative character of the gift.

Thus, when we observe the trajectories of objects across landscapes, we may account for this in a range of different ways. The interpretative space I have sketched here would draw attention to phenomena that may have been overlooked or appeared contradictory. Trade that mixes with rituals or marriage, displays of antagonism and feuding in contexts of peaceful exchange, the movement of cosmological ideas, gods and spirits may appear in a different light. The transfer of values and valuables along trade routes then is not so much a side effect of the satisfaction of commercial desires but an expansion of moral horizons which encompass the familiar and the strange in a single, asymmetrical movement.

References

Barraud, C., de Coppet, D., Iteanu, A. and Jamous, R. 1994 *Of Relations and the Dead. Four Societies Viewed from the Angle of Their Exchanges*. Explorations in Anthropology (Oxford)
Bourdieu, P. 1993 *Sozialer Sinn. Kritik der theoretischen Vernunft*, suhrkamp Taschenbuch. Wissenschaft 1066 (Frankfurt am Main)
Caillé, A. 2008 *Anthropologie der Gabe*. Theorie und Gesellschaft 65 (Frankfurt am Main)
Damon, F. H. 2000 From regional relations to ethnic groups? On the transformation of value relations to property claims in the Kula Ring of Papua New Guinea. *The Asia Pacific Journal of Anthropology* 1(2), 49–72
Därmann, I. 2010 *Theorien der Gabe zur Einführung* (Hamburg)
Garnier, F. 1996 *Further Travels in Laos and in Yunnan. The Mekong Exploration Commission Report (1866-1868)* II (Bangkok)
Godelier, M. 2011 *The Metamorphoses of Kinship* (London)
Graeber, D. 2001 *Toward an Anthropological Theory of Value. The False Coin of Our Own Dreams* (New York)
Graeber, D. 2012 *Schulden. Die ersten 5.000 Jahre* (Stuttgart)
Graeber, D. 2013 It is value that brings universes into being. *HAU. Journal of Ethnographic Theory* 3(2), 219–243
Gregory, C. A. 1982 *Gifts and Commodities* (London)
Grimm, C. 2018 *Der Wert der Alten. Multiple Wissensmodelle und Praktiken der Repräsentation in der Entwicklungszusammenarbeit Deutschland/Peru*. Comparative Anthropological Studies in Society, Cosmology and Politics 12 (Münster)
Hahn, H. P. 2015 Marcel Mauss als Ethnologe. In: H. P. Hahn, M. Schmidt and E. Seitz (eds), *Marcel Mauss. Schriften zum Geld*, suhrkamp Taschenbuch. Wissenschaft 2142 (Berlin), 9–24

Hart, K. 2007 Marcel Mauss. In pursuit of the whole. A review essay. *Comparative Studies in Society and History* 49, 473–485

de Josselin de Jong, J. P. B. 1983 Lévi-Strauss' theory on kinship and marriage. In: P. E. de Josselin de Jong (ed.), *Structural Anthropology in the Netherlands. A Reader.* Translation Series 17 (Dordrecht), 253–319

Kopytoff, I. 1986 The cultural biography of things. Commoditization as process. In: A. Appadurai (ed.), *The Social Life of Things. Commodities in Cultural Perspective* (Cambridge), 64–91

Lévi-Strauss, C. 1967 Die Struktur der Mythen. In: C. Lévi-Strauss, *Strukturale Anthropologie* (Frankfurt am Main), 226–254

Lévi-Strauss, C. 1993 *Die elementaren Strukturen der Verwandtschaft, suhrkamp Taschenbuch.* Wissenschaft 1044 (Frankfurt am Main)

Lindell, K., Samuelsson, R. and Tayanin, D. 1979 Kinship and marriage in northern Kammu villages. The kinship model. *Sociologus. Zeitschrift für empirische Ethnosoziologie und Ethnopsychologie* NS 29, 60–84

Malinowski, B. 1964 *Argonauts of the Western Pacific. An Account of Native Enterprise and Adventure in the Archipelagoes of Melanesian New Guinea* (London)

Mauss, M. 2016 *The Gift* (expanded edition, selected, annotated and translated by Jane I. Guyer). (Chicago IL)

McKinnon, S. 2001 The economies in kinship and the paternity of culture. Origin stories in kinship theory. In: S. Franklin and S. McKinnon (eds), *Relative Values. Reconfiguring Kinship Studies* (Durham NC), 277–301

Moebius, S. 2009 Die elementaren (Fremd-)Erfahrungen der Gabe. Sozialtheoretische Implikationen von Marcel Mauss' Kultursoziologie der Besessenheit und des 'radikalen Durkheimismus' des Collège de Sociologie. *Berliner Journal für Soziologie* 19, 104–126

Platenkamp, J. D. M. 2013 Sovereignty in the North Moluccas. Historical transformations. *History and Anthropology* 24, 206–232. <https://doi.org/10.1080/02757206.2012.697062> (accessed: 24 September 2021)

Platenkamp, J. D. M. 2016 Money alive and money dead. In: C. Haselgrove and S. Krmnicek (eds), *The Archaeology of Money. Proceedings of the Workshop 'Archaeology of Money', University of Tübingen, October 2013.* Leicester Archaeology Monograph 24 (Leicester), 161–181

Rio, K. 2014 Melanesian egalitarianism. The containment of hierarchy. *Anthropological Theory* 14, 169–190

Rio, K. M. and Smedal, O. H. 2009 Hierarchy and its alternatives. An introduction to movements of totalization and detotalization. In: K. M. Rio and O. H. Smedal (eds), *Hierarchy. Persistence and Transformation in Social Formations* (New York), 1–63

Robbins, J. 2015 Dumont's hierarchical dynamism. Christianity and individualism revisited. *HAU. Journal of Ethnographic Theory* 5(1), 173–195

Sahlins, M. 1972 On the sociology of primitive exchange. In: M. Sahlins, *Stone Age Economics* (Chicago IL), 185–275

Sahlins, M. 1985 *Islands of History* (Chicago IL)

Sahlins, M. 2000 The sadness of sweetness; or, the native anthropology of western cosmology. In: M. Sahlins, *Culture in Practice. Selected Essays* (New York), 527–583

Sahlins, M. 2008 The stranger-king or, elementary forms of the politics of life. *Indonesia and the Malay World* 36(105), 177–199

Sprenger, G. 2006 *Die Männer, die den Geldbaum fällten. Konzepte von Austausch und Gesellschaft bei den Rmeet von Takheung, Laos.* Comparative Anthropological Studies in Society, Cosmology and Politics 1 (Berlin)

Sprenger, G. 2016 Structured and unstructured misunderstandings. Towards an anthropological theory of misunderstanding. *Civilisations. Revue internationale d'anthropologie et de sciences humaines* 65, 21–38

Sprenger, G., Gregory, C., Retsikas, K., and Hahn, H.-P. 2017 Goods and Ethnicity. Trade and Bazaars in Laos from a Gift Perspective. A Discussion. *Heidelberg Ethnology Occasional Paper* 6, 1–31, <http://journals.ub.uni-heidelberg.de/index.php/hdethn/article/view/42017> (accessed: 6 September 2021)

Sprenger, G. 2019 Die konstitutiven Widersprüche der Gabe, *Paideuma. Zeitschrift für kulturanthropologische Forschung* 65, 139–156

Stirrat, R. L. and Henkel, H. 1997 The development gift. The problem of reciprocity in the NGO world. *The Annals of the American Academy of Political and Social Science* 554, 66–80

Strathern, M. 1988 *The Gender of the Gift. Problems with Women and Problems with Society in Melanesia.* Studies in Melanesian Anthropology (Berkeley CA)

Strathern, M. 1992 Qualified value. The perspective of gift exchange. In: C. Humphrey and S. Hugh-Jones (eds), *Barter, Exchange and Value. An Anthropological Approach* (Cambridge), 169–191

Viveiros de Castro, E. 2016 Claude Lévi-Strauss, Begründer des Poststrukturalismus. In: E. Viveiros de Castro, *Die Unbeständigkeit der wilden Seele. Aus dem brasilianischen Portugiesisch von Oliver Precht* (Vienna), 406–431

Weiner, A. B. 1976 *Women of Value, Men of Renown. New Perspectives in Trobriand Exchange* (Austin TX)

Weiner, A. B. 1988 *The Trobrianders of Papua New Guinea.* Case Studies in Cultural Anthropology (New York)

Yang, B. 2019 *Cowrie Shells and Cowrie Money. A Global History.* Routledge Approaches to History (Abingdon)

Znoj, H. 1995 *Tausch und Geld in Zentralsumatra. Zur Kritik des Schuldbegriffes in der Wirtschaftsethnologie,* Berner Sumatra-Forschungen (Berlin)

Part II

Re-evaluations

Chapter 8

Introduction to Part II: Re-evaluations

Anja Klöckner and Dirk Wicke

It is a wintry Saturday afternoon, in Vienna and we are on the site where the large flea market on the famous *Naschmarkt* has taken place since the early morning. All people are gone, dealers, buyers, curious onlookers, strollers, tourists. But various objects are left lying on the floor. They have not been sold and dealers did not care to repack them and take them along. There are, for example, a miniature model of the Eiffel Tower, various parts of tableware, a pair of shoes and of shoelaces, a clock, various brass objects, door mountings and gaskets or packing washers, some of them still in the original packaging (Figs 8.1a and 8.2a).

These objects were produced, offered for sale, partly used, partly never really used conforming to their original function. At some point, after having gone through many waypoints, they were resold or passed on and were now supposed to find new users via the flea market. However, apparently nobody needed such coat hangers or washers, as can be seen in our illustrations; nobody had been searching for a souvenir to remind them of a last trip to Paris. Nevertheless, even aside from functional, aesthetic and semantic aspects, some of these objects are not totally worthless, not even from a pecuniary point of view. The brass plates, for example, might earn proceeds with a scrap metal dealer. At least, these objects might have a certain tangible value. But here, they are rubbish; or, to use the well-known, even though highly disputed definition of Mary Douglas: 'a matter out of place'.[1] Yet, instead of being collected in a trash bin or finally stored on a dump, the objects are lying scattered on the pavement, clearly posing (minor) threats to traffic safety, at least attracting the attention of an engaged observer and causing public nuisance.

On this Saturday afternoon on the Vienna flea market, in any case, nobody ascribed any value to these objects. Someone would have just needed to pick them up – but nobody did. Nobody needed them, nobody wanted them; not even for free. These objects have become worthless and meaningless for individual practices of use. They

---

[1] Douglas 1966.

remained on the floor, unheeded. From there, they would have been removed by the road sweepers of the Viennese cleansing department and thereby further processed and recycled by administrative action or dumped.

Unless … they had not finally found an interested party who picked them up. The Swiss artist Daniel Spoerri has attended to these objects and arranged them to several assemblages creating works of art (Figs 8.1 a–b and 8.2 a–b). Partly bearing titles like *Das Allerletzte/The Very Last* or *Das Ende/The End*, rather subtly indicated by the lettering.

Mostly simply numbered like assemblage #19, *Das Allerletzte/The Very Last* has finally become a piece of artwork. Under the exhibition title *Was bleibt/What Remains*, the series was shown in several galleries and museums. Curator Kai Schupke[2] has described Spoerri's work as follows:

> Spoerri collects old things on garbage dumps and flea markets. By collecting unused things that have been marginalized, repressed, discarded by society, objects that have fallen out of their cycle of service, no longer have a place in the order of things he draws attention to the system of culture with its mechanisms of devaluation and exclusion.[3]

These works of Spoerri may demonstrate one essential, often repeated argument of Michael Thompsons *Rubbish Theory*:[4] the value of things does not lie within the object but is the result of social and cultural conventions. In our case, the habituated practices of art reception and the elaborate marketing strategies of the art market ensure that 'a real Spoerri' becomes an object of desire, although the objects themselves did not attract attention anymore in another context. We are dealing with an exponential enhancement in value, concerning both the monetary and the ideational aspect.

A transient object that declines in value and life span can linger in a valueless and timeless limbo of rubbish until it is discovered by a creative individual and transferred into something deemed durable. Unsaleable objects become high-priced products; formerly discarded things are now elaborately exhibited in galleries, carefully staged by curators, attentively observed by people interested in arts and intensively discussed by scholars. In this case, the objects have been passed through a process of drastic up-valuation. Such up-valuation has been achieved by staging and reframing single items. The loosely scattered and spurned articles are glued to a solid ground and thus become immovable and inextricably linked with each other. They have been permanently brought into a new context with other objects by the artist Spoerri, transformed into art. Spoerri changes the levels of perception and reality for the users by a simple interference: he tilts the objects' presentation from a horizontal to a vertical view. This demands a new interpretation of single object and collage. The rubbish on the ground is transformed to an *oeuvre d'art* hanging on the wall. Here, the cycle of usage contains use, re-use, de-use and re-use again, but also

---

[2] Curator in the Gallery Henze & Ketterer & Triebold, Wichtrach/Bern and Riehen/Basel.
[3] http://myartguides.com/exhibitions/daniel-spoerr-was-bliebtbildertollwut/.
[4] Thompson 1979.

8. Introduction to Part II: Re-evaluations

Figure 8.1. Daniel Spoerri: 30 WAS BLEIBT (Ende), Flohmarkt Vienna, Samstag 27.2.2016 16h, *Assemblage, 2016, 80 × 120 cm <https://www.galerie-krinzinger.at/exhibitions/30257/was-bleibt-bildertollwut/works/198183/30-was-bleibt-ende-flohmarkt-vienna-samstag-27-02-2016-16h/>.*

selling and repeated re-selling. The aura of the work of art opens a new dimension for the re-evaluation of the objects.

Taking this as a tangible starting point, we will now turn to some general remarks. Many objects and things are made for specific purposes and thus receive an initial or primary practical value in fulfilling those primary aims. Once they are removed from their primary context or fall into desuetude, objects or things can undergo a process of new ascription. This 're-ascriptive process' is not necessarily accompanied by a respective devaluation. Whereas putting the objects to waste may be the most extreme form of dis-use, namely non-use, recycling or secondary, sometimes even tertiary, use may result in new forms of value, which might constitute a higher, sometimes even a secondary value contrary to the primary one.[5]

There are many examples of such re-evaluations as a result of secondary uses during various social and ritual practices from antiquity until today. The ascription of symbolic and sacral value to previously profane objects, e.g. in the creation of religious relics, provides a case for the re-ascription of value by ritualising as social practice. In performing rituals – be it healing or harming rituals, purification, oath or divination rituals – objects are transformed into 'magical materials' (*materia magica*) outside of their primarily intended use and everyday context. In both processes, the change from the mundane to the sacral sphere is connected with an actual and striking up-valuation of re-used things. The reason for selecting specific objects for such up-valuation mostly remains unanswered, in particular when referring to events from the past. Similarly, the staging and reframing of objects in secondary use stresses particular, characteristic traits of things. Whether we deal with the aesthetic staging of antique ceramics in modern art museums or with the pronounced display of family heirlooms in domestic houses, former everyday objects receive new values irrespective of their primary value in order to create identity and legitimation of individuals, of smaller or larger groups. One frequent factor, however, remains a gain in social prestige – which in turn underlines the nature of re-evaluation as a social practice. Ritualising, staging and reframing are exemplar social practices in which not only objects but also places or acts can receive a redefinition of value – connoting devaluation, re-evaluation or up-valuation.

Following the cross-disciplinary structure of the Frankfurt Research Training Group, the 2017 conference *Re-Evaluations. On the Ascription of Value in Social and Ritual Practices*[6] intended to open various perspectives onto this phenomenon from archaeological and anthropological points of view. The conference brought together case studies from various disciplines in order to illustrate and discuss cases and phenomena from different disciplines. Papers delivered intended to address questions

---

[5] Cf. Thompson 1979 on his theory of rubbish.
[6] The conference took place on 23–25 November 2017 at the Goethe-University, Frankfurt am Main.

8. Introduction to Part II: Re-evaluations 147

Figure 8.2. Daniel Spoerri: 19 WAS BLEIBT, Flohmarkt Vienna, Samstag 2.1.2016, *Assemblage, 2015–2016, 110 × 140 × 40 cm <https://www.galerie-krinzinger.at/exhibitions/30257/was-bleibt-bildertollwut/works/833260/19-was-bleibt-flohmarkt-vienna-samstag-02-jaenner-2016/>*

such as 'Why are certain objects deemed fit to serve another purpose beyond the primary one?' or even contrast the primary and secondary contexts of use.[7]

A clear case for re-evaluation is illustrated by the study of Andreas Hartmann on the use of relics in Greek temples. Mythological stories and the perception of 'ancientness' – be it fiction or truth – played very important roles for the acknowledgment as relics. In particular, old objects were reframed with stories alluding to gods and heroes perpetuating the former glory to its new contexts.

Alexander Ahrens studies the presence of Egyptian imports in Syrian sites during the 2nd millennium BCE in elite, ritual or funerary contexts. Removed from their original context, Egyptian finds were reconceptualised in the Levant and in parts obviously equipped with a completely new function and meaning in Syria. It is particularly interesting to note a pattern of appropriation, in that there seems to be a reeling attitude towards Egyptian material culture, oscillating between embrace and rejection.

The use of *spolia* is a very common phenomenon in particular during Late Antiquity, with a growing scarcity of raw material and a quest for 'historic confirmation' by referring back to older, classical shapes and motifs. Gabrielle Kremer can demonstrate, however, that the use of *spolia* is much more than a simple re-use of stone but that there are cases of profound reflections and a deliberate handling of Roman artefacts. The range of practices and re-uses of earlier building materials at the site of Carnuntum illustrates the spectrum of secondary uses and re-evaluations in general, based on stone as a building resource.

Lucy Norris points out another range of approaches to re-used materials as a resource, namely at the example of textiles. From a local to international level, textiles provide an excellent example for the differing cultural attitudes not only as an economic but also as a social factor. Waste becomes a material resource or even a piece of artistic handicraft, as Spoerri has crafted the leftovers of a Viennese flea market into works of art.

Thomas Widlok approaches the issue of re-evaluation from a similar view, deriving from his ethnographic fieldwork. The used appearance of objects becomes a 'trademark' and sign for value in itself. In contrast to the frequent assumption, a second use can testify value in itself and objects therefore cannot be put to waste at all. Even broken objects are valuable and should be considered as an 'unbiased resource' – they simply might not have found their proper use yet. The 'used look' does not contain a pejorative meaning and is not an incidence of downgrading. This point of view, based on the notion that there is no primary value in the first instance but rather simply a change in use and value, questions the validity of a concept of re-evaluation at all.

---

[7] An initial workshop entitled 'Zwischen Pragmatismus und Inszenierung. Zur sekundären Nutzung von Objekten, Orten, Räumen und Landschaften in prähistorischen und antiken Gesellschaften' took place in Frankfurt in February 2017, yet solely focusing on archaeological phenomena.

A similar degree of reframing is addressed by James Whitley in his contribution, which is even more concerned with the consequences for the concept of art in general. He attempts to achieve a different, a new look onto the context, status and notion of art – in particular in classical archaeology – and warns against any objective or universal definition of art.

In sum, the contributions in the second part of this volume demonstrate the wide range of approaches and interpretations in judging the change of uses of objects. As a major strand from the discussion it can be argued that there is no clear direction in the perception of 'use-value' – be it upwards or downwards – neither in the continuous change of uses, nor even in case of periods of non-use. It seems as if use is a value in itself and the appreciation of such value depends on societal context.[8]

This leaves us with large variety of phenomena related to changes in value(s) (Fig. 8.3). Main factors remain time, space and (human) agents, which provide the frame for such phenomena depending on the range of time or space, in which the change in value takes place, or the kind or number of agents participating in the process of change. These factors will influence the identification of any phenomenon of change to a large extent. The nature of change is also depending on the societal scale and context: intra-cultural, inter-cultural or trans-cultural context can lead to differing phenomena of change and affect the spread of secondary values. The wider the gap in time, space or society, the more drastic such change can become. To that respect, change can even lead to complete breaks in use, the most drastic outcome of re-evaluation. In any case, there is a gradual range between break and change, without clear-cut limits for a distant observer. In turn, a perception of change or break of course depends on the above-mentioned factors of time, space and agent: the temporal and/or spatial separation of primary and secondary agents.

In case of intracultural re-evaluations, we are most likely dealing with the same actors or at least with a similar cultural background at least within a 'human' span of time. Because of that, an awareness of the primary value can often be assumed. Any radical break appears as a sudden 'twist of history', a revolution or catastrophe. In contrast, gradual change seems more connected to processes of forgetting and remembrance, influenced by factors of knowledge and awareness.

In contrast to this stand the constellations of trans- and intercultural re-evaluation of material culture, the ascription of value across societal borders. Here, the re-evaluating actors are different from the primary creators, which entails the issue of the relationship between those primary and secondary agents for a proper interpretation. Trans- or intercultural re-evaluation appears to be rather prone to radical breaks; re-evaluations seem to surface as appropriation or annexation. The (re-)ascribed value in inter- or transcultural secondary use is often rooted within this 'otherness'. This

---

[8] It appears as an interesting conclusion to muse about the re-evaluation not only of objects but also of ideas. Can we observe similar practices in the use and non-use of earlier body of thoughts or previous intellectual achievements? Can we recognise similar mechanisms of up- and downgrading of ideas according to changing societal environments and hermeneutics?

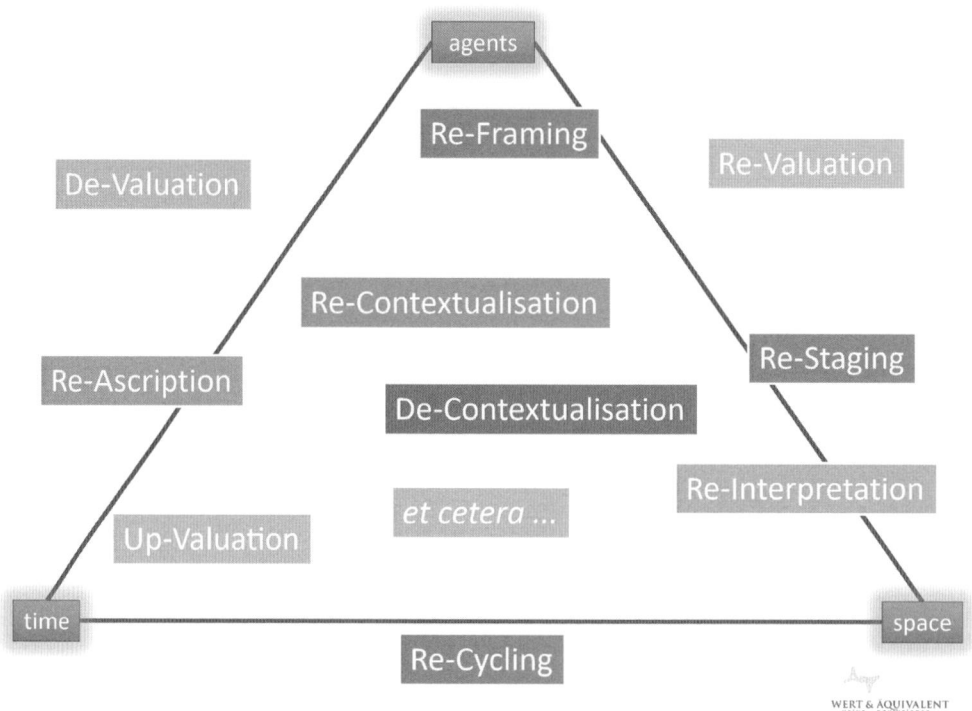

Figure 8.3. Exemplary modi of re-evaluations (layout: Dirk Wicke).

calls the topic of exoticism onto the stage, which is also addressed in the papers by Widlok or Ahrens. A third parameter, relevant to the understanding of phenomena of change remains space. Like time, space separates the agents and contributes to the degree, the quality and nature of change. Shifting agents and the widening of spatial and temporal distances prepare the grounds for profound phenomena of re-evaluations and a completely new horizon for their interpretation opens up to the thinker in particular once the change from material to immaterial value is studied.

References

Douglas, M. 1966 *Purity and Danger. An Analysis of Concepts of Pollution and Taboo* (London)
Thompson, M. 1979 *Rubbish Theory. The Creation and Destruction of Value* (Oxford)

Chapter 9

Recycling Egypt? The phenomenon of secondary re-use of Egyptian imports in the Northern Levant during the 2nd millennium BCE

Alexander Ahrens

> ... I have been all my life a dealer in antiquities, and I have imbibed the shadows of fallen columns of Balbec, and Tadmor, and Persepolis, until my very soul has become a ruin...
>
> (Edgar Allan Poe, taken from *MS. Found in a Bottle*, 1833)

Trash or treasure? Re-use, recycling or re-evaluation?

One of the most striking phenomena of the material culture of the Northern Levant during the 2nd millennium BCE is the presence of Egyptian objects in elite, ritual or funerary contexts. The presence of the Middle Kingdom Egyptian statuary and other inscribed Egyptian objects found in the Levant has been – and still is – the subject of much controversy. In the early days of Levantine archaeology and Egyptology, these Egyptian objects were used to synchronise and connect the Egyptian chronology with the, at that time still largely unknown, regional chronologies of the Levant. They were thus perceived as a secure means to give absolute dates for their finding, primarily based on the almost axiomatic assumption that they once were part of an existing gift exchange which took place between the Egyptian kings named on the objects and the Levantine rulers or even served as archaeological proof of an alleged 'Egyptian empire' in the Levant during the Middle Kingdom which exercised direct political control.

The seminal studies by James M. Weinstein[1] and Wolfgang Helck[2] presented a completely different approach to the statues' presence in the Levant and proposed a revised date for their dispatch from Egypt. According to Weinstein and Helck, most of the Egyptian statuary found in the Levant arrived there only later, i.e. during the

---
[1] Weinstein 1975.
[2] Helck 1971; 1976.

Second Intermediate Period, when statues and other inscribed objects dating to the Middle Kingdom were looted from temples, cultic installations and tombs alike. At that time, a similar scenario concerning Egyptian objects found in the Aegean had also already been put forward by Leon Pomerance.[3] Weinstein's as well as Helck's argumentation was based on the inscriptions of these statues – linking the titles, names, toponyms or gods and their associated cults mentioned in the inscriptions with the place of their original setup in Egypt – and the date of the objects' find contexts in the Levant.

Evidence of a dispatch of Middle Kingdom statuary and other inscribed objects to the Levant during the Second Intermediate Period may now be supported by new archaeological evidence from both Egypt and the Northern Levant. Clearly, most of these objects were brought to the Levant only after their initial and primary use and function in Egypt – judging on the basis of typology or the hieroglyphic inscriptions, i.e. their respective 'object biographies', to use a term coined by Igor Kopytoff[4] in Arjun Appadurai's influential volume *The Social Life of Things* – and thus apparently received a secondary and completely redefined function after their dispatch to the Bronze Age Northern Levant.

In many cases such observations are obstructed by undefined or unknown archaeological find contexts, hampering an exact identification of the objects' uses in the Levant; in other cases, missing inscriptions make tracing the specific objects' biographies impossible – yet, one needs to securely reconstruct both possible patterns of translocations and differentiating perceptions. Apart from chronological issues regarding the dispatch of these objects, an examination of the reception of these imports by the local elites, their appropriation within Northern Levantine material (and ritual) culture and incorporation into different contexts of use may help to shed new light on the modalities and strategies behind their re-use. The patterns seem to reveal a dialectic approach between the embrace and rejection of certain Egyptian objects and motifs of authority by the local Levantine elites.[5]

Concerning terminology, several general observations may be stated here. While the term 're-use' would seem to simply imply a second use of any given object, a 're-evaluation' would do so, too, but at the same time would also additionally imply a second – and different to the object's original conception – 'perception' being ascribed to the object in question. The term 'recycling' in turn would imply that an object is made of parts or components of one or even more objects, known or unknown in their original conception, thus creating an entirely new object with a different perception. It is apparent that it is not always easy to assign a specific object to just one of the categories described above, as in most cases, each object in question would seem to

---

[3] Pomerance 1973.
[4] Kopytoff 1986.
[5] Cf. also Ahrens 2020.

belong to many of these categories.[6] Also, an amalgamation of these categories is usually the case, e.g. the terms 're-use' and 'recycling' are being used in the same way when referring to material objects that have multiple life circles.

While it is out of scope of the present paper to cover all Egyptian objects found at various sites in the Northern Levant, a compilation of a selection of Egyptian finds with significant and meaningful find contexts from the site of Tell Mišrife/Qatna may suffice to emphasise the implications of the present argument. The Egyptian finds discussed here are finds from the Bronze Age royal palace and the Royal Tomb and Tomb VII at Tell Mišrife/Qatna, discovered in the years 2002 and 2010 respectively. To complement the picture of the re-use of Egyptian objects described in the present paper, one peculiar find from the site of Tell Mardikh/Ebla, which is also located in the Northern Levant, is also presented.

The Bronze Age Northern Levant and Tell Mišrife/Qatna – history, location and geographical setting

Already in the late 4th to early 3rd millennium BCE, intensive relations between Egypt and the Levant are well attested in the archaeological record. Primarily based on trade and the exchange of goods between the Levantine littoral and Egypt, a great number of various Egyptian imports in contexts dating to the 3rd millennium BCE were found at the important harbour city of Byblos and even farther inland at Tell Mardikh, ancient Ebla. During the 2nd millennium BCE, i.e. the Middle and Late Bronze Ages, these relations intensified, and there is a growing body of archaeological and historical evidence for the relations and political contacts between the two regions. While the Middle Bronze Age (c. 2000–1550 BCE) saw the emergence of mighty and powerful Levantine city states actively engaging and participating in trade networks spanning the entire Eastern Mediterranean, the Late Bronze Age (c. 1550–1250 BCE) in the Northern Levant was characterised by a period of Egyptian, Mittanian and later Hittite domination. Despite this political domination by these foreign powers, the Levantine rulers themselves managed to keep at least part of their political power and influence over the region at all times during the 2nd millennium,[7] As Egyptian control in the area was probably very benign, the local rulers reigned more or less

---

[6] Michael Thompson's *Rubbish Theory* (Thompson 1979) distinguishes between three types of things: durables, transients and rubbish. A durable is an object that does not lose its value over time and is not destroyed over time (at least not in the easily foreseeable future). A transient is an ordinary everyday object and rubbish is, well, rubbish. A transient can only transcend into the durable category by first becoming rubbish and then by being 'saved' by someone who gives new and perhaps (or likely) different meaning to it. Clearly, the Egyptian objects were indeed objects that once had a specific meaning, which at the time of their dispatch to the Levant was not deemed important anymore, because their original meaning, function and use was not known anymore, the individuals depicted or mentioned long dead (and probably forgotten). If these objects were considered 'rubbish' by the Egyptians, we simply do not know (it is unlikely, given the enormous amount of devotion for the past by the Egyptians), but they were certainly valued by the Levantine elites, although in a totally different way of perception.
[7] Helck 1971; Akkermans and Schwartz 2003.

autonomously as long as they continued to pay annual tribute to their overlords. In return, Egypt, but also Mittani and Hatti, benefitted from trade which passed goods through the region.

The site of Tell Mišrife, ancient Qatna, is located on the eastern side of the Wadi Zora in the upper Orontes Valley, approximately 17 km north-east of the modern city of Homs. The site, *c.* 110 ha in size, occupies the strategic crossing point of the important trade routes passing south to north, from the Southern Levant via the Beqaʿa Valley, and east to west along the southern route, from Mesopotamia via Mari and Tadmor towards the Mediterranean coast via the 'Gap of Homs' and the Akkar plain. The site emerges as one of inland Syria's and the Northern Levant's major urban centres during the Middle Bronze Age. During the Late Bronze Age, due to the alternating domination of the region by the empires of the Mittani, Egyptians and Hittites, Qatna's political power diminished, but the city remained one of the important city-states in Syria until its final destruction around 1340 BCE. The city's urban structure is dominated by public buildings, almost all of them identified as palaces and almost all clustered within the city's centre. Not much is known about the layout and structure of the rest of the city, which is surrounded by large earthen ramparts, each side measuring approximately 1 km.

As one of the most, if not *the* most, important city state in the Northern Levant during most of the Bronze Age, there is a large body of Egyptian imports found at the site. Not surprisingly, a concentration and clustering of Egyptian artefacts is found within the area of the royal palace.

From Egyptian princess to Near Eastern goddess? – the Sphinx of Ita and the shrine of the Belet-Ekallim (Nin-Egal) in the royal palace of Qatna

The most prominent Egyptian object found within the Bronze Age royal palace of Qatna is the so-called Sphinx of Ita, dating to the 12th Dynasty.[8] The sphinx was discovered in 1927 by the French archaeologist Robert Comte du Mesnil du Buisson[9] in the central area of the palace – more precisely within the so-called *sanctuaire* or the shrine of the goddess Belet-ekallim or Nin-Egal (*Bēlet-ekalli*[*m*], ^{d}NIN.É.GAL)[10] in the central part of the palace[11] (Figs 9.1–9.2).

Fragmented into more than 400 pieces, the sphinx, made of schist, was found within the debris of the Late Bronze Age palace and thus must have been displayed

---

[8] Paris, Louvre, inv. AO 13075.
[9] Count Robert du Mesnil du Buisson (9 April 1895, Bourges–8 April 1986, Caen) was a French archaeologist and soldier. He was the son of Auguste, Comte du Mesnil du Buisson and Berthe Roussel de Courcy. Interestingly, he named one of his daughters 'Ita'.
[10] For a thorough compilation of the historical sources pertaining to this specific goddess, see De Clercq 2003.
[11] Mesnil du Buisson 1928, 9–12 pls 6, 6; 12; 1935, 71–79.

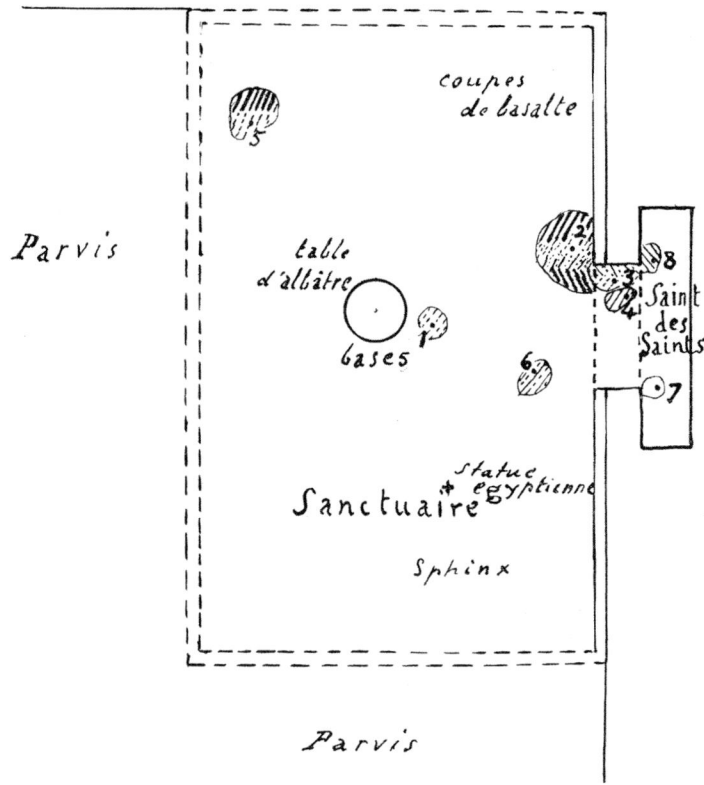

Figure 9.1. The sanctuaire *and the* saint des saints *with clusters of finds, including the findspots of the 'Sphinx of Ita' and the second Egyptian statue (after Mesnil du Buisson 1928, pl. 7).*

at the time of its destruction (Fig. 9.3).[12] In the immediate vicinity of the sphinx, several fragments of another statue made of calcite-alabaster were found, belonging to a royal statue, most probably that of a king of the Middle Kingdom (i.e. dating to the 12th–13th Dynasties) depicted in a kneeling position, presumably offering *nw*-pots in his hands (Fig. 9.4).[13]

An inscription is positioned between the forelegs of the sphinx, indicating that the sphinx once was used in a funerary context. It consists of a single column and reads:

---

[12] The object is now kept in the collections of the ancient Near East at the Louvre (Louvre, inv. AO 13075) and would require yet another study of recontextualisation in itself.
[13] Mesnil du Buisson 1928, 10 pl. 14, 1. The present location of the fragments of this statue is unknown.

Figure 9.2. The sanctuaire *and the* saint des saints *seen from the south-east; note that in the photograph the* saint des saints *has already been rebuild with a mudbrick structure by the excavator (after Mesnil du Buisson 1935, pl. 21, 1).*

> [1] jrj.t-pˤ.t sȝ.t njswt mrw.t=f n.t-ẖ.t=f Jtȝ nb.t jmȝḫ.w
> The hereditary princess, the king's beloved daughter,
> of his body, Ita, possessor of honour

The inscription makes it quite likely that the sphinx once was used in a funerary context. In Egypt, the tomb of Princess Ita was discovered in 1895 (12 February) by the French archaeologist and then Director of Egyptian Antiquities, Jacques de Morgan, within the precinct of the burial complex of Amenemhat II at Dahshur. Ita's tomb was part of a double tomb complex which also contained the tomb of another princess named Chnumit.[14] Interestingly, a statue of a princess with the name of Chnumit has been found at the site of Ras Šamra/Ugarit at the Northern Levantine coast but unfortunately comes from an unsecure find context.

Accepting that the Sphinx of Ita found at Qatna may have originated from a funerary context – possibly the princess's tomb complex underground or associated

---

[14] Ahrens 2006, 26–27; 2010, 20–21.

mortuary chapel above ground – such a late date for these tombs would also be of great importance for establishing a possible date of the dispatch of the sphinx from Egypt to Qatna. Apart from the uncertainties concerning the historical chronology and the exact position of this specific Princess Ita within the 12th Dynasty, her sphinx, in any case, most probably arrived at Qatna only at a later date. A scenario involving the looting of the princess's tomb or cultic installations also seems likely to have been the case here.[15]

The 'Shrine of Belet-ekallim' of Qatna – the lady of the palace, i.e. the goddess presiding over the religious activities and the fate of the palace of Qatna and its line of kings – is located in the north-eastern part of Hall C and consists of one single room – Room P – with an area in front of this room relabelled 'Enclosure GO' by the German mission and referred to more poetically as *saint des saints* and *sanctuaire* by the French excavator (Fig. 9.1).[16] Cuneiform documents (the 'Qatna inventories') were found within Room P and the adjacent Enclosure GO by the du Mesnil du Buisson list and describe the *šukuttum* (i.e. inventory of jewellery or literally 'jewel-box') belonging to the goddess Belet-ekallim and other 'gods of the king'.[17]

Enclosure GO, the '*sanctuaire*', clearly exhibits characteristics of a sacred area used for a cultic function which was separated by a low threshold of wood, indicated by a 10–15 cm wide groove in the lime floor.[18] This served as a visual border to separate Hall C from the cultic Enclosure GO and Room P. Within Enclosure GO, the Sphinx of Ita and the fragments of the above-mentioned second Egyptian statue were found – along with other cultic paraphernalia, such as basalt tripod bowls and a large platter apparently made of calcite-alabaster – not documented in any other part of the palace. It is probable that such objects were used in cultic rituals, perhaps serving as containers for offerings to the goddess and her cult. Room P, which was only accessible via Enclosure GO, served as an *adyton*, where apparently the jewellery of the goddess was once kept. Interestingly, there are references to a statue for some of the jewellery mentioned, making it possible that a large amount of jewellery actually adorned a statue or statues.[19] Yet, apart from the Sphinx of Ita and the other Egyptian statue, albeit male, other statues or fragments thereof were not discovered within this area. Apparently jewellery was found neither in Enclosure GO nor in Room P, but the scattered distribution of the cuneiform documents within Enclosure GO and Room P also shows that the tablets were probably taken from their original place of storage (most likely Room P) shortly before the destruction of the palace. This scenario would also make it highly likely that the jewellery, easy to carry away, would have been plundered, too.

---

[15] Ahrens 2006, 26–27; 2010, 20–21; 2011b.
[16] Mesnil du Buisson 1928, 9–16; 1935, 71–79; Pfälzner 2015, 425–428; Geith *et al.* 2019; Pfälzner and Schmid 2019.
[17] Virolleaud 1928; 1930; Bottéro 1949; 1950; Richter 2004; Roßberger 2015, 303–361.
[18] Pfälzner 2015, 426.
[19] Virolleaud 1928; 1930; Bottéro 1949; 1950; Richter 2004; Roßberger 2015, 308.

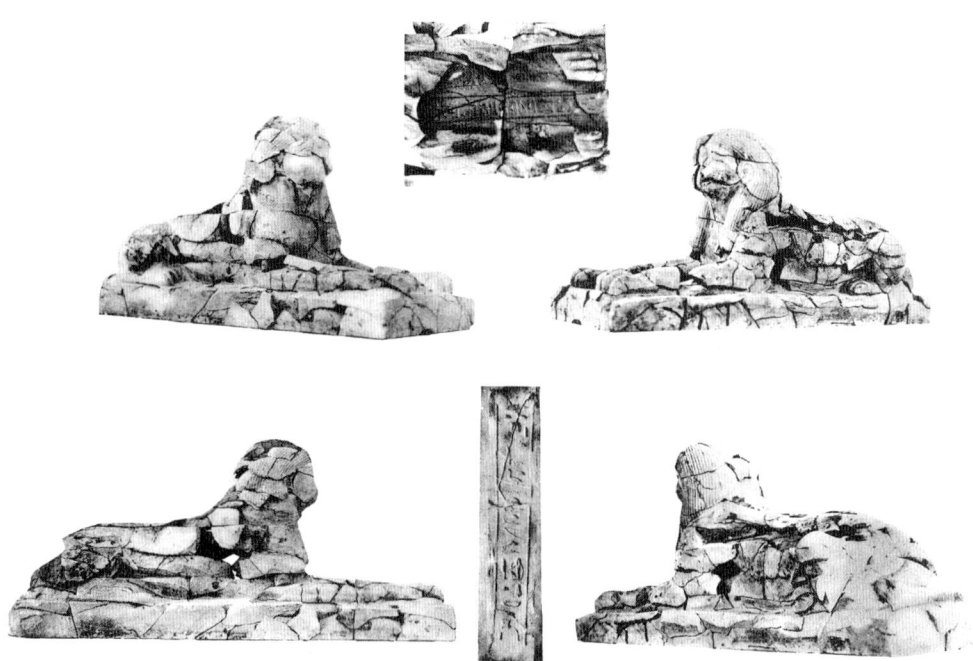

Figure 9.3. The restored 'Sphinx of Ita' with inscription (after Mesnil du Buisson 1928, pl. 12).

It is therefore possible that the Sphinx of Ita was considered a (presumably not the only) representation of the Belet-ekallim of Qatna, with the second Egyptian statue – that of a seated Egyptian king – maybe a representation of one of the kings of Qatna or perhaps a male god belonging to the royal sphere?[20] Located in the central part of the palace, the shrine was openly integrated into the layout of the palace, with the goddess residing in the epicentre of political power within the kingdom of Qatna – located between the throne and banqueting rooms and the large Hall C of the royal palace. In Hall C, a large number of people were thus able to witness ceremonies performed within Enclosure GO and Room P.

The objects, intriguingly, were presented within the cultic area until the destruction of the palace, i.e. *c*. 1340 BCE. This means that the sphinx – and possibly also the second Egyptian statue which is more difficult to date stylistically – were almost 500 years old, thus antiquities in their own right, at the time of the destruction of the palace

---

[20] While the cuneiform documents from the inventories explicitly mention a cultic statue made of red gold (Roßberger 2015, 308), this fact does not necessarily exclude the possibility that other statues, made of other materials, were also in use within the enclosure. Additionally, it is clear from the inventories that not only the goddess Belet-ekallim but also other gods, e.g. the 'gods of the king' were worshipped here, making it likely that other statues were present, too (also Roßberger 2015, 312–315).

Figure 9.4. Fragments of a kneeling statue from the sanctuaire, perhaps that of an Egyptian king, probably dating to the Middle Kingdom (after Mesnil du Buisson 1928, pl. 14, 1).

of Qatna. It is, however, unclear whether the royal elite of Qatna were fully aware of this fact and, for the purpose of re-evaluation and re-use of the statues within the palace, this may not have been of major significance since stylistic details and their intrinsic chronological implications concerning Egyptian statuary were most probably unknown at the court of Qatna. The interpretation of this peculiar context, admittedly not proven with certainty, is hampered but not refuted by the fact that thus far no other shrine dedicated to the goddess Nin-Egal with an original inventory has been identified in the entire ancient Near East, apart from many references within the historical sources.[21] The above proposed 'Egyptianising interpretation' of

---

[21] Novák 2002; De Clercq 2003 with a thorough compilation of the sources. While there are several mentions of the goddess in sources from Mari, Emar and even Ugarit, only one further archaeological attestation of a possible sanctuary of the goddess, apart from that at Qatna, has been proposed to have

a part of the shrine of Nin-Egal and the royal cult – i.e. the emulation of Egyptian motifs or use of Egyptian objects within the royal sphere – is also evidenced in the glyptic material found at the site, where a cuneiform tablet issued by one of the Late Bronze Age kings of Qatna – Addu-nīrārī – features a strongly Egyptianising seal impression with a cartouche, the emblematic presentation of royalty in Egypt.[22] This shows that during this period – since the destruction level of the shrine and the findspot of this cuneiform tablet date to the same period – the kings of Qatna were strongly emulating Egyptian motifs. This would then also seem to substantiate the interpretation presented above of the shrine and the Egyptian statues found within it, although it cannot be proven.

The two Egyptian statues, the female royal sphinx and the male royal statue, were not originally used as an ensemble in Egypt but only placed together at Qatna. This re-use is apparent not only because the statues were never conceived as an ensemble but also that, at least for the sphinx, a funerary context is applicable on the basis of the inscription, which links the object with the tomb of this princess in Egypt. Unfortunately, such a concise contextualisation cannot be established for the second statue. At Qatna, quite contrarily, both Egyptian statues were set up in the centre of the royal palace; not in a funerary context, albeit also in a cultic function. Apart from an apparent re-use of these objects within the shrine, a re-evaluation of the Egyptian objects is not easily detected, as their apotropaic and protective features may also well have been perceived by the rulers of Qatna.

Yet another Middle Kingdom princess – Itakayet and Tomb VII at Qatna

In 2009, a second undisturbed tomb (referred to as 'Tomb VII') was discovered underneath the north-western part of the royal palace. It consists of an antechamber and a double kidney-shaped chamber. The tomb contained at least 79 individuals in a striking contrast to the much bigger Royal Tomb VI which contained far fewer remains.[23] It has been suggested that Tomb VII was a place for reburial; the very long period of the Royal Hypogeum's usage meant that it needed to be cleared sometimes to make room for new interments, and the older remains were transferred to Tomb VII.

The tomb contained numerous precious objects, among them more than 100 Egyptian and Egyptianising stone vessels of various types and materials, including also one stone vessel with an inscription of yet another Middle Kingdom princess (Fig. 9.5).

The inscription reads:

---

existed in the royal palace at Tell Hariri/Mari, see De Clercq (2003, 91–94). It has to be noted here that the site of Mari, located at the Euphrates, is clearly too far away from the Levantine coast to have been influenced by Egyptian imagery. Therefore, an Egyptianising influence within the shrine of the goddess at Mari seems also unlikely.

[22] Elsen-Novák 2003, 153–154, fig. 16b.
[23] Pfälzner and Dohmann-Pfälzner 2011.

¹ jrj.t-pꜥ.t sꜣ.t njswt n.t-ẖ.t=f Jtꜣkꜣ<y>t nb.t jmꜣḫ.w
The hereditary princess, the king's daughter, of his body,
Itakayet, possessor of honour

Again, the inscription points to a funerary use of the vessel.²⁴ Apart from the implications of the inscription, which also strikingly resembles the inscription of Ita's Sphinx, the period of use of Tomb VII (Middle Bronze Age IIB–Late Bronze Age IA) suggests that the vessel must have been deposited within the tomb during the later part of the Middle Bronze Age or the very beginning of the Late Bronze Age, i.e. the Second Intermediate Period or the early 18th Dynasty. Given this time frame, a dispatch of the vessel during the Hyksos Period seems likely. Fortunately, a tomb of princess Itakayet is attested archaeologically. Unfortunately though, two tombs (pyramids) are known to have existed for a princess with that name, one within the pyramid precinct of Senwosret I ('Pyramid 2'), the other within the pyramid precinct of Senwosret III ('Pyramid 3'). Thus far, due to the scanty archaeological and inscriptional evidence found at these two pyramids, it cannot be determined with certainty who of the two princesses must be linked with the stone vessel from Tomb VII.²⁵ Both of the princesses' tombs, however, were plundered during the Second Intermediate Period (late 13th–15th Dynasty), leaving little doubt that the vessel from Tomb VII was part of the loot of one of these pyramids.

In this way, Egyptian objects may have reached the Levant well after their original deposition by 're-entering the life cycle' as valuable and prestigious objects. Following this argument, a date sometime after the 12th Dynasty would seem most plausible, since almost all the burial

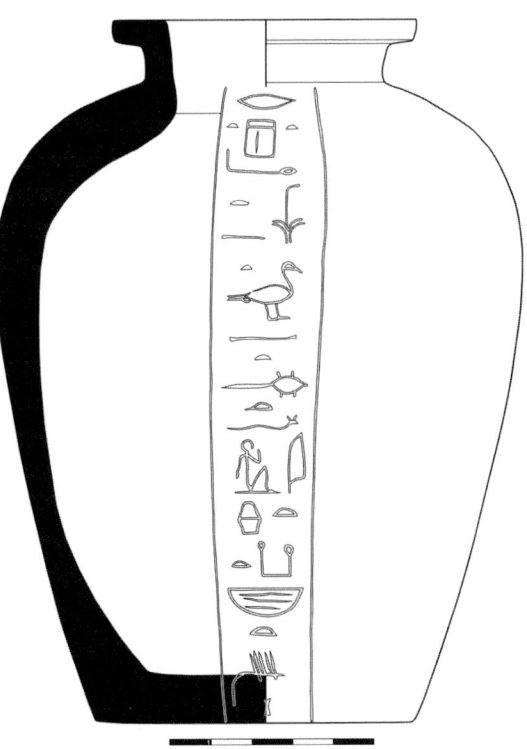

Figure 9.5. Stone vessel featuring the name of princess Itakayet of the 12th Dynasty from Tomb VII at Qatna (drawing by A. Gubisch; courtesy of the Qatna Excavation Project, IANES Tübingen).

---

²⁴ Ahrens 2010.
²⁵ Summarised in Ahrens 2010.

complexes of the Middle Kingdom kings and the tombs of their entourage were reused or plundered as early as the 13th Dynasty and the following Second Intermediate Period. Whether the stone vessel reached Qatna directly from Egypt or via another Northern Levantine kingdom is a moot point to discuss, since there is no conclusive archaeological evidence to prove or disprove any such hypothesis yet. The important harbour city of Gubla/Byblos, in strong contact with Egypt since the 3rd millennium BCE, would certainly be a likely candidate for a 'mediator' of Egyptian objects into inner Syria during the 2nd millennium.

Since Itakayet's vessel comes from a funerary context in Egypt, the question is whether or not the elites at Qatna knew of this and employed the vessel accordingly when depositing it within Tomb VII. This, however, seems unlikely, since knowledge of the vessel's original function is only understood via the hieroglyphic inscription and a profound knowledge of Egyptian funerary rites and customs by the Levantine elites.

Queens, kings and a crocodile god – the Royal Tomb of Qatna

The Royal Tomb of Qatna is located 12 m beneath the royal palace at the northern edge. The tomb consists of four chambers cut in the bedrock beneath the palace's foundations and a corridor, 40 m long, which connects it to Hall A of the royal palace. The corridor takes a turn to the east and stops abruptly; an antechamber 5 m beneath the floor of the corridor follows and a wooden stair is used to descend to it, after which a door leads to the burial chambers.[26] The tomb was in use for around 350 years, and bodies of both genders and different ages were interred; a minimum of 19-24 individuals were found in the tomb.

A drop-shaped alabastron made of serpentinite found in Chamber 3 of the Royal Tomb at Qatna carries a hieroglyphic inscription naming Amenemhat III of the late 12th Dynasty, consisting of three columns and one horizontal line (Fig. 9.6).

The inscription reads:

¹ s3 R ͨ (Jmn-m-ḥ3t) ² njswt bjtj (Nj-m3 ͨ.t-R ͨ) ³
mry Sbk Šd.tj ⁴ ḏj.w ͨnḫ mj R ͨ ḏ.t
¹ Son of Re: Amenemhat, ² King of Upper- and Lower Egypt: Ni-maat-Re, ³
beloved of Sobek Shedety, ⁴ given life like Re eternally

The inscription makes it likely that the vessel was originally part of the main temple of Sobek Shedety at Shedet (Crocodilopolis, Kīmân Faris) located in the Fayum.[27] When and how the vessel finally reached Qatna and its Royal Tomb remains an open question again but it is likely that the vessel – just like the Sphinx of Ita and Itakayet's stone vessel – reached Qatna at a later date, albeit difficult to pinpoint exactly.

---

[26] For the tomb in general, cf. Pfälzner 2011a; 2011b.
[27] Ahrens 2006, 18–20.

Figure 9.6. Stone vessel made of Serpentinite featuring the cartouches of Amenemhat III and mentioning the god 'Sobek of Shedet' from the Royal Tomb at Qatna (drawing by Gabriele Elsen-Novák; courtesy of the Qatna Excavation Project, IANES Tübingen).

Interestingly, the stone vessel was found in an accumulation of 14 stone vessels, all of them typologically dating to the Middle Bronze Age spectrum. Thus, one might argue that the vessel reached Qatna sometime during the second phase of the Middle Bronze Age, i.e. the Second Intermediate Period, since there are no clear Late Bronze Age types present in this body of stone vessels and since the Royal Tomb's last phase of use clearly dates to the Late Bronze Age, i.e. just before the palace's destruction at around 1350 BCE.

Chamber 3 of the Royal Tomb is symbolically linked to the throne room in the palace itself, with Chamber 1 imitating and resembling Hall C. Chamber 3 does not feature a large number of objects but apparently was the location of a wooden construction perhaps imitating a throne or the like. The entire tomb as such therefore could be considered a cultic *doublette* of the royal palace itself, reflecting not only its architectural layout but perhaps also its internal organisation, with the king at the top and at the centre and focal point of both ensembles.[28] In this respect, it is enlightening that the stone vessel made of green serpentinite – a material not attested in the Levant – and featuring a cartouche associated with royalty was deposited just here.

Not far from Chamber 3, in the south-western part of Chamber 1, another stone vessel with a hieroglyphic inscription was found on one of the stone benches located here. The inscription mentions Queen Ahmes-Nefertari of the early 18th Dynasty, along with the titles and name of chief treasurer Nefer-peret (Fig. 9.7).[29] The inscription makes it clear that the vessel was given to Nefer-peret by Ahmes-Nefertari as a 'gift of honour' by the queen.

The inscription reads:

¹ dj(.w) m ḥś(w).t n.t <ḥr> ḥm.t nṯr ḥm.t njswt mw.t njswt
(Iꜥḥ-ms-nfr.t-jr.j) ꜥnḫ.tj ² n (j)r(j)-pꜥ.t ḥꜣtj-ꜥ
smr wꜥ.tj jmj-rꜣ ḫtm.t sḏ.tj njswt Nfr-pr.t mꜣꜥ-ḫrw
¹ *Given as a gift of honour by the God's Wife, the King's Wife, the King's Mother, Ahmes-Nefertari, she may live,* ² *to the Iripat ('Noble'), the Hatia ('Count'), Sole Companion, the Chief Treasurer, the King's Fosterling, Nefer-peret, justified*

The connection between Ahmes-Nefertari and Nefer-peret becomes clear when you take a look at his titles: as a *sḏtj-njswt* – a king's fosterling – Nefer-peret probably was raised together with the later king Ahmose and his sister, later wife and royal consort Ahmes-Nefertari. As Chief Treasurer, Nefer-peret was in charge of important construction works in the country.

Clearly, the inscription shows no apparent connection of Nefer-peret – or Ahmes-Nefertari in that respect – with the Northern Levant or even Qatna in specific.[30] The

---

[28] Pfälzner 2011b.
[29] Ahrens 2006, 20–24.
[30] Ahrens 2006, 22–24; 2015b.

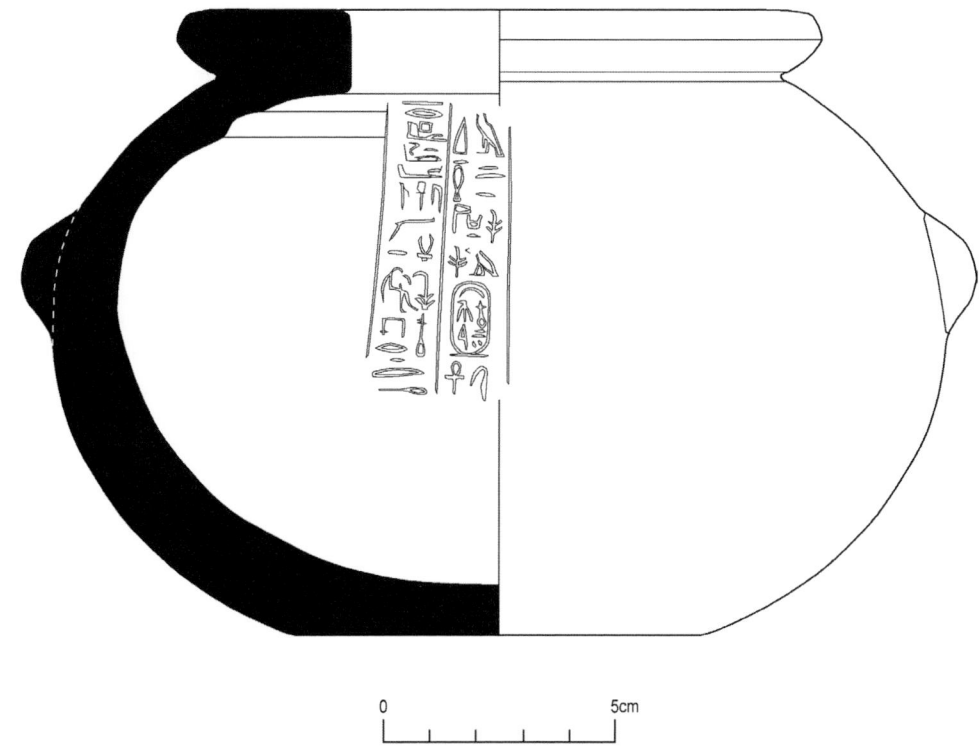

Figure 9.7. Stone vessel made of calcite-alabaster featuring the names of Queen Ahmes-Nefertari and Chief Treasurer Nefer-peret from the Royal Tomb at Qatna (drawing by Gabriele Elsen-Novák; courtesy of the Qatna Excavation Project, IANES Tübingen).

vessel must have belonged to Nefer-peret's tomb equipment, which may have been given partly to him personally or for his burial after his death by the queen. A later dispatch of the vessel – probably again as a result of tomb robbing[31] – seems highly likely, although a precise date for this cannot be given, since the Royal Tomb was used continuously from the MB IIB period (c. 1800 BCE), using the Northern Levantine periodisation, until the LB IIA period (c. 1350 BCE).

Just like Itakayet's vessel found in Tomb VII, the two Egyptian stone vessels found in the Royal Tomb were originally used in cultic contexts in Egypt and dispatched to the Levant and re-used there only at a later time. While the stone vessel with the cartouche of Amenemhat III most probably comes from a temple repository, the stone vessel of Nefer-peret clearly must come from his tomb in Egypt.[32] Again, the question as to whether or not the kings of Qatna knew of the origin of these two stone vessels

---

[31] Ahrens 2006, 22–24.
[32] As yet unlocated but most likely at Draʿ Abū el-Naga, cf. Ahrens 2006.

is a moot point to discuss, since it most likely was the emblematic appeal and impact of the hieroglyphic inscriptions – apart from the exotic appearance of the rare stone material – not their actual content, which made the vessels precious to the rulers of Qatna. In the case of the stone vessel of Amenemhat III, the fact that the vessel must come from a temple would also show that the original function and use was not known or understood.

Similar finds and find contexts at other sites in the Northern Levant. The 'ceremonial mace' of Hotepibre at Tell Mardikh/Ebla

Having looked at only one particular site so far, the question arises as to whether such secondary re-evaluations or re-uses of Egyptian objects can be observed at other sites in the Levant as well.

As mentioned in the beginning, in many cases such observations are obstructed by undefined or unknown archaeological find contexts, hampering an exact identification of the objects' uses in the Levant; in other cases, missing inscriptions make tracing the specific objects' biographies impossible – yet, one needs to securely reconstruct both possible patterns of translocations and differentiating perceptions. While it is clearly out of scope in this presentation to present more finds in more detail, one further example of this phenomenon from the site of Tell Mardikh/Ebla is enlightening in this respect.

The so-called ceremonial mace of the Egyptian pharaoh Hotepibre was found as part of a tomb assemblage within a princely – not the royal – tomb, the so-called Tomb of the Lord of the Goats, underneath Palace Q at the Middle Bronze Age site of Ebla/Tell Mardikh[33] (Fig. 9.8). Without being able to go into much detail here, the mace – with few, if any, parallels in Egypt itself but with a second almost identical mace without featuring hieroglyphs from the same tomb complex, i.e. 'Tomb of the Cistern'[34] – has been referred to as an Egyptian import by the excavators. However, this view has been questioned by a number of scholars ever since.[35]

Instead, the mace has been identified as a Levantine production, merging techniques and styles exclusively attested in the Middle Bronze Age Levant. What is striking is the use of Egyptian hieroglyphs forming the presumed name of a king 'Hotepibre', who admittedly is known to have shortly reigned during the 13th Dynasty. However, the arrangement of the hieroglyphs displays serious flaws and mistakes. While the excavators interpret this as a 'restoration' executed by a Levantine craftsman without knowledge of Egyptian script, it is argued here that the mace actually 'recycled' elements that once belonged to a different, and unknown, Egyptian object, perhaps a wooden chest or the like. Furthermore, it has to be noted that the hieroglyphs used here would also make up parts of the throne name of Amenemhat

---

[33] Scandone Matthiae 1979.
[34] Matthiae *et al.* 1995, 240.
[35] Already Lilyquist 1993; Ryholt 1998, 4; Ahrens 2011a.

I of the 12th Dynasty and also the name of an ephemeral and almost completely unknown king Sehotepibre (II or even III?) of the 13th Dynasty.³⁶ As an object 'recycling' parts of an unidentified Egyptian object, a missing hieroglyph would not surprise, especially since the Levantine craftsmen were unable to actually read and understand hieroglyphic writing, apart from conceiving its emblematic value. All in all, a secure identification with one of the Egyptian pharaohs mentioned above is far from clear, as is therefore also the assumed chronological value of the mace.

The fact that Levantine craftsmen at Ebla knew Egyptian iconography and incorporated it into locally manufactured items is not only shown by the highly Egyptianising iconography and motifs employed in the Middle Bronze Age glyptic material from the Northern Levant in general³⁷ but also clearly exemplified by the Middle Bronze Age Egyptianising ivories found within Palace P at Ebla, which were used as inlays as part of a wooden object not preserved.³⁸

Figure 9.8. The 'ceremonial mace' of Hotepibre from the 'Tomb of the Lord of the Goats' at Tell Mardikh/Ebla (after Scandone Matthiae 1979, fig. 39a).

The mace more probably must be considered to be a Levantine creation, not an Egyptian import. The mace from the tomb, itself being a symbol associated with the concepts of 'power', 'royalty' and perhaps 'kingship', also clearly reflects the prestige of the living rulers at Ebla (or future rulers, since the mace was found in the tomb of a prince, possibly named 'Immeya') or, more generally speaking, the Levant. Without proof, the original Egyptian object that was used for the mace, or even only parts thereof, in this case most likely must have come to Ebla via Byblos. Direct contacts are at least attested between both sites for the Early and Middle Bronze Age.³⁹

---

³⁶ Ryholt 1997; 1998, 4.
³⁷ Eder 1995; Teissier 1996.
³⁸ Scandone Matthiae 2002; 2006; also Ahrens 2011a.
³⁹ Nigro 2009; Pinnock 2012; Ahrens 2015a.

Re-using, recycling or re-evaluating Egypt? – Conclusions

To conclude with this brief survey of a selection of Egyptian objects found in find contexts in the Northern Levant, does the title of this paper 'recycling Egypt' hold true? It would seem that the answer is at least partly yes, since the majority of the Egyptian imports from clear find contexts were indeed re-used in secondary contexts in the Levant, and – as in the case of the mace of Hotepibre – were also indeed 'recycled' from another object (or perhaps even many different objects) that was dispatched to the Levant some time before it was then 'recycled' for a second time. A 're-evaluation' of Egyptian objects is much more difficult to reveal and prove, since the historical texts are silent on this issue, and the archaeological find contexts are ambiguous most of the time. It is striking at first that some of the Egyptian objects found in the Levant come from funerary contexts in Egypt and were also found in funerary contexts in the Levant, mostly – but not exclusively – tombs. Would this suffice to prove that the Levantine elites understood the objects' original function and contextual use and thus employed them accordingly? As mentioned above, this seems highly unlikely, as this would imply profound and in-depth knowledge of Egyptian funerary rites and customs, which clearly did not exist. However, since Egyptian objects and iconography had already been known and locally adapted – but probably not always understood in the correct way – for a long time and had become part of the indigenous material culture in almost all regions of the Levant at least since the Middle Bronze Age, such objects generally were thus not merely 're-used' in the truest meaning of the term – i.e. employed in their original function – but rather received a different function and use altogether, ascribing new 'uses' and 'functions' to these objects in the Levant, equally obstructing their original function and use. From an epistemological point of view, these objects were thus 're-evaluated' and 'recycled', although not in the conventional sense of the term. The Egyptian objects were presumably conceived as 'exotic foreign objects', carrying emblematic hieroglyphic inscriptions not necessarily understood and also made of precious rare materials not locally attested in the Levant. Due to the fact that not only royal but also private statuary seems to belong to the objects that were sent to the Levant during the Second Intermediate Period, it is clear that – on behalf of the recipient, i.e. the Levantine courts and its rulers – the actual content of the Egyptian inscriptions was not considered important; they probably were not understood in their original conception. The fact that the mobile objects presumably transported little knowledge regarding their primary functions or their origin is also exemplified by the fact that many Egyptian objects in the Levant, including those from Qatna presented in this paper, stem from funerary contexts in Egypt but were not always used in such contexts in the Levant. Thus, it is more plausible to conclude that the objects' original function was not known or recognised.

There probably was little to no knowledge within the Levantine elites concerning the origin of the Egyptian objects and their specific original functions, apart from their coming from Egypt, based on their distinctive stylistic traits, which were well known in the entire Levant due to constant political contacts between the two regions. As already mentioned, hieroglyphic writing and other characteristic traits of the Egyptian cultural sphere and artistic production were well known in the Levant – e.g. in the glyptic material[40] – and this was subsequently often emulated and even transformed into something distinctively 'Levantine' in certain objects, i.e. featuring a hybrid mix of Egyptian and Levantine motifs and imagery, including pseudo-hieroglyphic signs.

Without doubt, however, the phenomenon cannot and must not be conceived as evidence for the actual presence of these individuals in the Northern Levant or contact of these individuals with the Levantine rulers at this time. In all probability, these objects only reached the Levant after their initial use in Egypt, most probably as a direct result of tomb robbing of the major burial or temple complexes of the Middle Kingdom during the Second Intermediate Period, possibly even as early as in the 13th Dynasty. Historical sources – especially the Amarna correspondence of the Late Bronze Age (second half of the 14th century BCE) – show in great detail that an exchange of prestige goods and numerous other valuables was mediated through messengers and emissaries sent by the royal courts of the Late Bronze Age political powers. The fact that such an exchange of goods and personnel already took place during earlier periods of the Bronze Age is likely, as exemplified by a fragment of a cuneiform tablet found at Tell el-Dabʿa/Avaris in the Nile Delta and also a cylinder seal impression, both dating to the second half of the Middle Bronze Age.[41] How these objects finally reached Qatna is difficult to say with certainty. It is possible that at least some of the Egyptian objects found in the Northern Levant, and especially those found at sites in inland Syria, actually were 'mediated' via Gubla/Byblos, although this scenario cannot be proved on the basis of the scanty historical and archaeological record for this region during this period;[42] a seal impression with a name of a ruler of Byblos found at Tell el-Dabʿa, however, may now shed new light on the contacts between the coastal Levant and Egypt during the late Middle Bronze Age at least.[43]

The reason for the presence of Egyptian statuary, royal and private, may be seen in light of their 'emblematic' and 'exotic' character, regardless of the actual content of the objects' hieroglyphic inscription, their specific 'biographies' or whether the statues depicted royal or private individuals. In this regard, the objects naming Egyptian princesses thus actually belong to a larger corpus of imported Egyptian objects that were 'recontextualised', thus 're-used', and perhaps even 're-evaluated' and as such primarily served the local Levantine rulers' need for self-representation and negotiation of status and prestige. The translocation and apparent re-contextualisation

---

[40] Eder 1995; Teissier 1996.
[41] Bietak and Forstner-Müller 2009; Collon *et al.* 2012/2013; van Koppen and Lehmann 2012/2013.
[42] Ahrens 2011a; 2015a.
[43] Kopetzky and Bietak 2016.

of these objects thus clearly led to their re-evaluation and appropriation within a newly defined cultural background by the elites in the Levant.

In this regard, the objects assembled within the palaces (and associated tombs) might be seen as (clearly not directly related but used in a similar vein) 'intellectual precursors' of the 'cabinets of curiosities' during the medieval period in Europe (also known in German loanwords as *Kunstkabinett* or *Wunderkammer*), which were encyclopaedic collections of objects whose categorical boundaries were yet to be defined. Modern terminology would categorise the objects included as belonging to natural history (sometimes faked), geology, ethnography, archaeology, religious or historical relics, works of art (including cabinet paintings) and antiquities. These cabinets were regarded as a microcosm or 'theatre of the world' and conveyed symbolically the ruler's control of the world through its indoor, microscopic reproduction.[44] In this respect, it is important to note that apart from the Egyptian imports and Egyptianising Levantine objects – perhaps serving the same purpose – Aegeanising wall paintings were also discovered in Room N in the western part of the royal palace of Qatna.[45] This phenomenon is therefore not only restricted to the royal palace of Qatna but is also attested in the royal palace of Tell Atchana, Bronze Age Alalaḫ, located at the mouth of the Orontes and also at other palaces in the Levant.[46] Without doubt, these Aegeanising wall paintings with their motifs from yet another region of the Bronze Age world were also considered 'exotic' and 'foreign' by the Levantine rulers, albeit different mechanisms of exchange, adaptation and perception may have been applied in this specific case.[47]

While there clearly is abundant evidence for a re-use of Egyptian objects in use contexts displaying or underlining royal prestige in the Levant, there is also archaeological evidence for a cultic use of re-used Egyptian imports, as exemplified by the use of the Sphinx of Ita within the Shrine of the Belet-ekallim/Nin-Egal at Qatna, but likewise also the use of Egyptian forms and hieroglyphic script in the Temple of Obelisks at Byblos and perhaps the presence of Egyptian statuary within the Temple of Baal at Ugarit, among many other sites.[48] To add to this, the abundance of Egyptian imports within tomb assemblages, most of them belonging to the royal sphere, would clearly also have to be regarded as 'cultic' in a way, since the objects deposited here were probably all ascribed ritual functions in the afterlife.

Egyptian imports and other *aegyptiaca*, as demonstrated by the selection of examples given above, can be interpreted as evidence for distinction of status and rank because of their symbolic significance due to their foreign origin. The relatively limited number of Egyptian objects found in the Northern Levant may also show that these objects were highly valued and demanded local emulation, seen for example in

---

[44] Pomian 1998; cf. also Helms 1988; 1993.
[45] von Rüden 2011.
[46] von Rüden 2017.
[47] Feldman 2007.
[48] Cf. Ahrens 2011a; 2011b; 2020 for a thorough compilation of Northern Levantine sites and finds.

the repertoire of motifs in the corpus of Levantine glyptic material. Thus, the Egyptian objects found in the Northern Levant, among other 'exotica', also provide a unique and challenging opportunity to analyse the way Levantine elites sought to present themselves and their social rank and visualise their political power by accumulating foreign Egyptian objects and adapting Egyptian iconography, ignorant of their actual meaning at the time of the objects' conception but putting new perceptions into these at the same time.

References

Ahrens, A. 2006 A journey's end. Two Egyptian stone vessels with hieroglyphic inscriptions from the Royal Tomb at Tell Mišrife/Qaṭna. *Ägypten und Levante. Internationale Zeitschrift für ägyptische Archäologie und deren Nachbargebiete* 16, 15–36

Ahrens, A. 2010 a stone vessel of Princess Itakayet of the 12th Dynasty from Tomb VII at Tell Mišrife/Qaṭna (Syria). *Ägypten und Levante. Internationale Zeitschrift für ägyptische Archäologie und deren Nachbargebiete* 20, 15–29

Ahrens, A. 2011a Strangers in a strange land? The function and social significance of Egyptian imports in the Northern Levant during the 2nd millennium BC. In: K. Duistermaat and I. Regulski (eds), *Intercultural Contacts in the Ancient Mediterranean. Proceedings of the International Conference at the Netherlands-Flemish Institute in Cairo, 25th to 29th October 2008*. Orientalia Lovaniensia Analecta 202 (Leuven), 285–307

Ahrens, A. 2011b A 'Hyksos connection'? Thoughts on the date of dispatch of some of the Middle Kingdom Objects found in the Northern Levant. In: J. Mynářová (ed.), *Egypt and the Near East. The Crossroads. Proceedings of an International Conference on the Relations of Egypt and the Near East in the Bronze Age, Prague, September 1-3, 2010* (Prague), 21–40

Ahrens, A. 2015a Objects from Afar. The distribution of Egyptian imports in the Northern Levant. Parameters for ascertaining the character of diplomatic contacts between Egypt and the Levant during the Bronze Age? In: B. Eder and R. Pruzsinszky (eds), *Policies of Exchange. Political Systems and Modes of Interaction in the Aegean and the Near East in the 2nd Millennium B.C.E. Proceedings of the International Symposium at the University of Freiburg. Institute for Archaeological Studies, 30th May–2nd June 2012*. Oriental and European Archaeology 2 (Vienna), 141–156

Ahrens, A. 2015b The Early 18th Dynasty in the Northern Levant. New finds and a reassessment of the sources> In: J. Mynářová, P. Onderka and P. Pavúk (eds), *There and Back Again. The Crossroads II. Proceedings of an International Conference Held in Prague, September 15-18, 2014* (Prague), 353–371

Ahrens, A. 2020 *Aegyptiaca in der nördlichen Levante. Eine Studie zur Kontextualisierung und Rezeption ägyptischer und ägyptisierender Objekte in der Bronzezeit*. Orbis Biblicus et Orientalis. Series Archaeologica 41 (Leuven)

Akkermans, P. M. M. G. and Schwartz, G. M. 2003 *The Archaeology of Syria. From Complex Hunter-Gatherers to Early Urban Societies (c. 16,000-300 BC)*. Cambridge World Archaeology (Cambridge)

Bietak, M. and Forstner-Müller, I. 2009 Der Hyksospalast bei Tell el-Dabʿa. Zweite und dritte Grabungskampagne (Frühling 2008 und Frühling 2009). Mit einem Beitrag von F. van Koppen und K. Radner. *Ägypten und Levante. Internationale Zeitschrift für ägyptische Archäologie und deren Nachbargebiete* 19, 91–119

Bottéro, J. 1949 Les inventaires de Qatna. *Revue d'assyriologie et d'archéologie orientale* 43, 1–40. 137–213

Bottéro, J. 1950 Autres textes de Qatna., *Revue d'assyriologie et d'archéologie orientale* 44, 105–118

Collon, D., Lehmann, M. and Müller, S. E. M. 2012/2013 Tell el-Dabʿa Sealings 2009–2011. *Ägypten und Levante. Internationale Zeitschrift für ägyptische Archäologie und deren Nachbargebiete* 22/23, 95–104

De Clercq, G. 2003 Die Göttin Ninegal/Bēlet-ekallim nach den altorientalischen Quellen des 3. und 2. Jt. v. Chr. Mit einer Zusammenfassung der hethitischen Belegstellen sowie der des 1. Jt. v. Chr. Unpublished PhD. dissertartion Julius-Maximilians-Universität, Würzburg). https://opus.bibliothek.uni-wuerzburg.de/frontdoor/index/index/docId/1749 (accessed: 24 August 2021)

Eder, C. 1995 *Die ägyptischen Motive in der Glyptik des östlichen Mittelmeerraumes zu Anfang des 2. Jts. v. Chr.* Orientalia Lovaniensia Analecta 71 (Leuven)

Elsen-Novák, G. 2003 Glyptik, 152–155 in: M. Novák and P. Pfälzner, Ausgrabungen im bronzezeitlichen Palast von Tall Mišrife – Qaṭna 2002. Vorbericht der deutschen Komponente des internationalen Kooperationsprojektes. *Mitteilungen der Deutschen Orient-Gesellschaft zu Berlin* 135, 131–166

Feldman, M. H. 2007 Frescoes, exotica, and the reinvention of the Northern Levantine kingdoms during the second millenium B.C.E. In: M. Heinz and M. H. Feldman (eds), *Representations of Political Power. Case Histories from Times of Change and Dissolving Order in the Ancient Near East* (Winona Lake IN), 39–65

Geith, E., Abd el-Hay, T. and Schmid, J. 2019 *Der Königspalast von Qaṭna II. Architektur, Stratigraphie, Keramik und Funde des westlichen Zentralbereichs.* Qaṭna Studien. Forschungsergebnisse und vergleichende Untersuchungen des deutsch-syrischen archäologischen Projekts auf dem Tall Mišrife 6 (Wiesbaden)

Helck, W. 1971 Die Beziehungen Ägyptens zu Vorderasien im 3. und 2. Jahrtausend v. Chr. *Ägyptologische Abhandlungen* 5 (Wiesbaden)

Helck, W. 1976 Ägyptische Statuen im Ausland. Ein chronologisches Problem. *Ugarit-Forschungen. Internationales Jahrbuch für die Altertumskunde Syrien-Palästinas* 8, 101–115

Helms, M. W. 1988 *Ulysses' Sail. An Ethnographic Odyssey of Power, Knowledge, and Geographical Distance* (Princeton NJ)

Helms, M. W. 1993 Craft and the kingly ideal. Art, trade, and power (Austin TX)

Kopetzky, K. and Bietak. M. 2016 A seal impression of the green jasper workshop from Tell el-Dabʿa. *Ägypten und Levante. Internationale Zeitschrift für ägyptische Archäologie und deren Nachbargebiete* 26, 357–375

Koppen, F. van and Lehmann, M. 2012/2013 A Cuneiform sealing from Tell el-Dabʿa and its historical context. *Ägypten und Levante. Internationale Zeitschrift für ägyptische Archäologie und deren Nachbargebiete* 22/23, 91–94

Kopytoff, I. 1986 The cultural biography of things. Commoditization as process. In: A. Appadurai (ed.), *The Social Life of Things. Commodities in Cultural Perspective* (Cambridge), 64–91

Lilyquist, C. 1993 Granulation and glass. Chronological and stylistic investigations at selected sites, ca. 2500–1400 B.C.E. *Bulletin of the American Schools of Oriental Research* 290/291, 29–94

Matthiae, P., Pinnock, F. and Scandone Matthiae, G. (eds) 1995 *Ebla. Alle origini della civiltà urbana. Trent' anni di scavi in Siria dell'Università di Roma 'La Sapienzia'* (Milan)

Mesnil du Buisson, R. Comte du 1928 L'ancienne Qatna ou les ruines d'el-Mishrifé au n.-e. de Homs (Emèse). Deuxième campagne des fouilles (1927). *Syria. Revue d'art oriental et d'archéologie* 9, 16–24, 81–89

Mesnil du Buisson, R. Comte du 1935 *Le site archéologique de Mishrife-Qatna.* Collection de textes et documents d'Orient 1 (Paris)

Nigro, L. 2009 The eighteenth century BC Princes of Byblos and Ebla and the chronology of the Middle Bronze Age. In: A.-M. Maila Afeiche (ed.), *Interconnections in the Eastern Mediterranean. Lebanon in the Bronze and Iron Ages. Proceedings of the International Symposium. Beirut 2008.* Bulletin d'Archéologie et d'Architecture Libanaises. Hors-Série 6 (Beirut), 159–175

Novák, M. 2002 A shrine of Bēlet-Ekallim in the Palace of Qaṭna? *Occident & Orient. Newsletter of the German Protestant Institute of Archaeology in Amman* 7(2), 20–22

Pfälzner, P. 2011a Die Chronologie der Königsgruft von Qaṭna. In: P. Pfälzner (ed.), *Interdisziplinäre Studien zur Königsgruft von Qaṭna.* Qaṭna Studien. Forschungsergebnisse und vergleichende Untersuchungen des deutsch-syrischen archäologischen Projekts auf dem Tall Mišrife 1 (Wiesbaden), 55–67

Pfälzner, P. 2011b Die Königsgruft von Qaṭna als architektonisches Ensemble. In: P. Pfälzner (ed.), *Interdisziplinäre Studien zur Königsgruft von Qaṭna*. Qaṭna Studien. Forschungsergebnisse und vergleichende Untersuchungen des deutsch-syrischen archäologischen Projekts auf dem Tall Mišrife 1 (Wiesbaden), 69–84

Pfälzner, P. 2015 A house of kings and gods. Ritual places in Syrian palaces. In: A.-M. Maila Afeiche (ed.), *Cult and Ritual on the Levantine Coast and Its Impact on the Eastern Mediterranean Realm. Proceedings of the International Symposium. Beirut 2012*. Bulletin d'Archéologie et d'Architecture Libanaises. Hors-Série 10 (Beirut), 413–442

Pfälzner, P. and Dohmann-Pfälzner, H. 2011 *Die Gruft VII. Eine neu entdeckte Grabanlage unter dem Königspalast von Qaṭna*. Mitteilungen der Deutschen Orient-Gesellschaft zu Berlin 143, 63–139

Pfälzner, P. and Schmid, J. 2019 *Der Königspalast von Qaṭna I. Chronologie, Grundriss, Baugeschichte und Bautechniken*. Qaṭna Studien. Forschungsergebnisse und vergleichende Untersuchungen des deutsch-syrischen archäologischen Projekts auf dem Tall Mišrife 5 (Wiesbaden)

Pinnock, F. 2012 Some gublite artifact possibly made at Ebla, Syria. *Archéologie, art et histoire* 89, 85–100

Pomerance, L. 1973 The possible role of tomb robbers and viziers of the 18th Dynasty in confusing Minoan chronology. In: G. Rizza (ed.), *Antichità Cretesi. Studi in onore di Doro Levi I*. Cronache di archeologia 12 (Catania), 21–30

Pomian, K. 1998 *Der Ursprung des Museums. Vom Sammeln*. Wagenbachs Taschenbuch 302 (Berlin)

Richter, T. 2004 Ein Tafelfund der Grabungskampagne 2003 in Tall Mišrife/Qaṭna. *Mitteilungen der Deutschen Orient-Gesellschaft zu Berlin* 136, 217–222

Roßberger, E. 2015 *Schmuck für Lebende und Tote. Form und Funktion des Schmuckinventars der Königsgruft von Qaṭna in seinem soziokulturellen Umfeld*. Qaṭna Studien. Forschungsergebnisse und vergleichende Untersuchungen des deutsch-syrischen archäologischen Projekts auf dem Tall Mišrife 4 (Wiesbaden)

Rüden, C. von 2011 *Die Wandmalereien aus Tall Mišrife/Qaṭna im Kontext überregionaler Kommunikation*. Qaṭna Studien. Forschungsergebnisse und vergleichende Untersuchungen des deutsch-syrischen archäologischen Projekts auf dem Tall Mišrife 2 (Wiesbaden)

Rüden, C. von 2017 Producing Aegeanness. An innovation and its impact in Middle and Late Bronze Age Syria/Northern Levant. In: S. Burmeister and R. Bernbeck (eds), *The Interplay of People and Technologies. Archaeological Case Studies on Innovation* (Berlin), 223–247

Ryholt, K. S. B. 1997 *The Political Situation in Egypt during the Second Intermediate Period c. 1800–1550 B.C.* Carsten Niebuhr Institute Publications 20 (Copenhagen)

Ryholt, K. S. B. 1998, Hotepibre, a supposed Asiatic king in Egypt with relations to Ebla. *Bulletin of the American Schools of Oriental Research* 311, 1–6

Scandone Matthiae, G. 1979 Un oggetto faraonico della XIII dinastia dalla 'Tomba del Signore dei Capridi'. *Studi Eblaiti* 1, 119–128

Scandone Matthiae, G. 2002 *Gli avori Egittizzanti dal Palazzo Settentrionale. Con appendice di Barbara Wilkens*. Materiali e Studi Archeologici di Ebla 3 (Rome)

Scandone Matthiae, G. 2006 Nuovi frammenti di avori Egittizzanti di Ebla. In: E. Czerny, I. Hein, H. Hunger, D. Melman and A. Schwab (eds), *Timelines. Studies in Honour of Manfred Bietak* III. Orientalia Lovaniensia Analecta 149 (Leuven), 81–86

Teissier, B. 1996 *Egyptian Iconography on Syro-Palestinian Cylinder Seals of the Middle Bronze Age*. Orbis Biblicus et Orientalis. Series Archaeologica 11 (Fribourg)

Thompson, M. 1979 *Rubbish Theory. The Creation and Destruction of Value* (Oxford)

Virolleaud, C. 1928 Les tablettes cunéiformes de Mishrifé-Katna, Syria. *Revue d'art oriental et d'archéologie* 9, 90–96

Virolleaud, C. 1930 Les tablettes de Mishrifé-Qatna, Syria. *Revue d'art oriental et d'archéologie* 11, 311–342

Weinstein, J. M. 1975 Egyptian relations with Palestine in the Middle Kingdom. *Bulletin of the American Schools of Oriental Research* 217, 1–16

Chapter 10

Beyond the bones: relics in Greek temples

Andreas Hartmann

Pre-Christian relics are not a new topic in classical studies but scholarly discussion has often been pre-occupied with the development of heroic tomb cults. Apart from real or imagined human bones, however, there were other relics in Greek temples, namely objects that were supposed to have belonged to some important person of the past. In contrast to the bones, these secondary relics were actually on display.[1] The best point to start an exploration of this phenomenon is the ancient city of Lindos on the island of Rhodes. A lengthy inscription from the sanctuary of Athena Lindia, generally known as the *Lindian Chronicle*, opens a window into the world of ancient secondary relics.[2] In 99 BCE, the Lindians decreed that a catalogue of lost relics and divine epiphanies that had happened at the sanctuary should be compiled and published in stone. While the *Chronicle* is unique as an inscription, similar information was available elsewhere:[3] when Pausanias visited Sikyon, his local guides told him about two relics, the spear of Meleagros and the flute of Marsyas, which had been destroyed in the burning of the temple of Apollon.[4] According to a section in the *Liber memorialis* of Ampelius, this temple housed a collection of objects very similar to those recorded at Lindos.[5] At Samos, the local historian Leon wrote on the votive offerings in the Heraion and the epiphanies of the local deity[6] – exactly the topics of the *Lindian Chronicle*. Periegetic treatises have been written on the treasures of certain

---

[1] Thompson 1985, 27–30.
[2] Cf. Shaya 2002; 2005; Higbie 2003; Bresson 2006; Massar 2006; Robert 2010; 2015. Further bibliography can be found in Ampolo *et al.* 2014. All recent scholarship is dependent on the seminal work of Christian Blinkenberg: Blinkenberg 1912; 1915; 1941, 148–200.
[3] Cf. Blinkenberg 1912, 405–406; Higbie 2003, 258–273.
[4] Paus. 2, 7, 9.
[5] Ampelius, *Liber memorialis* 8, 5; Pfister 1914; Scheer 1996; Robert 2010, 183–184.
[6] Leon FGrH/BNJ 540 T1 ~ IG XII 6, 1, 285.

sanctuaries since the Hellenistic period.[7] These works may very well have contained references to objects already lost.[8]

Re-evaluation

According to the imagination of the Greeks, votive practices had always been the same. Dedications of weapons are mentioned in the Homeric epics,[9] and 'Homer' was taken as a reliable source for ancient history. Accordingly, weaponry allegedly dedicated by some hero could be seen at many sanctuaries.[10] The *Lindian Chronicle* lists offerings of this kind for Herakles (V), the companions of Tlepolemos (IX), Menelaos (X), Meriones (XIII), Teukros (XIV), the companions of Kleoboulos (XXIII), the inhabitants of Phaselis (XXIV), the pharaoh Amasis (XXIX), the generals of Dareios I. (XXXII), the Lindian people (XXXV. XXXVII), king Pyrrhos (XL), king Hieron (XLI) and king Phillip V. (XLII).[11] In fact, contemporary votive practices[12] were projected backwards into a heroic past. This constructed continuity had a welcome side-effect: when historical persons, e.g. Hellenistic kings, dedicated weapons to Greek sanctuaries, they ostensibly (or rather ostentatiously) followed heroic models. The heroic connotations of the royal votives in the *Chronicle* are further emphasised by the claim that Pyrrhos and Hieron had dedicated weapons they had actually used in battle. In other words, these were not ceremonial items but tools of personal valour.[13]

The same line of thought can be applied to the second important category of offerings in the 'mythic' section of the *Lindian Chronicle*: vessels. Dedications of this kind are reported for Lindos (I), the Telchines (II), Kadmos (III), Minos (IV), Tlepolemos (VI), Rhesos (VII), Telephos (VIII), Aretakritos and his sons (XVI), the inhabitants of Gela (XXV), Phalaris (XXVII) and the inhabitants of Soloi (XXXIII). The prominence of drinking cups may reflect the actual popularity of this kind of offering during the Archaic period.[14] In the 4th century BCE, scholars such as Theopompos of Chios and Phainias of Eresos were perfectly aware of the fact that Greek sanctuaries had

---

[7] Heliodoros FGrH/BNJ 373 (on Athens); Anaxandridas of Delphi FGrH/BNJ 404 and Alketas FGrH/BNJ 405 (on Delphi); Menodotos of Samos FGrH/BNJ 541 F 1–2 (on Samos). Polemon of Ilion wrote about offerings at Athens (Strab. 9, 1, 16; fr. 1–5 Preller), Sparta (fr. 18–20 Preller), Olympia (fr. 22 Preller), Delphi (fr. 27–28 Preller) and Dodona (fr. 30 Preller).
[8] Theopompos had written Περὶ τῶν συληθέντων ἐκ Δελφῶν χρημάτων (FGrH/BNJ 115 F 247–249). A late testimony (FGrH/BNJ 404 F 1) ascribes to Anaxandridas a book Περὶ τῶν συληθέντων ἐν Δελφοῖς ἀναθημάτων, but the title is rather doubtful (see Jacoby's commentary in FGrH).
[9] Hom Il. 7, 81–83; 10, 570–571.
[10] Cf. the catalogue in Pfister 1909, 331–332 and the index in Thompson 1985 on armour.
[11] Blinkenberg numbered the items in the catalogue part of the *Lindian Chronicle* and all later editors followed this system. When referring to Lindian relics, I will henceforth only cite this numbers in Roman numerals.
[12] Cf. Pritchett 1979, 240–276.
[13] Contrast the πανο|[πλία, ἣν Ἀ]λέξα<ν>δρος ὁ Πολυπ|[έρχοντ]ος ἀνέθηκεν· θώραξ π|[ομπικὸ]ς ἐντελής, πέλτη ἐπί|[χρυσος] ἐντελής, κνημῖδες χα|[λκαῖ ἀρ]γυ[ρ]ωταί in IG II² 1473 l. 6–11.
[14] Blinkenberg 1912, 388; 1915, 7.

not always been populated with statues but that cauldrons and tripods made from bronze had been prestigious votive offerings in former times.[15] While this insight certainly reflects some genuine knowledge deriving from observation, it also provided a framework to re-evaluate such objects as 'ancient' offerings. The fact that tripods are mentioned as valuable possessions in the Homeric epics readily suggested the idea that the heroes had dedicated such objects to the gods.[16]

It is a sensible guess that most of the relics in Greek temples were historical votive offerings which came to be re-interpreted in the due course of time.[17] Such a re-evaluation was not, however, a necessary outcome for every votive offering. The epigraphically transmitted temple inventories list many objects without suggesting that they were in any way regarded as especially important from a historical perspective, while their material value is specified exactly. In stark contrast, the *Lindian Chronicle* is interested in such quantification by the way of exception only (XXXV, XXXVI). Most of the heroic relics displayed in Greek sanctuaries were not very conspicuous objects in themselves:[18] even such mundane items as shoes, tools, steering-oars and toys could become treasured relics.[19] This begs the question why some objects were re-evaluated as 'relics' while others were not.

A very important factor in the process of identification was the perception of ancientness. I cannot delve here into the question whether antiquity knew an art history based on stylistic observation.[20] Ancient viewers undeniably were able to perceive the otherness of ancient monuments when compared with the artistic conventions of their own time. The *Lindian Chronicle* provides one of the finest examples: the catalogue mentions offerings of the three ancient Rhodian *phylai* which

---

[15] Theopompos of Chios: FGrH/BNJ 115 F 193; Phainias of Eresos: FGrH 1012 F 1 ~ fr. 11 Wehrli.
[16] Hom. Il. 8, 290; Hom. Od. 15, 84.
[17] Rouse 1902, 318; Higbie 2003, 164.
[18] Thompson 1985, 14–15. The frequent occurrence of items made of precious materials in the *Lindian Chronicle* is not representative: silver drinking cup (IV); golden goblet (VII); phiale with golden embellishments (VIII); bracelet (XI); silver quiver (XIII); earrings, necklace, tiara, bracelets (XXII); golden crown (XXIII); golden statues (XXIX); phiale with gilded embellishments (XXXIII); golden crown (XXXIV); golden necklace and bracelets (XXXV); golden statue (XXXVI). The list can be supplemented with a cup made of electron which Helena was believed to have dedicated and which was formed according to the shape of her breast: Plin. nat. 33, 81; cf. Blinkenberg 1912, 434–435; Robert 2015, 19. It is to be noted, however, that only the first five objects from the *Lindian Chronicle* fall into the 'mythic' section. It seems that valuable offerings from the 'historical' period distort the ratio.
[19] On shoes see Helena at a sanctuary of Athena in Japygia: Lykophr. Alexandra 852–855; Sch. ad loc. On tools see Epeios, the constructor of the Trojan horse, at Lagaria or Metapontum: Lykophr. Alexandra 930. 946–950; Aristot. mir. 840a; Iust. 20, 2, 1. On steering-oars see Kanopos, the helmsman of Menelaos, at Lindos: XII. On toys see Hippodameia in the temple of Hera at Olympia: Paus. 5, 20, 1 (the couch of Hippodameia is described by Pausanias as a toy (παίγνιον); it may have been a piece of miniature furniture); Palamedes in the temple of Tyche at Argos: Paus. 2, 20, 3.
[20] Cf. Furtwängler 1877/1878; Kalkmann 1898; Schweitzer 1932; Jucker 1950, 118–146; Pollitt 1964; 1974, 73–84; Pernice and Gross 1969; Preißhofen 1979; Settis 1993; 1995a, 44–46; 1995b; Rouveret 1995; Tanner 2006, 205–276; de Angelis 2015a. The hyper-criticism of Sprigath (2000) has been refuted by Bäbler (2002) and the publication of the *New Poseidippos* in 2001: Strocka 2007; Prioux 2009.

were believed to be very old (XV).[21] The basis for this assessment was that the people depicted on these images were all holding archaic stances (ἀρχαϊκῶς ἔχοντες τοῖς σχήμασι)[22] Pausanias describes the statue of the pancratiast Arrachion at Phigaleia in very similar terms.[23] Dionysios of Halikarnassos, Plutarch and Philostratos provide further instances of such observations.[24] The cauldron dedicated by Kadmos and listed in the *Lindian Chronicle* (III) is described by Diodoros of Sicily as being made after the ancient manner of composition (εἰς τὸν ἀρχαῖον ῥυθμόν).[25]

For an identification of heroic weaponry, the material was of prime importance.[26] Pausanias presented the spear of Achilles at Phaselis (in the temple of Athena) and the sword of Memnon at Nikomedeia (in the sanctuary of Asklepios) as evidence for a heroic Bronze Age.[27] Phainias of Eresos had already observed that all the ancient votive offerings in the sanctuary at Delphi were made of bronze.[28] Even remoter from contemporary Greek practices were shields made of wicker and leather caps, such as those mentioned in the *Lindian Chronicle* to have been dedicated by Herakles and Menelaos (V, X).[29] It is only consequent that the oldest offerings at Lindos, predating the Homeric heroes, are reported to be made from a mysterious unknown material (I, II).

The most explicit form of identification was provided by writing, of course.[30] The *Lindian Chronicle* meticulously reports the alleged dedicatory inscriptions for most of its entries.[31] Poseidonios relied on inscriptions to identify the helmets of Meriones and Odyseus in the sanctuary of Kybele at Sicilian Engyion.[32] The expectation that all objects in Greek temples were to possess a dedicatory inscription seems to have been quite strong: in the Athenian inventories, the ἀνεπίγραφα are duly noted.[33] When a

---

[21] The argument is not affected if the offerings were archaistic fabrications of the Hellenistic period, as is suggested by Cannistraci (2014). Archaistic imitation presupposes a knowledge about characteristic traits of ancient art. This does not mean that 'archaic art' from a Hellenistic perspective is necessarily equivalent to our modern notion of the term, of course. Blinkenberg (1912, 391-392) regarded the painted tablets themselves as genuinely archaic but the inscriptions as later additions.
[22] On σχῆμα as a technical term in ancient art criticism, see Pollitt 1974, 258-262; Koch 2000.
[23] Paus. 8, 40, 1.
[24] Dion. Hal. ant. 1, 48, 2; 1, 79, 8; 4, 40, 7; Plut. Publ. 19, 10; Philostr. Ap. 4, 28.
[25] Diod. 5, 58, 3. On ῥυθμός as a technical term designating 'shape' or 'composition', see Pollitt 1964, 321-323; 1974, 218-228. 260-261. Diodoros also recognised the similarity of composition between ancient Egyptian statues and 'those made by Daidalos' (Diod. 1, 97, 6).
[26] Pfister 1912, 505-506.
[27] Paus. 3, 3, 8; cf. Lacroix 1989, 87-98; Bouvier 2005. A similar conception is pre-supposed by Arr. per. p. E. 9, 2 where an alleged anchor of the Argonauts is rejected because it was made from iron.
[28] Phainias of Eresos FGrH 1012 F 1 ~ fr. 11 Wehrli.
[29] Wicker shields were used by the Persians: Hdt. 7, 61, 1; Xen. an. 4, 7, 26; Xen. Kyr. 1, 2, 9. 13; Paus. 10, 19, 4. The readers of the *Lindian Chronicle* might also have remembered the description of the shield of Aias in Hom. Il. 7, 219-223.
[30] Pfister 1912, 502-505; Thompson 1985, 33-34.
[31] Blinkenberg 1912, 400-401; Higbie 2003, 174-179.
[32] Poseidonios FGrH 87 F 43 ~ fr. 93 Theiler.
[33] Aleshire 1989, 232-233.

votive had no such inscription, descriptive labels could be attached.[34] It is easy to see how mere interpretations and learned guesswork could be turned into fact in this way.

While belief in the truth of anything written remained unquestioned in most cases, ancient letterforms and writing habits provided additional proof for the age of an artefact.[35] In the *Lindian Chronicle*, a vessel dedicated by Kadmos and the statues donated by Amasis are credited with paleographically notable inscriptions (III, XXIX).[36] When Dionysios of Halikarnassos substantiated his argument concerning the wanderings of Aineias with references to a long list of relics, he did not fail to mention that some of them bore 'ancient inscriptions' naming their dedicator.[37] The most compelling examples, however, come from the pages of Pausanias:[38] in his description of the chest of Kypselos at Olympia, the periegete recognises not only ancient letterforms,[39] but he also explains the archaic practice of *boustrophedon* writing.[40] Pausanias also comments on the peculiar circular arrangement of the inscription on the discus of Iphitos.[41] This interest in ancient letterforms can be traced back to Herodotus, who presented some epigrams in 'Kadmeian letters' on tripods in the Theban Ismenion as evidence for his theory about the Phoenician derivation of the Greek alphabet.[42]

Only rarely, however, can we get a glimpse at the actual process of re-evaluation. Herodotus reports that a golden vessel among the offerings of Kroisos at Delphi had been appropriated as a dedication of the Spartans in his time: 'The inscription was made by a certain Delphian, whose name I know but do not mention, out of his desire to please the Lacedaemonians.'.[43] In fact, a unique epigraphic monument from Lindos testifies to a similar occurrence: at the end of the 4th century BCE, a priest dedicated a group of statues in the sanctuary of Athena.[44] Approximately 500 years later, one of these statues acquired a new dedicatory inscription which declared it to be an offering of the eponymous hero Lindos himself.[45] It is almost certain that some (if not most)

---

[34] IG XI 2, 208 l. 12; cf. Aleshire 1989, 106.
[35] Hartmann 2013.
[36] On the statues of Amasis and their inscriptions see Francis and Vickers 1984, 120–122. The Phoenician inscription on the cauldron of Kadmos is also mentioned by Diod. 5, 58, 3. Blinkenberg (1912, 388; 1915, 9) pointed out that many fragments of bronze cauldrons, some of Near Eastern origin, were found during the excavations of the sanctuary at Lindos. The offering of Kadmos is perhaps the result of creative re-interpretation of an actual Phoenician inscription (cautious optimism also in Willi 2005, 170–171).
[37] Dion. Hal. ant. 1, 51. On Dionysius's use of monuments and inscriptions as historical evidence see Andrén 1960; Engels 2011.
[38] On Pausanias's use of inscriptions see Habicht 1984; Tzifopoulos 1991; Whittaker 1991; Bommelaer 1999; Modenesi 2001; Zizza 2006; Nafissi 2007.
[39] Paus. 5, 22, 3; 6, 19, 6; 8, 25, 1.
[40] Paus. 5, 17, 6.
[41] Paus. 5, 20, 1.
[42] Hdt. 5, 59–61. One of these tripods was still there to be described by Paus. 9, 10, 4, who gave another meaning to the apparently badly understood inscription, however. Cf. Volkmann 1954, 59–62; West 1985, 289–295; Pritchett 1993, 116–121; Higbie 1999, 58–59; Papalexandrou 2008, 256–259; Obradović 2009.
[43] Hdt. 1, 51, 3–4; cf. Volkmann 1954, 62.
[44] ILindos 57 Aa. B. C.
[45] ILindos 57 Ab; cf. Blinkenberg 1912, 433; Shaya 2002, 173–174.

of the dedicatory texts in the *Lindian Chronicle* were secondary additions or simply inventions of the historians who reported them.[46] All the dedications to Athena Polias and Zeus Polieus fall into this category because the veneration of Athena Polias is not securely attested at Lindos[47] and Zeus Polieus does not appear in Lindian inscriptions before *c*. 313–275 BCE.[48]

In the Delphian case reported by Herodotus, the re-interpretation amounted to an outright falsification. In other instances, the process may not have been so intentional, and obviously, creative explanation often played an important part. In the sanctuary of Athena Alea at Tegea, Pausanias found a *peplos* that had been dedicated by Laodike, a descendant of Agapenor who had led the Arcadians to Troy and ended up on Cyprus as the founder of Paphos.[49] Pausanias tells us that there was an identifying inscription 'on the dedication': 'This is the robe of Laodike; she offered it to her Athena, | Sending it to her broad fatherland from divine Cyprus.' The epigram is a product of the Hellenistic period.[50] One may wonder whether this inscription was weaved into the clothing or added later in some way, but even in the first case, the object was not necessarily an outright fake. It is to be noted that the inscription does not make any reference to Agapenor. The crucial link between the Laodike of the dedication and the mythical figure of Agapenor is an unproven supposition and could very well be the result of wishful thinking.[51] This becomes even clearer when considering that this Laodike is not attested in any other source than the report of Pausanias. The mostly very terse votive inscriptions from the Archaic period left ample room for this kind of speculation.[52] In the very similar case of one of the tripods at the Theban Ismenion, Herodotus was indeed rather cautious to identify the boxer Skaios named in the dedicatory inscription with his mythological homonym.[53]

It is easy enough for us to dismiss such re-interpretations of ancient objects but it would be wrong to suppose that all ancient observers were simply credulous. Pausanias was capable of rational criticism: he did not believe that the temple of Apollon at Lycian Patara housed a bronze bowl which had been made by Hephaistos himself and dedicated by the hero Telephos; Pausanias insisted that the Samians Theodoros and Rhoikos were the first to melt bronze.[54] Pausanias also dismissed the claim of the inhabitants of Pheneos to possess a statue of Poseidon Hippios dedicated by Odysseus, even if they pointed out its dedicatory inscription.[55] According to Pausanias, the

---

[46] Blinkenberg 1912, 400–404.
[47] ILindos 132. 482 probably relate to the city of Rhodes.
[48] ILindos 56–57.
[49] Paus. 8, 5, 3.
[50] Roy 1987, 196–197.
[51] Roy 1987, 197–200.
[52] Willi 2005, 164–165.
[53] Hdt. 5, 60.
[54] Paus. 9, 41, 1; cf. Pirenne-Delforge 2009, 45–46.
[55] Paus. 8, 14, 5–7.

technique used to produce the statue had not been known in the heroic age.[56] Along similar lines, Pliny dismissed the claim of Mucianus to have read a letter of Sarpedon written on papyrus which was kept in a sanctuary in Lydia.[57] He built his judgement on the fact that papyrus is never mentioned in Homer and his conviction that it simply had not been invented yet. Athenaios did not accept the identification of an object in the temple of Artemis at Capua as the famous cup of Nestor.[58] In this case, the presence of an inscription probably proved to be detrimental to the credibility of the interpretation: the object had the Homeric verses describing the cup inlaid in golden letters, thus suggesting a material reconstruction of the literary artefact. Efforts in this direction are attested, and Athenaios mentions the object at Capua exactly in this context.[59] Descriptions in archaic literature (especially the Homeric epics) often were regarded as decisive for the identification of relics: Pausanias attacked the claims of Cyprian Amathous to possess the necklace of Eriphyle because the object simply did not match the description given by Homer.[60]

Sometimes, the importance ascribed to a relic is increased by giving several notable possessors. This kind of object biography occurs several times in the *Lindian Chronicle*.[61] The prototypes of these object biographies are found in the Homeric epics.[62]

A final point concerns the ambiguity of these re-evaluations. Mythological stories were not unequivocally tied to a specific object, but local tradition was relatively free to connect them with a suitable artefact.[63] The shield of Euphorbos, e.g., was on display at Argos[64] and Miletus.[65] Possession of the notorious necklace of Eriphyle was claimed by Delphi, Delos and Amathous.[66] Ancient scholars might discuss the merits of this or that version but, in the end, there was no authority which could enforce a decision. Even the obvious device to direct an enquiry to an oracle, which was used

---

[56] A similar argument is put forward by Paus. 10, 38, 5–6 concerning a statue of Athena, allegedly brought to Amphissa from Troy by Thoas.
[57] Mucianus fr. 22 Peter ~ Plin. nat. 13, 88.
[58] Athen. 11, 30. 77. On ancient discussions about Nestor's cup see Robert 2010, 186–187; de Angelis 2015b.
[59] Athen. 11, 77 ~ Promathidas of Herakleia FGrH/BNJ 430 F 8.
[60] Paus. 9, 41, 2–5. Duffy (2013/2014) argues that the reliance on Homer is a peculiarity of Pausanias, but literary corrections of Homer, aptly classified as *Schwindelliteratur* (fake literature) in modern scholarship, do not provide an unproblematic parallel to periegetic writing.
[61] V: shields of Eurypylos and Laomedon, dedicated by Herakles; X: leather cap of Paris, dedicated by Menelaos; XIV: quiver of Pandaros, dedicated by Teukros; XVI: vase having served as price at the funeral games of Aigialeus, dedicated by Aretakritos and his sons; XXVII: krater given to Kokalos by Daidalos, dedicated by Phalaris; XXXV: gifts from king Artaxerxes, dedicated by the people of Lindos. Cf. Higbie 1995, 195–203; Robert 2010, 188–194.
[62] Hom. Il. 2, 101–108; 23, 740–748; Hom. Od. 4, 615–619; 15, 115–119.
[63] see the index in Thompson 1985 on conflicting claims.
[64] Heraion: Paus. 2, 17, 3; cf. Piérart 1996, 176–177.
[65] Didyma: Herakl. Pont. fr. 89 Wehrli; Diod. 10, 6, 2–3; Ov. met. 15, 163–164.
[66] On Delphi: Ephoros/Demophilos FGrH/BNJ 70 F 96; Theopompos of Chios FGrH/BNJ 115 F 248; Apollod. 3, 7, 5–7; Paus. 8, 24, 10; 9, 41, 2. On Delos: IDélos 104, 89; Rouse (1902, 319) believes this object to be an 'imitation' of the original relic, but this is not what the inventory says. On Amathous, sanctuary of Aphrodite and Adonis: Paus. 9, 41, 2–5.

to identify heroic primary relics, was not put into effect regarding secondary relics.[67] This, however, did not diminish the allure of relics, real or imagined. They were an integral part of Greek myth-historical thinking.[68] Herodotus provides many examples of stories tied to such objects,[69] and the *Lindian Chronicle* shows what could be culled from the pages of local historians.

Framing

Unfortunately, our knowledge about the framing of relics in ancient sanctuaries is rather limited.[70] Many objects were fastened to the temple walls. In the context of the battle of Leuktra, Kallisthenes mentions weapons on the wall of the temple of Herakles at Thebes.[71] Asklepiades of Myrleia found shields and ships' beaks that had been suspended from the walls in the temple of Athena at Odysseia in Spain.[72] The temple inventories, e.g. those of the Asklepieion at Athens, confirm this practice.[73] From this evidence, it becomes clear that the walls (at least halfway up) and the wooden beams of the roof construction often were crowded with objects.[74] Bigger objects such as 'giant bones' could be deposited in porticoes.[75] The chariot of Pelops was preserved on the roof of the so-called Anaktoron in the sanctuary of Demeter at Keleai.[76] Thus, the temples themselves and dedicated treasuries provided a monumental frame for the votive offerings.[77]

As is the case today, the value of certain objects could be further emphasised by gratings and visible means of preservation in general: the front and back porch of

---

[67] Cf. Thompson 1985, 23–26.
[68] Boardman 2002; Hartmann 2010, 409–496; 2014.
[69] e.g. at the Heraion of Samos: Hdt. 1, 70; 2, 182; 4, 88. 152.
[70] Cf. Rouse 1902, 342–347.
[71] Kallisthenes FGrH/BNJ 124 F 22a; cf. Xen. hell. 6, 4, 7; Diod. 15, 43, 4; Polyain. 2, 3, 8.
[72] Asklepiades of Myrleia FGrH/BNJ 697 F 7.
[73] The most important piece of evidence is IG II² 1534a. Cf. Aleshire (1989, 229, 235–237; 1991, 41–46), who also provides a graphical reconstruction (Aleshire 1991, pl. 11). Harris (1995, 3) has a similar reconstruction for the Parthenon, Krumeich 2008, 74 for the temple of Athena at Tegea. The situation at Delos was similar: e.g. IDélos 1421 Ab; 1432 Bb col. ii. Objects which were nailed to the walls are attested in IG XI 2, 165, l. 18 and IDélos 1444 Aa l. 48. Archaeological evidence for this practice is provided by the *tabulae ansatae* found in the Asklepieion at Pergamon: Albert 1972, 6–11. Sometimes, shelves were used: SEG 19, 129 (Chalkotheke, Athens); IG I³ 387 l. 14–16 (Opisthodomos, Athens). Cf. Aleshire 1989, 236. However, ῥυμός does not signify a shelf in every instance: Burr Thompson 1944, 186–187; Tréheux 1955/1956, 140.
[74] For dedications fastened to parts of the roof construction see IG II² 1532b l. 8 ([πρ]ὸς τῆι ὀροφῆ[ι]); IDélos 399 B l. 156; 407 l. 20–21; 442 l. 222; 443 l. 136; 444 B l. 56–57; 461 Bb l. 45; Paus. 3, 16, 1 (egg of Leda in the temple of Hilaeira at Sparta); Paus. 2, 10, 3; 8, 22, 7 (small statues). Cf. Aleshire 1989, 119–120.
[75] Paus. 2, 10, 2.
[76] Paus. 2, 14, 4.
[77] Cf. the dagger of Pelops in the treasury of the Sikyonians at Olympia: Paus. 6, 19, 6. Significantly, Polemon of Ilion fr. 20 Preller makes no distinction between the 'old temple of Hera' and the treasuries in his discussion of votive offerings at Olympia. All buildings fall into the category of ναός.

the Athenian Parthenon were protected by wooden grills.[78] The same is true for the Hephaisteion,[79] and similar gratings are attested in many Greek temples.[80] This must have been a device to regulate access for relatively good-willing visitors because such barriers would have been no obstacle to any serious intruder. For the same reason, it is improbable that these porches were used as a strong room for housing major assets of money and/or materially precious objects.[81] Such an arrangement would have made perfect sense, however, for the display of votive offerings that had become relics. In a discussion of barriers in front of cult images within Greek temples, Torsten Mattern has pointed out that in many cases these barriers enclose much more space than would have been necessary to protect the statues from unauthorised access: possibly, this space also was used for the presentation of relics.[82]

There is not much evidence on the accessibility of relics either. Lucian tells a story about Neanthos, the son of Pittakos, who wanted to play on the lyre of Orpheus which was kept at the temple of Apollon.[83] Neanthos had to bribe a priest who exchanged the relic for another instrument. Leaving aside the questionable historicity of this story, the legend pre-supposes an expectation that relics are not directly accessible to everyone. Herodotus reports that when the Persians advanced upon Delphi, weapons 'which no man was allowed to touch' moved outside the temple of Athena Pronaia in a miraculous fashion.[84] However, Mucianus saw only tiny remains of the linen corselet that Amasis had dedicated to Athena Lindia[85] because too many visitors had tested the fabric with their hands.[86] Needless to say, this did not prevent him from doing the same.

General restrictions did apply, of course: in some cases, temples were opened only on certain days of the year or for certain people.[87] In other cases, the right to enter a temple depended on the performance of certain ritual acts.[88] At Lindos, visitors

---

[78] Stevens 1940, 69–73; 1942.
[79] Stevens 1950.
[80] Büsing 1970, 65–67.
[81] Cf. Linders 2007, 778. The *pronaos* housed many objects made predominantly of silver until the end of the Peloponnesian War: Harris 1995, 64–80. In comparison with the inventories of the so-called Hekatompedon it becomes clear, however, that the mass of wealth was stored there: Harris 1995, 104–200. Silver ware was regarded as second-rate treasure: Thuk. 6, 46, 3.
[82] Mattern 2007, 156.
[83] Lukian. ind. 11–12.
[84] Hdt. 8, 37.
[85] Hdt. 2, 182; 3, 47, 2–3; *Lindian Chronicle* XXIX; Plin. nat. 19, 12; cf. Francis and Vickers 1984, 125–126; Moxon 2000. This type of breast-plate is known from Ramesside Egypt: Picard 1957, 365–367 (whose reconstruction of Amasis's corselet is based upon severe misunderstandings of the ancient sources, however); on technical aspects s. Törnkvist 1969; Gleba 2012; Aldrete et al. 2013.
[86] Mucianus fr. 25 Peter ~ Plin. nat. 19, 12. – Cf. the meticulous documentation of textiles in a miserable state of preservation in a Milesian inventory: IMilet 3, 1357; cf. Günther 1988. It goes without question that the corselet seen by Mucianus must have been heavily restored at least: cf. Graells i Fabregat 2016.
[87] Cf. Hewitt 1909; Corbett 1970; Nilsson 1974, 75–77; Paliompeis 1996, 437–447; Krumeich 2008, 76–77; Mylonopoulos 2011, 286–288.
[88] e.g. Eur. Ion 185–235.

who wanted to access the sanctuary had to be ritually clean not only regarding the body but also the soul.[89] More specifically, one had to wear clean clothes and had to do without any headdress.[90] Visitors had to come either barefoot or wearing white shoes not made of goatskin. In general, anything made of goatskin and tied belts were forbidden. Such regulations effected a habitus-related framing of the sanctuary and its relics.

The most explicit sort of framing will have been the oral instructions of local priests and guides.[91] Inscriptions often formed the starting point for such explanations,[92] and Pausanias makes it clear that he regarded stories backed up by inscriptions as more credible.[93] As we have already seen, the importance of inscriptions is perfectly obvious from the *Lindian Chronicle*. In all these instances, however, the inscriptions do not present themselves to be a device of explanation. They were or pretended to be a part of the original dedication. The problem was acknowledged by Prokopios with concern to a marble ship at Cap Geraistos at Euboea, whose heavily weathered inscription declared it to be a dedication of Agamemnon himself.[94] The late antique historian understood that the inscription could have been a later addition. This was obviously the case at Olympia, where an epigram dating to the Hellenistic period explained to visitors that they looked at the ruins of the palace of Oinomaos.[95] The same device was used with the bridal chamber of Alkmene at Thebes.[96] These inscriptions must have been authorised by the administrators of the sanctuary who could thus enforce some control over the canonisation of certain aetiological interpretations.

The single remaining wooden column of the palace of Oinomaos provides the most striking example for the framing of relics at all: it was held together by metal clamps and shielded from weather by a protective roof.[97] The ruinous building clearly was to be perceived as an important (myth-)historic monument. It has been suggested that what could be seen were in fact the remains of Dörpfeld's Bau VII extant at the time.[98] The re-evaluation of this archaeological monument was dependent on its context: the oldest statues of Olympic victors stood in its immediate vicinity.[99] When a Roman senator wanted to erect a memorial to his victory near the pillar of Oinomaos, digging work for the fundament turned up fragments of armour, bridles and curb-chains,[100] suitably recalling Oinomaos's habit to kill his daughter's suitors in a chariot race.

---

[89] LSCG, Suppl. 91/ILindos 487 l. 1–10, dating from the 3rd century CE. On regulations of ritual purity in general see Wächter 1910; Bremmer 2002.
[90] On clothing regulations in Greek sanctuaries see Wächter 1910, 15–24; Mills 1984; Brøns 2017, 325–359.
[91] Cf. Jones 2001.
[92] Plut. de Pyth. or. 2 ~ Plut. mor. 395a.
[93] Paus. 1, 37, 2; 4, 1, 8; 5, 2, 5; 6, 4, 6; cf. Whittaker 1991, 176–179.
[94] Prok. BG 8, 22, 27–29.
[95] Paus. 5, 20, 7; cf. Brulotte 1994, 56–58.
[96] Paus. 9, 11, 1–2.
[97] Paus. 5, 14, 7; 5, 20, 6.
[98] Rambach 2002, 132–133.
[99] Paus. 6, 18, 7.
[100] Paus. 5, 20, 8–9.

Finally, there is the question whether there was some sort of cultic framing of relics in Greek temples. Secondary relics did not, as a rule, receive cult in ancient Greece. They were not holy objects because they participated in the special qualities of their former owner but they had a sacral status only insofar as they were regarded as property of the god – as were indeed all votive offerings.[101] There are only few exceptions: the sceptre of Agamemnon was honoured with daily sacrifices by the inhabitants of Chaironeia.[102] Probably, an ancient aniconic image of a god had been re-interpreted as a heroic relic.[103] Some objects were carried around during processions but our fragmentary sources make it difficult to assess whether they became the object of cultic veneration. The cuirass of Timomachos, who had taught the Spartans the art of war, was paraded during the Hyakinthia.[104] The shield of Diomedes was carried in a procession at Argos.[105] In this case, however, the primary focus of veneration clearly was the image of Athena which was identified with the famous Palladion.[106] The connection with Diomedes was important because it strengthened local claims to possession of this famous statue. The Athenians used the ship of Theseus for their regular sacred embassy to Delos until the time of Demetrios of Phaleron[107] but there is no evidence for cultic veneration of the vessel itself.

At the same time, the sacral status of secondary relics is not merely accidental. There are no known instances of individuals claiming private possession of heroic relics in ancient Greece. Obviously, the process of re-evaluation was restricted to the sphere of communal sanctuaries.[108] The sanctuary, the buildings that were used to house smaller votives, the ritual regulations for visitors, the restrictions of accessibility – all this was essential for the re-evaluation of ordinary objects as priced relics. Sacred framing and myth-historical re-interpretation were intimately interlinked. It was only at Rome that this bond was broken: heroic relics became the object of antiquarian interest and collectionism;[109] Augustus had set the example when he decorated his villas with weapons of the heroes and the bones of giants.[110] From Tegea, he transferred the tusks of the Kalydonian boar to Rome where they added historical depth to his new-

---

[101] Scheer 1996, 354–356; Zografou 2005, 124.
[102] Paus. 9, 40, 11–12, accepted as the only authentic work of Hephaistos at 9, 41, 5; cf. Easterling 1989, 116–117; Pisano 2015, 11–13. The qualification of the sceptre as ἄφθιτον αἰεί in Hom. Il. 2, 46 may have been responsible for the identification of a fitting object. Its exceptional status is justly emphasised by Bouvier 2005, 82–84.
[103] Cf. Pfister 1909, 336–337.
[104] Aristot. fr. 532 Rose.
[105] Kall. h. 5, 35–37; Sch. Kall. h. 5, 1; cf. Piérart 1996, 177–194.
[106] Kleinknecht (1939, 306–315) identified the Palladion with the shield of Diomedes, but his theory has been refuted by Ziehen (1941).
[107] Plat. Phaid. 58a–b; Plut. Thes. 23, 1; Plut. an seni respublica gerenda sit 6 ~ Plut. mor. 786 f.
[108] Thompson 1985, 20.
[109] Hor. sat. 2, 3, 20–28; Mart. 8, 6; Stat. silv. 4, 6, 59–88.
[110] Suet. Aug. 72, 3; cf. Federico 1993. It is to be noted, however, that Augustus did not claim to possess the armour of a *specific* hero: *arma heroum* might just mean something as 'bronze weapons such as the heroes had'.

built forum.¹¹¹ When Pausanias looked for the objects, he had to ask the custodians of wonders (οἱ ἐπὶ τοῖς θαύμασιν): at Rome, the objects were no longer *sacra*, but just *mirabilia*.¹¹² But even then, the monumental framing provided by sanctuaries remained important for the perception of relics: Pliny stated that some objects were only contemplated as very valuable because they were on display in temples.¹¹³

Temple and museum

These observations lead to the question whether ancient temples functioned as equivalents of modern museums, to a certain extent at least.¹¹⁴ I am not concerned here with the exposition of works of arts and the presumed conversion of temples into art galleries.¹¹⁵ In modern historical museums, decontextualised objects are displayed not for their material worth or their aesthetical value but because they are regarded as significant as remains of the past. Greek and Roman temples did not collect significant objects on purpose, even if some of the available objects came to be perceived as such. This is demonstrated very clearly by the extant inventories: most dedications were no relics in any meaningful sense. However, every votive had its lifespan. When the walls of the sanctuary or its treasuries became too crowded, ancient offerings were stored away in boxes or even melted down.¹¹⁶ At this stage at least, there must have been some selection. The responsible magistrates or priests will have decided which objects to repair and keep on display for their memorial value and which objects to dispose of.¹¹⁷

This kind of selectivity is at work to an even higher degree in the *Lindian Chronicle*. The *Chronicle* gives no systematic or complete history, but neither is it a comprehensive catalogue of lost or damaged offerings.¹¹⁸ In fact, the *Lindian Chronicle* does not contain a single object without historical significance. The *Chronicle* is concerned above all with the dedications of important foreigners (mythical and historical), while foreigners constitute a small minority among the dedicators in the inventories.¹¹⁹ Even more,

---

[111] Paus. 8, 46, 1. 5; cf. Scheer 2010, 232–235. Tusks formerly at Tegea: Kall. h. 3, 218–220; hide remaining at Tegea: Paus. 8, 47, 2; Lukian. ind. 14. Cf. Jördens and Becht-Jördens 1994, 178–184. Prok. BG 5, 15, 8 saw tusks of the Kalydonian boar at Beneventum. It was believed that Diomedes had left the relic there when he founded the city. For another transfer of the remains of a mythical creature cf. the sea-monster that had been killed by Perseus in defence of Andromeda, whose bones were brought to Rome by M. Aemilius Scaurus: Plin. nat. 9, 11. On this see Harvey Jr. 1994.
[112] Paus. 8, 46, 5.
[113] Plin. nat. praef. 19: *multa valde pretiosa ideo videntur, quia sunt templis dicata*.
[114] The most explicit development of this comparison can be found in Shaya 2002; 2005; 2015.
[115] The *locus classicus* is Strab. 14, 1, 14 on the Heraion at Samos. Arafat (1995) assumes an analogous musealisation also for the Heraion at Olympia but against this see Krumeich 2008, 77–86.
[116] On storing see the index of Harris 1995, regarding box. On melting see Prêtre 2014.
[117] Cf. IG II² 995/LSCG 43, esp. l. 8–10 (Athens, 2nd century BCE).
[118] Cf. Chaniotis 1988, 54; Robert 2015, 11. 13.
[119] For the Parthenon and the Erechtheion, Harris 1995, 278 lists 77 personal names mentioned on the *stelai*, among them only eight foreigners. On famous donors see Harris 1995, 228–236.

the *Chronicle* includes not a single anonymous dedication. It is quite improbable that no such objects existed in the sanctuary at Lindos, but obviously persons were more important than things for the authors of the *Chronicle* – in fact they are even named first. The heading of the whole catalogue explicitly states that what is to follow is not a catalogue of things, but of persons: 'those who made an offering to Athena'.[120]

In reality, even at Lindos the relics must have been a small minority of all votives on display.[121] We have observed some strategies for framing, but there is no evidence for the exclusive accumulation of relics in certain parts of the sanctuary. This last step of musealisation is only taken by the *Lindian Chronicle* as a text creating its own reality. If the sanctuary of Lindos was not a museum, the virtual collection presented by the *Chronicle* certainly is.[122] We may compare this with the musealising gaze of Pausanias held against the more comprehensive outlook of Polemon of Ilion: while the latter lists for the treasury of the Metapontians at Olympia 132 silver cups plus three in gold, two silver jugs and a silver vase for drinking, the former focuses on a single statue of Endymion made of ivory.[123] Pausanias's lack of interest in the mass of dedications of vessels unrelated to some notable person is also evident in his description of the Heraion.[124] The periegete himself emphasises that he does not give a complete catalogue[125] but only a selection of the most interesting objects.[126] The museal character often ascribed to this temple is due more to the specific perspective of Pausanias than to the original arrangements.[127]

Perhaps, we should look to another analogy: one that is rather self-evident but has been pretty much avoided by modern scholarship. We should think about churches. While keeping in mind the crucial differences, many similarities emerge: churches are often historic monuments preserving traces of the community's history over the last hundreds of years, some Christian denominations being more inclined to this kind of heritage building than others. These traces are not the result of conscious collecting, and in most cases, there is no special framing. What we can see is rather the result of a slow and ongoing process of selection. While most of these traces of history do not claim a sacred status as 'relics', they are enclosed within a sacral space demanding special behaviour from its visitors, thus imposing an embedded mode of viewing on the viewer, even on visitors who come without any religious motives for purely art-historical or historical interests. In the end, the comparison

---

[120] *Lindian Chronicle* B l. 1. – In contrast, the inventories from Didyma (e.g. IDidyma 427 l. 6) start with the formula τάδε ἀνετέθη τῶι θεῶι.
[121] Krumeich 2008, 88–93.
[122] Krumeich 2008, 93; Robert 2015, 11.
[123] Polemon of Ilion: fr. 20 Preller; Paus. 6, 19, 11.
[124] Paus. 5, 16, 1 – 5, 20, 5.
[125] Confirmed by Polemon of Ilion fr. 20 Preller; cf. Angelucci 2011, 337–338; Angelucci 2014, 21–22.
[126] Admittedly, the fragment of Polemon is transmitted by Athenaios in a discussion of a specific form of vessel. We cannot be sure that Polemon did not mention the votive offerings described by Pausanias. It is certain, however, that Pausanias did not bother to count and list common vessels.
[127] Cf. Krumeich 2008, 83–85.

between temples and churches concerning their role as places of memory may prove more helpful than the traditional question about the continuity between pagan and Christian relic veneration.

References

Albert, W.-D. 1972 Die Tabulae ansatae aus Pergamon. In: *Pergamon. Gesammelte Aufsätze.* Pergamenische Forschungen 1 (Berlin), 1–42

Aldrete, G. S., Bartell, S. and Aldrete, A. 2013 *Reconstructing Ancient Linen Body Armor. Unraveling the Linothorax Mystery* (Baltimore)

Aleshire, S. B. 1989 *The Athenian Asklepieion. The People, Their Dedications, and the Inventories* (Amsterdam)

Aleshire, S. B. 1991 *Asklepios at Athens. Epigraphic and Prosopographic Essays on the Athenian Healing Cults* (Amsterdam)

Ampolo, C., Erdas, D. and Magnetto, A. (eds) 2014 La gloria di Athana Lindia, *Annali della Scuola normale superiore di Pisa. Classe di lettere e filosofia* (Serie 5) 6, 3–444

Andrén, A. 1960 Dionysius of Halicarnassus on Roman Monuments. In: *Hommages à Léon Herrmann.* Collection Latomus 44 (Brussels), 88–104

Angelis, F. de 2015a Greek and Roman specialized writing on art and architecture. In: C. Marconi (ed.), *The Oxford Handbook of Greek and Roman Art and Architecture* (Oxford), 70–83

Angelis, F. de 2015b La coupe de Nestor et l'imagination hellénistique. Artistes, antiquaires, rois dans les deux derniers siècles av. J.-C. In: P. Linant de Bellefonds, É. Prioux and A. Rouveret (eds), *D'Alexandre à Auguste. Dynamiques de la création dans les arts visuels et la poésie, Archéologie & culture* (Rennes), 57–68

Angelucci, M. 2011 Polemon's contribution to the periegetic literature of the II century B.C. ὅρμος. *Ricerche di Storia Antica* NS 3, 326–341

Angelucci, M. 2014 Reiseliteratur im Altertum. Die periegesis in hellenistischer Zeit. In: E. Olshausen and V. Sauer (eds), *Mobilität in den Kulturen der antiken Mittelmeerwelt. Stuttgarter Kolloquium zur Historischen Geographie des Altertums 11, 2011.* Geographica historica 31 (Stuttgart), 11–23

Arafat, K. W. 1995 Pausanias and the Temple of Hera at Olympia. *The Annual of the British School at Athens* 90, 461–473

Bäbler, B. 2002 Auf der Suche nach Xenokrates. Gab es 'Kunstgeschichte' in der Antike? *Seminari Romani di Cultura Greca* 5, 137–160

Blinkenberg, C. 1912 Exploration archéologique de Rhodes (Fondation Carlsberg) VI. La chronique du temple lindien. *Oversigt over det Kongelige Danske Videnskabernes Selskabs Forhandlinger* 5/6, 317–457

Blinkenberg, C. 1915 *Die lindische Tempelchronik.* Kleine Texte für Vorlesungen und Übungen 131 (Bonn)

Blinkenberg, C. 1941 *Lindos. Fouilles de l'acropole 1902-1914 II. Inscriptions.* Lindos. Fouilles et recherches (Berlin)

Boardman, J. 2002 *The Archaeology of Nostalgia. How the Greeks Re-Created Their Mythical Past* (London)

Bommelaer, J.-F. 1999 Traces de l'épigraphie delphique dans le texte de Pausanias. In: R. G. Khoury (ed.), *Urkunden und Urkundenformulare im Klassischen Altertum und in den orientalischen Kulturen.* Bibliothek der klassischen Altertumswissenschaften, Reihe 2 N. F. 104 (Heidelberg), 83–93

Bouvier, D. 2005 Reliques héroïques en Grèce archaïque. L'exemple de la lance d'Achille. In: P. Borgeaud and Y. Volokhine (eds), *Les objets de la mémoire. Pour une approche comparatiste des reliques et de leur culte.* Studia Religiosa Helvetica 11 (Bern), 73–93

Bremmer, J. N. 2002 How old is the ideal of holiness (of mind) in the Epidaurian Temple inscription and the Hippocratic Oath? *Zeitschrift für Papyrologie und Epigraphik* 141, 106–108

Bresson, A. 2006 Relire la Chronique du temple lindien, Topoi. *Orient and Occident* 14, 527–551

Brøns, C. 2017 *Gods and Garments. Textiles in Greek Sanctuaries in the 7th–1st Centuries BC*. Ancient Textiles Series 28 (Oxford)

Brulotte, E. L. 1994 The 'Pillar of Oinomaos' and the location of Stadium I at Olympia. *American Journal of Archaeology* 98, 53–64

Burr Thompson, D. 1944 The Golden Nikai reconsidered. *Hesperia. Journal of the American School of Classical Studies at Athens* 13, 173–209

Büsin, H. H. 1970 *Die griechische Halbsäule* (Wiesbaden)

Cannistraci, O. S. 2014 Il lemma XV e le offerte delle phylai nella Cronaca di Lindo. Ricostruire le origini tra realia di età arcaica ed ellenistica, *Annali della Scuola normale superiore di Pisa. Classe di lettere e filosofia* (Serie 5) 6, 259–294

Chaniotis, A. 1988 *Historie und Historiker in den griechischen Inschriften. Epigraphische Beiträge zur griechischen Historiographie*. Heidelberger Althistorische Beiträge und Epigraphische Studien 4 (Stuttgart)

Corbett, P. E. 1970 Greek temples and Greek worshippers. The literary and archaeological evidence. *Bulletin of the Institute of Classical Studies* 17, 149–158

Duffy, W. S. 2013/2014 The necklace of Eriphyle and Pausanias' approach to the Homeric epics. *Classical World* 107, 35–47

Easterling, P. E. 1989 Agamemnon's skêptron in the Iliad. In: M. M. Mackenzie and C. Roueché (eds), *Images of Authority. Papers Presented to Joyce Reynolds on the Occasion of Her Seventieth Birthday*, Cambridge Philological Society Supplement 16 (Cambridge), 104–121

Engels, D. 2011 Zur Bedeutung der Inschriften im Geschichtswerk des Dionysius von Halikarnassos. In: C. Deroux (ed.), *Corolla Epigraphica. Hommages au professeur Yves Burnand*. Collection Latomus 331 (Brussels), 470–489

Federico, E. 1993 Ossa di giganti ed armi di eroi. Sugli ornamenti delle ville augustee di Capri (Svetonio, Aug. 72). *Civiltà del Mediterraneo* 5, 7–19

Francis, E. D. and Vickers, M. 1984 Amasis and Lindos. *Bulletin of the Institute of Classical Studies* 31, 119–130

Furtwängler, A. 1877/1878 Plinius und seine Quellen über die bildenden Künste. *Jahrbücher für classische Philologie* Supplement 9 (Leipzig), 1–78.

Gleba, M. 2012 Linen-clad Etruscan warriors. In: M.-L. Nosch (ed.), *Wearing the Cloak. Dressing the Soldier in Roman Times*. Ancient Textiles Series 10 (Oxford), 45–55

Graells i Fabregat, R. 2016 Las corazas incorruptas y la permanencia en exposición de algunas armas en santuarios (s. VI a.C.–II d.C.). *Ostraka. Rivista di antichità* 25, 53–66

Günther, W. 1988 'Vieux et inutilisable' dans un inventaire inédit de Milet. In: D. Knoepfler (ed.), *Comptes et inventaires dans la cité grecque. Actes du colloque international d'épigraphie tenu à Neuchâtel du 23 au 26 septembre 1986 en l'honneur de Jacques Tréheux*. Université de Neuchâtel. Recueil de travaux publiés par la Faculté des Lettres. Quarantième fascicule 40 (Neuchâtel), 215–237

Habicht, C. 1984 Pausanias and the evidence of inscriptions. *Classical Antiquity* 3, 40–56

Harris, D. 1995 *The Treasures of the Parthenon and Erechtheion*. Oxford Monographs on Classical Archaeology (Oxford)

Hartmann, A. 2010 *Zwischen Relikt und Reliquie. Objektbezogene Erinnerungspraktiken in antiken Gesellschaften*. Studien zur Alten Geschichte 11 (Berlin)

Hartmann, A. 2013 Cui vetustas fidem faciat. Inscriptions and other material relics of the past in Graeco-Roman antiquity. In: P. Liddel and P. Low (eds), *Inscriptions and Their Uses in Greek and Latin Literature*. Oxford Studies in Ancient Documents (Oxford), 33–63

Hartmann, A. 2014 Tekmeria. Die Wanderungen der Heroen als Problem der antiken Historiographie. In: E. Olshausen and V. Sauer (eds), *Mobilität in den Kulturen der antiken Mittelmeerwelt. Stuttgarter Kolloquium zur Historischen Geographie des Altertums 11, 2011*. Geographica historica 31 (Stuttgart), 275–291

Harvey, P. B. Jr 1994 The death of mythology. The case of Joppa. *Journal of Early Christian Studies* 2, 1–14
Hewitt, J. W. 1909 The major restrictions on access to Greek temples. *Transactions and Proceedings of the American Philological Association* 40, 83–91
Higbie, C. 1995 *Heroe's Names, Homeric Identities*. Albert Bates Lord Studies in Oral Tradition 10/Garland Reference Library of the Humanities 1366 (New York)
Higbie, C. 1999 Craterus and the use of inscriptions in ancient scholarship. *Transactions of the American Philological Association* 129, 43–83
Higbie, C. 2003 The *Lindian Chronicle* and the Greek creation of their past (Oxford)
Jones, C. P. 2001 Pausanias and his guides. In: S. E. Alcock, J. F. Cherry and J. Elsner (eds), *Pausanias. Travel and Memory in Roman Greece* (Oxford), 33–39
Jördens, A. and Becht-Jördens, G. 1994 Ein Eberunterkiefer als 'Staatssymbol' des Aitolischen Bundes (IG XII 2, 15). Politische Identitätssuche im Mythos nach dem Ende der spartanischen Hegemonie. *Klio. Beiträge zur alten Geschichte* 76, 172–184
Jucker, H. 1950 *Vom Verhältnis der Römer zur bildenden Kunst der Griechen* (Frankfurt am Main)
Kalkmann, K. 1898 *Die Quellen der Kunstgeschichte des Plinius* (Berlin)
Kleinknecht, H. 1939 Λουτρὰ τῆς Παλλάδος. *Hermes. Zeitschrift für klassische Philologie* 74, 301–350
Koch, N. J. 2000 ΣΧΗΜΑ. Zur Interferenz technischer Begriffe in Rhetorik und Kunstschriftstellerei. *International Journal of the Classical Tradition* 6, 503–515
Krumeich, R. 2008 Vom Haus der Gottheit zum Museum? Zu Ausstattung und Funktion des Heraion von Olympia und des Athenatempels von Lindos. *Antike Kunst* 51, 73–95
Lacroix, L. 1989 Quelques aspects du 'culte des reliques' dans les traditions de la Grèce ancienne. *Bulletin de la Classe des lettres et des sciences morales et politiques* 75, 58–99
Linders, T. 2007 The location of the Opisthodomos. Evidence from the Temple of Athena Parthenos inventories. *American Journal of Archaeology* 111, 777–782
Massar, N. 2006 La 'Chronique de Lindos'. Un catalogue à la gloire du sanctuaire d'Athéna Lindia. *Kernos. Revue internationale et pluridisciplinaire de religion grecque antique* 19, 229–243
Mattern, T. 2007 Griechische Kultbildschranken. *Mitteilungen des Deutschen Archäologischen Instituts. Athenische Abteilung* 122, 139–159
Mills, H. 1984 Greek clothing regulations. Sacred and profane? *Zeitschrift für Papyrologie und Epigraphik* 55, 255–265
Modenesi, N. 2001 Pausania 'epigrafista' nell'itinerario della Periegesis. Il caso singolare di Atene. *Acme. Annali della Facoltà di lettere e filosofia dell'Università degli studi di Milano* 54, 3–35
Moxon, I. S. 2000 The linen breast-plates in Herodotus 3.47. *Ars textrina* 34, 159–165
Mylonopoulos, J. 2011 Divine images behind bars. The semantics of barriers in Greek temples. In: M. Haysom and J. Wallensten (eds), *Current Approaches to Religion in Ancient Greece. Papers Presented at a Symposium at the Swedish Institute at Athens 17-19 April 2008*. Skrifter Utgivna av Svenska Institutet i Athen/Acta Instituti Atheniensis Regni Sueciae, Series in 8° 21 (Stockholm), 269–291
Nafissi, M. 2007 Sotto il sole di Olimpia. Pausania interprete di epigrafi. Tradizioni locali e testo. *Mediterraneo Antico. Economie, società, culture* 10, 197–214
Nilsson, M. P. 1974 Geschichte der griechischen Religion II. Die hellenistische und römische Zeit. *Handbuch der Altertumswissenschaften* 5 (2) (München)
Obradović, M. 2009 Kadmeian letters or what did Herodotos really see in the Temple of Ismenian Apollo in Boiotian Thebes (Hdt. V 59–61)? *Journal of Classical Studies Matica Srpska* 11, 35–46
Paliompeis, S. 1996 Studien zur Innenausstattung griechischer Tempel. Skulptur und Malerei. Unpublished PhD dissertation Johannes Gutenberg-Universität Mainz
Papalexandrou, N. 2008 Boiotian tripods. The tenacity of a panhellenic symbol in a regional context, Hesperia. *Journal of the American School of Classical Studies at Athens* 77, 251–282
Pernice, E. and Gross, W. H. 1969 Die griechischen und lateinischen literarischen Zeugnisse. In: U. Hausmann (ed.), *Allgemeine Grundlagen der Archäologie. Begriff und Methode, Geschichte, Problem der Form*. Schriftzeugnisse, Handbuch der Archäologie (Munich), 395–496

Pfister, F. 1909 Der Reliquienkult im Altertum I. Das Objekt des Reliquienkultes. *Religionsgeschichtliche Versuche und Vorarbeiten* 5 (Gießen)

Pfister, F. 1912 *Der Reliquienkult im Altertum II. Die Reliquien als Kultobjekt. Geschichte des Reliquienkultes.* Religionsgeschichtliche Versuche und Vorarbeiten 5 (Gießen)

Pfister, F. 1914 Die Wunderliste bei Ampelius und die neue Chronik von Lindos. *Wochenschrift für klassische Philologie* 31, 475–478

Picard, M.-T. 1957 La thoraké d'Amasis. In: *Hommages à Waldemar Deonna.* Collection Latomus 28 (Brussels), 363–370

Piérart, M. 1996 Pour une approche du panthéon argien par la mythologie. Le bouclier d'Athéna. *Kernos. Revue internationale et pluridisciplinaire de religion grecque antique* 9, 171–194

Pirenne-Delforge, V. 2009 Under which conditions did the Greeks 'believe' in their myths? The religious criteria of adherence. In: U. Dill and C. Walde (eds), *Antike Mythen. Medien, Transformationen und Konstruktionen. Festschrift Fritz Graf* (Berlin), 38–54

Pisano, C. 2015 'Autorità senza autore' nella Grecia antica. Il caso dello scettro. *I Quaderni del Ramo d'Oro on-line* 7, 1–14 (http://www.qro.unisi.it/frontend/node/176).

Pollitt, J. J. 1964 Professional art criticism in ancient Greece. *Gazette des Beaux-Arts* (Serie 6) 64, 317–330

Pollitt, J. J. 1974 *The Ancient View of Greek Art. Criticism, History, and Terminology.* Yale Publications in the History of Art 25 (New Haven CO)

Preißhofen, F. 1979 Kunsttheorie und Kunstbetrachtung. In: H. Flashar and T. Gelzer (eds), *Le classicisme à Rome aux Iers siècles avant et après J.-C.* Entretiens sur l'antiquité classique 25 (Vandœuvres-Geneva), 263–277

Prêtre, C. 2014 Vie et mort des offrandes à Délos. *Technè. La science au service de l'histoire de l'art et des civilisations* 40, 35–41

Prioux, É. 2009 Le nouveau Posidippe. Une histoire de l'art en épigrammes? In: F. Le Blay (ed.), *Transmettre les savoirs dans les mondes hellénistique et romain,* Histoire (Rennes), 275–292

Pritchett, W. K. 1979 *The Greek State at War III. Religion* (Berkeley CA)

Pritchett, W. K. 1993 *The Liar School of Herodotus* (Amsterdam)

Rambach, J. 2002 Dörpfelds Bau VII in der Altis von Olympia. Ein früheisenzeitliches Apsidenhaus und 'Haus des Oinomaos'? *Archäologischer Anzeiger* 2002(1), 119–134

Robert, R. 2010 Histoire d'objets. Objets d'histoire. *Dialogues d'Histoire Ancienne* 41, 175–199

Robert, R. 2015 La Chronique de Lindos et l'origine des inventaires d'œuvres d'art. In: P. Linant de Bellefonds, É. Prioux and A. Rouveret (eds), *D'Alexandre à Auguste. Dynamiques de la création dans les arts visuels et la poésie.* Archéologie and Culture (Rennes), 11–29

Rouse, W. H. D. 1902 *Greek Votive Offerings. An Essay in the History of Greek Religion* (Cambridge)

Rouveret, A. 1995 Artistes, collectionneurs et antiquaires L'histoire de l'art dans l'encyclopédie plinienne. In: É. Pommier (ed.), *Histoire de l'histoire de l'art I. De l'antiquité au XVIIIe siècle. Cycles de conférences organisés au musée du Louvre par le Service culturel du 10 octobre au 14 novembre 1991 et du 25 janvier au 15 mars 1993* (Paris), 49–64

Roy, J. 1987 Pausanias, VIII, 5, 2–3 and VIII, 53, 7. Laodice Descendant of Agapenor; Tegea and Cyprus. *L'Antiquité Classique* 56, 192–200

Scheer, T. S. 1996 Ein Museum griechischer 'Frühgeschichte' im Apollontempel von Sikyon. *Klio. Beiträge zur alten Geschichte* 78, 353–373

Scheer, T. S. 2010 Arcadian cult images between religion and politics. In: J. Mylonopoulos (ed.), *Divine Images and Human Imaginations in Ancient Greece and Rome.* Religions in the Graeco-Roman World 170 (Leiden), 225–239

Schweitzer, B. 1932 *Xenokrates von Athen. Beiträge zur Geschichte der antiken Kunstforschung und Kunstanschauung.* Schriften der Königsberger Gelehrten Gesellschaft. Geisteswissenschaftliche Klasse 9(1) (Halle [Saale])

Settis, S. 1993 La trattatistica delle arti figurative. In: G. Cambiano, L. Canfora and D. Lanza (eds), *Lo spazio letterario della Grecia antica I 2. La produzione e la circolazione del testo. L'ellenismo* (Rome), 469–498

Settis, S. 1995a Did the ancients have an antiquity? The idea of renaissance in the history of classical art. In: A. Brown (ed.), *Language and Images of Renaissance Italy* (Oxford), 27–50

Settis, S. 1995b La conception de l'histoire de l'art chez les Grecs et son influence sur les théoriciens italiens du Quattrocento. In: É. Pommier (ed.), *Histoire de l'histoire de l'art I. De l'antiquité au XVIIIe siècle. Cycles de conférences organisés au musée du Louvre par le Service culturel du 10 octobre au 14 novembre 1991 et du 25 janvier au 15 mars 1993* (Paris), 145–160

Shaya, J. 2002 The Lindos Stele and the Lost Treasures of Athena. Catalogs, Collections, and Local History. Unpublished PhD dissertation University of Michigan Ann Arbor

Shaya, J. 2005 The Greek temple as museum. The case of the legendary Treasure of Athena from Lindos. *American Journal of Archaeology* 109, 423–442

Shaya, J. 2015 Greek Temple treasures and the invention of collecting. In: M. W. Gahtan and D. Pegazzano (eds), *Museum Archetypes and Collecting in the Ancient World.* Monumenta Graeca et Romana 21 (Leiden), 24–32

Sprigath, G. 2000, Der Fall Xenokrates von Athen. Zu den Methoden der Antike-Rezeption in der Quellenforschung. In: M. Baumbach (ed.), *Tradita et inventa. Beiträge zur Rezeption der Antike.* Bibliothek der klassischen Altertumswissenschaften, Reihe 2 N. F. 106 (Heidelberg), 407–428

Stevens, G. P. 1940 The setting of the Periclean parthenon. *Hesperia. Journal of the American School of Classical Studies at Athens* Supplement 3 (Athens)

Stevens, G. P. 1942 The sills of the grilles of the Pronaos and Opisthodomus of the Parthenon. *Hesperia. Journal of the American School of Classical Studies at Athens* 11, 354–364

Stevens, G. P. 1950 Grilles of the Hephaisteion. *Hesperia. Journal of the American School of Classical Studies at Athens* 19, 165–173

Strocka, V. M. 2007 Poseidippos von Pella und die Anfänge der griechischen Kunstgeschichtsschreibung. *Klio. Beiträge zur alten Geschichte* 89, 332–345

Tanner, J. 2006 *The Invention of Art History in Ancient Greece. Religion, Society and Artistic Rationalisation.* Cambridge Classical Studies (Cambridge)

Thompson, E. T. 1985 The Relics of the Heroes in Ancient Greece. Unpublished PhD dissertation, University of Washington, Washington DC

Törnkvist, S. 1969 Notes on linen corslets. *Opuscula Romana* 7, 81–82

Tréheux, J. 1955/1956 L'aménagement intérieur de la Chalkothèque d'Athènes. *Études d'archéologie classique* 1 (1958), 133–146

Tzifopoulos, I. Z. 1991 Pausanias as a Steloskopas. An Epigraphical Commentary of Pausanias' Eliakon A and B. Unpublished PhD dissertation Ohio State University, Columbus OH

Volkmann, H. 1954 Die Inschriften im Geschichtswerk des Herodot. In: *Convivium. Beiträge zur Altertumswissenschaft. Festschrift Konrat Ziegler* (Stuttgart), 41–65

Wächter, T. 1910 *Reinheitsvorschriften im griechischen Kult.* Religionsgeschichtliche Versuche und Vorarbeiten 9(1) (Gießen)

West, S. 1985 Herodotus' epigraphical interests. *The Classical Quarterly* 35, 278–305

Whittaker, H. 1991 Pausanias and his use of inscriptions. *Symbolae Osloenses* 66, 171–186

Willi, A. 2005 Κάδμος ἀνέθηκε. Zur Vermittlung der Alphabetschrift nach Griechenland. *Museum Helveticum* 62, 162–171

Ziehen, L. 1941 Das argivische Palladion. *Hermes. Zeitschrift für klassische Philologie* 76, 426–429

Zizza, C. 2006 *Le iscrizioni nella Periegesi di Pausania. Commento ai testi epigrafici.* Studi e testi di storia antica 16 (Pisa)

Zografou, A. 2005 Images et 'reliques' en Grèce ancienne. L'omoplate de Pélops. In: P. Borgeaud and Y. Volokhine (eds), *Les objets de la mémoire. Pour une approche comparatiste des reliques et de leur culte.* Studia Religiosa Helvetica 11 (Bern), 123–145

Chapter 11

The 'Altar of the Emperors' from Carnuntum

Gabrielle Kremer

Recycling and secondary use of architectural elements and other kinds of stone monuments in various forms is a very current phenomenon in the Roman Empire, especially from the late 2nd and 3rd centuries CE onwards and most notably in late antiquity.[1] The best-known examples of this practice are the prominent late Roman monuments such as the Arch of Constantine in Rome, erected in 315 CE and consisting in large parts of so-called *spolia*[2] which had been taken from former monuments and were partly recarved under Constantine in order to be staged in a new context.[3] The discussion is still ongoing as to whether this imperial re-use had an ideological motivation and significance or rather a mainly pragmatic, materialist one. It is, however, widely agreed that the two explanatory models are not necessarily mutually exclusive and that the particular historical context is the most important factor to be considered when evaluating the occurrence of secondary use.[4] There can be no doubt that in the late 3rd and early 4th centuries CE, handling of and maybe also reflection about resources in the Roman world underwent profound and sustainable changes which are also perceptible in the Roman provinces.

A prominent but barely discussed example of imperial re-use is known from Carnuntum: the so-called Altar of the Emperors (Figs 11.1 and 11.2). Carnuntum was the capital of *Pannonia superior* (*Pannonia prima* in late antiquity), situated on the southern bank of the Danube about 40 km east of Vienna. Ancient Carnuntum consists of a legionary camp and an auxiliary fort with their respective settlements (*canabae*) and a civilian town, the *municipium* and, later, *colonia*. It presents the typical features

---

[1] e.g. Deichmann 1975; de Lachenal 1995; Pensabene 2015.
[2] In archaeology, the (modern) term *spolia* is often used in the broadest sense of 're-used elements', notwithstanding the fact that it is originally 'borrowed from the semantic field of war' and used in a judgmental way in the sense of 'antiquities found in secondary (medieval) contexts' since the 16th century (Kinney 1997, 119). More specifically, the term serves in a narrower sense, denoting unreworked architectural elements re-used in full view or out of sight (Ward-Perkins 1999, 226).
[3] L'Orange and von Gerkan 1939; Pensabene and Panella 1999; Ward-Perkins 1999.
[4] e.g. Ward-Perkins 1999; Liverani 2004.

of a military centre at the northern Limes, becoming important with the stationing of the 15th Legion in the middle of the 1st century CE and growing considerably up to Severan times, when the civilian town became *colonia Aurelia Antoniniana Carnuntum* and underwent an increase in building activity.[5]

The recent study of the more than 750 registered sacral monuments from Carnuntum has shown that a surprisingly high number of objects had been transformed for secondary use in antiquity or later.[6] Considering the stone monuments from Carnuntum, different forms of secondary use may be distinguished, potentially corresponding with different periods of building activity.[7] The first category is the result of a kind of 'waste management' occurring as a typical situation in densely built-up urban areas, where fragments of architecture and sculpture have been recycled by incorporating them into structures under construction, mostly foundations. This was the case for instance in the sanctuary of Iuppiter Heliopolitanus in the *canabae* of Carnuntum, where fragmented altars and votive sculptures have been found in the foundations of a chapel.[8] This type of re-use was observed several times in buildings of the second half of the 2nd century CE, a period of important reorganisations in public spaces of the civilian and military town. In the case of some sanctuaries, we do not always understand well why it became possible to discard former sacral objects in this way, as they belonged to the deities they had been dedicated to. They possibly had a private character or had been destroyed previously for one reason or another. By leaving them inside the sanctuary where they had been dedicated the legal requirements seem to have been respected. This kind of archaeological evidence, however, necessitates a highly refined excavation technique in order to distinguish ritual practices from other processes of destruction – a condition practically never fulfilled by older excavations.

A second category of recycling is the re-use of whole blocks as building material without any effect on the appearance of the building because the blocks were not visible from outside. In contrast to the first category, this kind of re-use was motivated by the benefit of gaining cheap high quality building material. The phenomenon is very common in late antiquity and in medieval times. A well-known example in Carnuntum is the so-called 'Heidentor', a *tetrapylon* built in the middle of the 4th century (Fig. 11.2).[9] Votive and funeral altars are especially suitable for this kind of re-use because they may be incorporated as ashlars for structural stabilisation. As the 'Heidentor' was originally entirely covered with marble or limestone veneer the altars became visible only after the decay of the building, in this case during its

---

[5] Jobst 1983; Kandler 2004.
[6] Kremer 2012.
[7] This categorisation does not intend a typology of *spolia* but rather aims at differentiating various recycling processes documented at Carnuntum, taking into consideration the specific spatial and historical contexts.
[8] Gassner *et al.* 2010.
[9] Jobst 2001.

11. The 'Altar of the Emperors' from Carnuntum

Figure 11.1a. The 'Altar of the Emperors' from Carnuntum, left side. Vienna, Kunsthistorisches Museum, inv. ANSA III 123 (© Land Niederösterreich – Archäologischer Park Carnuntum, Bad Deutsch-Altenburg (photos: Niki Gail).

Figure 11.1b. The 'Altar of the Emperors' from Carnuntum, front view. Vienna, Kunsthistorisches Museum, inv. ANSA III 123 (© Land Niederösterreich – Archäologischer Park Carnuntum, Bad Deutsch-Altenburg (photos: Niki Gail).

11. The 'Altar of the Emperors' from Carnuntum

Figure 11.1c. The 'Altar of the Emperors' from Carnuntum, right side. Vienna, Kunsthistorisches Museum, inv. ANSA III 123 (© Land Niederösterreich – Archäologischer Park Carnuntum, Bad Deutsch-Altenburg (photos: Niki Gail).

Figure 11.2. Heidenthor von Carnuntum und Mithrasbasis, *copperplate, attributed to Franz Xaver Parcar, engraver Joseph Georg Mansfeld (1764-1817) (© Kunsthistorisches Museum, Vienna).*

restoration.[10] They also must previously have lost their primary function, as there were no legal claims to them, probably because the former owners or their heirs died or emigrated or because the respective pagan cults were not practiced anymore in the middle of the 4th century.

Large-scale recycling is a category of re-use with particularly rich evidence in Carnuntum.[11] Also partly for pragmatic reasons, it characteristically results in a systematic dismantling and reshaping of monuments in a previously abandoned surrounding or an area under reconstruction and pre-supposes a more or less radical change of settlement structures.[12] Such a radical change may be observed in Carnuntum after the middle of the 4th century, probably partly due to an earthquake which damaged or destroyed parts of the settlement around 350 CE.[13] Former excavations in the legionary fortress and more recent ones in the civilian town and in the *canabae* uncovered clearly visible damage on walls and certain kinds of monuments. After this

---

[10] Müller 2001, 183–196.
[11] Kremer 2014a; 2014b; Kremer and Kitz 2018.
[12] Gugl and Humer 2014.
[13] Kandler 1989; Humer and Maschek 2007; Konecny *et al.* 2019.

catastrophe, large parts of the cemeteries were abandoned and numerous funeral monuments were not maintained anymore. Funeral slabs and architectural elements of burial structures changed their cultural category, so to say, and became 'rubbish'.[14] Being salvaged, reshaped and recycled they regained a new value: in this case not a commemorative or an aesthetic one but rather a merely economic one because the comparatively cheap recycling material certainly had a considerable value for the people who had to rebuild Carnuntum and its vitally important infrastructure as quickly as possible. There is evidence that the large-scale recycling process of stone monuments in the 4th century was organised in a systematic manner by specialised workshops.[15] In 2009, a rescue excavation uncovered part of a large cemetery situated in the southern area outside the city walls of the civilian town.[16] In this area, a 170 m long section of a late Roman sewer was unearthed which had been covered by about 300 slabs coming from re-used monuments from the 1st and 2nd centuries CE (Fig. 11.3). It is very likely that the slabs were taken from funerary enclosures in the immediate vicinity of the water pipeline.[17] A very similar situation has been documented at the beginning of the 20th century in the legionary fortress, where a drain channel had been repaired probably around 375 CE. This context provided, among others, several early funerary slabs which had originally been erected during the 1st century CE by members of the 15th Legion along the roads outside the *canabae*.[18] In both cases, the recycling measures were taken in order to repair infrastructural buildings and the re-used material stayed out of sight once the construction was completed.

A fourth category of re-use observed in Carnuntum may be denoted as 'respectful re-use' of monuments, encountered in places of reverence, as e.g. sanctuaries, churches or certain public spaces. This kind of re-use does not necessarily entail the (partial) destruction or even the reworking of the former monuments but rather represents a valorisation and upgraded display in a changed setting. The different stages of appreciation or ruptures these monuments possibly underwent and the motives inducing the actual transformation processes cover a wide range of possibilities and have to be considered within their particular historical context. This type of 'respectful' and non-destructive use of *spolia* is barely documented in Carnuntum until now and provides striking examples only in medieval contexts, like the 13th century city walls in Hainburg or the parish church in Bad Deutsch-Altenburg.[19]

One secured and rather exceptional example of that kind of re-use in Carnuntum is the so-called Altar of the Emperors (Fig. 11.1 above).[20] The altar-shaped monument,

---

[14] Thompson 2017.
[15] Kremer 2019.
[16] Konecny 2012.
[17] Kremer 2014a.
[18] Kremer 2014b.
[19] On Hainburg see Jobst 2005. On Bad Deutsch-Altenburg see Farka 2000.
[20] The practice of secondary burials in sarcophagi or funerary architectures has to be considered independently, as there is no rupture in the type of usage. Sarcophagi cut into re-used votive altars

Figure 11.3. Covering of a late antique sewer made of re-used elements from former funerary monuments, excavation Andreas Konecny 2009. Land Niederösterreich – Archäologischer Park Carnuntum, Bad Deutsch-Altenburg (photo: Andreas Konecny).

nowadays housed in the Kunsthistorisches Museum in Vienna,[21] is made of three separate blocks of regional marble, extracted in quarries upstream on the Danube at about 140 km from Carnuntum.[22] The inscription of the early 4th century on the

---

or similar blocks as occurring in Carnuntum (e.g. Kremer 2012, 270 n. 621), in turn, usually were not visible after burial.
[21] Vienna, Kunsthistorisches Museum, inv. ANSA III 123. Currently on display at the Archäologisches Museum Carnuntinum, Bad Deutsch-Altenburg (for literature see Kremer 2012, 179–180 n. 351; Weber 2014; Humer *et al.* 2014, 224-225).
[22] Probably crystalline limestone from Hiesberg, see Uhlir and Unterwurzacher 2012.

front is addressed to *Deus Sol invictus Mithras*,²³ the Roman sun god with Persian origins, very frequently worshipped in the military environment of the northern frontier at the Roman Empire from the early 2nd century onwards. On both sides of the shaft are depicted the representations of the two torchbearers usually accompanying Mithras: Cautes and Cautopates. Their iconography corresponds to many other representations of that kind and may be roughly dated to the 2nd century by stylistic analogy. The upper side of the altar shows a rectangular cavity without traces of fire and four small holes at the front edge, probably of secondary origin and possibly destined to fix a vessel or some other device for sacrifice rather than a sculpture. The inscription indicates that the monument has been re-used for a very exceptional purpose because the clearly late antique letters have been carved into an abraded background, like a palimpsest carved in stone (Fig. 11.1). Nothing is left from the former inscription so that we do not know who originally erected the monument and dedicated it to Mithras. The fact that it was cut in marble points at least to a wealthy and probably rather important dedicator, in the sense of being someone who possibly exercised a higher military or civilian function. Marble, although of regional provenance in this case, has only about a 10% share in sacral stone monuments from Carnuntum and may thus be considered as a precious material.²⁴

The late antique inscription of the 'Altar of the Emperors' indicates that the *Augusti* and the *Caesares*, the so-called *Iovii et Herculii religiosissimi*, restored a sanctuary (*sacrarium*) dedicated to the sun god Mithras. The exceptional purpose of this measure is a well-known and well-documented historical event, namely the so-called Conference of the Four Emperors (*Augusti* and *Caesares*) of the year 308 CE.²⁵ This conference was held in Carnuntum at a very crucial moment in the history of the Roman Empire when the persistence of the tetrarchy was threatened by the rivalries of the aspirants. The location of Carnuntum might have been chosen as a compromise, because Licinius, the candidate who was to be made Augustus of the West on this occasion, was probably staying here.²⁶ Diocletianus, the already abdicated tetrarch, came from *Salona*/Split; Maximianus, who claimed to have come back as Augustus after the death of Constantius and the proclamation of Constantine in *Eboracum*/York, started from *Augusta Treverorum*/Trier or from southern France. Galerius, the emperor of the East, probably departed from his residence in *Serdica*/Sofia. As a result of this summit meeting on 11 November 308, the political system of the tetrarchy was once more prolongated, a last time before the rise of Constantine as a sole ruler. Maximianus succumbed,

---

²³ D(eo) S(oli) i(nvicto) M(ithrae) / fautori imperii sui / Iovii et Herculii / religiosissimi / Augusti et Caesares / sacrarium restituerunt (CIL III 4413). ('To the unconquered sun god Mithras, the patron of their reign, the Iovii and Herculii, the very pious emperors and co-rulers, have restored the sanctuary')
²⁴ Kremer 2012, 421–430.
²⁵ Weber 2014, 16–27; Kovács 2016.
²⁶ Kovács 2012.

Figure 11.4. Gold multiple minted in Ticinum/Pavia in 313 CE showing Constantine and Sol Invictus. Paris, Cabinet des médailles, coll. Beistegui 233 (© Wikimedia Commons (Siren-Com)).

Licinius was made Emperor of the West and Constantine remained as Caesar of the West, whereas Galerius and Maximinus Daia were the Augustus and the Caesar in the East, respectively.[27]

The altar was set on behalf of these four newly designated emperors, although they were not named explicitly and only two of them were present at the conference. It is noteworthy that the emperors did not sacrifice to Iuppiter as the traditional protector of the empire and eponymous deity of the *Iovii* but to *Sol invictus Mithras*, referred to as protector of the empire (*fautor imperii*). This extraordinary choice is considered to be a concession to the troops based at Carnuntum, comprising many followers of the Mithras cult. Considering the geo-political situation and the military dominance in Carnuntum, this interpretation seems convincing, in spite of the fact that the so-called Mithraeum III, where the altar was probably found, is located in the civilian town and that some of the most important dedicators in this sanctuary are only mentioned by their names in the votive inscriptions, without any military or other function.[28] Moreover, the choice of the sun god seems to anticipate the ambivalent symbolism Constantine used some years later, e.g. on the famous gold multiple from *Ticinum*/Pavia of the year 313, where the emperor appears together with the sun god in a sort of double identity (Fig. 11.4).[29] Some scholars even saw a hidden concession to the early Christian religion, considering its analogies to the Mithraic cult and having in mind the subsequent rise of Constantine and his religious politics.[30] However, although Constantine was one of the four dedicators of the inscription on the 'Altar of the Emperors', this is not likely to have been one of the main motives for the choice of the addressee in 308 CE.

---

[27] Demandt 2018.
[28] Kremer 2012.
[29] Wallraff 2011.
[30] Girardet 2006; Demandt and Engemann 2007.

The altar was found before 1795, most probably in the so-called Mithraeum III, one of at least three sanctuaries of the Mithraic cult evidenced in Carnuntum.[31] Unfortunately, there is no documentation of the archaeological circumstances of this find. The sanctuary was, however, excavated and documented at the end of the 19th century and once more in the 1990s.[32] With its length of 23 m, the anterooms excluded, it is one of the largest Mithraea known in the Roman world. The anterooms have probably been added in a later period, maybe in relation to the conference of 308, because the altar is said to have been found in the larger of the two anterooms. Inside the sanctuary, part of the original sculptures were still existent in 1895, among them the remains of a very large tauroctony relief, dedicated by a certain Titus Flavius Viator, and the famous 'Altar of the Seasons', dedicated by a man named Magnius Heracla (Fig. 11.5).[33] If the 'Mithraeum III' was the *sacrarium* mentioned in the votive inscription of the four emperors, it has been renovated around 308, and some presumed transformations of the tauroctony relief – as e.g. the radiate crown of Mithras which emphasises the assimilation of the sun god Sol and Mithras (Fig. 11.6) – are possibly also connected to the sacrifice of the emperors in this sanctuary. The sanctuary might already have been abandoned in the years before 308 because it had to be renovated (*restituerunt*). But if so, the interim period of abandonment may not have lasted long, as at least part of the former cult and votive objects were staying on-site until the end of occupancy. It is likely that the 'Altar of the Emperors' in its original state was also part of the equipment of the former sanctuary.

The usurpation of the votive was an imperial practice in this case and did certainly not encounter legal obstacles. The first message of the secondary inscription to be read by the ancient observer was the renovation of a sanctuary which without doubt was of special importance in the cultural landscape of Carnuntum. On a further level, the altar testified to the renovation and consolidation of the tetrarchy as the ruling political system and its reference to the traditional religious system being underlined by the designation of the emperors as *Iovii et Herculii*. A third level invokes *Sol invictus Mithras* – a pagan deity, but not Iuppiter! – as the protector of the Roman Empire. As mentioned before, the older inscription has been entirely erased, so that there is no apparent reference to the original context of the monument except for the reliefs on both sides referring to the cult of Mithras. We completely lack insight into the circumstances which could inform us about a possible appropriation of the monument and its former message by the four emperors; thus, a substantiated interpretation of the actual re-evaluation is basically impeded. It remains also questionable if such a reference existed in the perception of the ancient observer and how valid it may have been after the renewed dedication and display of the altar. If there was

---

[31] Kremer 2012, 330–336.
[32] Tragau *et al.* 1895; Cencic and Jobst 2005.
[33] Kremer 2012, nn. 189, 350.

Figure 11.5. Tauroctony relief with colour projection and 'Altar of the Seasons' from so-called Mithraeum III. Bad Deutsch-Altenburg, Archäologisches Museum Carnuntinum, inv. CAR-S-98 (Tauroctony relief); inv. CAR-S-104 ('Altar of the Seasons') (© ÖAI-IKAnt; photo: Gabrielle Kremer).

another message connected to the original purpose of the altar it could have been referring to the sanctuary and to its former splendour and to the monument and its initial dedicators. The display of the altar in this exceptionally huge Mithraeum might possibly go back to another important moment in the history of Carnuntum, for instance the visit of an emperor such as Hadrian, Marcus Aurelius or Septimius Severus. In this case, *translatio memoriae* would be an appropriate characterisation of the process. Unfortunately, the communicative content of the re-evaluation itself vanished with the original local context and with the possibility of contextualisation through archaeological investigation.

Figure 11.6. Mithras with the radiate crown of the sun god (restored), tauroctony relief from so-called Mithraeum III. Bad Deutsch-Altenburg, Archäologisches Museum Carnuntinum, inv. CAR-S-98 (© ÖAI-IKAnt. Photo: Gabrielle Kremer).

The altar as a monument of traditional shape stands for *pietas*, and it remains doubtful if and to what extent it was recognisable as a re-used item by the ancient observer, taking into account that a coloured surface rendered the erased background invisible. The re-assignment of the recycled monument was certainly a cheap and quick solution in an emergency situation, in a moment when the sculptor-workshops in Carnuntum hardly produced anymore, or better, were already mainly specialised in recycling and recarving. A glance at the dated sacral stone monuments from Carnuntum may illustrate the situation.[34] There is a significant

---

[34] Kremer 2012, 318.

decline after Severan times and a nearly total lack of monuments at the end of the 3rd and beginning of the 4th centuries. An increased activity during the tetrarchy is until now only documented in the sanctuary of Iuppiter on the Pfaffenberg, where several altars have been dedicated to *Iuppiter Optimus Maximus K(arnuntinus)* even in the early 4th century.[35] The poor artisanal quality of the products in this period is notable through the character of the inscriptions, the profiles and the whole shape of the monuments.

For this reason, a pragmatic reading seems to be convenient regarding the phenomenon of re-use in the case of the 'Altar of the Emperors'. However, its probable setting in the reconstructed historical and religious local context in late antiquity also must have had a strong ideological, maybe even revivalist connotation. The denotation of a possible message transported by the fact that a former monument was re-utilised and thereby re-evaluated is in this case substantially reliant upon the knowledge of the inscription and the circumstances of display of the initial monument. An interpretation focusing on the process of re-evaluation must insofar remain highly speculative.

Considering value transformation in general, we notice that the awareness of the historical value of the 'Altar of the Emperors' increased considerably during the last ten years due to the multiple memorial exhibitions and events around Constantine, starting with a large-scale exhibition in Trier in 2007.[36] This value is partly reflected by the insurance sums required in connection with the lending procedures. The zenith of these anniversaries having passed, the object goes back to its relatively inconspicuous reception in a local exhibition or even in a museum depository, and awakening its ideological message nowadays again requires increased scientific and mediating efforts.

References

Cencic, J. and Jobst, W. 2005 Bericht über die Grabungen 1994–1998 im Mithräum III von Carnuntum. *Carnuntum Jahrbuch. Zeitschrift für Archäologie und Kulturgeschichte des Donauraumes 2004*, 59–72

Deichmann, F. W. 1975 Die Spolien in der spätantiken Architektur. *Bayerische Akademie der Wissenschaften. Philosophisch-Historische Klasse. Sitzungsberichte* 1975(6), 3–101

Demandt, A. 2018 *Geschichte der Spätantike. Das Römische Reich von Diocletian bis Justinian 284–565 n. Chr.* Beck's Historische Bibliothek (Munich)

Demandt, A. and Engemann, J. (eds) 2007 *Imperator Caesar Flavius Constantinus. Konstantin der Grosse. Exhibition catalogue Trier* (Mainz)

Farka, C. (ed.) 2000 *Der Kirchenberg. Archäologie und Geschichte im Bereich der Marienkirche von Bad Deutsch-Altenburg. Niederösterreich* (Bad Deutsch-Altenburg)

Gassner, V., Kremer, G., Steigberger, E. and Tober, B. 2010 Die Anfänge des Heiligtums des Iuppiter Heliopolitanus in Carnuntum (Flur Mühläcker). Die Forschungen 2010. *Anzeiger. Österreichische Akademie der Wissenschaften. Philosophisch-Historische Klasse* 145(2), 11–36

---

[35] Piso 2003.
[36] Demandt and Engemann 2007.

Girardet, K. M. 2006 *Die Konstantinische Wende. Voraussetzungen und geistige Grundlagen der Religionspolitik Konstantins des Großen* (Darmstadt)

Gugl, C. and Humer, F. 2014 Carnuntum in der Spätantike. In: Humer *et al.* (eds) 2014, 34–43.

Humer, F. and Maschek, D. 2007 Eine Erdbebenzerstörung des 4. Jahrhunderts n. Chr. im sogenannten Peristylhaus der Zivilstadt Carnuntum. *Archäologie Österreichs* 18(2), 45–55

Humer, F., Kremer, G., Pollhammer, E. and Pülz, A. (eds) 2014 *A.D. 313. Von Carnuntum zum Christentum. Exhibition catalogue Carnuntum.* Katalog des NÖ Landesmuseums (N. F.) 517 (St Pölten)

Jobst, W. 1983 *Provinzhauptstadt Carnuntum. Österreichs größte archäologische Landschaft* (Vienna)

Jobst, W. 2001 *Das Heidentor von Carnuntum. Ein spätantikes Triumphalmonument am Donaulimes* (Vienna)

Jobst, W. 2005 Lindwurm und Zauberdrache. Zwei missverstandene Römersteine in Hainburg an der Donau. In: F. Beutler and W. Hameter (eds), *Eine ganz normale Inschrift… und Ähnliches zum Geburtstag von Ekkehard Weber.* Althistorisch-epigraphische Studien 5 (Vienna), 543–553

Kandler, M. 1989 Eine Erdbebenkatastrophe in Carnuntum? *Acta archaeologica Academiae scientiarum Hungaricae* 41, 313–336

Kandler, M. 2004 Carnuntum. In: M. Šašel Kos and P. Scherrer (eds), *The Autonomous Towns of Noricum and Pannonia/Die autonomen Städte in Noricum und Pannonien.* Pannonia II, Situla 42 (Ljubljana), 11–66

Kinney, D. 1997 Spolia. Damnatio and renovatio memoriae. *Memoirs of the American Academy in Rome* 42, 117–148

Konecny, A. 2012 Die südliche Peripherie der Zivilstadt von Carnuntum. Neue Evidenz aus den Grabungen 2001–2009. In: C. Reinholdt and W. Wohlmayr (eds), *Akten des 13. Österreichischen Archäologentages. Klassische und Frühägäische Archäologie Paris-Lodron-Universität Salzburg vom 25. bis 27. Februar 2010* (Vienna), 271–280

Konecny, A., Humer, F. and Decker, K. (eds) 2019 *Das Carnuntiner Erdbeben im Kontext. Akten des III. Internationalen Kolloquiums 17.-18. Oktober 2013 Kulturfabrik Hainburg.* Archäologischer Park Carnuntum. Neue Forschungen 14 (St Pölten)

Kovács, P. 2012 Kaiser Licinius und Carnuntum. In: P. Kovács and B. Fehér (eds), *In memoriam Barnabás Lőrincz.* Studia Epigraphica Pannonica 4 (Budapest), 79–85

Kovács, P. 2016 *A History of Pannonia in the Late Roman Period I (284–363 AD).* Antiquitas. Abhandlungen zur alten Geschichte (Reihe 1), 67 (Bonn)

Kremer, G. 2012 *Götterdarstellungen, Kult- und Weihedenkmäler aus Carnuntum. Corpus signorum imperii romani/Corpus der Skulpturen der römischen Welt. Österreich.* Carnuntum Supplement 1 (Vienna)

Kremer, G. 2014a Wiederverwendete Teile von Grabanlagen aus Carnuntum. Zu ausgewählten Neufunden aus dem Bereich südlich der Zivilstadt. *Carnuntum Jahrbuch. Zeitschrift für Archäologie und Kulturgeschichte des Donauraumes 2014*, 67–78

Kremer, G. 2014b Zur Wiederverwendung von Steindenkmälern in Carnuntum. In: E. Trinkl (ed.), *Akten des 14. Österreichischen Archäologentages am Institut für Archäologie der Universität Graz vom 19. bis 21. April 2012* (Vienna), 199–208

Kremer, G. 2019 Spätantike recycling befunde aus Carnuntum. In: Konecny *et al.* (eds) 2019, 112–118.

Kremer, G. and Kitz, I. 2018 Use and re-use of roman stone monuments in Carnuntum and its surrounding area. in: C. Coquelet, G. Creemers, R. Dreesen and É. Goemaere (eds), *Roman Ornamental Stones in North-Western Europe. Natural Resources, Manufacturing, Supply, Life & After-Life. Proceedings of the International Conference, Gallo-Roman Museum of Tongeren (Belgium) 20-22 April 2016.* Études et Documents. Archéologie 38 (Namur)

Lachenal, L. de 1995 *Spolia. Uso e reimpiego dell'antico dal III al XIV secolo.* Biblioteca di Archeologia 24 (Milan)

Liverani, P. 2004 Reimpiego senza ideologia. La lettura antica degli spolia dall'arco di Costantino all'età carolingia. *Mitteilungen des Deutschen Archäologischen Instituts. Römische Abteilung* 111, 383–434

L'Orange, H. P. L. and Gerkan, A. von 1939 *Der spätantike Bildschmuck des Konstantinsbogens*. Studien zur spätantiken Kunstgeschichte 10 (Berlin)

Müller, K. 2001 Die Bauforschung am Heidentor. In: Jobst 2001, 183–196

Pensabene, P. 2015 *Roma su Roma. Reimpiego architettonico, recupero dell'antico e trasformazioni urbane tra il III e il XIII secolo*. Monumenti di antichità Cristiana (Serie 2) 22 (Vatican City)

Pensabene, P. and Panella, C. (eds) 1999 *Arco di Costantino. Tra archeologia e archeometria*. Studia Archaeologica 100 (Rome)

Piso, I. 2003 *Das Heiligtum des Jupiter Optimus Maximus auf dem Pfaffenberg/Carnuntum. Die Inschriften*. Der römische Limes in Österreich 41 Sonderband 1 (Vienna)

Thompson, M. 2017 *Rubbish Theory. The Creation and Destruction of Value* (London)

Tragau, C., Reichel, W. and Bormann, E. 1895 Das dritte Mithraeum. *Archaeologisch-Epigraphische Mittheilungen aus Oesterreich-Ungarn* 18, 169–201 = Bericht des Vereins Carnuntum in Wien 1892-1894, 19–51

Uhlir, C. and Unterwurzacher, M. 2012 Monumente aus Marmor – Materialanalyse und Herkunfstbestimmung. In: Kremer 2012, 421–430

Wallraff, M. 2011 Konstantins 'Sonne' und ihre christlichen Kontexte. In: K. Ehling and G. Weber (eds), *Konstantin der Große. Zwischen Sol und Christus*. Zaberns Bildbände zur Archäologie (Darmstadt), 42–52

Ward-Perkins, B. 1999 Re-using the architectural legacy of the past, entre idéologie et pragmatism. In: G. P. Brogiolo and B. Ward-Perkins (eds), *The Idea and Ideal of the Town between Late Antiquity and the Early Middle Ages*. The Transformation of the Roman World 4 (Leiden)

Weber, E. 2014 Fünf Jahre, die die Welt veränderten - vom 11. November 308 bis zum 13. Juni 313. In: Humer *et al.* (eds) 2014, 16–27

Chapter 12

How do materials matter?

Lucy Norris

This chapter focuses on perceptions of materials and technologies as they are disassembled and reassembled as part of the sacrificial exchange and revaluation of old clothing and textile waste. It revisits previous long-term ethnographic fieldwork in India and the UK that examined the meaning and value found in old clothing, how it is remade and recycled and how these material transformations in turn make and remake social relations. Exploring different cultural attitudes to discarded clothing, this research also mapped the exchange circuits created at the local, national and international levels and the social and political hierarchies of power that they help to constitute, through the lens of anthropological theories of waste, value and materiality.

This earlier work is then contrasted with more recent field research in Berlin and the UK that focuses on how various actors in the fashion industry are responding to the undeniable crisis in social and environmental sustainability in the sector, from grassroots activism among independent designers to larger-scale business initiatives. The chapter briefly introduces concepts of the circular economy now being explored by the global fashion industry which, to date, are largely being pursued by multinational corporations and framed within a model of resource security and continued economic growth. Finally, it references briefly ongoing fieldwork amongst design activists who are developing alternative modes of production and putting the value of materials and textile-making at the heart of their practice, one that uses the properties of those recycled materials once again to foster social ties through local collaboration and community building.

Revisiting the remains of fieldwork

Recently I came across a tattered pink silk and silver brocade waistcoat, packed in a trunk in my cellar in Berlin (Fig. 12.1). I thought it had been acquired by the Pitt-Rivers Museum as part of a collection of recycled Indian clothing I had made years ago but it had been left out. This might be considered to be a dormant object, an 'absent presence',[1] hidden away in a liminal domestic space, in limbo, waiting for me to find a use for it. But as it has no functional use I now think of it as part of my own collection of textiles, odd pieces of clothing and scraps of fabric that I have acquired while travelling, inherited from family and found through years of rummaging among remnants and cast-offs. These accumulated things have been taken out of circulation; I sometimes look through them for a particular piece, and they are occasionally shown to others, but could it be said that have they been made sacred? Do they, as Krzysztof Pomian suggests, have exchange value because they mediate between the realms of the visible and invisible?[2] Pomian gives us the example of precious objects in royal treasure houses that represent the invisible through the rare materials from which they were made, the particular forms that they were given and their association with spatially or temporally distant people or events. Such collections forge connections to people and events in the past, to distant places where they were made or acquired, and can signal their former roles as parts of other wholes, their periodic re-assembling into new orders allowing for the opening up of alternative futures.[3]

Or, like orange peel and cheese rinds, are these things in the cellar just 'remains'. Are they the surplus or left-overs from consumption, the 'remnants of life past and fragments of lost cultural corpora' described by Francesco Pellizzi?[4] They may last longer because they were discarded not consumed but remains may also be what one keeps, a sort of capital to be preserved and treasured. Pellizzi writes that there is a sacrificial relation between *what is discarded*, the unconsumed leftovers, and *what is set aside*, the 'discarded-through-treasuring', where the status of 'remains' changes to that of something kept apart, made sacred – in other words, offerings. He describes a Mexican village in the Chiapas in the 1960s that had no remains, no debris – things were either organic, perishable and quickly consumed or utensils that were too precious to be discarded; these closed circuits could maintain a precarious condition without growth, or rather, a situation where growth closed in on itself, where instead of aiming to preserve surpluses, one turned them, again and again, into offerings, thus eliminating any chance for real accumulation. He writes that 'in a sacrificial economy, there are no remains, and nothing is wasted'[5] (Fig. 12.1).

I confess to being rather ambivalent about this waistcoat's value – does it have transcendent value as part of my collection, so important to my own sense of self, or is it merely a leftover from fieldwork that I have failed to deal with properly? Once it belonged to Priya, an elderly lady living in the middle-class housing association in East Delhi where I was doing fieldwork on the life-cycle of clothing in 1999–2000.[6] No

---

[1] Hetherington 2004.
[2] Pomian 1990.
[3] Cf. Küchler 1997.
[4] Pellizzi 1995, 5.
[5] Pellizzi 1995, 6.
[6] Norris 2004.

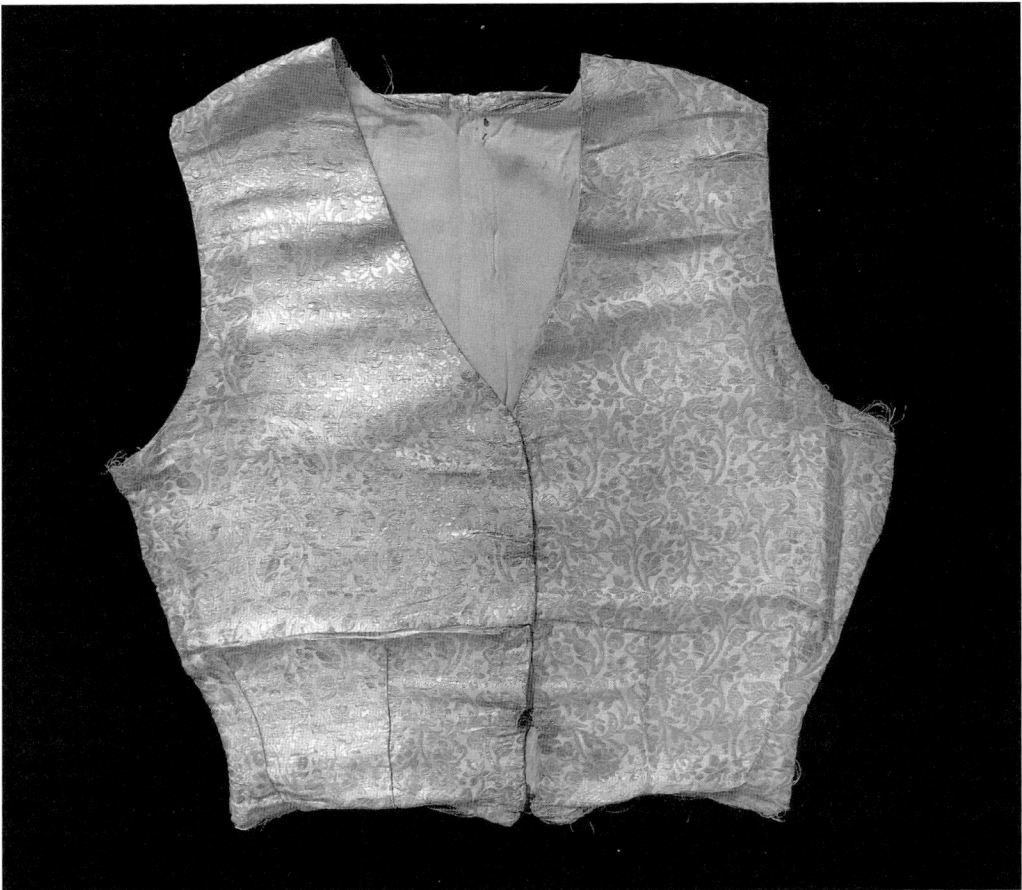

Figure 12.1. Priya's pink waistcoat, originally made in 1938 as part of her wedding trousseau (© Lucy Norris).

longer wearable, it had been in limbo in *her* flat for years; it had been irritating her, but she had had a difficult time trying to give it away. Hand-woven in salmon-pink silk with silver *zari* work in the heavy Banarasi style, this expensive, treasured piece was from her trousseau in the late 1930s, an unusual, iconic item that had been key to her self-image. I recap briefly here the story of how she tried to rid herself of it.

Indian women tend to have well-established strategies for re-using old clothing for children's clothing and around the house, offering them to close family, younger sisters, daughters and nieces. The belief that one should conserve old cloth is rooted in thriftiness, a concern for the household economy and the turning of waste into a surplus. But it is also linked to the belief that material things have the capacity to convey the essence of the people and places that have previously come into contact with them, making them a crucial connector with the capacity to tie together people, place and event through time and space. Cloth is a particularly porous, malleable and absorbent material and materials are believed to be morally coded substances. Flows of materials across the surfaces and through the bodies of persons, especially through the mediums of food[7] and clothing,[8] transform those who come into contact with them through their previous associations, with farmers and producers, givers and receivers, wearers and recyclers. Passing on clothing through the family, and making and remaking garments along the way, is a means of distributing one's personhood through the agency of cloth,[9] to make and remake the ties that connect people and create mutuality through gifting and receiving.[10] Wardrobes contain collections of clothing that are often not viewed as individual property to be worn or disposed of at will,[11] but rather as elements that constitute the relationality of extended family and kin. As has been observed for collections in general,[12] there is always a process of sorting, of identifying gaps, filling holes and getting rid of certain items that appear redundant. These unwanted things are never simply thrown away, they are too valuable a resource in multiple ways, and a great deal of effort goes into finding strategies for 'using them up' through handing them on or recycling them (Fig. 12.2).

To return to the pink waistcoat, Priya was unhappy to find that her only daughter-in-law did not want it and neither did her maid. Gifts of used clothing are part of payments to servants; they create hierarchies between giver and receiver that are always in the process of being negotiated through the frequency and quality of such gifts.[13] Handing on used cloth within family can pass on auspiciousness but passing it out of the family carries the risk for the receiver that it will carry inauspiciousness and transmit the ritual pollution associated with *jutha*, leftovers, that materially constitutes hierarchy.[14] Servants have a liminal status, part of the household but not part of the family. Refusing such clothing can be a refusal to accept inferior status; it contests dominant value systems and the gifts that materially constitute the social hierarchy and opens up the potential for alternative configurations of relative power.

Priya's next option was to see if she could barter it in return for kitchen pots via the *bartanwale*, the itinerant Gujarati women dealers who trade in old clothing and sell them into the second-hand markets where the poor buy their clothing. This marks the shift in its potential value from the auspiciousness of a family gift, through the difficult social terrain of gifts-as-payments to social inferiors, to the market value of old cloth. Thrifty households who barter unwanted clothes replace an object of transient value for a more durable one, translating its rubbish value into a different

---

[7] Appadurai 1981.
[8] Bayly 1986.
[9] Cf. Gell 1998.
[10] Norris 2010.
[11] Cf. Tarlo 1996.
[12] Benjamin 1992; Stewart 1993; Pearce 1995.
[13] Cf. Gordon 1996.
[14] Parry 1986.

12. How do materials matter? 213

Figure 12.2. Silk saris and valuables are often kept in metal almariya, lockable cupboards that are often part of a woman's dowry (© Lucy Norris).

Figure 12.3. A shop selling stainless steel utensils located in the Delhi suburb where the traders live and work. Old clothes' dealers often obtain these pots on credit (© Tim Mitchell and Lucy Norris).

register.[15] This transaction is a one-off exchange with strangers, entailing none of the longer-term reciprocal obligations expected in the complex gift economy that the clothes help to constitute. I also argue that barter, rather than the market economy organised through monetary payments, facilitates the sacrificial exchange of one representation of a woman's, and a household's, status through cloth for another representation via pots, an exchange controlled by women on both sides who manage these resources themselves.[16]

Women try to get the best pot they can from the dealer, pointing out the quality and finer details of the clothing they are getting rid of while swapping material registers in order to fill a perceived gap in a parallel collection in pots. Saris and pots are both essential elements in the trousseau which women bring with them in marriage, along with gold and jewellery, and, like saris, pots are a favourite category of accumulation: many women like to have ranks of pots in every size on display in their kitchens – they too are vehicles of women's status.[17] This has been elevated in the Gujarati custom of *mand*, practised by the women dealers themselves, where

---

[15] Thompson 1979.
[16] Cf. Gell 1992.
[17] Gell 1986.

Figure 12.4. Dealers in Old Delhi's jewellery market test the metal threads used to decorate silk saris for purity, then burn the clothing to reclaim the silver and gold (© Tim Mitchell and Lucy Norris).

series of highly polished metal utensils are part of a wider aesthetic appreciation of the qualities of brilliance and reflection found in mirror work, gold and silver embroideries, gems and certain colour combinations.

Women complain of being emotionally exhausted after these encounters, where their own estimation of the clothing is derided and they struggle to achieve a desirable pot in return. A friend of Priya's offered to see what she could get for the waistcoat and she said that she wanted one of the recently introduced non-stick *Tefal* frying pans she had seen, which cost about 200–300Rs. However, the *bartanwallah* inspected the tatty garment and offered her only 50Rs, which Priya refused. Since she was upset by the incident, I offered to make one last effort to obtain something for it. I took it to the crowded lanes of the jewellery bazaar in Old Delhi. Here it was weighed for its silver content, so that it could be burnt in a crucible to reduce the silk to ashes, leaving the remaining twisted and tangled metal threads to be turned into grains of solid silver. This would then be sold back to the traditional makers of precious *zari* threads whose workshops are still in the nearby streets. I was offered 250–300Rs for it. I later gave Priya 300Rs in return for my keeping her waistcoat, so that she could buy the *Tefal* frying pan and the waistcoat later returned with me to London. Priya's waistcoat had to be sacrificed quite literally by it going up in smoke in order for its complex social, material and iconic value to be fully realised in its next incarnation; through iconoclasm its status in her sartorial collection could be replaced by something equally valuable on display in her kitchen, the iconic modern frying pan (Fig. 12.4).

The garment slashers. From 'cooked' to 'raw'

How then do migrant women, working in the industrial textile recycling factories in Panipat, north of Delhi, make sense of the towering heaps of imported cast-offs they are employed to process into recycled woollen yarn? What stories and images travel along with clothing cast-off in richer nations? What do the Indian factory workers think about us, our values, culture and lifestyles, through their engagement with our discards? In contrast to much Indian clothing that wraps the body in lengths of cloth rather than cuts the cloth to fit the body, tailored Western clothing is extremely complicated to disassemble and recycle due to the zips, buttons, shoulder pads, stiffening, mixed fibre fabrics and unidentifiable materials it contains. The wool fibre recycling industry still largely relies on manual skills to sort, cut up and deconstruct used garments and it has ended up in India, a country which does not produce enough virgin wool for its needs and has an abundant source of cheap labour. These women workers sit on the floor chopping up cast-offs bit-by-bit, slicing off unwanted elements using traditional vegetable cutters. Their engagement is intimate, sensory, disassembling the dirty garments stitch by stitch (Fig. 12.5).

Figure 12.5. Migrant women living in Panipat work in the woollen mills, chopping up winter clothing imported from the developed world so that it can be recycled into yarn and woven into blankets for the local market (© Tim Mitchell and Lucy Norris).

> Everyone says that the clothes come over because there's a water shortage in the West. Water is just as expensive as clothes are for these people, that's why they wear their clothes a couple of times, then throw them away. That's what everyone says, and what we always hear ... I wouldn't know why else they come ... who knows, maybe they just don't like washing their clothes![18]

These are the comments of low-paid women workers taking a break as they sort through mountains of used clothing in a Special Economic Zone on the west coast of India. They are trying to imagine the privileged lives of Western women that they see on the *Discovery Channel* while picking through the unfamiliar clothing that they discard, commenting that they are free to live their lives as they want to. How else can they make sense of a value system that results in over US $4 billion worth of used

---

[18] In Gupta 2012.

clothing discarded from the world's richer nations circulating the globe annually? Over the course of repeated short visits to Panipat and wholesale markets while living in Delhi in 1999–2000, again in 2004–2005 and an intensive two months of research in the factories in 2009 assisted by Meghna Gupta, I traced the reverse supply chain of used clothing itself, mapping out how it is traded, processed and made into recycled products. Having previously researched how the local used clothing trade worked, I also talked to the men and women working in the Indian recycling industry to find out how they made sense of their work.

These women's job is to slash the imported garments to make them unwearable and thereby prevent them from being sold for re-use in the Indian black market: India's indigenous textile industry is protected by high tariffs on imported second-hand clothing. These mutilated clothes will be downcycled into reclaimed fibres, regenerated into yarn and woven into one-season 'shoddy' blankets, using technologies developed in Yorkshire over 200 years ago and now embedded in India's cheap informal economy. These blankets are sold to the poor across Asia but international charities are also major buyers, stockpiling them ready to be distributed to disaster victims worldwide.[19] When asked for their own views as to why Indian factories were importing this old clothing, a group of women explained that they were transforming them (back) into raw materials for Indian manufacturers and consumers.

This unregulated industry, characterised by subcontracted labour arrangements where women earn far less than the living wage and bring small children along to play in the hot, stinking, dusty piles of cast-offs, has the dubious distinction of using up the waste products of a number of local industries. To soften the rags before they are fed into the machines they are soaked in a mixture of solid wastes from the local ghee factory, various adulterated chemicals and unrefined used transformer oil from the local power station. Thinner blankets might have their weight bulked out with salt or chapati flour from local mills. Synthetic fibres may be over-dyed: the boilers are stoked with scraps of plastic, fabric, old pallets, and vibrant waste-water runs along the channels at the side of the road. Spindles for the antiquated spinning machines are hand-rolled from recycled newspaper. And the metal zips cut from the clothing, the polyester linings, bundles of cardboard packaging and scraps of plastic sheeting are sold back onto the recycling market. This is a Dickensian parody of the environmental efficiency of 'industrial symbiosis', where industries feed each other's waste products into their production cycle to improve efficiency of resource and energy use.

Ironically, many of these garments will originally have been donated to charities in the world's richest countries which now sell them in bulk to textile recyclers rather than distribute them directly to those in need – this distinction is still not understood by many who donate clothing to a textile bank.[20] The recyclers finely hand-sort these piles of random donations into hundreds of categories and find buyers

---

[19] Norris 2012.
[20] Tranberg Hansen 2008.

Figure 12.6. Warehouses in Panipat import over 100,000 tonnes of used winter clothing annually. Each garment is first sorted by hand into a 'colour family', then fine sorted into shades (© Tim Mitchell and Lucy Norris).

in highly networked secondhand markets. Their profits depend upon keeping the labour costs of sorting extremely low (often employing workers who are 'far from the labour market', a euphemism for immigrants and the chronically disadvantaged) and finding niche buyers for exceptionally high-value garments such as vintage and retro-styles and collectible t-shirts. Less than one-fifth of used clothing is resold within the wealthier nations in which it is collected; the bulk, around three-fifths, is exported to poorer economies across the globe, where it is sold to end users via networks of local dealers. The top grades, or 'creamy layer', of nearly new, high quality brands are sent to Eastern Europe, good quality summer clothing is in demand in Africa, while the lowest grades are shipped to Pakistan. The remaining fifth is recycled into wiping cloths and reclaimed fibres, for example in northern India (Fig. 12.6).

Having started as a free 'gift', used clothing appears to magically make money for everyone along the value chain, from western charity to petty sub-Saharan dealer, and this is often described as a 'win-win system'.[21] However, those brokers running huge sorting operations at the beginning of the chain are able to profit through buying high volumes of cheaply obtained stock. Clothing for export is vacuum-packed into huge bales which are then often sold unopened in destination markets to smaller traders. These dealers in developing rural markets, often women, cannot afford to invest much at a time and they have to take a risk on what is inside the vacuum-packed bale of secondhand clothing. Their livelihoods are far more vulnerable to the vagaries of quality in the unopened bale.[22] It is the process of sorting that creates exchange value, and this ability to generate value has been monopolised by those who can invest capital into accumulating abundant stocks of heterogeneous discards, infrastructure for transporting them around the globe, warehouses to store them in, labour to manually categorise each and every garment and the political connections to ensure that regulatory devices and trade tariffs are not a hindrance.[23] If the risk is taken by the smaller dealers buying sealed bales, it is the end buyer who eventually pays for the western charity's cut, the textile recycler's profits, the importer's fee and the local dealer's meagre margins.[24]

The structural inequalities of the global secondhand clothing economy mirrors those characterising the economics of global fast fashion,[25] where, as with many global commodities, wastes are externalised and reprocessing is hidden in less-developed countries, out of sight from consumers.[26] Garment production is concentrated in low-wage economies and exported to consumers in wealthier nations, a function of a free market economy that is often championed for lifting millions out of poverty.[27] Once they have been 'used up' or more likely simply used and discarded, richer nations burn or bury their cast-offs as rubbish or re-export them back to poorer countries. The effects of exporting used clothing to countries that have, or used to have, an indigenous textile industry is also highly contentious but beyond the scope of this paper;[28] many developing countries have imposed high tariffs or outright bans, and the proposal by a group of East African nations wishing to ban all imports of secondhand clothing by 2019 led to threats of economic retaliation by the US. However, banning imports but turning a blind eye to smuggling simply increases the profits for all. Many regional import/export hubs and Special Economic Zones are located near to countries that have imposed protective bans on imports, facilitating cross-border smuggling.[29]

The enduring social injustice of a global economic system that depends upon poorly-paid workers to produce goods for wealthier consumers while they themselves

---

[21] Cf. Tranberg Hansen 2000.
[22] Brooks 2012.
[23] Crang *et al.* 2013; Norris 2019.
[24] Norris 2019.
[25] Brooks 2015.
[26] Alexander and Reno 2012.
[27] Rivoli 2005.
[28] Cf. Norris 2015.
[29] Cf. Abimbola 2012.

often consume the leftovers afterwards is not reflected in the environmentally-orientated focus of current waste policies in wealthier nations. In UK policy, for example, much of the governmental concerns expressed about rising amounts of post-consumer clothing waste have been framed by the need to meet measurable targets, to reduce carbon footprints, water usage and the quantity of waste and improving collection rates in the light of the EU Landfill Directive's 2020 deadlines. WRAP (Waste & Resources Action Programme) estimated that about 1.13 million tonnes of clothing were purchased in the UK in 2016, lasting for an average active lifetime of 3.3 years.[30] Comparing the figures of what is bought with how it is disposed of, WRAP estimated that about 48% are re-used (70% of which are exported overseas with little or no traceability), 14% recycled, 7% incinerated, but 31% simply end up in landfill every year. The figures for exporting are therefore part of the re-use category which is being promoted through targets, yet there are still no incentives for exporting nations to really find out what impact millions of tonnes of used clothing are having on markets in importing countries; some reports suggest that the leftovers of fast fashion are simply dumped illegally in landfills overseas.

Georges Bataille's theory of a general economy is based upon the need to eliminate surplus through useless or excessive consumption, or non-productive 'expenditure', and 'go against judgements that form the basis of a rational economy'.[31]

> Indeed, the imperative to waste and the related glorious modes of expenditure that fascinate Bataille are inimical to the calculations that define a restricted economy based on the tenets of limited resources and concern for securing future interests. But it is this consideration of the future, of advantageous utility, that deprives humans of sovereignty. Sovereignty, by Bataille's account, is linked with experience of the sacred, and refers to escape from the realm of work, subjugation to labour, calculation, and instrumental reason – in short, the realm of the profane.[32]

The excessive consumption and disposal of fashion can be understood as a type of sacrificial expenditure, and that the transformation work that turns those leftovers back into materials and things with value takes place in the rational, calculative realm of the profane, which re-introduces rational concern for the future. The global rise of fast fashion has made large volumes of cheap clothing accessible. The *Inquiry into the Sustainability of the Fashion Industry* launched by the UK Parliament's Environmental Audit Committee on 22 June 2018 has found that, while clothing purchases have doubled in the last ten years, spending on clothing has not significantly increased.[33] The fashion industry is being urged to become more 'sustainable', i.e. more calculative, rational and future-orientated. Strategies include both supporting approaches that develop an alternative economics of resource circulation and social exchange on local

---

[30] WRAP 2017.
[31] Bataille 1991, 22; Biles 2011.
[32] Biles 2011, 131.
[33] Environmental Audit Commission, UK Parliament n.d.

and regional scales, and encouraging multi-national corporations to develop along circular economy principles, keeping resources in circulation partly through a service economy model which emphasises ownership by business.[34]

Closing the loop

A new conceptual umbrella, the circular economy (CE), has been promoted most vocally by supranational institutions such as the Ellen MacArthur Foundation and the World Economic Forum and adopted as a policy objective by the EU and many national governments. CE models are explained at this level as a business-led solution to problems of resource security and global sustainability; fostering economic growth without resource depletion is a key tenet and the goal is to live as a global society within planetary boundaries. Waste is seen as a loss of material and technological resources; these are externalities that could be profitably brought within a closed loop system or could, instead, cascade through a series of related industries with one using the by-products of another.

With growing pressure on the availability of resources such as water, energy and oil required to produce both natural and synthetic oil-based fibres, fashion brands are beginning to sign up to the circular economy[35] and to find ways to recapture the value of pre- and post-consumer waste through investment in new technologies to guarantee control over resources. However, to achieve their stated goal of 'designing out waste', these fashion brands are now turning their attention to understanding their customers' attitudes and beliefs so as to encourage people to return their unwanted clothing and help the company recoup these precious materials, thereby 'closing the loop'. This involves trying to understand how cultural concepts are expressed through everyday habits and routines in order to 'change mindsets'. In the terminology of the growing service economy, consumers are being framed as users and international brands appear to see these users as weak points in emerging systems of control of materials circulation.

Despite its solid foundations in concepts of sustainability such as industrial symbiosis and industrial ecology,[36] cradle-to-cradle principles,[37] bio-mimicry and the service (performance) economy,[38] mainstream iterations of the CE model have been embraced by global capitalism; they continue to promote economic growth as a fundamental objective and have paid little attention to issues around social justice and equality. Key questions are how emerging circular economy models encapsulate property relations and the democratic control of resources and at what scale these systems will be developed. CE modelling foregrounds material flows stripped of their sociality; little account is taken of the ontological significance of the relationships

---

[34] Norris 2019.
[35] Ellen MacArthur Foundation 2017; Global Fashion Agenda 2017.
[36] Graedel 1996.
[37] McDonough and Braungart 2002.
[38] Stahel 2010.

between people, materials and technologies in shaping life-worlds and the processual nature of their unfolding. As Kersty Hobson points out, these initiatives have tended not to address the socio-political implications of moving towards a CE, have obscured other transformative pathways and practices and have not considered what forms and processes of governance would facilitate an effective and equitable CE.[39]

Kersty Hobson asks how social science approaches to materiality, emergence and everyday activism can engage with CE topics and investigate the possibilities for citizen engagement and reconfigured material practices around the CE.

Alternative economies

Social activists are fighting to change the terms on which these material and technical reconfigurations are taking place. They use open source principles to foster collaboration, question how much transparency is needed within a system in order to transition to full circularity, to grow social participation, shape alternative visions of society and start by placing people in the centre. Initiatives to encourage Europeans and North Americans to stop simply throwing clothes away have been focused on strategies to make us buy better quality and value our clothing for longer, now known as 'slow fashion'. Clothing sustainability experts and designers exhort us to invest in more durable, sustainable clothing,[40] profiling schemes such as the establishment of community projects which encourage the growth of clothes swapping as social events and pop-up repair cafes. Fashion hacktivists promote confidence in our own capacity to re-imagine and reskill ourselves so that we can upcycle, alter and repair our own clothing as radical anti-capitalist engagement,[41] often framing this mode of production as activism.[42] Collaborations such as Fibreshed, which aim to produce textiles from locally sourced materials and labour and design approaches that focus on locally abundant materials, foster personal contacts and regional production networks.

But at the same time, the boundaries between economic modes related to for-profit and not-for-profit, buying and swapping, renting and giving are being obscured. The emerging service economy model is capitalising on these ideas, integrating itself into previously non-marketised, domestic practices of thrift, from setting up platforms that provide alteration and repair services to developing profit-based exchange systems. New business models for leasing clothing, clothing take-back schemes and clothing lending libraries are all being trialled at local levels, sometimes by independent local businesses, other times by global chains experimenting with new ways of connecting with their customers, profiting from these blurred distinctions.

---

[39] Hobson 2016, 89.
[40] Fletcher 2016; Cobbing and Vicaire 2017.
[41] Graeber 2012.
[42] von Busch 2008; Hirscher 2015.

Conclusion

The example of the pink waistcoat highlights, at a particular point in the recent past in India, how difficult it could be to rid oneself of old clothing, how concepts of proper re-use and recycling are bound up with culturally specific beliefs and values about the entanglements of bodies, morals and materials and how sacrificial exchange is a central part of reconfiguring the moral, social and political order. Emerging large-scale corporate business models founded in circular economy thinking tend to focus on materials simply as economic resources and fail to take account of their social uses, associated values and the importance of practices of making and remaking for social relationships. There is a wealth of new entanglements between people, materials and things that emerge from desires to reshape our societies and build very different, sustainable economies in the future. These alternative social and political visions of sustainable living in socially embedded economies include people and practices operating in the interface between the market and non-market economies. Its proponents believe that only by being transparent and using the principles of exchange of knowledge about materials, design principles and technologies, can the complex problems posed by transitioning to a circular economy be solved. Arturo Escobar has called for a radical autonomous design practice, rooted in community-building and place-making activities, in contrast to design purely for capitalist ends.[43] As one fashion designer put it to me: 'it means working out what one wants to do and finding the gaps in current systems and ways of thinking', her own thinking grounded in a future-orientated design activism that begins, where this chapter began, with a deeper understanding of the social and cultural value of materials.

References

Abimbola, O. 2012 The international trade in second-hand clothing. Managing information asymmetry between West African and British traders. *Textile. The Journal of Cloth and Culture* 10, 184–199

Alexander, C. and Reno, J. (eds) 2012 *Economies of Recycling. The Global Transformation of Materials, Values and Social Relations* (London)

Appadurai, A. 1981 Gastro-politics in Hindu south Asia. *American Ethnologist* 8, 494–511

Bataille, G. 1991 The Accursed Share. An Essay on General Economy (transl. R. Hurley) (New York)

Bayly, C. A. 1986 The origins of Swadeshi (home industry). Cloth and Indian society, 1700–1930. In: A. Appadurai (ed.), *The Social Life of Things. Commodities in Cultural Perspective* (Cambridge), 285–321

Benjamin, W. 1992 Unpacking my library. In: W. Benjamin, *Illuminations* (London), 61–69

Biles, J. 2011 The Remains of God. Bataille/sacrifice/community. *Culture, Theory and Critique* 52, 127–144

Brooks, A. 2012 Riches from rags or persistent poverty? The working lives of secondhand clothing vendors in Maputo, Mozambique. *Textile. The Journal of Cloth and Culture* 10, 222–237

Brooks, A. 2015 Clothing poverty. The hidden world of fast fashion and second-hand clothes (London)

---

[43] Escobar 2018.

Busch, O. van 2008 *Fashion-Able. Hacktivism and engaged fashion design.* Unpublished PhD dissertation, University of Gothenburg)

Cobbing, M. and Vicaire, Y. 2017 *Fashion at the Crossroads. A Review of Initiatives to Slow and Close the Loop in the Fashion Industry* (Hamburg). <http://www.greenpeace.org/international/Global/international/publications/detox/2017/Fashion-at-the-Crossroads.pdf?utm_campaign=Press%20Release&utm_source=Link&utm_medium=HK> (Accessed: 9 August 2021)

Crang, M., Hughes, A., Gregson, N., Norris, L. and Ahamed, F. 2013 Rethinking governance and value in commodity chains through global recycling networks. *Transactions of the Institute of British Geographers* 38, 12–24

Ellen MacArthur Foundation. 2017 *A New Textiles Economy: Redesigning Fashion's Future* (Updated 1–12–17) (Cowes).<https://ellenmacarthurfoundation.org/a-new-textiles-economy> (Accessed: 9 December 2021)

Environmental Audit Commission, UK Parliament. n.d. Sustainability of the Fashion Industry Inquiry 2017-19. https://old.parliament.uk/business/committees/committees-a-z/commons-select/environmental-audit-committee/inquiries/parliament-2017/sustainability-of-the-fashion-industry-17-19/ (Accessed: 9 December 2021)

Escobar, A. 2018 *Designs for the Pluriverse. Radical Interdependence, Autonomy, and the Making of Worlds, New Ecologies for the Twenty-First Century* (Durham NC)

Fletcher, K. 2016 *Craft of Use. Post-Growth Fashion* (Abingdon)

Garmulewicz, A., Holweg, M., Veldhuis, H. and Yang, A. 2018 Disruptive technology as an enabler of the circular economy. What potential does 3D printing hold? *California Management Review* 60(3), 112–132

Gell, A. 1986 Newcomers to the world of goods. Consumption among the Muria Gonds. In: A. Appadurai (ed.), *The Social Life of Things. Commodities in Cultural Perspective* (Cambridge), 110–138

Gell, A. Inter-tribal commodity barter and reproductive gift-exchange in Old Melanesia. In: C. Humphrey and S. Hugh-Jones (eds), *Barter, Exchange and Value. An Anthropological Approach* (Cambridge), 142–168

Gell, A. 1998 *Art and Agency. An Anthropological Theory* (Oxford)

Global Fashion Agenda. 2017. *Pulse of the Fashion Industry* (Copenhagen) https://www.globalfashionagenda.com/publications-and-policy/pulse-of-the-industry/ (Accessed: 9 December 2021)

Gordon, S. 1996 Robes of honour. A 'transactional' kingly ceremony. *The Indian Economic and Social History Review* 33, 225–242

Graeber, D. 2012 Afterword. The apocalypse of objects. Degradation, redemption and transcendence in the world of consumer goods. In: Alexander and Reno (eds) 2012, 277–290

Graedel, T. E. 1996 On the concept of industrial ecology. *Annual Review of Energy and the Environment* 21, 69–98

Gupta, M. 2012 *Unravel. Documentary.* <https://aeon.co/videos/this-is-the-final-resting-place-of-your-cast-off-clothing> (accessed: 20 September 2021)

Hetherington, K. 2004 Secondhandedness. Consumption, disposal, and absent presence. *Environment and Planning D. Society and Space* 22, 157–173

Hirscher, A.-L. 2015 Open fashion & code. Interview with Cecilia Palmer. In: A. Fuad-Luke, A.-L. Hirscher and K. Moebus (eds), *Agents of Alternatives. Re-Designing Our Realities* (Berlin), 182–189

Hobson, K. 2016 Closing the loop or squaring the circle? Locating generative spaces for the circular economy. *Progress in Human Geography* 40(1), 88–104

Küchler, S. 1997 Sacrificial economy and its objects. Rethinking colonial collecting in Oceania. *Journal of Material Culture* 2, 39–60

McDonough, W. and Braungart, M. 2002 *Cradle to Cradle. Rethinking the Way We Make Things* (New York)

Norris, L. 2004 Shedding skins. The materiality of divestment in India. *Journal of Material Culture* 9, 59–71

Norris, L. 2010 *Recycling Indian Clothing. Global Contexts of Reuse and Value, Tracking Globalization* (Bloomington IN)

Norris, L 2012 Economies of moral fibre? Recycling charity clothing into emergency aid blankets. *Journal of Material Culture* 17, 389–404

Norris, L. 2015 The limits of ethicality in international markets. Imported second-hand clothing in India. *Geoforum* 67, 183–193. <http://dx.doi.org/10.1016/j.geoforum.2015.06.003> (accessed: 9 August 2021)

Norris, L. 2019 Urban prototypes. Growing local circular cloth economies. *Business History* 61, 205–224. <https://doi.org/10.1080/00076791.2017.1389902> (accessed: 30 August 2021)

Parry, J. 1986 The gift, the Indian gift and the 'Indian gift'. *MAN. The Journal of the Royal Anthropological Institute* N. S. 21, 453–473

Pearce, S. M. 1995 *On Collecting. An Investigation into Collecting in the European Tradition* (Abingdon)

Pellizzi, F. 1995 Remains. *Res. Anthropology and Aesthetics* 27, 5–10

Pomian, K. 1990 *Collectors and Curiosities. Paris and Venice. 1500-1800* (Cambridge)

Rivoli, P. 2005 *The Travels of a T-Shirt in the Global Economy. An Economist Examines the Markets, Power, and Politics of World Trade* (Hoboken NJ)

Stahel, W. R. 2010 *The Performance Economy* (Basingstoke)

Stewart, S. 1993 *On Longing. Narratives of the Miniature, the Gigantic, the Souvenir, the Collection* (Durham NC)

Tarlo, E. 1996 *Clothing Matters. Dress and Identity in India* (Chicago IL)

Thompson, M. 1979 *Rubbish Theory. The Creation and Destruction of Value* (Oxford)

Tranberg Hansen, K. 2000 *Salaula. The World of Secondhand Clothing and Zambia* (Chicago IL)

Tranberg Hansen, K. 2008 Charity, commerce, consumption. The international second-hand clothing trade at the turn of the millennium. Focus on Zambia. In: L. Fontaine (ed.), *Alternative Exchanges. Second-Hand Circulations from the Sixteenth Century to the Present* (New York), 221–234

Waste & Resources Action Programme (WRAP) 2017. *Valuing Our Clothes. The Cost of UK Fashion* (London)

Chapter 13

From antiquities to art: why has classical archaeology ignored Marcel Duchamp?

James Whitley

Introduction. The context of art

In May 2016 two teenage boys (as teenage boys will do) played a prank. They left a pair of glasses (spectacles) on the floor of an art gallery in San Francisco.[1] Visitors to the gallery were puzzled. Were these glasses art, or not? The setting (the art gallery) suggested that they *were* art, though there was nothing particularly special about the glasses themselves – they were not conspicuously well made, nor were they signed by any artist, nor was there a convenient label 'explaining' the point of the glasses to the uninitiated visitor.

This prank was of course far from original. Art historians, critics, archaeologists and many members of the general public are now used to the idea that anything found within an art gallery must be art – for us it is principally (though not exclusively) the gallery setting that defines what is art (as opposed to what is not). Now one could of course argue that the placing of the spectacles in a gallery space was an ill-conceived example of 'minimalism' or 'conceptual art'. This prank does, however, have bearing on the theme of this volume. For, however inept, it was still an attempt at a 're-evaluation through recontextualisation'. It was a comment on the widespread assumption that anything found within a gallery space (and much that is found in a museum) counts as art; it could then have been understood as a critique of the idea that it is purely context (rather than skill, or material, or genre, or indeed genius) that divides the category of 'art' from that of 'non-art'. As a father of two teenagers, I much prefer this, more generous, interpretation of this intervention.

This contextual definition of art is, however, relatively new.[2] Before the latter part of the 19th century, art was defined largely by material and genre and not by setting.

---

[1] Hunt 2016.
[2] Of course, galleries and museums have a longer history than this – their consolidation dates to around 1800 rather than 1900. My point is that it was only by 1900 that these institutions had gained the cultural authority to enforce such distinctions.

A painting in oils (such as Michelangelo Merisi da Caravaggio's *Supper at Emmaus*)[3] is presumptively considered to be art not so much through its subject but through the genre it belongs to (painting), regardless of whether its setting is an art gallery or a church. Works by Caravaggio can be found in both churches and art galleries – their context is not taken to have any bearing on their status as art. That *Supper at Emmaus* is by Caravaggio rather than another mannerist painter working in and around Rome in the early 17th century may be a factor in what distinguishes great art from minor, not what distinguishes art from non-art. The canonical status of the oil painting remained a stable feature of Western European culture until the end of the 19th century – after which things changed radically. That they did so is down to the activities of a number of artists working in and around Paris in the early years of the 20th century – Pablo Picasso, the Cubists, the Surrealists and the Dadaists.

Of these artists no-one had a greater impact than Marcel Duchamp (1887–1968). Duchamp (in some accounts at least) started out as a Cubist, though one of a rather ironic and saturnine cast. Of his most famous works – *Nude Descending a Stair*, *The Large Glass* and *Fountain* – only the first could conceivably be described as Cubist (in the sense we might apply to works by Picasso or Georges Braque).[4] He is also linked to the Surrealists – though nothing of his remotely resembles the works of Salvador Dalí, René Magritte, Max Ernst or Yves Tanguy. His two most celebrated works – *The Large Glass* and *Fountain* – are usually classified as Dadaist – conceptual art *avant la lettre*. It is these two works which, more than anything else, questioned the established practice of defining art by genre.

Fountain (Fig. 13.1) is not the first but perhaps the best-known of Duchamp's 'ready-mades' (*objets trouvés*). These are not quite 'objects devoid of aesthetic interest but classified, by context, as art', of which Robert Hughes found *Fountain* the 'most aggressive'.[5] Rather the ready-made 'challenges our idea of value'.[6] 'These veritable fetishes' are 'invested with a power that is evidently real, for since their consecration they have never ceased to inspire a devoted cult'.[7] These 'ready-mades' then changed our definition of art through a process which Duchamp called 'transubstantiation'.[8] It is not too much to say that *Fountain* was the work that re-defined art for the 20th century. Table 13.1 provides a crude summary of this change pre- and post-Duchamp.

The idea that it is largely (if not solely) spatial context that can define art is, however, something that many people today find unsettling. For to call something 'art' is to make an ontological claim about that object – it is to state that the object is

---

[3] London, The National Gallery, inv. NG172.
[4] In the *catalogue raisonnée* (Lebel 1959, 154–176) these are nos 87–90 (there are several versions), no. 118 and no. 132 respectively.
[5] Hughes 1980, 66.
[6] Lebel 1959, 35.
[7] Lebel 1959, 36.
[8] Duchamp 1959, 78.

 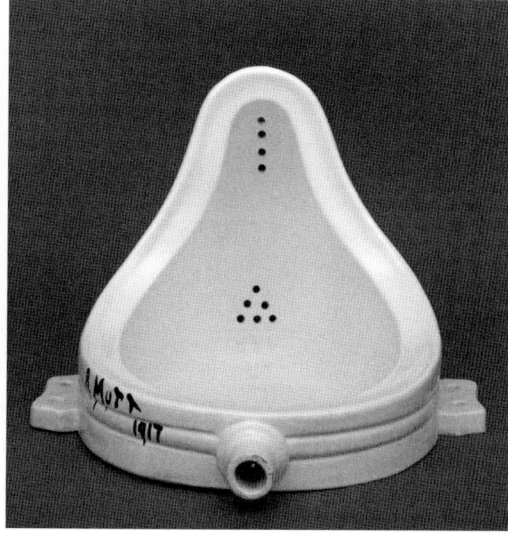

Figure 13.1. Original and copies: a) the only surviving photograph of the original Fountain *(photo: Alfred Stieglitz, from Wikimedia Commons); b) the exact copy in Tate Modern in London. London, Tate Modern, inv. T07573 (© Tate London 2019)*

Table 13.1. The differing definitions of art, pre- and post-Duchamp

Pre-1900 (pre-Duchamp)	Post-1900 (post-Duchamp)
Definition of art by genre (painting, sculpture, architecture)	Definition of art by setting (chiefly an art gallery, or art space)
Art closely related to materials involving skills linked to particular materials (e.g. sculpting in bronze)	Art related to concepts, as a vehicle for a 'concept'; weaker link to materials
Working and referencing within an established tradition (e.g. landscape painting)	Emphasis on novelty and 'originality' – including novel media and forms
Artist important – but minor works within established genres possible	Artist central – crucial to what distinguishes art from non-art

essentially different from a mere thing. Hence the controversies that originally arose about such 'works of art' as *Equivalent VIII*.[9] When this was bought by the Tate in London in 1973, many members of the public were outraged – 'it's just a pile of bricks' or 'why pay so much public money for a pile of bricks?'– were the kind of criticisms that were voiced. The artist's (Carl André's) insouciant response to this controversy

---

[9] London, Tate Modern, inv. T01534.

('it's just art') compounded the problem for the museum authorities, a problem which the elaborate Tate (Tate Modern) gallery label seeks to allay.

> Each of André's *Equivalent* series consists of a rectangular arrangement of 120 firebricks. Although the shape of each sculpture is different, they all have the same height, mass and volume, and are therefore 'equivalent' to each other. André's sculptures are often assembled using common industrial materials, which he arranges into a simple geometric pattern. His sculptures are always placed on the floor rather than on plinths. Not simply objects to look at, they become part of the environment, altering the viewer's relationship to the surrounding space.[10]

Elaborate inscriptions such as these, which describe at length how these bricks are not just any old bricks but are rather carefully chosen and indeed *crafted* bricks, are there to provide re-assurance that the object in question is indeed art. But such labels – labels which tell the gallery-goer who may as yet be unschooled in the mysteries of minimalism what the object is (or means) – inevitably patronise the visitor (especially in its assumptions that he or she is incapable of realising that bricks are, generally speaking, of the same size and shape).

This gallery label, at least, has not worked as the Tate curators intended. *Equivalent VIII* is, more often than not, not referred to by its title, nor by its originator/artist ('a work by Carl André'). The bricks are, more often than not, simply referred to as 'The Tate Bricks' or 'The Bricks' – an ironic commentary on the idea that is purely context that defines this assemblage as art. No critique is perhaps more withering than that of Hughes, written and spoken with characteristic Australian bluntness:

> The essential difference between a sculpture like André's *Equivalent VIII* ... and any that had existed in the past is that André's array of bricks depended not just partly, but entirely, on the museum for its context. A Rodin in a parking lot is still a Rodin; André's bricks in the same place can only be a pile of bricks. The museum alone supplies the etiquette that identifies it as art, slotting the bricks into the formal debate about contexts which enables a visually inert heap of material to be seen as part of an art movement called "Minimalism". The paradox of such works is that they staked everything on the institutional context for their effect, while claiming to have the density and singularity of things in the real world.[11]

So much for Minimalism!

The (ontological) status of art in the 20th century

Much remains at stake in the use of the term 'art'. We may no longer be attached to any mimetic theory of what might constitute art, but we remain deeply attached to the notion that some kind of ontological difference exists between everyday objects (non-art) and aesthetic objects (art) – that there is an ontological-cum-aesthetic-

---

[10] *Gallery label*, October 2016 (https://www.tate.org.uk/art/artworks/andre-equivalent-viii-t01534 [accessed: 28 July 2021]).
[11] Hughes 1980, 392-394.

cum-spiritual divide between art and non-art. That is, most visitors to galleries or museums would agree with Howard Morphy's definition of 'high art' as:

> a set-apart category of objects viewed independently of their function, housed in institutions of fine art, and appreciated for their aesthetic value, on the basis of disinterested viewing and judgement.[12]

Such objects would include this 1886 painting by Vincent Van Gogh (Fig. 13.2).[13] This is the subject of one of the 20th century's most sustained philosophical attempts to understand precisely what art is. This is a painting of a pair of shoes, shoes that have been heavily worn and used. Van Gogh made several such paintings. This one[14] was the subject of an extended meditation by Martin Heidegger:

> From the dark opening of the worn insides of the shoes the toilsome tread of the worker stares forth. In the stiffly rugged heaviness of the shoes there is the accumulated tenacity of her slow trudge through the far-spreading and ever-uniform furrows of the field swept by a raw wind. On the leather lie the dampness and richness of the soil. Under the soles slides the loneliness of the field-path as evening falls. In the shoes vibrates the silent call of the earth, its quiet gift of the ripening grain and its unexplained self-refusal in the fallow desolation of the wintry field. This equipment is pervaded by uncomplaining anxiety as to the certainty of bread, the wordless joy of having once more withstood want, the trembling before the impending childbed and shivering at the surrounding menace of death. This equipment belongs to the earth, and it is protected in the world of the peasant woman. From out of this protected belonging the equipment itself rises to its resting-within-itself.[15]

There is an interesting ambiguity in Heidegger's description. Heidegger here is at one level describing the shoes *in* the painting as if they were actual shoes real and present in his gaze, while at the same time he implies that such an evocation could not have been prompted by the shoes themselves (mere things, or mere equipment) so much as their incarnation (my term, not his) in Van Gogh's painting.

Incarnation is not very far from transubstantiation – they are both theological terms applied, not to God but to art. Which brings us back to Duchamp and, in particular, to his 'lost' work – *Fountain* (Fig. 13.1). It goes without saying that the San Francisco prank, *merde 'd'artiste*, Andy Warhol's *Brillo Boxes* and *Equivalent VIII* – indeed any example of conceptual art – would be quite impossible without this piece. Readers should all know the story.[16] In 1917 this standard, factory-produced men's urinal was modified, placed on its side, and 'inverted', so turned from a commonplace *pissoir* into a *Fountain*. As most people have since understood, this

---

[12] Morphy 2010, 268–269. Morphy does not really believe in this definition. He uses it as a foil to develop an argument about how the term art still has value within anthropological and archaeological discourse.
[13] Amsterdam, Van Gogh Museum, inv. s0011V1962.
[14] One of two now in Amsterdam (https://www.vangoghmuseum.nl/en/collection/s0127V1962?v=1 [accessed: 28 July 2021]).
[15] Heidegger 1978, 159–160.
[16] Lebel 1959, 35–41.

Figure 13.2. Pair of Shoes *by Van Gogh (1886). Amsterdam, Van Gogh Museum, inv. s0011V1962. (image courtesy Van Gogh Museum, Amsterdam).*

was an ironic inversion. Its status as 'art' was confirmed by the inscription – authored and so authenticated by the 'artist' R. Mutt (a pseudonym of Duchamp). Before it was exhibited, it was photographed – and this is the only image we have of the 'original'. In the standard account, the intention was to exhibit this piece alongside other examples of contemporary art in a gallery in New York. But it never was – as soon as Duchamp's purpose became known, other artists objected on the grounds that it could not be considered a true artwork. Its presence in an exhibition would then detract from the aesthetic status of their own 'works of art'.

After this *contretemps* the original *Fountain* rather mysteriously disappeared – whether destroyed or sold or otherwise lost we do not know. We do know there was an original because we have the photograph.[17] After this a number of copies were made: some of these (such as the one in the Tate)[18] appear (judging by the photograph) to be 'faithful' copies; others (such as the one in Edinburgh) are decidedly less so. All these copies of a lost original were authorised by Duchamp himself. They are – whatever their degree of fidelity to the original *Fountain* – authorised copies.

Fountain is, of course, an act of blasphemy against the very notion of art.[19] However much we may want to point out that Duchamp is drawing attention to the sculptural properties of a men's urinal and the underlying principles of good design we may find in an everyday object (IKEA like: 'finding beauty in the everyday'); however much we may want to interpret it as 'challenging the boundaries and definition of art', not art *tout court*,[20] it remains a comment on the arbitrary way in which we assign objects to the category of 'art' versus 'non-art'. In this respect it both attacks deeply held notions

---

[17] Lebel 1959, pl. 80; Fig. 13.1a.
[18] Lebel 1959; Fig. 13.1b.
[19] One should note, however, art historian Jeremy Tanner's objections to this statement (pers. comm.) 'Well: yes and no. Certainly against some conceptions of art; but what Duchamp was doing was challenging the boundaries and definition of art, not art tout court; hence his desire to have his work displayed in art galleries and museum'.
[20] Tanner, pers. comm.

of art and questions the 'regimes of value' that make ontological distinctions between art and non-art. That it was given a false signature – the authenticating inscription is a lie – underscores this. Discussion, in art historical and critical circles, has tended to concentrate on this aspect of the work: *Fountain* de-mystifies notions of 'art'.[21] It may well do this – but so does a pair of spectacles in a San Francisco art gallery. *Fountain* does much more than that. There is another dimension to this 'ready-made' which has hardly been commented on at all. As well as being an act of blasphemy it is also an act of commentary. And here we come to classical archaeology (*Archäologie* or *Klassische Archäologie*).

Fountain and *Kopienkritik*. Modern art and classical archaeology

One of the features that has always puzzled art historical/cultural critical observers is the idea that the 'original' *Fountain* must have been lost and/or destroyed, while the 'copies' remain (and indeed have proliferated). But if you are a classical archaeologist, then the reference seems plain. One of the main activities of traditional classical archaeology from the 19th century until the present day has been the practice of *Kopienforschung* or *Kopienkritik*. This is the attempt to define a 'lost' Greek original (usually if not invariably in bronze) by making careful comparisons of its various Roman copies (usually if not invariably in marble). Examples abound, but the numerous copies of the lost Demosthenes of Polyeuktos (set up in bronze around 280/279 BCE in the Agora of Athens) illustrate the practice (Fig. 13.3). Gisela Richter counts two full marble copies (one in Copenhagen, the other in the Vatican)[22] and 45 heads (such as the fine example in the Ashmolean Museum).[23] For Ulrich Sinn at least, this form of scholarly endeavour remains central to what classical archaeology is.[24] The proliferation of copies of *Fountain* (authorised by Duchamp himself), 16 in all, is thus analogous with the process by which marble 'copies' of lost Greek originals proliferated in the ancient world – and indeed how plaster copies of Roman copies proliferated in late 19th and early 20th century museums (such as the Cast Gallery in Oxford[25] and the Museum of Classical Archaeology in Cambridge). With this understanding Duchamp's *Fountain* – which, among other things, in its 'whiteness' echoes the materiality of marble 'copies' (and plaster copies of these copies) –

---

[21] As in Hughes 1980.
[22] Copenhagen, Ny Carlsberg Glyptotek, inv. 2782; Vatikan, Vatikanische Museen, inv. 2255.
[23] The Ashmolean museum head (Oxford Ashmolean Museum 1923.764) is one of the finest heads; Robertson 1975, pl. 159c. For a complete list of the heads see Richter 1965b, 215–223; 1970, 233; Richter and Smith 1984, 109–113; cf. Pollitt 1990, 112. For its significance see discussion in Pollitt 1986, 61–63.
[24] Sinn 2000. Of course there is now an alternative perspective in German classical archaeology; see Borbein *et al.* 2000.
[25] This has recently been attached to the Ashmolean but was for a long time a separate museum (and contains a fine copy in plaster of the Vatican Demosthenes (Ashmolean Museum CG.C.212). Cast galleries attached to departments of Classics and Classical Archaeology can be found in London (at University College) and even in Greece (in Thessaloniki).

Figure 13.3. Roman marble copy of the Demosthenes of Polyeuktos (in Copenhagen). Copenhagen, NY Carlsberg Glyptotek, Inv. 2782; neg. nr. 436a (photo J. Selsing; Courtesy NY Carlsberg Glyptotek, Copenhagen).

becomes both much more sophisticated, less reductively scatological ('he was just taking the piss') and much, much funnier (much funnier that is than any other piece of conceptual art).

This joke (or this aspect of the joke) seems to have been lost on cultural critics and art historians. What artists, art historians and cultural critics have taken from this is that 'art' can no longer be defined by genre or material. Art is what museum/gallery curators deem it to be – objects worthy to be placed within their sacred spaces. But just as the cultural critics/art historians seem to have missed Duchamp's joke (his act of commentary), so classical archaeologists seem not to have taken on board the intellectual consequences of his act of blasphemy. Many classical archaeologists remain firmly wedded to a pre-Duchampian notion of art – where art is defined by material and genre.[26] Whereas the art history of the 20th and 21st centuries has had, in some way, to accommodate itself to new kinds of art – to new things in new media – classical archaeology (in its most traditional form, under the livery of 'classical art history') has continued to study painting, sculpture and architecture.[27] This is odd. For classical archaeology and art history have, especially in the German tradition, always been fields of study with very close ties. Jeremy Tanner refers to them as 'sib-disciplines', a claim that has warrant in Erwin Panofsky's remark that classical archaeology is art history's 'elder and more conservative sister'.[28]

Many classical art historians working in Britain would balk at being described as either elderly or conservative. For have not Jeremy Tanner, Jas Elsner, Michael Squire and Robin Osborne fully embraced the theoretical dimension of the study of ancient art? Certainly they have, and much has been usefully brought in to 'classical art history' from the study of both literature and sociology.[29] But in their definition of what might constitute 'art', and in their insistence that art must be kept firmly at a distance from mere material culture, their approach remains deeply conservative. For all their theoretical sophistication, their approach to ancient art remains firmly pre-Duchampian. That is to say, ancient art can still be defined principally by the major genres of painting, sculpture, mosaics and glyptic; and that ancient art is, almost by definition, representational. The practical definition of art (in the ancient world) thus corresponds very closely with those genres that defined 'art' in Western Europe before 1900. Table 13.2 summarises the points of similarity.

That the ancient Greeks had no notion of 'art' is not, for them, a difficulty. This problem is, after all, not new. As long ago as 1942, Ernst Buschor had stated *Kunst ist nicht immer "Kunst" gewesen* (art has not always been art).[30] Classical art

---

[26] e.g. Meyer and Lendon 2005.
[27] I am referring here mainly to the Greek rather than the Roman sub-division of classical archaeology – or rather my generalisations require fewer qualifications in the 'Greek' rather than the 'Roman' sphere.
[28] Panofsky 1993 [1955], 370; Tanner 2018, 197.
[29] see Tanner 1994; and in particular contributions to Osborne and Tanner 2007.
[30] Buschor 1942, 7. This is the opening clause of Buschor's *Vom Sinn der griechischen Standbilder*. The full quote is less bald, more qualified: 'Kunst ist nicht immer "Kunst" gewesen, und so sind auch die

historians are fond of pointing out that, while Greeks had no notion of art in our sense, they clearly appreciated fine craftsmanship and technical accomplishment and praised complex, skilfully made artefacts such as Homer's (imaginary) Shield of Achilles. Richard Neer argues that many of the great works of the 5th and 4th centuries BCE would have been seen as 'wonders to behold', θαῦμα ἰδέσθαι.[31] Just as economic historians moreover can talk about the ancient economy, regardless of the absence of a Greek term for economy, and religious historians can continue to talk about Greek religion, regardless of the absence of a Greek equivalent for our term 'religion', so classical art historians can continue quite happily to talk about art.[32] Similarly the fact that both the major works of sculpture of classical Greece, and the sculptors (such as Polykleitos of Argos) who crafted them, enjoyed a relatively high standing – and that their agency as 'artists' was recognised – has for these scholars formed the clinching argument.[33]

For most of these scholars then that art is our term and not theirs presents no real epistemological or hermeneutic difficulty. We can continue to use it to make comparisons across cultures.[34] Comparisons across cultures, however, imply that there can be an 'etic' definition of art – that is a scientific one (science here understood in the French/German sense of a systematically organised body of knowledge, a form of *Wissenschaft*). Here and elsewhere Tanner has tried to redefine art as 'expressive symbolism', an idea borrowed from Talcott Parsons.[35] Certainly, such a concept helps to explain how Kresilas's 'Perikles'[36] became such an effective 'type' and used as a model for other portraits of generals.[37] Here portraits are enmeshed in a system of rewards for civic virtue that helped to sustain the *polis* of Athens particularly during the strains of the 4th century BCE. Tanner develops these ideas in his important 2006 book where he placed ancient sculptures, such as works by Polykleitos or Praxiteles made to commemorate athletic victories at Olympia, back in their original setting (that is, together with their original inscriptions).[38]

---

plastischen Bildwerke der Griechen zu verschiedenen Zeiten so verschieden in ihrem tieferen Ursprung und in ihrer inneren Zielsetzung, daß es dem aufmerksamen Betrachter nicht leicht ist, sie insgesamt mit demselben Wort, als Kunstwerke, als plastische Bildwerke zu bezeichnen. Es ist nicht ein anderes Verhalten zur gleichen Aufgabe, das eine frühe Tonfigur von einem spätantiken Standbild abhebt, sondern eine völlige Verschiebung des Ursprungs und der Bestimmung des plastischen Bildwerks.' ('Art has not always been "art". This is why the sculpted pictorial representations of the ancient Greeks differ so profoundly from period to period in their deeper original meaning and their purpose. An attentive observer would not find it easy to refer to them indiscriminately as sculptures, as if they represented a single body of works of art. It is not merely a difference in purpose that distinguishes, say, an early clay figurine from a late antique statue but a total shift in origin and purpose'; translation: Josef Lossl).

[31] Neer 2010.
[32] e.g. Osborne 2010; Squire 2010; Tanner 2010, 271.
[33] Tanner 2006, 141–204.
[34] e.g. between Chinese paintings and Greco-Roman and Renaissance marble sculptures; Tanner 2018.
[35] Tanner 1992; 2005; 2006.
[36] Richter 1965a, 102–104; Richter and Smith 1984, 173–175.
[37] Tanner 1992.
[38] Tanner 2006, 153–158; see also Tanner 1999. For an alternative theoretical approach to the 'agency' of classical sculpture see Whitley 2011.

Table 13.2. Genres of art objects in Art History (pre-Duchamp) and Classical Archaeology/Classical Art History

Art in art history (pre-Duchamp)	Art in Classical archaeology
Architecture (public and religious)	Architecture (religious and public)
Painting – oil painting and wall painting	Painting – wall painting and vase painting
Sculpture – marble, stone and bronze	Sculpture – marble, stone and bronze
Minor arts (various)	*Kleinkunst* (glyptic, terracottas etc.)
Lasted up until 1900	Still relevant in 'Classical Art History'

'Expressive symbolism' then provides insights into how sculpture 'worked' within the social and political order of classical Greece, dominated as it was by the civic demands of the *polis* and the arenas for inter-*polis* competition provided by panhellenic sanctuaries. There are still problems, however, with the concept. For both busts (or perhaps originally statues) of generals and honorific inscriptions (of which there are many in the 4th century BCE)[39] were both equally enmeshed in this system of rewards for civic virtue in 4th century Athens. They both serve the same purpose. Are honorific inscriptions then art since they seem to share the same 'expressive symbolism' as honorific statues (they certainly share the same agency)?[40] What is it that inscriptions lack that portraits possess that gives the latter 'expressive symbolism'? Is it simply that portraits, unlike inscriptions, are representational?

It is not only classical scholars who have difficulty with the notion of art. So too do prehistorians, who habitually use the term for things that are more or less representational (such as petroglyphs), while classifying the bulk of the objects they study as 'material culture'. This too brings with it a degree of conceptual confusion, confusion which John Robb has recently tried to resolve by use of different typefaces for the various meanings of 'art'.[41] So, for Robb, 'art' is a general topic under discussion; **ART** is a term for a set of modern, Western institutions and practices; and ART is what archaeologists (by which he means prehistorians) refer to when talking about the petroglyphs and bronzes of Late Bronze Age Scandinavia. Robb tries to maintain a thoroughly 'etic' separation between these terms. What this scheme conspicuously ignores, however, is the history and etymology of the term 'art' and its necessary, original link to a very specific ethnicity ('Greek art').

Art, ethnicity and Eurocentrism

Here we return to the general difficulty in defining what exactly is art. The etymology at least is plain. Our term 'art' derives from the Latin 'ars' – it has a genealogy that is more Roman than Greek. Art then is not an 'insider' (emic) category – we

---

[39] Lambert 2011.
[40] *Sensu* Gell 1998.
[41] Robb 2017.

cannot, in using the term, pretend that we are reproducing the terms in which the Greeks discussed the sculptures and paintings they themselves produced.[42] Nor is it an outsider's *scientific* term (an etic one) – such as 'state' where we agree on what constitutes a 'state' and use that term to provide some basis for comparison across cultures in time and space. It appears both to be indispensable and to resist precise definition. As such it must fall into another category – neither fully scientific, nor simply part of our everyday discourse about everyday 'emic' things. What kind of discourse might this be?

Here we run into another difficulty – and that is that the term 'Greek Art' has an ethnic and 'civilisational' charge. Greek art is, in art historical discourse, more art-like than anyone else's art in the ancient world, by virtue of its being Greek. This fact causes a whole set of problems when we look at things which, in the ancient world, look like they are examples of 'Greek Art' but in fact are not – such as south Italian red-figure pottery. That such things as Apulian red-figure are regularly included in general surveys of Greek art (or at least Greek painted pottery)[43] does not, in general, raise any concerns. This problem is compounded when we look at the art of other peoples who regularly came into contact, and borrowed from, the Greeks – such as the Phoenicians.[44] The notion of 'Greek Art' has led us profoundly to misinterpret such things as the so-called Alexander Sarcophagus (originally from Sidon, but now to be found in Istanbul).[45] Elsner has neatly summed up the problem:

> We know that "art" (whatever that means) was somehow borne there [ancient Greece] (differently, perhaps more "Europeanly", from its Indian, Egyptian and Mesopotamian origins), and for centuries – but especially after Winckelmann – we have been busy trying to be a bit more precise about what I have deliberately phrased in the woolliest terms with a touch of Eurocentric racism, which no amount of politically correct genuflections can ever wholly eradicate.[46]

This fact seems to have troubled members of Western cultural elites who remain deeply attached to the notion of art. Some might also have realised that we have tended to treat different kinds of 'art' differently.[47] Ethnographic or primitive art is 'contextualised', seen in terms of its role in social life[48] and displayed in ethnographic museums such as the Pitt Rivers in Oxford or the American Museum of Natural History in New York; 'Western' and 'Greek' art (and indeed increasingly the art of all 'civilised' countries) is aestheticised – treated as something that is intended, and indeed does, evoke a pure aesthetic response in the viewer (and is usually to be found in museums like

---

[42] see Whitley 2012.
[43] see Cook 1972.
[44] Martin 2017a.
[45] Istanbul, Archäologisches Museum, inv. 370; Martin 2017b.
[46] Elsner 2010, 290.
[47] Faris 1988; Price 1989.
[48] see also Gell 1998.

the Metropolitan Museum in New York or the Ashmolean in Oxford). So, a New York schoolteacher, on first seeing the works of the Berlin Painter displayed all together in Princeton[49] thinks of John Keats and produces her own odes to Grecian urns.[50]

I am not trying to belittle Helaine Smith's aesthetic response to the works of the Berlin Painter – it is quite genuine and contains some insight into how the best Athenian red-figure works. But it is not quite an innocent response, since it takes it for granted that what is being viewed is 'art'. Art remains central to modern, metropolitan notions of the civilised life, at least in the English-speaking world. And metropolitan cultural elites, troubled by charges of Eurocentrism, are keen to show that their view is now global.[51] Witness the recent television series *Civilisations*, which aired on BBC2 in Britain in the spring of 2018. This was an attempt, in one sense, to update Kenneth Clark's *Civilisation* (originally broadcast in 1969) for the 21st century. Whereas Clark had just covered 'the West' from the Fall of Rome down to the end of the 19th century, *Civilisations* scope was global – it attempted to cover all civilisations from the appearance of *homo sapiens* down to the present. If its global scope was broader than Clark's, in another sense its focus was narrower. It concentrated solely on the visual arts – on sculpture, painting and architecture (the pre-Duchampian trinity). Whereas Clark had brought in Byron, Beethoven and Balzac in his study of Romanticism (Episode 13, 'The Fallacies of Hope'), the only composer to appear in *Civilisations* was Wagner, and that was as the backing track for lingering shots of the vast canvases of Anselm Kiefer. And, while Clark attempted to define Western 'civilisation' by demonstration, the complete concentration on the visual arts (with only the vaguest references to music, literature or religion)[52] made this task an impossible one for the three presenters of *Civilisations*.

What this recent series did demonstrate, if inadvertently, was the religious fervour that now surrounds art amongst anglophone, metropolitan elites. 'Art' is considered to be the sum total of the visual arts, and the visual arts now stand in the place once occupied by music, literature and poetry. How has this come to be? Why is 'Art' in the sense of the visual arts so venerated? This brings us back to Duchamp. It was Duchamp's *Fountain*, after all, that first drew attention to the arbitrariness of what we define as art and to the absurdity of valuing 'the original' over the 'copies'.

What then about the question in my title – why has classical archaeology ignored Duchamp? A critic might turn this around – why should classical archaeologists pay any attention at all to Duchamp? My answer is that his *Fountain* presents a

---

[49] Padgett 2017.
[50] Smith 2017.
[51] By 'metropolitan cultural elites' I mean those based in major cities such as New York, London, Paris or Berlin who have a major role in the museum/gallery world, or work for major broadcasting organisations, or who act as commentators/critics on art or who are academics with privileged access to organs of metropolitan opinion (e.g. the *New York Review of Books*, the *London Review of Books*, or the *Times Literary Supplement*). Most lecturers in archaeology do not fall into any of these categories.
[52] One of the presenters, Mary Beard, did try to deal with the problem of 'the art of religion'. But in doing so she made the mistake of thinking that her metropolitan perspective was somehow not in any way religious.

direct challenge to established notions of art in general and is, in a more particular sense, both a commentary on and an (oblique) critique of *Kopienforschung*, a practice central to traditional *Archäologie*. One could argue, of course, that in a field which is as conservative as classical archaeology, scholars were simply not paying attention. Those who worked in the academic bubble of a *Seminar für Klassische Archäologie* in Marburg, Freiburg or Hamburg would have little reason to take notice of what was happening in the Paris art world. My response to this is that the conservatism of classical archaeology has been exaggerated. In Germany, moreover, conservatism in scholarly practice cannot be equated with indifference to philosophical questions. It was not for nothing that Buschor labelled his course of Greek sculpture 'Greek Sculpture from Parmenides to Plotinos'.[53]

It is worth digressing a little on how *Kopienkritik* was practised in the early 20th century and how this provides a kind of context for Duchamp. Let us look at one scholar, Bernhard Schweitzer. Schweitzer's career began with the study of Geometric pottery, to which he provided some order that had hitherto been lacking[54] and to which he returned later in life.[55] This was material on the very edge of 'Classical Archaeology' – its study being, of necessity, entirely archaeological since no texts (even Homer) were of much use in its interpretation. Schweitzer could happily continue to move from the study of Greek Geometric painted pottery to exercises in *Kopienkritik* such as his fundamental work on a celebrated Hellenistic sculpture, the Pasquino group[56] without being bothered by what was going on in New York or Paris (so this argument might run). I do not find this (hypothetical) argument convincing. Schweitzer's identification of the Pasquino Group as representing Menelaos carrying the body of the dead Patroklos[57] demanded more than a comparison of photographs;[58] it required autopsy of various fragments in Florence and Rome and a close demonstration of their relationship. This is one reason why modern scholars find his interpretation (including his placing this work within a 'Pergamene' school of sculpture) convincing.[59] *Kopienforschung* then requires extensive travel to look at the various copies that exist in European (and some American) museums. *Kopienforschung* is inherently cosmopolitan. Schweitzer, moreover, like Buschor, was interested in the philosophy of art and in particular how Greek art might express or embody concepts.[60] He was not working in an academic bunker.

Conservatism is not the real reason for classical archaeology's indifference to Duchamp. The real reason, I think, is an obsessive desire to hold on to a notion of art that emphasises art's intrinsic aesthetic (and so spiritual) qualities.

---

[53] Noted in Heidegger 2005, 18. 69.
[54] Schweitzer 1917; 1918.
[55] Schweitzer 1969.
[56] Schweitzer 1938.
[57] From Hom. Il. 17, 580–581.
[58] Schweitzer 1938.
[59] Pollitt 1986, 117–118.
[60] Schweitzer 1934; for criticisms see Tanner 2018, 201–207.

There are strong *religious* reasons – within an overall religious framework of contemporary metropolitan secularism – to this desire to hold on to a pure aesthetic notion of art. Art has become one of Heidegger's gods. Linked to the desire to hold on to the intrinsic aesthetic qualities of art is a parallel motive – to deflect attention from the consequences of decontextualisation and recontextualisation. For it is this process of contextualisation and recontextualisation where we can find the origins of art itself. Art is a Roman term that came to be applied to Greek things. It was the elder Pliny who provided the first canon of (Greek) objects to which the word 'ars' could be attached. While not quite being 'art' in our modern sense, the Latin ars differs from *technē* (τέχνη) (the Greek term) in that it be applied to a whole body of work, a whole category of objects. Pliny's *deinde cessavit ars* simply cannot be retranslated back into Greek.[61] Tanner has argued that this notion of an independent aesthetic realm emerges in Greek thought and practice at some point in the Hellenistic era as part of an autonomous intellectual and cultural process.[62] He points out that the first 'canon' of works of art was by Poseidippus, not Pliny, and that this canon appeared at some point in the 3rd century BCE. Tanner finds a precedent for the Roman habit of 'decontextualising' statues – removing them from the inscription which would identify (say) the athlete being honoured in 'Myron's Dyskobolos' and placing them in a new setting that made them unintelligible in relation to their original religious and civic purposes – in the practices of the kings of Pergamon in the middle of the 2nd century BCE.

These are all fair points. Yet there is a lot that Tanner leaves out. We have to think ourselves back to the material and political conditions in which the term 'ars' first emerged. This process was not simply an intellectual one, but one where a new set of relationships emerged between people and things.[63] In classical Greece sculptures in particular served a range of civic and commemorative functions and these functions depended on their setting. Sculptures were accompanied by inscriptions that indicated which person was being honoured (as in Kresilas's statue of Perikles) and what he was being honoured for. As Tanner has forcefully argued, classical sculpture in particular was enmeshed in a cycle of 'honour'.[64] It was not yet 'art'.

Art emerged out of a century of unprecedented destructiveness. The 2nd century BCE was probably the most violent era of ancient Mediterranean history. It was the century in which the Romans reached their final solution to their Epirot and Carthaginian problems – cities were sacked and territories ruined with a thoroughness that had not been seen before (something that can easily be verified by a trip to Epirus today). It was a time when an unprecedented quantity of wealth and loot reached the cities of Italy from the East producing a consumer revolution.[65] It was against this background that art appeared.

---

[61] Plin. nat. 32, 52.
[62] Tanner 2005; 2006, 205–276.
[63] *Sensu* Hodder 2011.
[64] Tanner 1992.
[65] Wallace-Hadrill 2008, 315–355.

Art could not have arisen without acts of radical decontextualisation. From 196 BCE Roman generals were campaigning throughout Greece. Campaigning involved looting – the most notorious act of which was Lucius Mummius's sack of Corinth in 146 BCE. This event was crucial for the 'history of art', for Mummius did not only take sculptures and paintings from their original settings (where their civic meaning would be plain) but also redistributed them to the various allies of Rome (allies in Italy like Pompeii, allies in Asia such as Pergamon).[66] It was in this way that many sculptures came to be dedicated in the sanctuary of Athena Nikephoros in Pergamon.

This process is perhaps a bit more than straightforward theft. Nor was this appearance of 'art as high culture'[67] a purely conceptual or intellectual process since it resulted in a reconfiguration of peoples' relationship with things (and so of their meaning). This Roman/Pergamene process involved the removal of bronze statues from a major sanctuary and their recontextualisation in an entirely different setting – originally perhaps a sanctuary, but eventually a large house or palace. In changing the setting (and the institutions that framed them), the Romans also changed the meaning of these 'works of art'. Crucial to this process was the removal from the statues of the inscriptions that explained what they were for.[68] We cannot now relate 'Myron's Dyskobolos' to the athlete whose victory it must have commemorated. This context – and meaning – have been lost. They became famous for the skill of the sculptors who created them rather than the persons or events whose fame they were intended to perpetuate. It is only after this century of violence that the Greeks can be looked at, not as political rivals to the Romans, but as a people uniquely gifted in the crafting of objects in bronze and marble *excudent alii spirantia mollius aera/ (credo equidem) vivos ducent de marmore vultus.*[69] In Ian Hodder's terms 'ars' requires a completely new form of 'human/thing entanglement', that differentiates the world of the 'Roman Revolution' sharply from the situation in classical Greece.[70] It was this new institutional and conceptual setting that authorised the production of 'copies' of Greek originals – creating the 'problem' that *Kopienforschung* set out to solve.[71]

While some scholars affect to be shocked (shocked!) to discover that art and looting have always been intimately linked, others are quite up front about this relationship. Witness Neil MacGregor's justification for exhibiting just one piece of the pedimental sculpture from the Parthenon in St Petersburg a few years ago.

> Two hundred years ago, when the Parthenon sculptures came to London, they transformed Europe's understanding of ancient Greek art. Until then, they had been *architectural*

---

[66] Tanner 2006, 222–231; Yarrow 2006; Wallace-Hadrill 2008, 131–134.
[67] As in Tanner 2005.
[68] Squire 2012; Whitley 2012, 591–594.
[69] Verg. Aen. 6, 847–848. A rough translation might read, '[Let] others cast softly breathing bronzes (so I believe) and carve living faces from marble'.
[70] Hodder 2011.
[71] Tanner 2018, 197–207.

decoration, adjuncts to a great but ruined building. Now they became independent sculptures, *works of art in their own right.* A new life, with new meanings and different stories, had begun.[72]

Only through its removal from its architectural context could, so it was claimed, the 'aesthetic value' of the torso of this river god be revealed. For those former students of Anthony Snodgrass (like myself) who have worked to make classical archaeology a little more like archaeology in general, MacGregor's remarks (and the idea that these ideas still command much public support) are profoundly depressing. MacGregor's words moreover seem to re-enforce the divide between 'primitive' (ethnographic/non-Western) and 'civilised' (Western/Greek) art, since he assumes that the response to this torso must be primarily aesthetic – an appreciation of the beautiful shorn of any consideration for what the figure represents or what the original pedimental ensemble might have meant to 5th century BCE Athenians.

Outside the gallery/museum. Objects in context and the agency of objects

Duchamp's work, however, undercuts this notion of intrinsic aesthetic interest advocated by MacGregor. In so doing it also opens up avenues to looking at the agency of objects in new ways. Let us look at two objects, one clearly a 'work of art', the other known primarily to archaeologists. The first is a portrait of Dr Gachet by Van Gogh painted in 1890 (Fig. 13.4). In 1990 it was acquired by Mr Ryoei Saito, a Japanese businessman, who paid $82.5 million for the privilege of owning it.[73] When Mr. Saito died, the painting mysteriously disappeared. In many respects this painting fulfils the essential condition of a modern work of art – it sold for several million dollars at auction. In another though it seems to have been treated in a very different way. It has been rumoured (though we do not know this for sure) that the painting was cremated together with the man himself at his funeral.[74]

One of the persistent misconceptions sustained by the notion of 'art' is that complex, carefully made artefacts such as the portrait of Dr Gachet must always have been made to *last* rather than being made to be *destroyed*. That one of the necessary ontological conditions for something being considered 'art' is that it must be preserved in perpetuity, preferably within a well-defined 'art' space, was proven by the online fuss created by the disappearance of this Van Gogh painting – its (possible) destruction in a funeral was considered an act of sacrilege against art by the predominantly New York online community that discussed it.[75] But if we widen our scope to other things classified as

---

[72] MacGregor 2014, 4 (emphasis mine).
[73] It is one of two portraits of Dr Gachet by Van Gogh. One is in the Musée d'Orsay in Paris (Paris, Musée d'Orsay, inv. RF 1949 16), the location of the other (once in the possession of Mr Saito) is unknown. Wikipedia (https://en.wikipedia.org/wiki/Portrait_of_Dr._Gachet [accessed: 28 July 2021]) at least does not believe that this portrait was cremated with Mr Saito but rather was sold on. To whom is unknown.
[74] Usborne 1999.
[75] Usborne 1999.

Figure 13.4. Portrait Dr Gachet *by Vincent Van Gogh (1890), whereabouts unknown (photo: Wikimedia Commons).*

'art', this idea that the gallery/museum is an object's natural home begins to look a little strange. Let us take as our example Malangan, objects which have been made and continue to be made in New Ireland for funerals.[76] Some of these objects have ended up in Western museums – but that is far from being their 'natural' home. As Alfred Gell explains:

> Conceptually, from the New Ireland point of view, a Malangan carving which has fulfilled its ritual role has rotted away and is no more, and its future as a museum piece is irrelevant. Malangan only 'exist' as socially salient objects, for a very short period, during the mortuary ceremonies for important persons, during which they are gradually imbued with life by being carved and painted, brought to perfection and displayed for a few hours at the culminating point of the mortuary ritual – only to be 'killed' with gifts of shell money. Once they have been 'killed' they no longer exist as ritual objects (which is why they may subsequently be sold to collectors).[77]

[76] Küchler 1987; Gell 1998, 223–228.
[77] Gell 1998, 224–225.

Malangan in Western museums are therefore objects out of place – but no more so than many 'Greek' objects which have found themselves into many 'art' museums. In the Ashmolean museum in Oxford there is a case devoted to Athenian white-ground *lekythoi*, a case juxtaposed to another which explains how John Beazley managed to attribute so many Athenian vases to particular artists.[78] These beautiful objects perhaps give us the best idea of the achievements of ancient painters in the 5th century BCE (since wall paintings by such famous figures as Polygnotos have been lost).[79] They have colour as well as line. But they were never meant to be seen, still less placed in a museum or gallery. Their purpose was to be buried with an Athenian man or woman in a cist, coffin or chest. Like the Malangan they would only be 'seen' at the funeral, and perhaps as offerings for the dead. Their iconography (with frequent scenes of parting, such as to be found in many examples painted by the Achilles painter) and their agency are thus strictly circumscribed. In a museum they are as much 'out of place' as any piece from Melanesia.

Even more shocking for Western art lovers and Western art theorists is the notion that many highly crafted artefacts manufactured in antiquity were made to be destroyed. The late Paul Rehak observed of the stone *rhyta* of neopalatial Bronze Age Crete that the more elaborately and finely decorated they had been made, the more likely they were to be found in pieces, as if to be broken and killed was the natural end of the life of these objects.[80] And there are parallels in the archaeological record for the violent end that Mr Saito's Van Gogh painting may have suffered. In other times and places, no-one would have bothered much with the ostentatious destruction of complex, skilfully made objects with extended biographies. This after all, was the fate of this Cypriot bronze stand (Fig. 13.5), carefully crafted and decorated with sphinxes, found in Tomb 201 of the North Cemetery at Knossos.[81] This kind of object is, quite possibly, one of the inspirations behind Homeric descriptions of highly crafted artefacts with a divine pedigree. Appreciation of high-quality craftsmanship and participation in the ostentatious 'killing' of such objects can, in many cultures outside of the modern West, often go hand in hand.

Such examples should lead us to doubt our notion of art as a clear-cut ontological category that automatically ascribes a different value to one set of objects (art) as against another (non-art). I would argue that the concept gets in the way of our understanding of objects from different cultures. Art simply reinforces Western ethnocentrism.

Let us consider two objects both for a time held in the Metropolitan Museum in New York. One is a humble piece of clothing used by women in Mali – it is not on display

---

[78] Beazley 1922; Arrington 2017.
[79] Kurtz 1975.
[80] Rehak 1995.
[81] This is KMF 201.f1, originally published by Coldstream and Catling 1996, 194. 517–518. For the class of stand see Papasavvas 2001, 82–85. For the wider significance of 'breaking and burning' such objects see Whitley 2013; 2016; Papasavvas 2017; Kotsonas 2018.

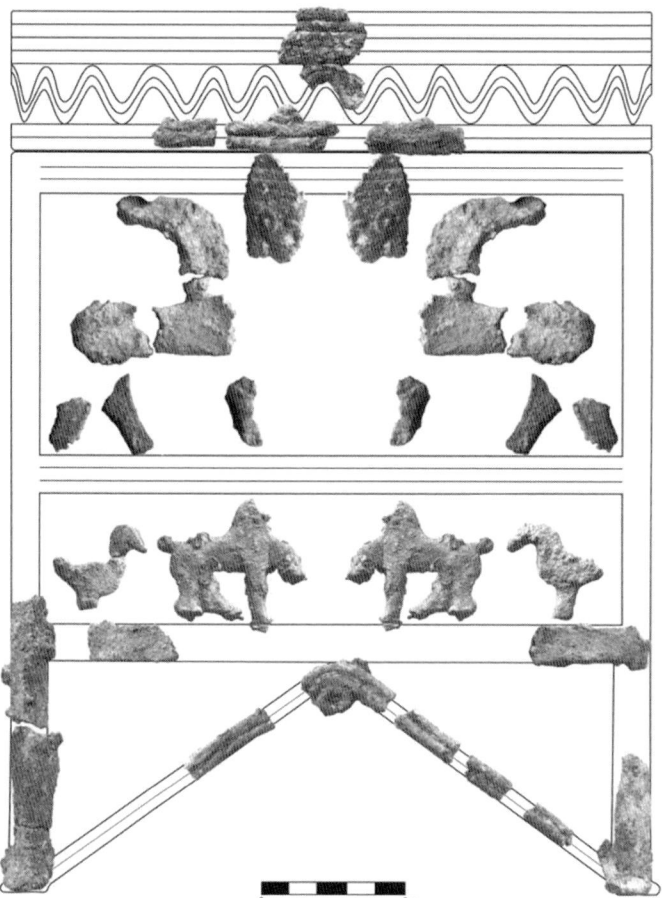

Figure 13.5. Reconstructed drawing of Late Bronze Age four-sided Cypriot stand from KMF tomb 201 (KNC 201.f1) in the North Cemetery of Knossos (courtesy British School at Athens and Georgios Papasavvas).

(so perhaps its status as art is suspect) but accessible through the online catalogue.[82] It is clear, however, that, though it was very carefully crafted by women, its survival is down to chance and the exceptional preservation properties of very dry caves. The online photograph is perhaps intended to disclose hitherto undiscerned no doubt aesthetic qualities – qualities such as were revealed when 'Vogel's net' was put on show in the early 1990s.[83] The other is of course an object which is presumptively considered

---

[82] New York, Metropolitan Museum, inv. 1998.478.4. The catalogue (https://www.metmuseum.org/toah/works-of-art/1998.478.4/ [accessed: 28 July 2021]) gives the following information: Cache-Sexe, Tellem people, 12th Century CE Mali. Gift of Jerome Vogel.
[83] Gell 1999.

to be art because it is an example of Late Archaic red-figure – the Euphronios *krater* that the Metropolitan Museum spent much time, effort and money to retain in New York.[84] Its Greekness (and its authorship by Euphronios, an attribution by Dietrich von Bothmer) guaranteed its status as art; in the view of the museum's previous director, all you needed to know or see about it was 'on the vase'. In this case this 'aesthetic' justification impeded our understanding of this object, an object that had been on its travels and (like Homer's *kraters*) was perhaps made with these travels in mind.[85]

I have suggested (and it is not a new suggestion) that museums and galleries are modernity's sacred spaces; a place where art is not simply celebrated but venerated.[86] In this respect they may be held to be like the sacred spaces of the ancient world, which retained the property of a god, images of the god and objects dedicated to a god. Are then modern 'art' objects like ancient dedications? Well, one major difference between the ancient world and the modern is that ancient objects were not, necessarily, made to last. Nor were exotic objects that had been dedicated to a god necessarily the subject of special treatment. Consider the contents of well 17 underneath the third stadium at Olympia.[87] These included a number of exotic Babylonian bronzes reworked as *sphyrelata* statues along with a number of parts of several different trophies of captured armour (some with inscriptions), accompanied by some rather plain painted pots. While we might consider the statues and buckets art, this is plainly not how the Late Archaic/Early Classical Greeks used these objects. In a sense they are rubbish (being deposited in a pit), but they are also sacred rubbish (as they had been dedicated and were deposited within the Altis). The concept of 'art' is simply not useful here if we want to understand how the 'exotic' came to occupy such a lowly status (it seems).

Let us return to Duchamp, who would (I think) would have been very interested in the theme of this volume.

> In the last analysis the artist may shout from the rooftops that he is a genius; he will have to wait for the verdict of the spectator in order that his declarations take a social value and that, finally, posterity includes him in the primers of art history.[88]

There can then be no objective or universal definition of art, still less a scientific (etic) one. Art is not then a scientific but a religious category. Art is a goddess who has taken her place in the pantheon of Western Metropolitan Secularism. But neither as deity nor as concept is art something we share with the ancient Greeks; nor is it a lens through which we can better understand the perennial

---

[84] New York, Metropolitan Museum, inv. 1972.11.10; von Bothmer 1976; Watson and Todeschini 2006.
[85] see Whitley 2012, 586–591; 2018, 63–66.
[86] This is not an entirely new argument (see discussion in Tanner 2005). Tanner argues that the 'sacral' character of art has its roots in Protestantism. I disagree. I would argue that secularisation has, since the time of the French Revolution, been and still is constantly creating new gods (the latest being Inclusion, which joins Equality and Diversity to form a modern trinity within British universities).
[87] Borrell and Rittig 1998.
[88] Duchamp 1959, 77–78.

achievements of Greek culture. Art too often gets in the way of both archaeology and history. Asking of an ancient object 'is it art' is a question that only makes sense within a particular institutional and cultural setting that has little to do with knowledge as such. It can serve no scientific (that is to say historical or anthropological) purpose. Whether a sculpture or a painted *krater* counts as 'art' is rarely the right question to ask about anything from antiquity. Duchamp has drawn our attention to this fact.

Acknowledgements

I would like to thank both Anthony Snodgrass and Jeremy Tanner for very helpful comments on an earlier draft of this paper. Neither, however, must be held to be complicit in the views I put forward here. I also thank the anonymous reviewer for his comments and pointing me towards Ernst Buschor.

References

Arrington, N. T. 2017 Connoisseurship, vases, and Greek art and archaeology. In: Padgett 2017, 21–39
Beazley, J. D. 1922 Citharoedus. *The Journal of Hellenic Studies* 42, 70–98
Borbein, A. H. Hölscher, T. and Zanker, P. (eds) 2000 *Klassische Archäologie. Eine Einführung* (Berlin)
Borell, B. and Rittig, D. 1998 *Orientalische und griechische Bronzereliefs aus Olympia. Der Fundkomplex aus Brunnen 17.* Olympische Forschungen 26 (Berlin)
Bothmer, D. von 1976 Der Euphronioskrater in New York. *Archäologischer Anzeiger* 1976, 485–512
Buschor, E. 1942 *Vom Sinn der griechischen Standbilder* (Berlin)
Coldstream, J. N. and Catling, H. W. (eds) 1996 *Knossos North Cemetery. Early Greek Tombs.* The British School at Athens Supplement 28 (London)
Cook, R. M. 1972 *Greek Painted Pottery* (London)
Duchamp, M. 1959 The creative act. In: Lebel 1959, 77–78
Elsner, J. 2010 Myth and chronicle. A response to the values of art. *Arethusa* 43, 289–307
Faris, J. C. 1988 ART/Artifact. On the museum and anthropology. *Current Anthropology* 29, 775–777
Gell, A. 1998 *Art and Agency. An Anthropological Theory* (Oxford)
Gell, A. 1999 Vogel's Net. Traps as artworks and artworks as traps. In: A. Gell, *The Art of Anthropology. Essays and Diagrams.* London School of Economics Monographs on Social Anthropology 67 (London), 187–214
Heidegger, M. 1978 The origin of the work of art. In: D. F. Krell (ed.), *Martin Heidegger. Basic Writings. From Being and Time (1927) to The Task of Thinking (1964)* (London), 139–212
Heidegger, M. 2005 *Sojourns. The Journey to Greece* (trans. J. Panteleimon Manoussakis, foreword J. Sallis (Albany NY)
Hodder, I. 2011 Human-thing entanglement. Towards an integrated archaeological perspective. *Journal of the Royal Anthropological Institute* 17, 154–177
Hughes, R. 1980 *The Shock of the New. Art and the Century of Change* (London)
Hunt, E. 2016 Pair of glasses left on US gallery floor mistaken for art. *The Guardian* 27 May. <https://www.theguardian.com/us-news/2016/may/27/pair-of-glasses-left-on-us-gallery-floor-mistaken-for-art> (Accessed: 26 July 2021)
Kotsonas, A. 2018 Homer, the archaeology of Crete and the 'Tomb of Meriones' at Knossos. *The Journal of Hellenic Studies* 138, 1–35

Küchler, S. 1987 Malangan. Art and memory in a Melanesian society. *MAN. The Journal of the Royal Anthropological Institute* N. S. 22, 238–255

Kurtz, D. C. 1975 *Athenian White Lekythoi. Patterns and Painters.* Oxford Monographs on Classical Archaeology (Oxford)

Lambert, S. 2011 What was the point of inscribed honorific decrees in classical Athens? In: S. D. Lambert (ed.), *Sociable Man. Essays on Ancient Greek Social Behaviour. In Honour of Nick Fisher* (Swansea), 193–214

Lebel, R. 1959 *Marcel Duchamp* (trans. G. Heard Hamilton) (New York)

MacGregor, N. 2014 Russia must see this marble ambassador for European values. *The Times* 5 December, 4

Martin, S. R. 2017a *The Art of Contact. Comparative Approaches to Greek and Phoenician Art* (Philadelphia PA)

Martin, S. R. 2017b Ethnicity and Greek art history in theory and practice. In: L. C. Nevett (ed.), *Theoretical Approaches to the Archaeology of Ancient Greece. Manipulating Material Culture* (Ann Arbor MI), 143–163

Meyer, E. A. and Lendon, J. E. 2005 Greek art and culture since *Art and Experience in Classical Greece*. In: J. M. Barringer and J. M. Hurwit (eds), *Periklean Athens and Its Legacy. Problems and Perspectives* (Austin TX), 255–276

Morphy, H. 2010 Art as action, art as evidence. In: D. Hicks and M. C. Beaudry (eds), *The Oxford Handbook of Material Culture Studies* (Oxford), 265–290

Neer, R. 2010 *The Emergence of the Classical Style in Greek Sculpture* (Chicago IL)

Osborne, B. 2010 The art of signing in ancient Greece. *Arethusa* 43, 231–251

Osborne, R. and Tanner, J. (eds) 2007 *Art's Agency and Art History, New Interventions in Art History* (Malden MA)

Padgett, J. M. 2017 *The Berlin Painter and His World. Athenian-Vase Painting in the Early Fifth Century B.C. Exhibition Catalogue Princeton* (New Haven CO)

Panofsky, E. 1993 [1955] *Meaning in the Visual Arts,* Penguin Art and Architecture (Harmondsworth, reprint)

Papasavvas, G. 2001 Χαλκινοι Υποστατες απο την Κυπρο και την Κρητη. Τριποδικοι και Τετραπλευροι Υποστατες απο την Υστερη Εποχη του Χαλκου εως την Πρωιμη Εποχη του Σιδηρου (Nicosia)

Papasavvas, G. 2017 Breaking and burning the Sphinx. In: V. Vlachou and A. Gadolou (eds), ΤΕΡΨΙΣ. *Studies in Mediterranean Archaeology in Honour of Nota Kourou*. Études d'Archéologie 10 (Brussels), 481–500

Pollitt, J. J. 1986 *Art in the Hellenistic Age* (Cambridge)

Pollitt, J. J. 1990 *The Art of Ancient Greece. Sources and Documents* (Cambridge)

Price, S. 1989 *Primitive Art in Civilized Places* (Chicago IL)

Rehak, P. 1995 The use and destruction of Minoan stone bull's head rhyta. In: R. Laffineur and W.-D. Niemeier (eds), POLITEIA. *Society and State in the Aegean Bronze Age. Proceedings of the 5th International Aegean Conference. University of Heidelberg, Archäologisches Institut, 10-13 April 1994.* Aegaeum 12 (Liège), 435–460

Richter, G. M. A. 1965a *The Portraits of the Greeks I* (London)

Richter, G. M. A. 1965b *The Portraits of the Greeks II* (London)

Richter, G. M. A. 1970 *The Sculpture and Sculptors of the Greeks* (New Haven CO)

Richter, G. M. A. and Smith, R. R. R. 1984 *The Portraits of the Greeks* (Oxford)

Robb, J. 2017 'Art' in archaeology and anthropology. An overview of the concept. *Cambridge Archaeological Journal* 27, 587–597

Robertson, M 1975 *A History of Greek Art* (Cambridge)

Schweitzer, B. 1917 Untersuchungen zur Chronologie der geometrischen Stile in Griechenland I. Unpublished PhD dissertation, Ruprecht-Karl-Universität Heidelberg

Schweitzer, B. 1918 *Untersuchungen zur Chronologie und Geschichte der geometrischen Stile in Griechenland II.* Mitteilungen des Deutschen Archäologischen Instituts. Athenische Abteilung 43, 1–152

Schweitzer, B. 1934 Mimesis und Phantasia. *Philologus. Zeitschrift für das klassische Altertum* 89, 286–300

Schweitzer, B. 1938 Die Menelaos-Patroklos-Gruppe. Ein verlorenes Meisterwerk hellenistischer Kunst. *Die Antike. Zeitschrift für Kunst und Kultur des klassischen Altertums* 14, 43–72

Schweitzer, B. 1969 *Die geometrische Kunst Griechenlands. Frühe Formenwelt im Zeitalter Homers* (Cologne)

Sinn, U. 2000 *Einführung in die Klassische Archäologie* (Munich)

Smith, H. L. 2017 On black ground. The Berlin Painter at Princeton. *Arion. A Journal of Humanities and the Classics* 25(H. 1), 213–236

Squire, M. 2010 Introduction. The art of art history in Greco-Roman antiquity. *Arethusa* 43, 133–163

Squire, M. 2012 Greek Art through Roman eyes. In: T. J. Smith and D. Plantzos (eds), *A Companion to Greek Art.* Blackwell Companions to the Ancient World 90 (Hoboken NJ), 599–620

Tanner, J. J. 1992 Art as expressive symbolism. Civic portraits in classical Athens. *Cambridge Archaeological Journal* 2, 167–190

Tanner, J. 1994 Shifting paradigms in classical art history. *Antiquity* 68, 650–655

Tanner, J. 1999 Culture, social structure and the status of the visual artists in classical Greece. *Proceedings of the Cambridge Philological Society* 45, 136–175

Tanner, J. 2005 Rationalists, fetishists, and art lovers. Action theory and the comparative analysis of high cultural institutions. In: R. C. Fox, V. M. Lidz and H. J. Bershady (eds), *After Parsons. A Theory of Social Action for the Twenty-First Century* (New York), 179–207

Tanner, J. 2006 *The Invention of Art History in Ancient Greece. Religion, Society and Artistic Rationalisation.* Cambridge Classical Studies (Cambridge)

Tanner, J. 2010 Aesthetics and Art History Writing in Comparative Historical Perspective. *Arethusa* 43, 267–288

Tanner, J. 2018 *Revixit ars.* Artistic 'rebirth' in Greco-Roman antiquity and early modern China and Europe. In: L. Nevett and J. Whitley (eds), *An Age of Experiment. Classical Archaeology Transformed. 1976-2014.* McDonald Institute Monographs (Cambridge), 197–222

Usborne, D. 1999 Missing Van Gogh feared cremated with its owner. *The Independent* 26 July. <https://www.independent.co.uk/news/world/missing-van-gogh-feared-cremated-with-its-owner-1108973.html> (accessed: 26 July 2021)

Wallace-Hadrill, A. 2008 *Rome's Cultural Revolution* (Cambridge)

Watson, P. and Todeschini, C. 2006 *The Medici Conspiracy. The Illicit Journey of Looted Antiquities. From Italy's Tomb Raiders to the World's Greatest Museums* (New York)

Whitley, J. 2011 *Hybris* and *Nike.* Agency, victory and commemoration in panhellenic sanctuaries. In: S. D. Lambert (ed.), *Sociable Man. Essays on Ancient Greek Social Behaviour. In Honour of Nick Fisher* (Swansea), 161–191

Whitley, J. 2012 Agency in Greek art. In: T. J. Smith and D. Plantzos (eds), *A Companion to Greek Art.* Blackwell Companions to the Ancient World 90 (Hoboken NJ), 579–595

Whitley, J. 2013 Homer's entangled objects. Narrative, agency and personhood in and out of Iron Age Texts. *Cambridge Archaeological Journal* 23, 395–416

Whitley, J. 2016 Burning people, breaking things. Material entanglements, the Bronze Age/Iron Age transition and the Homeric dividual. In: M. Mina, S. Triantaphyllou and Y. Papadatos (eds), *An Archaeology of Prehistoric Bodies and Embodied Identities in the Eastern Mediterranean* (Oxford), 215–223

Whitley, J. 2018 The krater and the pithos. Two kinds of agency. In: L. Nevett and J. Whitley (eds), *An Age of Experiment. Classical Archaeology Transformed. 1976-2014.* McDonald Institute Monographs (Cambridge), 59–73

Yarrow, L. 2006 Lucius Mummius and the spoils of Corinth. *Scripta Classica Israelica* 25, 57–70

Chapter 14

When secondary is primary: on *Halbzeug* and other objects of continual re-evaluation

Thomas Widlok

This paper looks at artefacts which take the shape of semi-finished products (*Halbzeug*), items left half-finished for later use by others (or by oneself). As a consequence of these practices objects can actually be improved upon and gain value after they have been in use by others and before they are taken out of usage and become singularised as nostalgic or ritually loaded items. Based on my ethnographic field research with contemporary hunter-gatherers, I argue that, in contra-distinction to the now dominant conception, the objects in question are evaluated primarily because they have the property of being secondary. This need not be a ritual re-evaluation since it is a more fundamental view of objects as generally pre-owned, as typically unfinished and as valuable for the fact that they can be 're-owned' and reshaped at a later stage.

Introduction. The value of things

What influences changes in the value of things? Anthropologists tend to focus on the inverse form of this question, namely how the value of things influences the position and relation of people. Research that follows Pierre Bourdieu's work on distinction[1] seeks to establish how people create and alter their positions through consuming and using certain objects. Work in the highly influential gift exchange paradigm is largely about the role of objects for establishing and maintaining social relationships. According to the dichotomous distinction that Christopher A. Gregory proposed (based on Karl Marx and Marcel Mauss), commodity exchange establishes a relationship between the objects exchanged, whereas gift exchange establishes a relationship between the subjects.[2] The rich research tradition following this dictum tended to treat the value of objects in gift exchange as unproblematic, since the frequent value changes that we find in the price-forming process would only apply to commodities,

---

[1] Bourdieu 1979.
[2] Gregory 1982.

not to gifts. More recently, however, changes of value have also become interesting to those working on gift economies in Melanesia[3] and beyond.[4] Value, Nancy Munn emphasised, is 'relational' rather than 'substantive', i.e., it is subject to social practices and the social construction of meaning, as it is not simply given.[5]

In archaeology, multiple or shifting values of objects in pre-capitalist societies have been subject to debate for much longer, probably because of a less pronounced dichotomy between 'us' in the commodity economy and 'them' in the gift economy. Michael Schiffer and James Skibo's 'performance based theory' of the relation between 'people and things' recognises that objects have utilitarian and substantive 'techno-' properties but that they do fulfil a variety of functions, some social and ideational, and that people associate alternating uses and multiple utilitarian and symbolic values to things.[6] This complexity of multiple and shifting values in their view applies as much to ceramic pots used in subsistence agriculture as to complex technical objects, such as cars, in a national capitalist economy. Just as clay pots mean different things to different people, the fact that petrol-driven cars outran electricity-driven cars in the US in the 20th century is not due to a higher value associated with intrinsic technological properties but rather a consequence of the choices made by consumers on the basis of their social positions and their social practices.[7]

Michael Thompson's 'dynamic theory of rubbish' goes one step further by underlining that agents and their ideas are also, to some extent, materially 'thing-like' and that, conversely, we as social and cognisant beings never see objects as 'raw and unprocessed' but rather as they are constantly reshaped in social processing.[8] Again, he applies this to durables as in the sudden rise in value of Victorian Stephengraphs (pictures industrially and commercially made from woven silk) but also to transient items as in the gradual decline of a car to zero value or, more extremely, to faeces and snot. The transfer of objects from transient items with declining value to the limbo of rubbish with no value and (possibly) on to durable items (such as antiques) with increasing value, Thompson shows, is a social process subject to power struggles and cultural reclassifications.[9]

The existing anthropological and archaeological work suggests that our everyday observation that the value of objects can change frequently is therefore not simply a result of living in a capitalist market system with its changing prices. In fact, changes in value can be much more fundamental than what participants in a market economy are used to when they see changing prices. Although it has become the default assumption that the value of an object can go up or down, in economist thinking about these

---

[3] Munn 1992.
[4] Otto and Willerslev 2013.
[5] Munn 1992, 8.
[6] Skibo and Schiffer 2008.
[7] Skibo and Schiffer 2008, 4.
[8] Thompson 2017, 88.
[9] Thompson 2017, 28.

transactions, the market itself is usually envisaged as a unified process of producing a value, more specifically *the* value of something at a certain point in time. The value is variable only insofar as it is relative to the trade partners' willingness to give up a thing for another. These preferences may vary and change, but the deliberation and negotiation between them constitutes a single invariable process as far as mainstream economic theory is concerned. The value of an object is not intrinsic to this object but it is a product of its transaction(s). However, given a certain constellation of preferences, there is only one possible outcome that economic theory envisages, namely that each item will receive its specific value as a consequence of supply and demand at a given time and space. In other words, people's *values* may change, but the mechanism that produces *the value* of an object in a market situation is thought to be invariable and stable.[10] As markets grow more complex and interconnected it has become difficult to trace what exactly affects the value of items, making it a reasonable assumption that it is the abstract, impersonal and underlying 'market forces' which make things gain or lose value or, more generally, be evaluated differently across time and space. For example, with rare exceptions, these forces would attribute higher value to new and unused items unless they happen to be old *and* rare things. Re-evaluation in terms of current economic theory would therefore have to be primarily located at the impersonal level of the economic system at large.

This could lead to the parallel impression that frequent changes of value are a recent thing and that the values of objects were somehow more stable before the world got saturated by features such as market logic, pricing or inflation. The prevalent anthropological theories of gift exchange nurture this impression. For Gregory, as mentioned above, one of the main differences between commodity exchange and gift exchange is that in the former, there is a relationship of objects changing values and of agents remaining constant and untouched by the transaction, while in the latter case, the value of objects is kept constant while the evaluation of giver and receiver is altered in the exchange.[11] This reinforces an underlying assumption that re-evaluations were previously rare (i.e. before market integration). Things may have been produced for their main purpose and received their value from that 'primary purpose', which would be fairly stable. Only occasionally, and after long periods of serving their main purpose, may things be expected to undergo re-evaluation, when they were taken out of their primary use and got re-evaluated, for instance as ritual items, heritage items or otherwise singled out from the category of objects to which they previously belonged.

For both, current economic theory and dominant gift exchange theory, re-evaluations at the personal level would therefore be the exception and rather difficult to explain. Against the background of my own field research with hunter-gatherers in southern Africa, this is a rather unsatisfactory state of affairs. During my research, I

---

[10] Graeber 2001; see also Widlok 2013.
[11] Gregory 1982.

frequently encountered individuals who put a lot of effort and interest into obtaining a particular item but who would also dispose of things that were demanded by others or for which they had no immediate use anymore. Many things actually gained value by being in use. Stones used for nut-cracking, for instance, would improve through being used, as they became smoother through frequent touching or because frequent use creates cavities in the stone which keep the nuts to be cracked in the right position.[12] Personal re-evaluations were not rare and in some domains there was very high interpersonal variation in evaluation, too. I shall therefore argue that an assumed stability of evaluations with only occasional re-evaluations may carry the bias of the farming way of life which dominated many parts of the world in the last centuries and continues to dominate a lot of contemporary thought. Before I engage in that argument, however, I want to give an example of a re-evaluation that seems to fit the image of the process between primary and secondary (re-)evaluation as being rather special, infrequent and unidirectional.

Re-evaluations in the social life of things

On my bookshelf is an old stoneware beer mug; it is probably the oldest item in our house, definitely much older than the house itself and one of the few pre-war items that I own (Fig. 14.1). It can be easily dated to 1926 because on its front it commemorates and dates the 700 year anniversary of the town of Zülz in Upper Silesia. Silesia is (or at least was) a beer producing and consuming region, so it is fair to assume that the primary value of this mug was that one could drink beer from it when the town celebrated its anniversary. The mug shows clear signs of long and intensive use as a kitchen utensil (to be described in more detail below). However, I have never drunk beer from it and it is no coincidence that the mug is not in our kitchen but in my study, on the book shelf. Apart from being old, it is also one of the very few items which were owned by my paternal grandmother who was born in Zülz but who was an economic migrant, leaving Silesia for the faraway *Ruhrgebiet*, which was a booming industrial area around the time that Zülz was celebrating its 700 year anniversary. It is not clear whether she had the mug with her then or whether she or other relatives took it along later, possibly during the war when Silesia was not bombed and the family had sent children (including my father) to their grandparents. In any case, I value this mug because it belonged to my grandmother, whom I was very close to and who had managed to lead an honest, modest and self-respecting life under very tough circumstances. I have therefore revalued this item as a family heirloom, not of great monetary but of substantial emotional value. As such, it is a prototypical case of what we may consider the re-evaluation of material objects. At the end of this paper, I shall critically assess whether this initial assessment can be upheld or not. But for the time being, the re-evaluated beer mug can also help to

---

[12] Widlok 2016.

Figure 14.1. Stoneware mug commemorating the 700 year anniversary of the town of Zülz. The inscription reads 700 Jahrfeier der Stadt Zülz – 1225–1925 – 27 Juni–3 Juli 1926 *(photo: Thomas Widlok).*

illustrate what is probably the most influential anthropological theory in this domain, namely that of the 'social life of things'.

The contributors to the volume *The Social Life of Things*[13] managed to breathe new life into the anthropology of material objects at a point in time when it was seriously undertheorised and neglected. With this new social and dynamic theory of objects, material items were no longer the dusty and passive pieces of museums, but they were re-appreciated (dare I say re-evaluated) as being constitutive to social relationships and as undergoing biographical changes themselves as a consequence of being subject to diverse social practices. In particular, Igor Kopytoff's contribution on the 'biography' of things[14] and Arjun Appadurai's introduction to the volume suggested that any item could be described as being subject to two contrastive practices, namely *singularising* and *commoditisation*, and could therefore shift repeatedly between being an item that was sold and exchanged as opposed to an item that was inalienable and almost personal in character. This, the authors showed, could be true of material

---

[13] Appadurai 1986.
[14] Kopytoff 1986.

objects such as household items (e.g. beer mugs) but also for human beings who could enter and leave the status as slaves, items to be bought and sold. In other words, there was nothing 'essential' which made something a commodity or essentially an heirloom because everything could become subject to the social practices of making it either common and commercial or by 'singularising' it, taking it out of market or other types of exchange. Items like the beer mug may have been bought directly by individual users or, more common nowadays, they may have been bought by companies who would then give them away as a promotion item – in both cases, the beer mug was produced in order to be traded on the market. By contrast, we could say, following Kopytoff, that more than half a century later I 'singularised' it as I would not want to sell it. It probably could not easily be sold as a mug for drinking beer (its 'primary purpose') anyway, since it has lost its glazing and has become brittle, not much of a use for beer drinkers.

When secondary is primary

This practice-oriented approach to material culture has been very productive for many different types of items over the last few decades but, like all dichotomising concepts, it has its limits. This I had to find out during my field research with the ≠Akhoe Hai//om in Namibia who, in the 1990s, still very much lived a hunter-gatherer lifestyle. Part of that hunter-gatherer way of life was the production of metal knife blades and arrowheads (Fig. 14.2). As blacksmiths (Fig. 14.3), the ≠Akhoe Hai//om occupied an economic niche in the north of Namibia, surrounded by agropastoralist neighbours who had a demand for various types of ironwork and for game meat which was hunted with tools such as iron-headed arrows. Producing arrows is a laborious task and usually takes some days or even weeks. The iron arrowheads are heated up, beaten, allowed to cool down, inspected before being heated up again and so forth. ≠Akhoe Hai//om today do not smelt iron, so finding an appropriate piece of metal to convert into an arrowhead is already part of the work.

In the 1990s, the main source of metal was abandoned army gear from the independence war. One could say that the ≠Akhoe Hai//om were busy converting 'swords to ploughshares' but also occasionally swords (and ploughs) to 'hunting gear'. What should be noted is that the 'primary' production of the iron was far removed in terms of space and time. The metal army gear of those days was very much like many globalised products today. For instance, any Toyota car that I have used over the years to visit the ≠Akhoe Hai//om has multiple components with 'primary values' of various sorts, a 'value chain' impenetrable to me as the person who bought or rented the car. The chassis of the car was likely to have been assembled in South Africa, its design originally created in some office in Japan, but the metal could come from steel plants in the *Ruhrgebiet* or some other place in Germany who, in turn would have gotten the iron ore from South America or elsewhere. Such a vehicle, whether military or civilian, could be said to be the

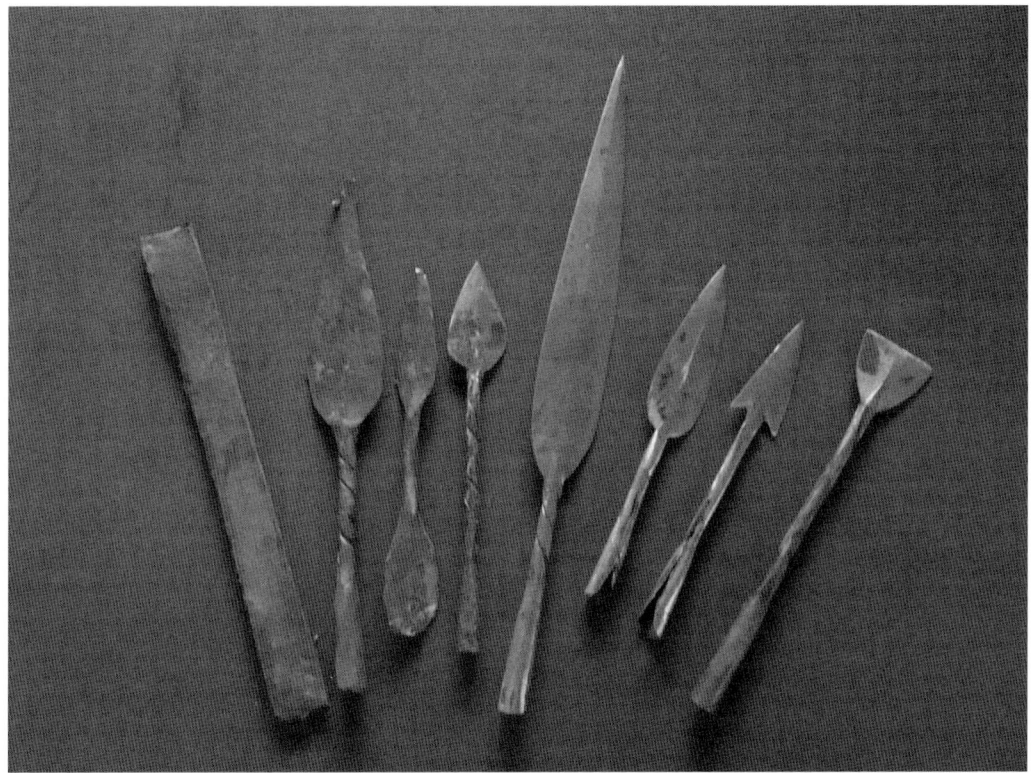

Figure 14.2. Halbzeug. Iron arrowheads at various stages of production and reworking, collected among the ≠Akhoe Hai//om San of Namibia (photo: Thomas Widlok).

product of an ultimately endless chain of inventions and productions across time and space, involving not only individual inventors like Nikolaus Otto (who designed the internal-combustion engine in Cologne back in the 19th century) but countless others who prepared the ground, so to speak, for cars to be able to drive – all the way to the ≠Akhoe Hai//om.

Ultimately, this is a case that substantiates Peter Kropotkin's argument that it is an illusion to assume that inventions and most items that we use as infrastructure in our lives are created from something 'primary', out of nothing. Kropotkin has pointed out, for large products like the railways, that 'Whole generations … have handed on this immense inheritance'[15] so that individuals could not legitimately claim them as property or as having created their value. With objects frequently changing hands and being worked on by a number of people over a longer period of time, this seems to hold true also for much of the inventory of the ≠Akhoe Hai//om. The first person may find a piece of iron, another may transport it to a camp, a third person may divide

---

[15] Kropotkin 1995, 14.

Figure 14.3. A group of ≠Akhoe Hai//om men doing blacksmith work at Mangetti-West, northern Namibia (1990s) (photo: Thomas Widlok).

it and a fourth may start working on it but put it aside, leaving it to others to pick it up again for reworking. Even finished arrowheads can serve as *Halbzeug* because they may deteriorate over time and need refreshing/sharpening or they may break, which would still allow someone to pick them up in order to create a smaller and finer type of arrowhead from it.

Figure 14.2 illustrates such *Halbzeug* at various stages of reworking and Figure 14.3 shows a blacksmith community of practice in which individuals work on pieces to create half-baked items – what I have called *Halbzeug*[16] – that others may pick up, let go of, pick up again and so forth.

The ≠Akhoe Hai//om effort to turn the 'raw iron' of military vehicles into arrowheads is not 'primary' in the absolute sense, even though the arrowheads could subsequently become subject to a long chain of further exchanges and secondary uses which may lead to some of these arrows being re-evaluated and ending up on bookshelves of anthropologists or tourists or indeed in museum collections. A lot of the social life of these things remains invisible in that the underlying dynamic processes defeat a single watershed distinction of 'primary' and 'secondary' evaluation. Much of what we see in the domain of tools and their 'primary uses' is in fact at

---

[16] Widlok 2017.

least secondary if not further removed, leaving the 'primary' as pretty much an illusion. The 'secondary' in the strict sense of the term is turned into one of many subsequent uses and re-evaluations. In the remainder of this paper I want to challenge the conventional view which distinguishes 'wild' or 'raw' or 'primary' things from 'domesticated', 'valorised' or 'secondary'.

The social life of *Halbzeug*

What I observed in the field was not only the frequent re-evaluation of things but also an alternative perspective of the process of re-evaluation itself. The ≠Akhoe Hai//om did not entertain an ideology of seeing themselves as the sole agents who convert 'raw' natural things into things of primary value and then possibly re-evaluate them and attach secondary value. Rather, they were constantly on the lookout for things that already had some form and therefore some value due to the affordances they possessed. Pieces of scrap metal were only one example, the same holds true for other items needed for making arrows, for instance sticks of various kinds.[17] But not every stick is suitable for becoming an arrow and when coming across a stick, or rather a branch of a tree, one would not know for sure whether it had the appropriate affordances or not. Some sticks may be amenable for starting work on them, 'inviting' the artisan to start carving them and turning them into an arrow as straight as possible. But sometimes they did not turn out the way it was anticipated and they ended up as sticks that were only good for stirring food on the fire or ultimately only as firewood. Alternatively, they may also be used for the arrows that one sells to tourists, arrows that can be crooked without any value-loss, since no one would ever seriously try to hunt animals with them.[18]

What is true for small things also holds true for the ≠Akhoe Hai//om settlements, their largest artefacts, and probably for much of their material culture along that spectrum. As for the settlement and the huts it was made of, bushes and trees of a certain given form could become walls or lean-tos. There is a seamless transition between what was a 'natural given', such as a trimmed tree, and a hut carefully designed from wood (Fig. 14.4). The ≠Akhoe Hai//om did not buy into the farmer ideology that out there was a 'wilderness' that needed to be tamed or converted into something valuable. Like many other hunter-gatherers, they rather seemed to see the bush as a kind of a ready-made pool of more-or-less valuable things that one could tap into.

What I have just outlined for material items from the bush would apply equally to non-material items, including those that were clearly 'man-made'. For instance, the ≠Akhoe Hai//om would similarly use bits and pieces of folklore that they 'found' (or found useful) and would combine that with their own experiences and sentiments in

---

[17] Widlok 2015.
[18] see Widlok 2015.

Figure 14.4. ≠Akhoe Hai//om camp in northern Namibia (1990s) (photo: Thomas Widlok).

their storytelling.[19] In all these cases, there is a sense of 'making' as 'doing' which is very different from the farmers' ideal of turning the wild into a domesticated product. The hunter-gatherer perspective, it seems, is one in which the form (and 'primary' value) of everything is beyond human control, an ultimate creation, maybe by God, but basically beyond human grasp. Since then, humans are surrounded by things with form and value, they pick things up and shape them further, often they just leave them somewhere (or share them upon demand), they let go of things which others take up again and shape further, and these things eventually may end up in their hands again at a later stage. The blacksmithing of arrowheads already mentioned proved the point: much of what outsiders considered to be rubbish around ≠Akhoe Hai//om camps was in fact *Halbzeug*, stuff discarded for the moment and for the current purpose but ready to be picked up by someone else (or by the same person at a later stage) in order to do something with it.

How does the arrowhead example (or, for that matter, the other above-mentioned examples) that we observe among the ≠Akhoe Hai//om affect the singularising/commoditising dichotomy with which we started off? Is it simply a case, another case, of hunter-gatherers being very flexible culturally, switching cognitively and

---

[19] Widlok 2018.

practically, frequently and readily, between a domain in which things are made common and comparable to one another and the opposite domain in which things are made singular? While I do suggest that the hunter-gatherer ethnography is useful to counter a particular ('farming') bias in our research, I shall point out below that this is not simply a matter of it being a 'special case'. Rather, I take this example to show how our thinking about evaluation and re-evaluation has been 'over-dichotomised'.

Modes of transactions and modes of (re-)evaluation

As pointed out above, the two practices of singularisation and commoditisation have been aligned with two modes of exchange, namely gift exchange and market exchange. Since Mauss it has become common to lump all modes of transfer that are somehow different from what we see in capitalist markets together under the rubric of 'gift exchange'. As I have pointed out elsewhere,[20] this does not adequately and appropriately capture the spectrum of transfers that we find in human societies and, in fact, within our own contemporary society and its manifestations of the so-called sharing economy. Modes such as sharing, pooling, redistributing, lending and others do form alternatives to both gift exchange systems and market systems. We have also been too quick in equating the exchange of objects in markets with the conversion of objects into profits that in turn become capital assets for producing more market objects. There is a historical reason for that: in the course of European industrialisation, markets and capitalism expanded largely together. However, the two processes need not go together. There have been markets in many parts of the world and for long periods without market items receiving the status of capital assets. And there are capitalist conditions in which markets are very limited, as for instance with the large internet-based monopolies which are clearly capitalist in character without being subject to market competition. It is worthwhile recalling that the distinctive feature of capitalism, as opposed to market economy, is the underlying process of evaluation. In markets, things are evaluated in relation to the degree to which they are able to address demands and needs, competitively if you like. In capitalist settings, things are made common with one another in the sense that they are exchanged in order to create assets for further capital accumulation. In other words, when items become capital assets, their value is independent of any intrinsic property that they may have (like being edible, being usable as a tool or for living in etc.) so that only their extrinsic property for allowing accumulation of more capital is retained.

The singularising/commoditising dichotomy, I argue, emerged at the point in history when commoditisation meant 'putting on the market' *and* 'turning into an asset for capital accumulation'. The social thinkers who were critical of this process only saw one alternative, namely 'singularisation', keeping things out of the market

---

[20] Widlok 2017.

and out of capital accumulation. They contrasted a situation in which an object (or any other item) could be converted into anything else with a situation in which an object could not be converted or alienated at all. If we broaden our perspective, however, we see many situations in which neither of these extreme conditions apply, when objects can be neither exchanged or converted into *everything* nor remain *singular* and incapable of being converted into *anything* else. Instead, what we find is that they are converted into something *particular*. Pre-capitalist and pre-monetary markets in Africa typically were of this kind. They allowed the conversion and trade of items within certain *spheres of exchange*. Probably the most well-known example is that of the Tiv who practiced conversion within three spheres – first everyday subsistence items, secondly 'prestige' items like slaves, cattle, ritual offices and brass rods and thirdly rights in humans, in particular rights in women.[21]

However, these markets with formalised and separate spheres of exchange are not the only exception to the full integration into a capitalist and market economy. There are many other ways in which the conversion of items was neither banned completely nor opened up entirely. This is what we see in and around ≠Akhoe Hai//om camps. The half-finished arrowheads and other items are not singular. Quite the reverse, they receive multiple uses, sequentially but also in parallel. There are very few single-purpose items in forager material culture and there are very few items that in their social life are only owned by a single person. Whatever you may possess at a point in time can be subject to demand by others. Typically, items have a number of owners in the course of their 'biographies' and they are subject to multiple uses. They can even be said to have 'uses' and value before humans stumble across them. After all, sticks are branches of trees and trees are used by animals and they have their 'value' as providers of shade, orientation and whatever other affordances they may have before humans decide that this makes good construction wood for building huts or making arrows.[22] And such items are never considered completely and utterly useless and valueless, since the expectation is that someone some time will have some use for the item, be it another human or an animal.

This is a far cry from the conversion into a common asset – with omni-usage for the accumulation of more capital – that we find in capitalist settings. Outside such settings, at any point in time, an item is characterised by some particular value that is attached to it; not a single value though, but often a limited range of value for a limited set of uses. This connects to what Africanists have described as 'spheres of exchange'.[23] Even under the incorporation into the money economy and capitalist relations, peasants in many parts of Africa continued to insist that not everything can be exchanged for everything else or purchased with money, for that matter. Mary Douglas reported from the Lele that they converted raffia cloth to money but only under very specific circumstances 'in a limited range of transactions'.[24] Money would

---

[21] Bohannan 1959.
[22] see Ingold 2000 for a discussion of affordances in the anthropology of tools and other objects of use.
[23] Douglas 1958; Bohannan 1959.
[24] Douglas 1958, 115.

go along raffia exchanges among kin as a kind of 'acknowledgement fee' which did not constitute a price, since money alone could not buy raffia.[25] As Douglas put it, this 'would be as absurd as the imaginary case of an Englishman reduced to buying Christmas cards to adorn his mantelshelf',[26] which only proves the point that the idea that Englishmen would be willing to reduce all transactions to buying and selling is also 'imaginary'.

If it is not just a 'hunter-gatherer thing' to depart from the singular versus commercial dichotomy, where does this leave our, my, beer mug from Silesia? When we look at the mug a little more carefully (Fig. 14.5), we notice that its base is badly burnt, as if it had often been used on an oven. In this case I can testify that it has been used to keep soup and other liquids warm on my grandmother's old coal oven. I do not know whether there was ever any beer drunk out of this mug, possibly not. My grandmother moved westwards in 1927, one year after the anniversary of Zülz. She was poor and she did not bring much over from Silesia. Possibly, she was given the mug as a memorial item from her home town; after all, chances were that she would not see her homeplace again, at least not any time soon. In that case, my use of the mug as a memorial item would not be much of a re-evaluation but simply a continuation of the value it already had when it was taken from its place of origin. The fact that it was used to contain soup and other liquids later on may therefore be a case of its *secondary* usage and re-evaluation and not a primary use, as you may expect. Only after she lost most of her kitchenware in bombing raids, may my grandmother have re-evaluated the memorial mug accordingly, since it was one of the few unbroken items left which could be used to hold liquids. Similarly, my use of the mug as a pencil holder goes back to one of its 'primary' affordances as a hollow open container of a certain height and size (perfect for pens and pencils) but which was certainly not intended when it was produced. All of this would question any simple-minded distinction between primary and secondary evaluation.

Moreover, it points to a multiple re-evaluation that goes beyond the singularising/commoditising dichotomy. The mug, one could argue, was double or multiple from the start, a common commercial beer mug, in competition with other things that could hold beer, and a 'singular' memorial item through its inscription. But there is more to it. During my grandmother's lifetime, the vessel was repeatedly re-evaluated to serve not only as an emergency cooking utensil but also for other purposes without ever entirely losing its other values that remained latent or dormant. Since I have the vessel in my possession, it has also served various purposes, not only as a pencil holder but also as a piggy bank, a book support and various other purposes, such as being an object of scholarly reflection. And my expectation is that my children may find other uses for it in the future. Sure enough, there are limits to what one can do with it. It would not receive a high price if one was to sell it. It probably will not be good for drinking beer or other liquids from (anymore) because the glazing

---

[25] Douglas 1958, 115.
[26] Douglas 1958, 117.

Figure 14.5. Burned bottom of the Zülz mug (photo: Thomas Widlok).

is now brittle and it would probably leak. The development of a memorial value is also somewhat unpredictable, as it can go up and down and up again. After 1945, the name of Zülz was changed to Biała and the German part of its heritage (just like previously its strong Jewish part of the heritage) was supressed. Since the Wall has come down, this seems to be changing again, so that it is not impossible that such a mug may become a sought-after museum item at some stage, maybe at its 800 year anniversary, which is approaching fast.

Conclusion

In this contribution, I have dealt with objects that have frequently been (re-)evaluated rather than only rarely or unilinearly converted from primary to secondary use. I have argued that the distinction between primary and secondary evaluation is problematic and that this is not only true for the case of hunter-gatherers who are known to be very flexible in their handling of material culture. Material items have multiple and changing affordances. Thus, the 'beer mug' from Silesia can be said to have lost some of its affordances and gained others, just as the wooden arrowshafts and iron arrowheads that constantly get (re-)shaped and (re-)valued by the ≠Akhoe Hai//om. To make things even more complicated, both have now a virtual existence, like many material objects, as photographed and documented items. Even if the mug and the arrowheads were lost for good, the photos and my description may be sufficient to create a replica, for a Zülz/Biała local museum or for a Hai//om exhibition. I could sell the picture of the mug but keep the mug itself, or vice versa, and so forth.

All these considerations not only 'complicate' the picture but, in my view, they also shed serious doubt on a dichotomisation between things that are singular and that belong to a home base versus things that are common and that are traded on markets. Re-evaluations are not only taking place along this unidimensional axis between the singular base and the commoditised exterior. Rather, evaluations frequently take place laterally, as it were, as items are moved from one set of relations to another and from one set of practical purposes to another.

References

Appadurai, A. (ed.) 1986 *The Social Life of Things. Commodities in Cultural Perspective* (Cambridge)
Bohannan, P. 1959 The impact of money on an African subsistence economy. *Journal of Economic History* 19, 491–503
Bourdieu, P. 1979 *La distinction. Critique sociale du jugement* (Paris)
Douglas, M. 1958 Raffia cloth distribution in the Lele economy, Africa. *Journal of the International African Institute* 28, 109–122
Graeber, D. 2001 *Toward an Anthropological Theory of Value. The False Coin of Our Own Dreams* (New York)
Gregory, C. A. 1982 *Gifts and Commodities* (London)
Ingold, T. 2000 *The Perception of the Environment. Essays on Livelihood, Dwelling and Skill* (Abingdon)
Kopytoff, I. 1986 The cultural biography of things. Commoditization as process. In: Appadurai (ed.) 1986, 64–91
Kropotkin, P. 1995 *The Conquest of Bread and Other Writings* (ed. M. Shatz). Cambridge Texts in the History of Political Thought (Cambridge)
Munn, N. D. 1992 *The Fame of Gawa. A Symbolic Study of Value Transformation in a Massim (Papua New Guinea) Society* (Durham NC)
Otto, T. and Willerslev, R. 2013 Introduction. Value as theory. Comparison, cultural critique, and guerilla ethnographic theory. *HAU. Journal of Ethnographic Theory* 3(1), 1–20
Skibo, J. M. and Schiffer, M. B. 2008 *People and Things. A Behavioral Approach to Material Culture* (New York)
Thompson, M. 2017 *Rubbish Theory. The Creation and Destruction of Value* (London)
Widlok, T. 2013 Sharing. Allowing others to take what is valued. *HAU. Journal of Ethnographic Theory* 3(2), 11–31
Widlok, T. 2015 Kulturtechniken. Ethnographisch fremd und anthropologisch fremd. Eine Kritik an ökologisch-phänomenologischen und kognitiv-modularisierenden Ansätzen. In: T. L. Kienlin (ed.), *Fremdheit. Perspektiven auf das Andere*. Universitätsforschungen zur prähistorischen Archäologie 264/Kölner Beiträge zu Archäologie und Kulturwissenschaften 1 (Bonn), 41–59
Widlok, T. 2016 Steine, die Nüsse zum Knacken bringen. In: J. Reuter and O. Berli (eds), *Dinge befremden. Essays zu materieller Kultur*. Interkulturelle Studien (Wiesbaden), 133–143
Widlok, T. 2017 *Anthropology and the Economy of Sharing* (Abingdon)
Widlok, T. 2018 A practice approach to Hai//om storytelling. In: K. Beyer, G. Boden, B. Köhler and U. Zoch (eds), *Linguistics Across Africa. Festschrift for Rainer Vossen* (Cologne), 349–362